LANGUAGE AND LITERACY SERIES

Dorothy S. Strickland, Founding Editor
Donna E. Alvermann and María Paula Ghiso, Series Editors
ADVISORY BOARD: Richard Allington, Kathryn Au, Bernice Cullinan, Colette Daiute,
Anne Haas Dyson, Carole Edelsky, Mary Juzwik, Susan Lytle, Django Paris, Timothy Shanahan

continued

For volumes in the NCRLL Collection (edited by JoBeth Allen and Donna E. Alvermann) and the Practitioners Book-
shelf Series (edited by Celia Genishi and Donna E. Alvermann), as well as other titles in this series, please visit www.
tcpress.com.

Language and Literacy Series, *continued*

The **ADMINISTRATION** and **SUPERVISION** of **LITERACY PROGRAMS**

SIXTH EDITION

EDITED BY

Shelley B. Wepner
Diana J. Quatroche

Foreword by Jack Cassidy

TEACHERS COLLEGE PRESS

TEACHERS COLLEGE | COLUMBIA UNIVERSITY

NEW YORK AND LONDON

Published by Teachers College Press,® 1234 Amsterdam Avenue, New York, NY 10027

Library of Congress Cataloging-in-Publication Data is available at loc.gov

ISBN 978-0-8077-6593-7 (paper)
ISBN 978-0-8077-6594-4 (hardcover)
ISBN 978-0-8077-7986-6 (ebook)

Printed on acid-free paper
Manufactured in the United States of America

If your actions inspire others to dream more, learn more, do more, and become more, you are a leader.

—John Quincy Adams, 6th U.S. President

Again, to our parents, our first role models and supervisors:
Carole and the late Bernard Markovitz
Katie and Norman Frost

To our families for giving us the opportunity to continue the legacy of our parents:
Husband, Roy Wepner; daughters, sons-in-law, and grandchildren—Leslie, Marc,
Teddy, and Sloane Regenbaum and Meredith, Judd, Eliza, and Sydney Grossman

In memory of my sons, John and Michael, and husband, John Robert;
and to my grandson, Johnathan

To the late Dorothy S. Strickland for being the ultimate role model
in promoting literacy leadership

Contents

Foreword

A few years ago, a colleague at a local university approached me to teach a course on the administration and supervision of reading programs. Although it had been some time since I taught that course, I was tempted because I had been a reading supervisor overseeing the literacy curriculum at a large Eastern school district, and I had taught such a course for many years. My colleague went on to say, "We use the Wepner and Strickland book, *The Administration and Supervision of Reading Programs,* in this course." "Of course you do," I thought. "It's the best book out there."

Although I would ultimately decline the offer to teach, the encounter triggered a memory. Long ago, I met a young college professor, Dr. Shelley Wepner, teaching a course on the administration of reading programs. Like me, she was using a series of duplicated handouts rather than a text. We challenged each other to produce a book on that topic. Soon after that meeting, Shelley joined with the late Dr. Dorothy Strickland, arguably one of the foremost literacy authorities in the world, and the late Dr. Joan Feeley to produce the first edition of *The Administration and Supervision of Reading Programs,* which appeared in 1989. I was honored to write the Foreword for that edition and even more honored when I saw the stellar group of chapter authors whom Shelley, Dorothy, and Joan had assembled. Over 3 decades later, I am equally impressed with the chapter authors of this volume—the sixth edition. The fact that this is the sixth edition of the work is equally noteworthy. Only the most valuable of academic texts get to a sixth edition. For this edition, Shelley and Dr. Diana Quatroche are sharing editing responsibilities. As in the fifth edition, this volume includes Reflection Questions and a Project Assignment at the end of each chapter. As a former university professor and reading supervisor, I value these sections the most because they facilitate staff development in a college course or a school district

classroom. These components, along with the advance organizers, encourage the reader to reflect on and to apply the knowledge presented.

Like the previous editions of the book, this volume is organized into four sections: Overview of Program Components and Personnel; Program Development; Program Implementation and Evaluation; and Interconnections. Drs. Wepner and Quatroche have recruited the foremost authorities in their respective areas of literacy to write each chapter in these sections.

It is fitting that Dr. Rita Bean of the University of Pittsburgh authors the first chapter in the first section of this volume. In addition to being one of the leading authorities on the role of the specialized literacy professional, she is constantly called on to consult with districts and state departments across the country. Her chapter on "Developing a Comprehensive Literacy Program" highlights the three key components in any reading plan: standards and curriculum, instruction, and assessment. In the second chapter, Drs. Wepner and Quatroche follow up with a discussion of the key role specialized literacy professionals play as leaders in the administration and supervision of literacy programs. Jacy Ippolito then follows up in Chapter 3 with the context and practice for effective literacy coaching.

The second section of this volume opens with a chapter by literacy icons D. Ray Reutzel and Parker C. Fawson focusing on new opportunities and initiatives for creating a cohesive literacy-learning, knowledge-based curriculum for children during the early years. Timothy Rasinski and his colleagues follow with a great chapter on improving literacy achievement in the elementary grades that is based on scientific and evidence-based findings.

William G. Brozo, a prominent author and researcher on content area/disciplinary literacy, completes this section with a focus on principles to follow in order to promote meaningful and sustainable secondary literacy reform. All of the chapters in this section emphasize the importance of literacy leadership in successful program development.

In the third section of this volume, focusing on program implementation and evaluation, Wepner and Quatroche have again assembled, as chapter authors, a *Who's Who* of the literacy world. The topics dealt with include selection of materials, assessment of students, teacher evaluation, professional development, and program evaluation. As with the other sections in this volume, there is a focus on the role of the literacy leader in implementing successful programs.

The last section of this book, titled Interconnections, has chapters dealing with program topics closely connected to successful literacy development in students. Fittingly, the first chapter discusses writing and its close interconnection with reading. In addition, there are chapters on linguistically diverse students, and on students with reading disabilities. There is also a focus on the role of online technologies in the literacy curriculum—Zoom, the Internet, and any of thousands of mobile apps. Finally, this section concludes with a chapter on productive parent and community involvement.

For many years, along with various collaborators, I wrote a column called "What's Hot, What's Not in Literacy" for the ILA publication *Literacy Today*. For that column, I surveyed literacy leaders around the country to ascertain those topics that were currently receiving attention and received attention in the recent past. Readers were then encouraged to research the topics in more depth. This latest edition of *The Administration and Supervision of Literacy Programs* provides that depth. Readers will gain insight into the research behind important literacy topics and why they are particularly relevant to the 21st-century classroom. More importantly, one sees how these various topics should be operationalized in schools and classrooms—always with a good literacy leader guiding the way. If I were to do a column on "What's Hot in Literacy Texts," this volume would undoubtedly be at the top of the list. Kudos again to Dr. Wepner and Dr. Quatroche for giving us such a fine work.

—Jack Cassidy
Emeritus Member,
Specialized Literacy Professionals
Past President,
International Literacy Association
Past President,
Association of Literacy Educators and Researchers
Past President,
Texas Association for Literacy Education (TALE)
Past President,
Diamond State Reading Association

Acknowledgments

We pinch ourselves every time we think of the quality of the authors for this sixth edition. These authors have spent years, even decades, conducting research by themselves and with others to learn as much as possible about their chapter topics. As a result, they have earned prominence in the field for their ability to shed light on critical components of school- and districtwide literacy programs. Just as important as these authors' expertise is their professionalism. They were gracious about following specific guidelines for sharing their unique and compelling messages so that their chapters were consistent with the book's overriding theme. They also were willing to adhere to the book's structural formula for presenting information and ideas. These authors inspired us to work hard on their behalf to create just the right message with just the right tone so that their chapters blended perfectly with the others. We acknowledge with deep admiration the enormous contribution of each of our authors for their significant role in helping this edited book come together.

We pay tribute to Jack Cassidy, who has written the Foreword for every single edition of *The Administration and Supervision of Reading Programs*. In truth, this book would not exist if it were not for Jack, because he challenged Shelley to write the first edition in the mid-1980s. Sadly, Jack passed away soon after he wrote this edition's Foreword. We are deeply indebted to Jack and his wife, Drew Cassidy, for preparing the Foreword during a difficult time in their lives. We also acknowledge one of our original editors, the late Joan T. Feeley, who was instrumental in developing the book's content. Shelley is grateful to Joan for introducing her to the late Dorothy S. Strickland nearly 40 years ago to begin their writing collaborations.

We especially acknowledge the late Dorothy S. Strickland, another of the original editors who served in this capacity up through the fifth edition. In addition to authoring the chapter on early childhood in earlier editions, she was instrumental in helping to update the book's content and format to reflect changes in the field. To say that she was passionate about literacy for all is an understatement. She lived and breathed literacy and did extraordinary things on behalf of our profession because of her influential advocacy across the nation. Shelley acknowledges with enormous gratitude the honor of co-editing all previous editions of this book with Dorothy, one of the giants in the field.

We also acknowledge the work of graduate assistant Jennifer Choe for her help in conducting research on the status of the field and the personnel within the field.

We recognize that this sixth edition would not exist without the kind, sincere, and insightful support of our acquisitions editor, Emily Spangler. Without fail, Emily was responsive to our questions, encouraging with our plans, and tactfully helpful with our mission. From the beginning, we knew that Emily was in our court, and quite naturally, we are deeply appreciative of her efforts to make sure that this book would be published. We are in awe of the talents of our developmental editor, Susan Liddicoat, who used her microscopic and telescopic lens to help us see ways in which we could present thoughts and ideas more comprehensibly and effectively.

We acknowledge the work of our production editor, John Bylander, who made the entire book that much stronger because of his unusually strong editing abilities and precise attention to detail. We also appreciate the support of Brian Ellerbeck, executive acquisitions editor at Teachers College Press, who enabled us to publish this sixth edition. His belief in this book's mission, even with an increasingly competitive market of other books on this topic, inspired us to provide the most current and informative book possible.

On a more personal level, we are grateful every day for the love and support of our families, friends, and colleagues. They have been incredibly accepting of our need to write this latest edition and our less than remarkable attention to other areas of our lives. Since most of this book was written during the pandemic, the shelter-in-place mandate actually gave us an excuse to focus on writing and editing.

As our families and friends attended to long-ignored home projects and connected virtually for social sustenance, we often chose to be holed up in our offices because of our desire and need to attend to some aspect of this book.

Finally, and once again, we thank you, our readership, for letting us know that a current edition was needed and would be read.

Looking Forward, Looking Back

Shelley B. Wepner and Diana J. Quatroche

The sixth edition of *The Administration and Supervision of Literacy Programs* addresses the eternal quest of literacy leaders to prepare *all* students for 21st-century literacy demands. The most recent definition of literacy includes writing, speaking, listening, viewing, and visually representing in both print and digital realms. This expanded definition reflects the prominent role of technology in developing and promoting students' literacy, integrated curriculum models in schools, and new responsibilities for literacy leaders, who are now called specialized literacy professionals (International Literacy Association, 2018).

Unlike the circumstances surrounding previous editions, this volume was written during the coronavirus pandemic of 2020 that transformed the educational system overnight. Debates about how to best teach, develop, and assess literacy were overshadowed by the need to help children and adolescents learn with synchronous and asynchronous online instruction. Teachers, administrators, and parents struggled to survive in a new teaching and learning environment that was often lonely, confusing, and challenging.

Specialized literacy professionals realized rather quickly that the inequities in education were having an especially deleterious effect on those students who did not have access to the technology or to the at-home support needed to continue learning when schools were closed. However, they also discovered that those teachers who were motivated and dedicated to figuring out how to help their students access and use technology effectively were able to counterbalance some of the inequities with opportunities for learning.

The long-term effect of the pandemic most likely will be reflected in students' high-stakes test scores, graduation rates, and career and college readiness.

Even though states now have jurisdiction over the standards and tests that they use as a result of the Every Student Succeeds Act (2015), they nevertheless will have to navigate literacy proficiency expectations in the face of existing inequities. Teachers' knowledge and effectiveness will continue to be key determinants for promoting pre-K–12 students' literacy development (International Literacy Association, 2020).

Specialized literacy professionals will need to be present and available more than ever to help teachers adapt to students' complex needs in relation to standards, learning gaps, and lived experiences. Specialized literacy professionals will need to work with school and district stakeholders to oversee literacy programs and ensure that administrative policies and instructional practices continue to change to ensure that data-driven instruction and culturally responsive teaching are being used with and for all types of students at all different grade levels.

THE EVOLVING LANDSCAPE OF ADMINISTERING LITERACY PROGRAMS

Today's expectations and responsibilities for specialized literacy professionals are vastly different from our original portrayal in the first edition of this book, published 32 years ago, in 1989. Then, intense debates took place about the nature of literacy instruction (holistic versus skills-based) and the types of materials to use to promote literacy. Teachers and administrators viewed assessment as an opportunity, not a mandate, to promote sound instructional practices. Teachers and administrators were just beginning to appreciate process writing and technology as exciting innovative instructional practices.

Each new edition has reflected important research, new policies, and state and national mandates about literacy development. Over the decades, teachers and administrators began to use a balanced approach to literacy instruction, understand how to support literacy development from early childhood through the adolescent years, make use of process writing and technology in promoting and extending literacy, and, most important, realize that high-stakes testing and accountability were central components for an increasingly diverse student population. When the fifth edition was published, there was widespread adoption of the Common Core State Standards that placed a new emphasis on having students read more challenging narrative and informational texts to help prepare them to be college and career ready. High-stakes testing and standards-based education, an outgrowth of the No Child Left Behind Act of 2001 (NCLB), were the centerpiece of administrative thinking about schools and districts.

This sixth edition reflects a shift away from national standards to state standards, renewed interest in the science of reading, and a deep concern for closing the achievement gap that has become more prevalent across the nation, even in suburban schools. High-stakes testing, standards-based education, and accountability continue to be major concerns, especially with the nation's consistently disappointing results for reading achievement on the National Assessment of Educational Progress (National Center for Education Statistics, 2019).

Even with the changing landscape, certain themes prevailed and persisted in each edition, namely, that teachers are the linchpin to student achievement; program change must be systematic, ongoing, and collaborative; communication among colleagues and with the community is essential; sound programs must take into account the needs of all children; and administrators cannot be experts in all functions of their schools and need specialized literacy professionals to help them initiate, implement, and evaluate their literacy programs.

This sixth edition reflects both the gradual evolution of instructional and assessment practices and unswerving confidence in the power of teachers, collaborative processes, and specialized literacy professionals to help students achieve.

OVERVIEW OF THE SIXTH EDITION

This sixth edition aims to help prospective and current specialized literacy professionals understand how to organize and supervise literacy programs within the context of current state and federal mandates. How administrators and teachers can and should provide instruction at all levels and for different types of learners is the focal point of the book. Specific program elements are explored related to materials selection, teacher evaluation, professional development, student assessment, writing, technology, schoolwide evaluation, and parent and community outreach. The 36 authors of this sixth edition (17 of whom are new to this book) provide new insights as they articulate what specialized literacy professionals should know and be able to do. Familiar terms such as literacy leaders, literacy specialists, reading specialists, and reading professionals are used instead of specialized literacy professionals in some chapters because of the authors' current situations. Examples, observations, and research are used to make this text both practical and readable. As with previous editions, the book is divided into four parts.

Part I provides an overview of literacy supervision by describing the components and process for developing a comprehensive pre-K–12 literacy plan that is based on standards, and the specialized literacy professionals involved in developing, implementing, and sustaining such plans. Part II presents guidelines for developing literacy programs for early childhood, childhood, and adolescence. Part III describes five critical areas for program implementation and evaluation: instructional materials selection and use, teacher evaluation, professional development, student assessment, and school- and districtwide assessment. The focus of these five chapters is more critical than ever for helping teachers to succeed with data-driven instruction for all types of learners. Part IV addresses connections with different components of the literacy program—writing and technology—and with linguistically diverse students, students with reading disabilities, parents, and the community. The chapter on working with parents and the community communicates the indisputable recognition that student success depends on parent engagement and community support.

To facilitate readability, discussion, and follow-up projects, this edition includes

- Advanced organizers at the beginning of each chapter to highlight the chapter's major points
- Reflection questions at the end of each chapter to promote thoughtful discussion
- A project assignment at the end of each chapter to encourage application of the content presented

What follows is a summary of the themes that recur across the four parts of the book. Presented as connections and directions, these themes represent the key ideas presented by the chapter authors. This introductory section serves two purposes: (1) to foreshadow overarching concepts and (2) to reflect back on authors' ideas. We encourage you to use this discussion to frame your thoughts for reading and then return to it after you complete the book to reframe your thinking.

CONNECTIONS

1. Increased racial, cultural, linguistic, and academic diversity in the schools requires that specialized reading professionals, classroom teachers, and administrators work together to create comprehensive school- and districtwide literacy programs that both subscribe to statewide standards and address student needs. Students' capacity to function in 21st-century America and compete in a globally competitive society depends on high-level literacy skills. Schools must have in place comprehensive and integrated literacy programs that use statewide standards as a framework for addressing students' diverse needs. Such programs must focus on preparing students to read, listen to, and comprehend complex narrative and informational text in print and digital formats; evaluate critically what they read, see, and hear; and respond in written and visual formats to what they read, see, and hear. These programs need to be aligned vertically and horizontally; in other words, spiral through the grades so that there is increasing complexity from grade to grade. Specialized literacy professionals, teachers, and administrators need to work together to develop and align the standards-based curriculum with instruction and assessment through the grades.

School- and districtwide literacy programs need to account for the neighboring community so that students' and parents' needs are addressed. If administrators, specialized literacy professionals, and teachers acknowledge and recognize parents' cultural, linguistic, and economic differences, they will develop strategies and practices that can involve parents in ways that support students' success.

All types of students—those beginning to read, those struggling with reading because of their special needs as learners or their language differences that interfere with understanding English, those developing as readers, and those advancing as readers—need to be included in a comprehensive literacy program.

Teacher beliefs and knowledge about literacy need to be reflected in literacy programs because of teachers' pivotal role in students' literacy achievement. At the same time, teachers' instructional and assessment practices need to be in alignment with state-mandated standards so that students are given the opportunity to meet standards and succeed, as best as possible, with standardized assessment instruments. Materials, resources, and emerging technologies must be reviewed and adopted in light of program changes. Professional development opportunities also must be reviewed and revised so that they are relevant and useful for developing teachers' competencies.

Those responsible for guiding the development of comprehensive literacy programs need to convince key personnel and the community that standards provide a focus for a rigorous curriculum and revised instructional practices that will help students to function in the 21st century. Any meaningful change requires a time-consuming and painstaking, collaborative process of rethinking and retooling that is based on a shared vision. Such reform efforts, which are organic and based on the organization, require leaders who have the knowledge, skills, and leadership qualities to guide such changes.

2. Administrators and specialized literacy professionals are responsible for creating the culture and ethos for change. Although administrators and specialized literacy professionals cannot expect to be expert in all the disciplines, developmental levels, and areas of concern for which they are responsible, they need to have their own set of competencies to serve as credible leaders. This entails having knowledge about the field, instructional and assessment mandates, methodologies, and materials, and using such knowledge to promote change. Such knowledge about the field comes from reading current research, getting involved with professional associations, attending and speaking at conferences and workshops, working with vendors to stay informed about new tools and products being developed, learning about new technological developments that have implications for classroom practice, and working closely with classroom teachers and faculty from colleges and universities. Competent administrators and specialized literacy professionals understand the dynamics of leadership and the change process with an awareness of the conflicting demands and needs of different constituencies. They have sufficient intellectual and emotional stamina to work well with all types of people to get the most from them. Specialized literacy professionals need to know enough about a school or district to establish and communicate realistic expectations, and to know when to call on the expertise of others. Specialized literacy professionals must possess certain leadership characteristics to be effective, such as enthusiasm for the job and a thick skin.

A major responsibility of administrators and specialized literacy professionals is to guide the change process so that teachers perceive it as supportive rather than burdensome. An ongoing and strategic program of professional development enables teachers to keep current about reading and writing instruction, and to understand how data-driven instruction helps to promote congruence between what is taught and what is tested. Administrators and specialized literacy professionals must provide resources and value teachers' voices in planning both the process and the content of professional development. Consideration should be given to how observations, observation conferences, coaching, demonstration lessons, and professional portfolios help to assess and document accomplishments, and how action research helps to develop a problem-solving mindset for answering questions about instructional practices. Because teachers are recognized now more than ever as the essential component of literacy achievement, administrators and specialized literacy professionals need to do all that is humanly possible to promote teachers' involvement with and investment in changing expectations. Administrators and specialized literacy professionals play a pivotal role in supporting the advancement of teachers as professionals, the success of instructional reforms, and the quality of educational opportunities offered to students. They should engage in pursuing partnerships with colleges, universities, businesses, and community agencies to bring to their schools and districts additional professional development resources. Administrators and specialized literacy professionals also need their own professional development to keep abreast of current developments in effective literacy practices, technological applications, and assessment tools, and learn new ways to coordinate the complexities of school- and districtwide literacy interventions.

3. *Administrators and specialized literacy professionals should remember at all times that the teacher is the key to students' literacy achievement.* Teachers should be knowledgeable, skillful, and invested in students' achievement because teachers have a profound impact on students' learning. Teachers are responsible for providing students with the tools and knowledge that are needed to develop as literate persons in the 21st century. They must be able to provide explicit instruction in the major components of reading (phonological awareness, fluency, word recognition, vocabulary, and comprehension) in the early years; exposure to varied genres of high-quality text, especially informational text; and instruction in critical reading strategies so that students can comprehend as well as critique, value evidence, and understand other perspectives and cultures. Teachers should use digital media strategically and capably so that their students can learn to use such resources to enhance their reading and writing skills. Teachers now must know how to teach online effectively, both synchronously and asynchronously. They also are responsible for differentiating instruction so that all types of learners can become independent readers of increasingly complex printed and digital text. Even though a simple solution will not emerge for helping students to meet standards, there will be different types of programs, models, and instructional practices that teachers can use to help students function as effectively as possible in and out of school. Early prevention and intervention programs will continue to help identify young children who need additional support to meet grade-level standards. Multi-Tiered Systems of Support (MTSS) will become more commonplace to focus on academics, behavior, and social emotional learning to prevent academic failure.

These systems are especially effective when students have qualified teachers who know how to offer appropriate intervention, monitor and reinforce students' efforts, and expose students to effective practices. These same teachers are able to work effectively with specialized literacy professionals and special educators to provide supplemental instruction for those students still struggling with reading. These teachers also are equipped to be culturally responsive to English learners by using appropriate teaching strategies and assessments.

Effective teachers of adolescents understand that they need to expose students to a wide variety of material, both print and digital; use a variety of strategies to help with reading comprehension and study strategies across the curriculum; and create literacy environments that are responsive to adolescent students' needs and differences.

All teachers will know how to use assessment data to determine instructional plans. They will be able to make decisions about next steps based on their own assessment of students' performance results.

Teachers will grow and change when they are engaged in professional development that is relevant to the contexts in which they teach. Peer collaboration, peer coaching, observations in one another's classrooms, and mentoring programs for new teachers are some of the many ways to promote teacher growth. Literacy coaches, as teachers' teachers, can provide the professional development support that teachers need through co-teaching and modeling.

4. Communication and collaboration among colleagues and with the community are essential. Dynamic literacy programs emanate from strong leadership within the school as well as from sincere efforts by school personnel to reach out and involve parents and the community. When colleagues communicate and collaborate regularly, they are better able to understand and plan for the varied complexities of literacy programs. Specialized literacy professionals can then take stock of the successes and failures with students, and the conditions surrounding each. Communication and collaboration also provide for better coordination within and across grade levels, and between regular and special programs. Communication and collaboration enable teachers to address grade-specific standards in tandem with the broader goals of college and career readiness. In

other words, teachers work together to *spiral* their curriculum so that they use similar standards with increasing complexity from grade to grade. When teachers work together, they can maintain their vision of literacy development and make instructional decisions accordingly. They can figure out ways to use data to gain insights about their instruction and their students' learning. When teachers work with specialized literacy professionals, administrators, and other stakeholders, they learn to respect one another's expertise as they collect, analyze, and use data to improve programs.

Communication with parents helps them to understand the literacy program. Collaboration with the community helps bring about important initiatives that extend a school's resources. Forming professional development schools and other types of partnership networks between the pre-K–12 and higher education communities helps bridge the gap between theory and practice as higher education faculty and students work directly with pre-K–12 faculty and students.

In sum, these four themes communicate that specialized literacy professionals help to determine the quality of a literacy program. Leaders administer with care and competence when they possess the necessary knowledge and skill to help schools set appropriate and realistic goals; when they create a culture that values teachers' professionalism and parents' contributions in support of students' literacy; and when they do everything in their power to provide a balanced yet meaningful literacy program. Just as there is no best program for all learners at every level, nor at any level, there is no best way to supervise under all circumstances. A key to administering a program is to create a balance of one's goals, one's abilities, and one's realities.

DIRECTIONS

This sixth edition of *The Administration and Supervision of Literacy Programs*, prepared 7 years after the publication of the fifth edition, contains 15 directions that speak to major shifts in thinking about educating our youth. These directions account for areas of both rapid change and steady state. They are, in fact, a set of hypotheses about the next steps needed to build on existing opportunities and discoveries. Implicit in these directions is the recognition that specialized literacy professionals will need to know more, be more, and help more as schools change their expectations for teachers and students.

1. Continued recognition of the need to improve students' literacy achievement calls for the study and *development of schoolwide comprehensive literacy programs* (CLPs) that reflect current research and theories about instruction and assessment, incorporate state standards and curricular goals, address students' unique abilities and characteristics, reflect local district and community needs, and focus on teachers as the linchpin for student achievement. Rita M. Bean (Chapter 1) describes the major components of CLPs and a systematic process for development that school and district leaders of literacy should consider as they collaboratively develop written action plans.

2. Comprehensive literacy plans require that *schools will have literacy leadership teams* to provide direction for the schoolwide literacy effort. The teams should be comprised of principals, specialized literacy professionals, teachers, parents, and community members. Timothy Rasinski, Chase Young, and Meghan Valerio (Chapter 5) describe how such teams can create a schoolwide horizontal and vertical approach to literacy instruction at the elementary level that is based on the science of reading and is responsive to the school culture.

3. Given that *teachers' abilities will continue to have a profound impact on students' success*, new evaluation models for determining teachers' success will be developed, implemented, and validated. Douglas Fisher and Nancy Frey (Chapter 8) describe the current state of teacher evaluation and how to make the process useful. Recognizing the importance of professional development for teachers' success with these new teacher evaluation models, Maryann Mraz, Jean Payne Vintinner, and Miranda S. Fitzgerald (Chapter 9) offer guidelines for creating a wide variety of professional development options and programs that are perceived as relevant and useful to teachers' instructional situations.

4. *Specialized literacy professionals will need to play a significant role with teacher professional development and student achievement.* They should work closely with principals, classroom teachers, and other stakeholders to ensure their position's viability. Shelley B. Wepner and Diana J. Quatroche (Chapter 2) look at the various and varied roles and responsibilities that specialized literacy professionals have and can have within and across schools focused on teaching, coaching, and leading.

5. *Literacy coaching, a major role of specialized literacy professionals, will continue to emerge as a powerful lever for improving literacy teaching and learning in schools.* Jacy Ippolito (Chapter 3) provides a new frame for effective coaching that highlights the contextual nature of coaching success and situates both the coach and the principal as collaborative artisans crafting a successful coaching model.

6. The *early years of schooling will continue to receive attention* because of accumulated data indicating that early learning experiences are linked with later school achievement. D. Ray Reutzel and Parker C. Fawson (Chapter 4) discuss what school and district administrators and literacy supervisors need to know about the science of how young children learn to read and write so that they can help teachers provide effective early literacy instruction.

7. *Effective secondary literacy reform can and will occur* if system and school leaders work together to create structures that help teachers acquire the necessary knowledge and practices of effective literacy instruction. William G. Brozo (Chapter 6) offers five principles of effective literacy leadership as a guide to an organizational approach that ultimately develops adolescents' literacy proficiency.

8. *Assessment of students' reading development and reading achievement will continue to evolve*, as Peter Afflerbach, Hyoju Ahn, and Moonyoung Park (Chapter 10) explain, with an eye toward ensuring that assessments serve all audiences and purposes. They offer ideas on how to select a balance of formative and summative assessments, develop students' self-assessment routines, and incorporate online reading and scenario-based reading assessment.

9. *Schools will use Multi-Tiered Systems of Support to meet the needs of students with diverse reading and writing needs.* Jennifer L. Goeke and Kristen D. Ritchey (Chapter 14) explain how administrators and supervision professionals can use MTSS as the "umbrella" system that incorporates Response to Intervention (RTI) and Positive Behavioral Interventions and Supports (PBIS) to support the whole child.

10. The *exponential growth of a diverse group of English learners in pre-K–12 schools will require teacher support* for using new instructional approaches and programs that help such students to succeed. MaryEllen Vogt (Chapter 13) discusses six principles of exemplary teaching that specialized literacy professionals and administrators can use as a framework for helping teachers to work effectively with emerging bilinguals/multilinguals to develop language, literacy, and academic content.

11. *Instructional materials, including the use of technology, will need to correlate with standards and foster equity.* Alejandro Gonzalez Ojeda, Toni Faddis, and Diane Lapp (Chapter 7) discuss the role of specialized literacy professionals in helping their schools and districts to apply an equity lens to the selection, purchase, and implementation of literacy materials that support a culturally relevant curriculum to meet all students' needs.

12. *Teachers will need to learn how to provide effective writing instruction for students from a variety of diverse backgrounds.* Julie K. Kidd and M. Susan Burns (Chapter 12) explain the need for effective professional development that will help teachers remain current on trends, issues, research, and policies in writing. They explain what administrators and specialized literacy professionals can do to help teachers integrate writing into the curriculum and promote learning across the content areas.

13. *New online technologies will continue to appear for literacy that redefine reading, writing, communication, and learning.* As a result, it is important to think about literacy in a new way. Elena Forzani, Clint Kennedy, and Donald J. Leu (Chapter 15) provide 10 principles as a backdrop for describing how administrators and specialized literacy professionals can help classroom teachers include instruction in the new literacies so that students are fully prepared for a continuously shifting landscape of new literacy requirements.

14. Specialized literacy professionals will become increasingly focused on *school- and districtwide evaluation of literacy programs* to help teachers reflect on and modify their instructional and assessment practices to accommodate students' diverse learning needs. Misty Sailors and James V. Hoffman, with Jimmie Walker and Yadira Palacios (Chapter 11), demonstrate how to use a specific evaluation model that involves all stakeholders and creates a culture of change within a school and district that is ongoing and sustainable.

15. Teachers, specialized literacy professionals, and administrators will need to *become deeply knowledgeable about students' families* so that they are fully aware of parents' intellectual, emotional, cultural, and social resources at their disposal. Patricia A. Edwards, Lisa Domke, and Marliese Peltier (Chapter 16) discuss ways to develop clear profiles of families, their resources, and their challenges to use in creating responsive and imaginative plans of action for effective parent engagement.

In looking back to look ahead, we recognize that the components for administering and supervising a literacy program remain essentially the same; however, the degree of focus on each component will shift as political mandates, national health and financial crises, social justice issues, achievement gap analyses, and research breakthroughs unfold. Consequently, the way in which specialized literacy professionals develop and revise school and district literacy plans depends on what has been discovered, what has been determined as an urgent need, *and* what has been mandated. A critical factor for responding effectively to changing expectations is *collaborative leadership* with teachers, other literacy personnel, administrators, school districts, the community, colleges and universities, businesses, and social agencies. This collaborative leadership will continue to evolve as each constituent recognizes the value and importance of the others. Collaborative leadership is referenced throughout this book as the hallmark for identifying and implementing special plans, programs, projects, and processes to support specific goals.

We fully recognize that "the times they are a-changin'," but at the same time we as a field have made considerable progress in understanding the critical elements for administrating and supervising a literacy program. We must always take heed to "what's going on" as we piece together the major elements for ensuring that our teachers are prepared to enable our increasingly diverse pre-K–12 student population to meet literacy standards. While aware of the challenges ahead, our expert authors use their knowledge, experiences, and research to describe existing pursuits and offer realistic possibilities for creating educational environments that subscribe to existing mandates *and* honor all that already works. We hope that you will join us with this new edition in using and reusing our authors' glorious insights and ideas about reaching for our next developmental milestone in developing 21st-century literacy for all types of learners.

REFERENCES

Every Student Succeeds Act, 20 U.S.C. § 6301 (2015). https://www.congress.gov/bill/114th-congress/senate-bill/1177

International Literacy Association. (2018). *Standards for the preparation of literacy professionals 2017*. https://literacyworldwide.org/get-resources/standards/standards-for-the-preparation-of-literacy-professionals-2017

International Literacy Association. (2020). *What's hot in literacy report*.

National Center for Education Statistics. (2019). *NAEP report card: Reading: 2019 NAEP reading assessment*. https://www.nationsreportcard.gov/reading?grade=4

Part I

OVERVIEW OF PROGRAM COMPONENTS AND PERSONNEL

The three chapters in Part I provide an overview of the components and personnel needed to administer an effective literacy program. In Chapter 1, Rita M. Bean offers a framework for districts to consider in developing a pre-K–12 comprehensive literacy program (CLP) that includes three essential components: standards and curriculum, instruction, and assessment. She explains why a CLP, which reflects shifts in how literacy is defined, is needed to create a road map for an aligned, consistent, and equitable curriculum for all students. She shows that it is essential to incorporate professional learning, shared leadership, and families/communities into literacy action plans, and offers a 4-step process for districts to use as they work collaboratively with their constituencies to develop such plans.

In Chapter 2, Shelley B. Wepner and Diana J. Quatroche explain that *specialized literacy professional* (SLP) is now the overarching term for three major roles in today's schools: reading/literacy specialist, literacy coach, and literacy coordinator/supervisor. The type of work professionals in these positions perform is illustrated with vignettes. The authors describe each role's qualifications and responsibilities within the context of teaching, coaching, and leading school literacy programs. They discuss the skills and characteristics that specialized literacy professionals should have to be effective leaders and emphasize the importance of working collaboratively with various partners and stakeholders to promote literacy across schools and districts. Suggestions for documenting and highlighting the significance of specialized literacy professionals are provided to ensure the position's viability

In Chapter 3, Jacy Ippolito provides a new frame for literacy coaching so that it can become one of the most powerful ways for schools to support the continual improvement of literacy teaching and learning. His frame focuses on both the knowledge, skills, and work of the coach (the foreground) and the context of school and district leaders who support coaching (the background). He describes essential elements for successful coaching, with an emphasis on the need to have clear lines of communication among coaches, principals, and teachers around what constitutes effective coaching to promote powerful progress with teaching.

These three chapters together illustrate the importance of having in place a comprehensive framework and qualified personnel to be able to develop, implement, and sustain a successful literacy program.

CHAPTER 1

Developing a Comprehensive Literacy Program

Rita M. Bean

- Developing a comprehensive literacy program requires an understanding of literacy, its importance for learning, and the rationale for creating a pre-K-12 plan.
- Careful consideration must be given to the many components contributing to an effective pre-K-12 plan for a comprehensive literacy program.

A systematic process that involves all stakeholders is crucial for the success of a comprehensive literacy program. This introductory chapter describes the rationale for developing a district comprehensive literacy program (CLP), and the importance of designing a framework and making sure that the program takes into consideration its essential components. Key concepts about these components are identified and explained. Finally, I describe the various stages of a process that districts can use to develop their comprehensive literacy plan, which is the written document that describes the program.

WHY A COMPREHENSIVE LITERACY PROGRAM?

A comprehensive literacy program provides a road map or framework that allows the district and its schools to provide an aligned, consistent, and equitable curriculum for all students. Although individual teachers may work effectively in the classroom with students, their individual efforts do not ensure that students will receive pre-K–12 instruction that has been thoughtfully considered and orchestrated, aligned vertically and horizontally. A comprehensive literacy program provides a well-developed and articulated vision of what literacy is from its early stages; it requires all professionals to make a concerted effort to work toward a shared vision. The development of such a program also requires knowledge of the school or district's community and communication with parents to ensure their participation in decision-making.

A CLP is critical given that there continue to be students in our schools who are not learning to read, write, or communicate effectively. Student literacy performance has generally been stagnant over the past decade; the results of the 2019 National Assessment of Educational Progress (National Center for Education Statistics, 2019) indicated that only 35% of 4th-graders and 34% of 8th-graders were proficient in reading. Further, the inability of many schools across the nation to address the achievement and opportunity gaps (Kostyo et al., 2018) that exist between majority students and others—for example, English learners, low-income students, students of color, or those with special needs—continues to be a challenge. Even legislation such as the No Child Left Behind Act of 2001 (2002) and its programmatic initiative, Reading First, which provided funds for high-poverty, low-achieving schools, did not achieve the high goals set for it (Gamske et al., 2008). Further, given that all graduates must be prepared to meet the high expectations of our technological, global, and competitive society, and that schools are educating more students and more diverse students than they did in the past, schools must get better at getting better (Bryk et al., 2015).

WHAT IS A COMPREHENSIVE LITERACY PROGRAM?

In previous editions, this chapter was titled "Developing a Comprehensive Reading Plan." Several factors have influenced the change in title and content. First is the need for a curriculum that recognizes the importance of teaching all components of the language arts, not only reading. Such a curriculum promotes instruction that takes advantage of the interrelationships or connections among the language arts to develop deep learning and facilitate transfer (Fisher et al., 2016). A recent metanalysis conducted by Graham et al. (2017) supports the notion that "balancing reading and writing instruction can strengthen reading and writing and that the two skills can be learned together profitably" (p. 279). At the same time, these authors raise an important point: that although reading and writing share common processes, they are not "identical skills" (p. 300), and that some time must be spent on teaching them separately. Langer (2001), in describing features of higher-performing schools, highlights the importance of literacy instruction as both an integrated and a separated set of experiences.

Second, and closely aligned with the notion that teachers have a responsibility to teach all the language arts, is the shift in how literacy is defined. Although a narrow definition of literacy might include just reading and writing, current definitions place an emphasis on more than these two essential components; rather, literacy addresses "a broader scope of skills, processes, and applications . . . . [including] oral language development, writing, digital and multiple literacies, visual literacy, and the power of literacy learning to change lives" (Fisher, 2018, p. xi). Also significant is that literacy instruction is viewed as the responsibility of educators across the disciplines, pre-K–12. This broader perspective reflects an integrated perspective of literacy instruction, evident in recent student standards, both those developed by the Common Core State Standards (CCSS) for English Language Arts and Literacy in History/Social Studies, Science, and Technical Subjects (Common Core Standards Initiative, 2010) and those created by states. Current standards acknowledge that a single rich task (e.g., reading, drafting a written response to that text, and then editing it) can provide students with the opportunity to achieve several standards. Essentially, there has been a shift from a narrow focus on reading to a broader perspective of literacy instruction.

COMPONENTS OF A COMPREHENSIVE LITERACY PROGRAM

A district should have a CLP that its schools can use to develop action plans to address district goals and vision while, at the same time, taking into consideration each school's unique context (e.g., student and family demographics, teacher knowledge and experience, and student learning outcomes). The schools can use the district plan as a guide for addressing their own specific goals, needs, and approaches to achieving those goals. The district CLP is a composite of many different factors—it is more than the purchase of a core literacy program, provision of supplemental materials or additional instructional time, or a change in the assessment measures used in the school. It is all of these and more! Figure 1.1 graphically portrays each of the major components to be considered by districts as they think about their current status. The overlapping circles highlight the three broad components of Standards and Curriculum, Instruction, and Assessment. Three additional and important considerations are included: Professional Learning, Shared Leadership, and Families/Communities. An effective program must attend to these considerations to ensure successful implementation and sustainability.

Figure 1.1 Major Components of a Comprehensive Literacy Plan

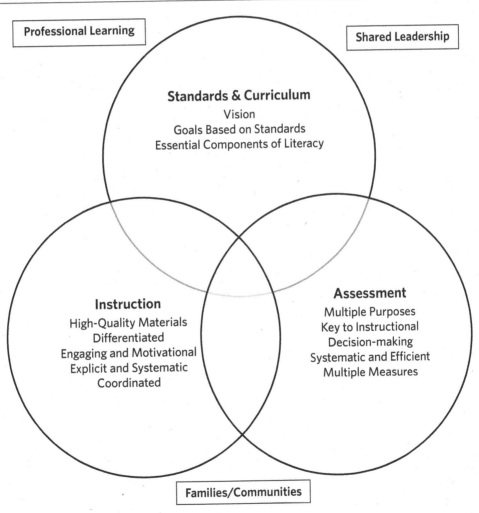

Standards and Curriculum

A Vision

The vision for literacy teaching and learning in a district guides the decisions that the district and schools make and helps them stay focused on what matters. It ensures systemic thinking that can lead to literacy success for all students. School/district faculty can ask themselves questions like those identified by Fountas and Pinnell (2018): What do we think literacy teaching and learning should look like in our classrooms and schools? What would students and teachers be doing in 1st grade? Third grade? Twelfth grade?

Goals Based on Standards

As mentioned previously, state standards provide districts with a comprehensive list of standards (pre-K–12) for all the language arts and literacy in the disciplines. At the local level, districts can then use the state standards to create a version that helps them identify goals that address the specific needs of students in their schools. Goal setting requires that teachers within and across grade levels have discussions about vertical and horizontal alignment of the curriculum. These discussions can help upper-grade teachers better understand what students are learning in the early grades; likewise, teachers in the lower grades can become more cognizant of the expectations of teachers who work with intermediate and adolescent students. Questions relating to how curriculum needs to be structured so that students have opportunities to learn how to read, write, and think effectively in the various disciplines must be asked—and answered. Below are important guidelines for developing a comprehensive pre-K–12 curriculum. It should be:

- Standards-based, reflecting research-based knowledge about literacy instruction
- Systematically and deliberately designed to provide for horizontal and vertical alignment, including alignment across all instructional programs available to students (supplemental, interventions)
- Free of gaps and unnecessary repetition
- Supported via the use of high-quality instructional materials that address standards

and the cultural, linguistic, and instructional needs of students

Essential Components of Literacy

In developing the CLP, educators will have the task of thinking about the many domains of literacy learning. Figure 1.2 categorizes these domains into two broad categories, *constrained* and *unconstrained* (Paris, 2005). The constrained skills identified in the graphic are generally learned more quickly, and mastered entirely; they need close attention, especially at the earlier grades. They are also necessary, but not sufficient, for developing the unconstrained skills that continue to develop throughout our lifetimes and are unique to individuals and their experiences. Below, several curricular issues are addressed that often require extended discussion by both those developing the plan and educators who will be responsible for implementing it.

Oral language. Language and literacy experiences at the preschool level provide the basis for successful reading and writing in later years. Research findings (National Early Literacy Panel, 2009; Snow et al., 1998) indicate that oral language, including vocabulary development, is highly related to proficient literacy; thus, districts must consider, in their planning, the experiences of young children in their homes and communities. Oral language and literacy experiences are also necessary for building world knowledge, contributing to literacy learning (Neuman, 2006; Paratore, 2019). These important language skills must continue to be developed throughout the grades to facilitate students' ability to talk, listen, read, and write in a thoughtful, critical way, as they continue to learn new concepts.

Figure 1.2. Major Domains of Literacy Learning

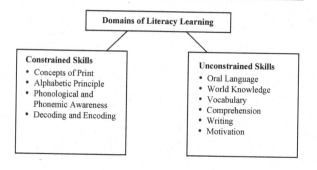

Word recognition and language comprehension. As described by Scarborough (2002), effective reading instruction requires attention to both word recognition (i.e., decoding) and comprehension and to recognizing the interactive nature of these two strands. A comprehensive plan calls for the systematic development of foundational skills that includes a systematic and explicit phonics program (Duke & Mesmer, 2018; Foorman et al., 2016; National Reading Panel, 2000; Paratore, 2019). Such a phonics program provides students with opportunities to analyze word parts actively and deliberately (Paratore, 2019), to read them, spell them, and write them. Students can keep journals in which they write some of the words that they have analyzed or built (Beck & Beck, 2013). Students also need to develop automaticity, to be able to read words accurately, fluently, and with expression; thus, opportunities for oral reading of text are important (i.e., repeated readings and partner reading). In fact, fluency serves as a bridge between basic foundational skills and comprehension. Further, a comprehensive program provides opportunities for students to apply their decoding skills in a meaning-based, language-rich curriculum with rich exposure to various genres of text (Foorman et al., 2016; International Literacy Association, 2019; National Education Policy Center & Education Deans for Justice and Equity, 2020). Not only should attention be given to constrained skills at the early levels, but, in addition, older students need learning experiences that enable them to analyze multisyllabic words—e.g., syllabication, prefixes, suffixes, Latin and Greek roots—as approaches for obtaining meaning.

Disciplinary literacy. Aligned closely with the importance of language and knowledge in learning to read is the premise that from early ages, students must not only learn to read, but must have opportunities to use reading to learn (Pearson et al., 2020). At all grades, there is a need to develop a curricular structure that provides for content area and disciplinary skills. The CLP should address the responsibilities of teachers of the disciplines in engaging students in learning the content and developing the "skills and strategies necessary to read, write and communicate in discipline-specific ways" (International Literacy Association, 2018, p. 85). Further, there is increasing agreement that disciplinary literacy instruction work can and should begin as early as kindergarten (Ippolito et al., 2019); these authors suggest that teachers of young children can introduce age-appropriate disciplinary ways of thinking and working (e.g., predict and ask questions about topics in informational texts and practice close observation and description).

Digital literacies. Digital use has increased exponentially, not only in schools, but in society as a means of communication, especially because of the restrictions placed on physical proximity by the COVID-19 pandemic in 2020. Therefore, an effective CLP should include information about what skills and knowledge students need to be effective and critical users of these digital tools. The definition by the American Library Association of "digital literacy" as "the ability to use information and communication technologies to find, evaluate, create, and communicate information, requiring both cognitive and technical skills" provides a useful starting place for thinking about digital literacies (from International Literacy Association Glossary, n.d.). Further, given that not all students have equal access to digital tools or learnings, schools are responsible for providing students with both the tools and the skills they need to be proficient users of these new literacies (International Literacy Association, 2017a). This has implications for teachers who, from the early grades on, need to know about how to use technology as an integral part of their instructional practices.

Writing. The literacy curriculum must address writing, not only as a means of enhancing reading instruction, but as an important dimension of literacy itself. As mentioned above, basic writing activities are key for enhancing foundational skills. But in addition, students need many opportunities for composing that go beyond the conventions of grammar, mechanics, and usage. Possible activities to enhance writing include the following: engage students in daily writing for different audiences and purposes, highlight the importance of writing as a means of learning (e.g., note-taking and summarizing), encourage peer collaboration, provide teacher and peer feedback, teach writing explicitly, and use technology in promoting writing (Graham & Harris, 2016).

Instruction

Let us turn now to the second component of a CLP, instruction. For instruction to be effective, schools will need to consider many different factors: an organization that provides for meeting needs of individual students; learning tasks or activities and strategies; grouping arrangements; resources, including print and nonprint instructional materials; and available support personnel. Research findings also indicate the importance of allocating sufficient time to literacy instruction (Puccioni, 2015; Taylor et al., 2000; Taylor & Peterson, 2003).

An individual teacher working with one student might be effective in meeting that student's needs; however, teachers are responsible for instruction for 20 or more students whose range in literacy performance varies tremendously. Teachers must be able to select or develop appropriate academic tasks, and then teach using them in ways that enable each student to grow and learn in an environment that promotes risk-tasking and guarantees success. District personnel should consider the following key, research-based features essential for planning an effective instructional program.

High quality. Selecting or developing materials for instruction requires educators to think carefully about whether such materials address the district goals, describe evidence-based strategies and activities, and meet the needs of all students in that context. Key points include the following:

- Although a core reading program may be used as a basic framework for instruction, it serves only as a guide. Students in the classroom may need additional scaffolding, supplemental support, or additional practice, beyond those suggested in the selected or district-developed program. Teachers in the classroom must have the expertise to decide whether the core program is meeting the needs of their students and how the program might be modified if it does not.
- All students should have exposure to material that relates to their own experiences and culture; at the same time, they should also read about cultures other than their own.
- Students should have experiences with multiple genres as well as types of text,

print and digital. Digital technologies have "transformed literacy practices, which have . . . . expanded the ways learners read texts, access information, and interact with each other" (International Literacy Association, 2018, p. 5).

- The purpose for reading influences texts used for instruction. Although the CCSS are explicit in the expectations that all students engage in reading high-quality literary and informational texts, they also acknowledge that some students will need additional support and scaffolding to access these texts. Further, at times, teachers may expose students to texts that give them opportunities to practice fluent reading or apply their developing decoding skills. Beginning readers especially will need opportunities to read decodable text (i.e., text that includes many phonetically regular words that students can successfully read) to develop fluency (Foorman et al., 2016). But such decodable texts may not generate students' motivation to read. They will need opportunities to grapple with more complex, interesting texts that support the development of language, vocabulary, and world knowledge.

Differentiated. Instruction should be responsive to the diverse needs of students. In planning instruction, educators need to address important questions such as: What does the student need to learn? How should they be taught? Research conducted by Connor and Morrison (2016) suggests that students will vary in how they respond to specific instructional approaches, depending on what they bring to the reading process. Modifications in intensity, group size, and materials should be considered, especially when students are experiencing difficulties with reading tasks. International Literacy Association (2017b) and Vogt (2020) address issues related to teaching English learners, and Connor & Morrison (2016), International Literacy Association (2016), and Scanlon et al. (2020) present ideas for helping students experiencing difficulties learning to read. (See also Chapter 13 in this book.)

Motivational and enthusiastic. Instruction should be engaging and meaningful. Such instruction enables students to make connections between what they know and what they are learning. Peer-group collaboration reinforces the importance of literacy learning as a social experience and can increase motivation, as well as help students develop self-directed learning (Botel & Paparo, 2016). Also, giving students choices in activities and reading materials has been found to be highly related to student engagement, motivation, and achievement (Guthrie & Humenick, 2004).

Explicit and systematic. In addition to developing instruction that is motivational and engaging, instruction that is explicit can provide students with a greater understanding of what they are to learn. By explicit, I mean that teachers model or demonstrate what they are teaching (I do), they work with students to assist them (we do), and then provide opportunities for students to work in small groups and individually (we/I do) to provide necessary practice, application, and feedback. Instruction that is systematic is carefully paced and sequenced, with easier skills taught first.

Coordinated. Many students receive instruction beyond that provided by the classroom teacher. In fact, most schools use some sort of Multi-Tiered System of Support (MTSS)/Response to Intervention (RTI) framework that addresses both the academic and emotional social needs of students. Students experiencing difficulties with core classroom instruction may need interventions provided by specialized literacy personnel. One of the important aspects of a CLP is congruence between the specialized literacy programs in schools and the classroom literacy program.

Assessment

Schools will use assessment results of student learning for multiple purposes: accountability or outcome results, instructional decision-making for teachers, feedback to students, classification and certification, and reform (Goatley et al., 2020). Often assessment programs are "high-stakes," that is, decisions about resources, sanctions, and rewards may be based upon the results (Popham, 2005). At the same time, an important use of assessment results is that of *informing instruction* at the school, classroom, and individual levels. In fact, results of school reform studies indicate that successful schools use data to support and guide instruction (Bryk et al., 2010; Goatley et al., 2020; Reeves, 2005). To develop a well-articulated system of assessment, one that is both systematic and efficient, a district or school must review the measures that they use pre-K through grade 12 and ask questions about the value of those measures: Is the information being used, and for what purpose? Is there redundancy? How important is the measure at that grade level? Developing an assessment system requires stakeholders to engage in thoughtful discussion about who and what will be assessed, what instruments or measures will be used, and how to use the measures to inform instruction. By developing an assessment system, time given to test administration can be reduced and greater emphasis can be placed on interpreting and using the results of assessment more meaningfully. When developing or selecting the assessment measures, consider the need for various types of assessment measures, including those focused on outcomes, screening, diagnostic, and progress monitoring. Further, look for measures that provide for overlap between what is taught and what is tested; otherwise, the tests are not a fair and valid measure of what students know or what teachers have taught.

Multiple measures, beyond the usual standardized and formal measures, for assessing student literacy learning can provide useful information about student performance. Students can use technology to demonstrate learning (e.g., a PowerPoint presentation summarizing the characteristics of specific rock types or a video of high school seniors' interviews about the community in which they live). Further, assessment tools such as retellings, in which students listen to or read a story and then tell or write all that they remember, may be used as an indication that students have a sense of story and can identify relevant elements (characters, plot, setting, and resolution). By listening to a child read orally, a teacher can identify the reader's accuracy, rate, and fluency. The number and type of books that a student reads in one year can be monitored to determine students' interests and desire to read. What is essential is that students and their parents are given feedback and suggestions on improving students' learning, and that teachers use the results to modify and adapt classroom instruction. (For further discussion of assessment, see Chapter 10 in this book.)

PROCESS FOR DEVELOPING A COMPREHENSIVE LITERACY PROGRAM

In this section, a 4-step process for developing a comprehensive literacy plan is described. As part of that process, I discuss the important topics of professional learning, shared leadership, and families/communities.

Step 1. Determining the Status Quo: A Team Effort

The literacy leadership team. As part of any curricular change process, an initial step is assessing where the school or district is and where it wants to be (its goals) to determine where there is a need for change. A *literacy leadership team* representing district constituents can be instrumental in promoting teacher ownership of the CLP, ensuring that there is a common understanding and language about literacy instruction and assessment. Parent representatives on the leadership team often can provide key insights about what they value and believe about their children, schooling, and literacy.

The literacy leadership team should work closely with teachers to develop a sense of ownership of the program being designed. Teacher knowledge and beliefs greatly influence the ways that a program will be perceived, and, as importantly, how it will be implemented. Begin by allowing teachers to discuss their own beliefs and values about literacy teaching and learning as they formulate goals and design or select curricula for students in their school. Teachers' own lives and school experiences, as well as their cultural backgrounds, influence their beliefs and actions. Beliefs are often resistant to change, and opportunities must be provided for teachers to think and reflect on what they believe, to read articles that present new ways of thinking about teaching literacy. Also, teachers must be supported as they attempt to relate what they are learning to what they already know. Opportunities should be provided for reflective discussions in a low-risk environment, where they can speak freely about issues related to the proposed goals. For example, teachers might have little knowledge about how to teach students who are English learners, they may not understand how they as content teachers can "teach" literacy in their classrooms, or they may not believe that formal literacy instruction should be part of a preschool program. They may have little understanding of how to address issues of equity and diversity. Discussing topics like these, although difficult,

is important for developing teacher ownership and can lead to effective implementation of the literacy program. Further, such reflective conversations are necessary to build knowledge that leads to shifts in beliefs—which contribute to changes in instructional practices. Figure 1.3 provides a list of questions that team members and teachers might consider as they reflect on the comprehensive literacy plan's design.

Figure 1.3. Questions to Consider When Developing a Comprehensive Literacy Program

Curriculum

1. Does the school have a vision and mission for its literacy program? Has the school established goals and standards (pre-K–12)? Has it considered:
   - The amount of time for literacy instruction at the primary and intermediate levels?
   - The relationship between reading and the other language arts?
   - The role of content-area teachers at all levels, but especially at the middle school/high school levels, in helping students address the literacy demands of their classrooms?
2. Do standards address the need for a developmental continuum that considers the student at all stages of reading and writing: emergent, beginning, transitional, intermediate, and skilled? Do they recognize the needs of learners at the middle school and secondary levels?
3. Are the standards based on what is known about effective literacy instruction and assessment; that is, are they evidence-based?
4. Do the standards address the essential elements of effective literacy instruction?
5. Have instructional resources (print and nonprint) been selected that enable teachers to address the goals and standards? Do these resources address the needs of all learners (students experiencing reading and writing difficulties, English learners, etc.)? Do they provide for the varying reading levels of students? Is a variety of materials available (narrative, informational, poetry, etc.)? Do they provide students with opportunities to read about students like themselves and others?
6. Is there a written framework or guide that makes the curriculum visible and usable?

Instruction

1. Has consideration been given to how literacy instruction will be organized, including how the differing needs of students will be met? Grouping options? Instructional resources? Additional time?

Additional support of specialized professionals?

2. Is there coordination and coherence among the literacy programs in the school (the core, the various tiers of instruction?) Is support provided to various learners (English learners, students experiencing reading and writing difficulties, etc.)?

3. Are teachers given opportunities to gain knowledge and understanding of the current research and literature about effective, evidence-based literacy instruction?

4. Is there coherence between the written curriculum of the school and actual classroom practices?

Assessment

1. Is there an assessment system (pre-K–12) that is coordinated across the grades? Is there provision for outcome measures? Screening measures? Diagnostic measures? Progress monitoring measures?

2. Is there alignment between the standards of the district and the assessment system; that is, is the assessment system measuring what is being taught?

3. Do the assessment measures address high-level cognitive thinking?

4. Do the classroom assessment measures assist teachers in instructional decision-making? Do they assist teachers in identifying the needs of struggling readers, English learners, and high achievers?

Process for Change

1. Is the committee or group assigned the task of developing the comprehensive plan a representative one; that is, does it include constituents at all levels? To what extent are teachers involved in the curriculum development process? Have they had opportunities to discuss their beliefs and understandings and learn more about how literacy can be taught effectively?

2. Is there leadership support for the development of the comprehensive literacy plan? Is time provided for meeting as a group and are the necessary resources available to members of the group? Do leaders encourage and support the work of the group members?

3. Have teachers been provided with the professional learning (PL) they need to implement the program effectively? Does this PL include opportunities for support and feedback (e.g., literacy coaching)?

4. Do PL activities provide teachers with opportunities to learn from each other, to collaborate? In other words, are teachers working together so that change can occur at the system level?

5. Are administrators supportive and involved in the change effort? Do they understand what is required of their teachers so that they can provide the necessary support?

Collecting and interpreting data. Data from multiple sources—e.g., outcome data, perceptual data, demographics, and school process data (Bernhardt, 2013)—should be collected to determine the strengths and weaknesses of the current program. Insights provided by families and the community can provide a stronger bond between the school and its constituents. Relevant information about current trends or research findings is also an important source of data, as is information about state standards or guidelines. Teachers who agree to work with the CLP development can select or be given articles to read that can then be discussed and debated.

Teachers who elect or are selected to work with the literacy team on the CLP must share and discuss what they are doing with other members of the teaching staff; the more understanding and ownership there is of the proposed changes, the more likely it is that implementation will be successful. Thus, there should be an intentional and deliberate process for involving all faculty—to obtain their input and seek their ideas. A set of guidelines or a template can assist leaders in their efforts to work with the planning group. Various states have developed needs assessments for assessing the literacy program in schools (pre-K–12); these are generally available on state websites. The document prepared by the Massachusetts Department of Secondary Education, *Guidelines for Developing an Effective District Action Plan* (Meltzer & Jackson, 2010), describes three key steps: organizing for action, assessing current status, and developing a plan.

A final step in this process of assessing the current program is interpreting and summarizing the data so all can see what the strengths of the district are, where pieces are missing, and what this means for future planning and implementation.

Step 2: Moving Forward with an Action Plan

Data from the survey and needs assessment are used to develop an action plan that identifies priorities for moving forward. In developing an action plan, keep in mind "the power of simplicity, clarity, and priority" (Schomker, 2011). Processes for achieving each goal should be described, including who will do what, when, and how. (For an example of an action guide, see Bean & Ippolito, 2015, Appendix I). An action plan may also require a district to select or develop a new curricular plan for literacy; in Figure 1.4, Celia Banks, a literacy coordinator in a large district, offers the lessons learned from leading such a literacy change effort in her district.

Step 3: Implementing a Plan for Sustainability

The comprehensive literacy program and its accompanying action plan are meant to be dynamic documents that may be modified as districts move through the implementation process and as districts monitor their impact on teaching and learning. Fixsen et al. (2007) describe implementation as the missing link between research and practice. They indicate that implementation may take 2 to 4 years to complete, and discuss the various stages of implementation, including exploration,

installation, initial implementation, full implementation (doing it with fidelity), innovation (making it work for the school), and, finally, sustainability. Often implementation of a specific initiative may require adaptation, given differences in context, such as resources, demographics, leadership support, and so forth (McLaughlin, 1990). Developing a systematic plan for obtaining ongoing feedback from teachers is especially important to make the modifications necessary for success in a specific context.

Professional learning. Given that the teacher is an important factor in determining whether students will be successful learners (Goldhaber & Anthony, 2004; Rice, 2003; Risko & Vogt, 2016), any change effort in the school, including curricular change, must provide opportunities for teacher learning.

Figure 1.4. Lessons Learned from Leading a Literacy Change Effort, Created by Celia Banks, Coordinator of Language Arts, K–6, Bilingual

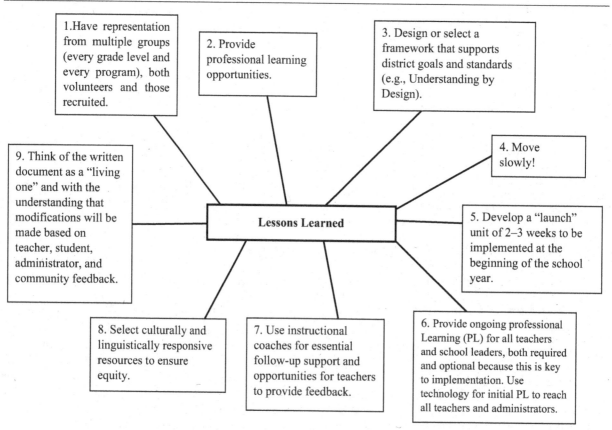

Decisions about what professional learning (PL) should be provided for teachers will depend on a district's goals as well as the beliefs and current expertise of teachers.

Fixsen et al. (2007) emphasize the importance of professional learning for those involved in implementing an initiative. Too often, good ideas that are placed in curriculum guides or district manuals are not implemented appropriately or at all by classroom teachers. Often this is caused by inadequate PL for teachers, who need practice and feedback in developing their skills. Such professional learning should reflect what is known about effective adult learning; that is, it provides meaningful activities that can be applied, opportunities for choice, active engagement, and collaborations with others (Bean & Goatley, 2020). PL should also provide for ongoing job-embedded support, such as coaching (Bean & Goatley, 2020; Bean & Ippolito, 2015).

Shared leadership. School leadership has been found to have a strong influence on student learning; moreover, leadership is more effective when it is shared collectively by principals and other school professionals, as this leads to a culture of collaboration and mutual accountability (DiGisi et al., 2020; Louis et al., 2010; Supovitz et al., 2010). Those in leadership positions must be sensitive to the complexity of bringing about long-lasting change and remember that change is difficult. Individuals involved in the change process will come to it with differing perceptions of how literacy should be taught. Thus, school leaders must be involved, not only in the CLP design, but in its implementation. They should attend PL sessions so that they understand what is expected of teachers and students and support the initiative by providing necessary resources, including time for ongoing PL, grade/academic department meetings, and coaching. At the same time, they must hold their faculty accountable for implementation.

Families/communities. Districts should use an asset-based approach that acknowledges and respects the resources that families bring to schooling (Paratore et al., 2020). This means that schools and teachers must "seek opportunities to uncover families' experiences, interests, achievements, problems and challenges, and to share children's classroom and school experiences" (p. 354).

Step 4. Evaluating the Program

An evaluation plan should be developed in the initial stages of curricular planning. As goals are identified, developers can think about ways to assess the accomplishment of those goals—in both formative and summative ways. There should be formative evaluation that documents how well the efforts to implement the change are working and provide ideas about what might need to be changed and modified during program implementation. Evaluation can come from classroom assessment measures used frequently, from teacher surveys, and from observation visits to the classrooms. In addition, a process for determining the effects of the changes should be identified (summative evaluation). This stage calls for specific attention to assessing the success or impact of the changes (Do they make a difference?) and the degree to which the changes have become institutionalized (Are teachers using the programmatic approaches?). The cyclical nature of the change process is also evident. As stated by Fullan and Miles (1992), "Change is a journey, not a blueprint. . . . One should not plan, then do, but do, then plan . . . and do and plan some more" (p. 749).

CONCLUSION

The development of a comprehensive pre-K–12 literacy program is an exciting and challenging task that requires the cooperation and collaboration of all concerned. The process is ongoing and cyclical, and it must include teachers and other constituents as part of the process if understanding and ownership are to occur. When developing a school comprehensive literacy program, the first task is to address the vision and accompanying goals that form the basis for curriculum, instruction, and assessment. Developing such a vision calls for a deep understanding of the research and literature to assist schools in making decisions about literacy instruction. It also calls for professional learning that enables teachers to increase their knowledge and understanding of literacy instruction. The development of a comprehensive literacy program can and should be a professional learning experience itself. When teachers are involved in developing the program, there is more likelihood that they will also have an investment in implementing it in their classrooms.

REFERENCES

Bean, R. M., & Goatley, V. (2020). *The literacy specialist and coach: Leadership in classroom school, and community*. Guilford Press.

Bean, R. M., & Ippolito, J. (2015). *Cultivating coaching mindsets: An action guide for literacy leaders*. Learning Sciences International.

Beck, I. L., & Beck, M. E. (2013). *Making sense of phonics: The hows and whys* (2nd ed.). Guilford Press.

Bernhardt, T. (2013). *Data analysis for continuous school improvement* (3rd ed.). Routledge.

Botel, M., & Paparo, L. B. (2016). *The plainer truths of teaching, learning, and literacy: A comprehensive guide to reading, writing, speaking and listening Pre-K–12 across the curriculum*. Owl Publishing.

Bryk, A.S., Gomez, L.M., Grunow, A. & LeMahieu, P. G. (2015). *Learning to improve: How America's schools can get better at getting better*. Harvard Education Press.

Bryk, A. S., Sebring, P. B., Allensworth, E., Luppescu, S., & Easton, J. Q. (2010). *Organizing schools for improvement: Lessons from Chicago*. University of Chicago Press.

Common Core State Standards Initiative. (2010). *Common Core State Standards for English language arts and literacy in history, social studies, science and technical subjects*. http://www.corestandards.org/the-standards

Connor, C. M., & Morrison, F. J. (2016). Individualizing student instruction in reading: Implications for policy and practice. *Policy Insights from the Behavioral and Brain Sciences*, 3(1), 54–61.

DiGisi, L. L., Meltzer, J., Schade, L., & Maze-Hsu, S. (2020). Sustaining literacy practices that transform teaching and learning. In A. Swan Dagen & R. M. Bean (Eds.), *Best practices of literacy leaders: Keys to school improvement* (pp. 387–410). Guilford Press.

Duke, N. K., & Mesmer, H. A. E. (2018). Phonics faux pas: Avoiding missteps in teaching letter-sound relationships. *American Educator*, 42(4), 12–16.

Fisher, D. (2018). Foreword: International Literacy Association sets the standard. In International Literacy Association, *Standards for the preparation of literacy professionals 2017* (pp. xi–xii).

Fisher, D., Frey, N., & Hattie, J. (2016). *Visible learning for literacy: Implementing the practices that work best to accelerate student learning*. Corwin Press.

Fixsen, D. L., Naoom, S. F., Blasé, A., & Wallace, F. (2007). Implementation: The missing link between research and practice. *APSAC Advisor*, 19(1&2), 4–11.

Foorman, B., Beyler, N., Borradaile, K., Coyne, M., Denton, C. A., Dimino, J., . . . Wissel, S. (2016). *Foundational skills to support reading for understanding in kindergarten through 3rd grade* (NCEE 2016-4008). National Center for Education Evaluation and Regional Assistance (NCEE), Institute of Education Sciences, U.S. Department of Education. https://ies.ed.gov/ncee/wwc/Docs/PracticeGuide/wwc_foundationalreading_040717.pdf

Fountas, I., & Pinnell, G. S. (2018). Every child, every classroom, every day: From vision to action in literacy learning. *The Reading Teacher*, 72(1), 7–19.

Fullan, M. G., & Miles, M. B. (1992). Getting reform right: What works and what doesn't. *Phi Delta Kappan*, 73(10), 745–752.

Gamske, B. C., Jacob, R. T., Horst, M., Boulay, B., & Unlu, F. (2008). *RF Impact Study Final Report* (NCEE 209-4038). National Center for Education Evaluation and Regional Assistance, Institute of Education Sciences, U.S. Department of Education.

Goatley, V. J., Dozier, L., & Puccioni, J. (2020). Using literacy assessments to improve student learning. In A. Swan Dagen & R. M. Bean (Eds.), *Best practices of literacy leaders: Keys to school improvement* (pp. 135–153). Guilford Press.

Goldhaber, D., & Anthony, E. (2004). *Can teacher quality be effectively assessed?* Urban Institute. http://www.urban.org/url.cfm?ID=410958

Graham, S., & Harris, K. R. (2016). A path to better writing: Evidence-based practices in the classroom. *The Reading Teacher*, 69(4), 359–365.

Graham, S., Liu, X., Aitken, A., Ng, C., Bartlett, B., Harris, K. R., & Holzapfel, J. (2017). Effectiveness of literacy programs balancing reading and writing instruction; A meta-analysis. *Reading Writing Quarterly*, 53(3), 279–304. https//doi:10.1002/rrq.194

Guthrie, J. T., & Humenick, N. M. (2004). Motivating students to read: Evidence for classroom practices that increase motivation and achievement. In P. McCardle & V. Chabra (Eds.), *The voice of evidence in literacy research* (pp. 329–354). Paul Brookes.

International Literacy Association. (n.d). *Glossary*. https://literacyworldwide.org/get-resources/literacy-glossary

International Literacy Association. (2016). *Dyslexia* (Research advisory).

International Literacy Association. (2017a). *Overcoming the digital divide: Four critical steps* (Literacy Leadership Brief).

International Literacy Association. (2017b). *Second language learners' vocabulary and oral language* (Literacy Leadership Brief).

International Literacy Association. (2018). *Standards for the preparation of literacy professionals 2017*.

International Literacy Association. (2019). *Meeting the challenges of early literacy phonics instruction* (Literacy Leadership Brief).

Ippolito, J., Dobbs, C. L., & Charner-Laird, M. (2019). *Disciplinary literacy inquiry and instruction*. Learning Sciences International.

Kostyo, S., Cardichon, J. & Darling-Hammond, L. (2018). *Making ESSA's Equity promise real: State strategies to close the opportunity gap*. Learning Policy Institute.

Langer, J. (2001). Beating the odds: Teaching middle and high school students to read and write well. *American Educational Research Journal*, 38(4), 837–880.

Louis, K. S., Leithwood, K., Wahlstrom, K. L., & Anderson, S. E. (2010). *Investigating the links to improved student learning: Final report of research findings.* Unpublished document, University of Minnesota, Minneapolis. https://conservancy.umn.edu/bitstream/handle/11299/140885/1/Learning-from-Leadership_Final-Research-Report_July-2010.pdf

McLaughlin, M.W. (1990). The RAND change agent study revisited: Macro perspectives and micro realities. *Educational Researcher*, 19(9), 11–16.

Meltzer, J., & Jackson, D. (2010). *Guidelines for developing an effective district literacy action plan* (version 1.1). Massachusetts Department of Elementary and Secondary Education and Public Consulting Group. https://www.publicconsultinggroup.com/media/1265/literacy-guidelines.pdf

National Center for Education Statistics. (2019). *Nation's Report Card*. https://www.nationsreportcard.gov/reading/nation/scores/

National Early Literacy Panel. (2009). *Developing early literacy: Report of the National Early Literacy Panel*. https://lincs.ed.gov/publications/pdf/NELPReport09.pdf

National Education Policy Center & Education Deans for Justice and Equity. (2020). *Policy statement on the "Science of Reading."* National Education Policy Center. http://nepc.colorado.edu/publication/fyi-reading-wars

National Reading Panel. (2000). *Teaching children to read: An evidence based assessment of the scientific research literature on literacy and its implication for literacy instruction*. National Institute of Child Health and Human Development.

Neuman, S. (2006). The knowledge gap: Implications for early education. In D. Dickinson & S. Neuman (Eds.), *Handbook of early literacy research* (Vol. 2, pp. 29–40). Guilford Press.

No Child Left Behind Act of 2001. Pub. L. no. 107–110, 115 Stat. 1425 (2002).

Paratore, J. R. (2019). Looking back: Lessons learned about making literacy instruction matter. *Primer*, 47(2), 7–18.

Paratore, J. R., Steiner, L. M., & Dougherty, S. M. (2020). Developing effective home-school literacy partnerships. In A. Swan Dagen & R. M. Bean (Eds.), *Best practices of literacy leaders: Keys to school improvement* (pp. 346–363). Guilford Press.

Paris, S. G. (2005). Reinterpreting the development of reading skills. *Reading Research Quarterly*, 40(2), 184–202.

Pearson, P. D., Palincsar, A. S., Biancarosa, G., & Berman, A. I. (Eds.). (2020). *Reaping the rewards of the Reading for Understanding Initiative*. National Academy of Education.

Popham, W. J. (2005). *America's "failing" schools: How parents and teachers can cope with No Child Left Behind*. Routledge.

Puccioni, J. (2015). Predictors of reading achievement: Time on reading instruction and approaches to learning. *Literacy Research: Theory, Methods, and Practice, 64*(1), 249–266.

Reeves, D. B. (2005). High performance in high-poverty schools: 90/90/90/ and beyond. In J. Flood & P. Anders (Eds.), *Literacy development of students in urban schools* (pp. 362–388). International Literacy Association.

Rice, J. K. (2003). *Teacher quality: Understanding the effectiveness of teacher attributes.* Economic Policy Institute. https://www.epi.org/publication/books_teacher_quality_execsum_intro/

Risko, V. J., & Vogt, M. E. (2016). *Professional learning in action: An inquiry approach for teachers of literacy.* New York: Teachers College Press.

Scanlon, D. M., Goatley, V. J., & Spring, K. (2020). Literacy leadership in special education. In A. Swan Dagen & R. M. Bean (Eds.), *Best practices of literacy leaders: Keys to school improvement* (pp. 281–303). Guilford Press.

Scarborough, H. S. (2002). Connecting early language and literacy to later reading (dis)abilities: Evidence, theory, and practice. In S. B. Neuman & D. K. Dickinson (Eds.), *Handbook of early literacy research* (pp. 97–110). Guilford Press.

Schomker, J. (2011). *Elevating the essentials to radically improve student learning.* Association for Supervision and Curriculum Development.

Snow, C. E., Burns, M. S., & Griffin, P. (Eds.) (1998). *Preventing literacy difficulties in young children.* National Academy Press.

Supovitz, J., Sirinides, P., & May, H. (2010). How principals and peers influence teaching and learning. *Educational Administration Quarterly, 46*(1), 31–56.

Taylor, B. M., Pearson, P. D., Clark, K., & Walpole, S. (2000). Effective schools and accomplished teachers: Lessons about primary-grade literacy instruction in low-income schools. *The Elementary School Journal, 101*(2), 121–166.

Taylor, B. M., & Peterson, D. S. (2003). *Year 3 Report of the CIERA School Change Project.* University of Minnesota, Center for Reading Research.

Vogt, M.E. (2020). *Academic language and literacy development for English learners.* In A. Swan Dagen & R.M. Bean (Eds.), *Best practices of literacy leaders: Keys to school improvement* (pp 325–343). Guilford Press.

CHAPTER 2

Specialized Literacy Professionals as Leaders

Shelley B. Wepner and Diana J. Quatroche

- Specialized Literacy Professionals have various and varied roles and responsibilities within and across schools, focused on teaching, coaching, and leading.
- Specialized Literacy Professionals who are successful as leaders demonstrate intellectual, emotional, social, and moral characteristics and competencies.
- Specialized Literacy Professionals need to work closely with principals, classroom teachers, and other stakeholders, and document their achievements to ensure their position's solvency.

We begin this chapter by introducing Susan Green and Paula DiDomenico. Both are certified in reading; however, their specific coaching roles and responsibilities are shaped by their positions and themselves. They share a common purpose in promoting students' literacy and learning development, one at the districtwide elementary level and one at the schoolwide high school level.

Susan Green is the district literacy coach for K–5 schools in Rock Hill, South Carolina, where she works primarily with the coaches and teachers in the district's Title I schools. Susan has been a classroom teacher, reading teacher, and English as a second language (ESL) teacher in New York, North Carolina, and now South Carolina. As the district literacy coach, she works in the schools by meeting with the coaches of every school and performing several functions: helping the coaches plan professional development (PD); conducting classroom observations with the coaches; and engaging in coaching cycles with a coach and a classroom teacher. She also provides professional development at the district level. If asked by a principal, she might provide PD for a particular school or do a coaching session with one of the teachers. Susan's role is a partnership role rather than a supervisory role. She and a coach will look at school or classroom data and use the information to focus PD on the actual needs of the school. One of her biggest challenges is time. All the schools schedule their literacy blocks at the same time, and the teachers do not have a special period designated for professional learning. This is especially challenging when a building coach or an administrator asks for help to implement a new program. Since the teachers do a good job of differentiating instruction for their students, one of Susan's goals is to provide targeted professional development. She knows that one of the most important parts of her position is to build relationships with the principals, coaches, and teachers.

Paula DiDomenico is an instructional coach for a large high school in Franklin Park, Illinois, where she works with teachers of all disciplines. She has been a coach for 11 years and the head of the student-support department for the past 6 years. In this role, she oversees the three other coaches, the math and writing center, and the library. Paula and the coaches focus their professional development on helping teachers to prepare students to be confident

problem solvers, which is the district's broad goal. On a typical day Paula will collaborate with content-area teachers about the reading of rigorous text, the use of discussion for problem solving, the composing of original thought, or the constructing of an argument. She will collaborate with the social studies teacher on how to use an inquiry lens in social studies and the science teacher on the use of notebooks to compose original thought. She might do a demonstration lesson in the classroom, co-teach, or review student work. For those teachers who do not want modeling, she might serve as another set of eyes focused on the relationship between instruction and student success. She might include the school librarian as part of the collaboration. Paula studies the standards and curriculum for each content area but relies on her teachers to help her know their needs in supporting the district focus. Paula finds that while coaching is not easy, it is worth the effort.

WHAT IS A SPECIALIZED LITERACY PROFESSIONAL?

Specialized literacy professional (SLP) is an overarching term for three major positions in today's schools: reading/literacy specialist, literacy coach, and literacy coordinator/supervisor (International Literacy Association, 2018). All SLPs have advanced preparation and experience in literacy with the goal of improving students' literacy achievement in a classroom, school, or district. The reading/literacy specialist works primarily with students, especially those who have difficulty with reading and writing. The literacy coach works primarily with teachers and facilitates efforts to improve school literacy programs. The school coordinator/supervisor works primarily with teachers and administrators across schools within a district to lead, coordinate, and/or evaluate the literacy program (International Literacy Association, 2015). An SLP can be called reading specialist, reading teacher, literacy coach, reading coach, reading consultant, literacy liaison, literacy facilitator, reading supervisor, or reading coordinator (International Literacy Association, 2018; Quatroche & Wepner, 2008). Specific titles and responsibilities depend on the context in which SLPs work, their teaching experience, and their educational background.

Advanced preparation and experience in reading typically means that an SLP has a valid teaching certificate, previous teaching experience, and a master's degree with a concentration in reading and writing that leads to statewide certification. The master's degree usually includes graduate credits in literacy and related courses, hours of a supervised practicum experience that includes work with struggling readers and writers, and collaborative and coaching experiences with teachers (International Literacy Association, 2015; International Reading Association, 2010). State regulations and standards determine the distribution of coursework and fieldwork requirements and stipulate the number of years of previous teaching experience that a candidate must have to be eligible for licensure.

SLPs work with early childhood, elementary, adolescent, or adult learners. They help preschoolers to emerge as readers, elementary children to develop as readers, adolescents to use reading to learn across content areas, and adults to continue to read or to develop as readers, depending on their previous experiences and abilities. While most SLPs work at the elementary level, many serve an important role at the middle and high school levels (International Reading Association, 2000). In fact, secondary reading specialists are needed to help students who do not have the necessary literacy skills to keep up with the secondary curriculum and so have difficulty with the more complex reading and writing skills required by high-stakes tests (AASA The School Superintendents Association, 2019). Poor literacy skills have been identified as the most common factor for high school dropouts (Carlson, 2011). SLPs work in public and private schools, commercial schools, reading resource centers, and reading clinics.

WHAT ARE THE ROLES OF SPECIALIZED LITERACY PROFESSIONALS?

Specialized literacy professionals have three primary roles: teaching, coaching, and leading school literacy programs (International Literacy Association, 2018). Each role, as described below, contributes to promote student learning.

Teaching

Teaching is at the heart of reading/literacy specialists' responsibilities. They provide supplemental instruction for students who are experiencing difficulties with reading and writing. Such instruction, which can be within and outside students' classrooms, tends to go beyond what is provided by classroom teachers to help students with specific learning needs. Reading/literacy specialists participate in making decisions about the kinds of interventions that students need and then provide targeted instruction to students individually and in small groups throughout the day. They typically use a combination of instructional strategies and models and a wide range of traditional print, digital, and online resources. (International Literacy Association, 2015; International Reading Association, 2010; Pletcher et al., 2018).

Reading/literacy specialists' work as instructors is important because of their ability to help students acquire enough skills and strategies so that they no longer need the additional assistance. Reading/literacy specialists have different orientations in the way that they provide instruction because of their own training and the focus of their schools and districts.

Jeannemarie Cregan is a reading/literacy specialist in a 4th- to 6th-grade school in Westchester County, New York, where she provides reading instruction and interventions to students. She is called a reading teacher in her school and is one of three who have been charged with helping the nearly 65% of students who need support with literacy development. Jeannemarie has a master's degree in reading and has been trained beyond her master's degree in multisensory approaches to help develop students' word fluency.

Every student in her school is assessed each year to determine their instructional and independent reading levels. If students have decoding challenges, they are further assessed for their word identification, spelling, and sound-symbol knowledge. These assessments identify those students who are placed with Jeannemarie for individual and small-group instruction. Jeannemarie collaborates with the English Language Arts teachers to ensure instructional consistency. She works closely with parents and families to communicate the importance of having their children practice and apply their developing literacy skills at home. She is very proud that her school and district have evolved to focus on literacy. She attributes this newfound mission to the leadership. The district now has a literacy director who meets regularly with Jeannemarie and the other reading/literacy specialists to discuss and plan for each school's progress with students' literacy development. Jeannemarie is encouraged to continue to develop professionally so that she is proficient in using research-based methodologies. As someone who thrives on witnessing students' progress, Jeannemarie shares with pride that her originally self-doubting students now enjoy reading novels, and they have participated with great success in nationwide literacy competitions.

The instructional role allows reading/literacy specialists to have a direct impact on students' literacy achievement; their teaching also serves as a model for classroom teachers when they teach directly in the classroom. Critically important for students' literacy development is the coordinated instructional effort of the reading/literacy specialist and the classroom teacher so that their objectives, strategies, assignments, and materials are aligned to maximize students' learning.

The instructional role helps to establish credibility with classroom teachers because reading/literacy specialists can communicate their understanding of students' needs and their knowledge of ways to help. By having access to teachers to discuss both students and the literacy program, reading/learning specialists have a pathway to serving as leaders (Bean et al., 2003). Jeannemarie uses this access to teachers to share with them her interpretation of their students' instructional needs, based on the results of her individual assessments of students, so that they can coordinate instructional tasks that support word fluency and comprehension.

Coaching

Coaching means providing professional development support for teachers to help them implement programs and practices that improve student learning. Literacy coaches help teachers reflect on their practices to improve classroom instruction (Bean & Kern, 2018).

Coaching is a form of instruction involving an ongoing relationship between an experienced and a less experienced person in which the coach provides training, guidance, advice, support, and feedback to the protégé. Coaching helps teachers learn to use new ideas, tools, and strategies, and to practice what they learn within their own contexts. Practicing within their own contexts allows teachers to see whether such ideas and techniques are relevant for their unique teaching situations.

Coaching that impacts teacher practice comes from a shared vision, commitment, positive interactions in a safe environment, and trusting relationships (Brownell et al., 1997; Edwards, 2015; Ferguson, 2014; Toll, 2018). With coaching, teachers can develop a heightened sense of self-efficacy, an improved knowledge base, and a better understanding of how to improve learning for students. Coaching is most effective when there are clear guidelines, these guidelines are discussed, and the coach maintains a flexible schedule to be available for collaborative work with teachers (Guth & Pettengill, 2005; Pletcher et al., 2018).

As the district leader coach, Susan Green engages in coaching cycles with a coach and a classroom teacher. Susan works with the district's coaches and teachers to strengthen instruction. Coaching cycles usually begin with a coaching conversation where the coach and teacher meet to discuss data and come up with a plan to adjust classroom instruction. The coach and teacher then collaborate and teach together for a determined amount of time. These demonstration lessons are followed up with debriefing conversations where the teacher is able to provide input and determine next steps.

As a high school instructional coach, Paula DiDomenico appreciates the need for teacher input for any type of coaching that she provides. Her problem-based coaching approach focuses on what teachers request. Her teachers might want her to help them study data or figure out ways to incorporate writing into the classroom to conform to the district's writing standards. She knows that teachers feel better when they are collaborating with her and working together to solve problems.

Students are best served when teachers are aided in building their capacity to educate. Coaching is one element of professional development that helps build that capacity in teachers.

Leading School Literacy Programs

Leading school literacy programs usually means leading, coordinating, and evaluating the school or district reading program to meet the needs of all students (International Literacy Association, 2015). Literacy coordinators/supervisors work with teachers and administrators to

- Develop curriculum and special initiatives
- Develop and lead short- and long-term professional development programs
- Identify, select, and develop reading material
- Evaluate the literacy program in general
- Assess the reading strengths and needs of students
- Coordinate the reading and writing program across grade levels
- Engage in systemic changes that occur across the school or district
- Collaborate with various school personnel such as special educators, psychologists, and speech therapists (Bean, Kern, et al., 2015; Galloway & Lesaux, 2014; International Literacy Association, 2015)

An important aspect of leading school or district reading programs is knowledge about and application of assessment. Literacy coordinators/supervisors are responsible for helping teachers understand the purpose of assessment in relation to instruction. Literacy coordinators/supervisors must know the types of assessment instruments and what they measure, know how to use such assessment instruments, know test preparation strategies, and know ways to interpret and report assessment data in relation to intervention practices and students' responses to instruction and intervention. Susan Green, as a district leader coach, has knowledge of assessment that enables her to work with principals to share data so that professional development for their teachers is targeted to what the data show. This collaborative effort helps her principals to avoid PD that is not supported by the data.

Literacy coordinators/supervisors often conduct assessments for individuals or groups of students. For example, they might assess the reading skills of all entering kindergartners, test all those who participated in a special program, or test those recommended by classroom teachers. They also help teachers develop assessments. Susan Green worked with her teachers to develop formative and summative assessments along with pacing guides for grades 3, 4, and 5.

SLPs also use and help teachers use test-preparation strategies. Some of the strategies include using testlike material to help students develop the skills needed to be successful with the test; familiarizing students with a specific test format; modeling test-taking so that students can listen to a respected person respond to test questions; and simulating testing conditions (McCabe, 2003).

HISTORICAL CONTEXT AND CURRENT STANDARDS FOR SPECIALIZED LITERACY PROFESSIONALS AS LEADERS

The role of the specialized literacy professional as a leader is not new. In the 1960s and 1970s, when the role of reading specialist developed to address post-*Sputnik* concerns about literacy in the United States, these professionals served as resource persons, advisors, and in-service leaders (Robinson & Rauch, 1965; Vogt & Shearer, 2003). A shift in the reading specialist position occurred in the early 1980s when the role evolved into functioning primarily as a remedial reading teacher with the primary responsibility of assessing and instructing students. A downward trend in the use of reading specialists as leaders continued until the late 1990s and early 2000s. Studies conducted in these decades suggested that reading specialists should again be given leadership responsibility in order to improve literacy for all students (Allington & Walmsley, 1995; Bean et al., 2002; Ippolito et al., 2019; Long, 1995; Quatroche et al., 2001).

The 2004 International Reading Association (IRA) standards for reading professionals called for the leadership role because, as Pipes (2004) reported, working with classroom teachers would help to ensure that they know how to provide quality instruction. Widespread recognition of the leadership role occurred with the emergence and hiring of literacy coaches when Reading First, one of the many outgrowths of No Child Left Behind, required that such professionals be available to work with classroom teachers as they implemented best practice in relation to the five components of reading: phonemic awareness, phonics, fluency, comprehension, and vocabulary.

One of the categories in the 2004 IRA standards was reading specialist/literacy coach (International Reading Association, 2004). The responsibilities included serving as a resource to teachers, paraprofessionals, administrators, and the community; collaborating and working cooperatively with other professionals; providing professional development; and advocating for students.

The 2010 IRA standards gave more prominence to the leadership role by including the roles of literacy coach and literacy supervisor or coordinator as part of the overall set of standards. Reading specialists as coaches meant providing professional development support for teachers to help them implement programs and practices that improve student learning. Reading specialists as leaders of school reading programs meant developing, implementing, and evaluating the school or district reading program to meet the needs of all students (International Reading Association, 2010).

The latest standards, issued in 2018, reflect the new name of the association, which is now the International Literacy Association (ILA). This name change occurred in 2013 to communicate a broader definition of literacy beyond reading to include writing, speaking, listening, viewing, and visually representing in both print and digital realms. This broader emphasis is consistent with the integrated literacy curriculum in today's schools. The leadership role is still an integral part of the new standards, with literacy coach and school coordinator/supervisor considered two of the three major roles of the SLP. While all three roles have distinct responsibilities, they also are interconnected in the work that they do in the schools (International Literacy Association, 2018).

Literacy Coach

A literacy coach is primarily responsible for working with teachers to help improve school literacy programs. A literacy coach might work with one or more teachers to support them in their efforts to improve classroom instruction. In addition to serving as a resource to teachers, a literacy coach might lead teachers through observation–feedback cycles to provide suggestions for changes in instructional practice. A literacy coach might also be responsible for developing curriculum and selecting instructional materials to help with the schoolwide literacy program (International Literacy Association, 2015; Stover et al., 2011).

The concept and importance of literacy coaches emerged from the No Child Left Behind Act so that teachers would receive the necessary professional development to implement evidence-based reading instruction. There has been a noticeable decrease in the numbers of coaches employed in schools because of diminished funding for literacy coach positions (Bean, Dole, et al., 2015). Yet many districts have found ways to fund coaching by shifting the responsibilities of reading/literacy specialists, identifying teacher leaders to assist their colleagues in improving literacy instruction (Steinbacher-Reed & Powers, 2011), or shifting Title I funds to support the role (International Literacy Association, 2015).

Literacy coaches should have the knowledge, skills, and dispositions expected of reading/literacy specialists in order to be successful. Otherwise, they will find it difficult to provide the effective job-embedded professional development that improves literacy instruction (Bean, Kern, et al., 2015; L'Allier et al., 2010). The expectation for literacy coaches to have the necessary qualifications to work with teachers applies to both elementary and secondary levels. Even though the focus might be different, with elementary teachers focused on the development of literacy and secondary teachers focused on the development of discipline-specific content knowledge, the coaching processes are similar (Edwards, 2015; Ippolito & Lieberman, 2012).

Joseph Franks became a literacy coach for his middle school teachers in southern Pennsylvania. Previously, he was a language arts teacher in the same school, but decided to get a master's degree and reading specialist certification so that he would be qualified to serve as a coach. He works directly with his teachers during grade-level and content-area team meetings. He helps his teachers plan curriculum units and lessons in different content areas. He goes into their classrooms to model lessons, co-teach, or observe lessons about which he provides feedback. His work with teachers is based on their collaborative analysis of student work. He has found that a key ingredient for serving as a successful literacy coach is his ability to apply adult learning principles to his professional development efforts by honoring teachers' experiences, expertise, and purposeful learning styles. Even though he was a teacher in the building prior to becoming a coach, he has had to spend a great deal of time building trust so that they know that he is not there to judge them but to assist them with what they need. He also has discovered that his coaching work is not linear; it is a circuitous process of working with teachers, and it does not necessarily translate into a "quick fix" for higher student achievement scores but instead offers a qualitatively different way of helping students to learn.

Literacy Coordinator/Supervisor

As the most recent ILA standards (2017) indicate, some reading/literacy specialists have a specific focus that further defines their duties. One such role is that of a literacy coordinator/supervisor who possesses the skills of reading/literacy specialists plus the supervisory skills and certification to officially observe teachers. They are responsible for leading the entire district literacy program and facilitating the work of other reading/literacy specialists.

Literacy coordinators/supervisors lead committee efforts to develop and implement the school literacy program, collaborate with parents or community agencies to increase the effectiveness of school literacy efforts, write and manage proposals for Title I or other grants, and work with school leaders to assist in school change efforts. These professionals may also be asked to work closely with administrators to implement a system of teacher performance evaluation to improve teaching practices (Bean, Kern, et al., 2015; Galloway & Lesaux, 2014). When they evaluate teacher performance, they are serving in a supervisory capacity, which means that they need a minimum number of years as a reading/literacy specialist or coach and, if possible, at all levels that they supervise (International Literacy Association, 2015).

See Figure 2.1 for a brief overview of very general similarities and differences of the positions of reading/literacy specialists, literacy coaches, and reading coordinators/supervisors. Although there are specific roles and responsibilities for each job title, SLPs tend to play multiple roles, depending on the context in which they serve (Bean et al., 2018; International Literacy Association, 2015; Ippolito et al., 2019).

WHAT SPECIAL SKILLS AND CHARACTERISTICS SHOULD SPECIALIZED LITERACY PROFESSIONALS POSSESS?

Charged with the responsibility of improving literacy achievement in their assigned school or district positions, SLPs should possess the skills and characteristics that are reflective of good leaders. They need to have the expertise to deliver exemplary instruction (Allington, 2006). They also need to be able to get their teacher colleagues to work with them to deliver high-quality instruction that meets students' needs.

SLPs with credibility as leaders are able to do what they are charged to do. In addition to the necessary educational and professional background, SLPs have certain leadership skills that enable them to succeed in their roles. Borrowing from a

Figure 2.1. Comparison of Reading/Literacy Specialists, Literacy Coaches, and Reading Supervisors/Coordinators

	Reading/Literacy Specialist	Literacy Coach	Literacy Coordinator/ Supervisor
Qualifications	• Graduate coursework that leads to a master's degree • Reading/literacy specialist certificate • Prior teaching experience	• Graduate coursework that leads to a master's degree • Reading/literacy specialist certificate • Prior teaching experience • Prior experience working with teaching peers (e.g., leading professional development sessions)	• Graduate coursework that leads to a master's degree • Reading/literacy specialist certificate • Prior teaching experience • Prior experience as a reading/literacy specialist or coach • Prior experience with curriculum development and teacher observation
Roles and responsibilities	• Instruct students • Assess students and reading program • Work with teachers	• Sometimes instruct students • Sometimes analyze student test results • Primarily work with teachers	• Work with and supervise teachers • Facilitate the work of other reading/ literacy specialists and/or literacy coaches • Oversee literacy program in the district
Level of responsibility	School-based	School-based	District-based

conceptual framework about the leadership of education deans (Wepner, D'Onofrio, & Wilhite, 2003, 2008; Wepner, Wilhite, & D'Onofrio, 2011), it appears that SLPs who are successful as leaders possess characteristics that enable them to function in four dimensions: *intellectual, emotional, social,* and *moral* (see Figure 2.2).

The *intellectual* dimension refers to SLPs' knowledge of the various facets of their job and their ability to juggle each responsibility within their own contexts. The assumption with this dimension is that SLPs have the necessary knowledge about the field of literacy and about their own school and district literacy program. They know how their literacy program addresses, for example, digital literacy and assessment mandates, and how to modify their plans accordingly. They know how to administer and interpret multiple assessment instruments. They are aware of trends, research, and alternative methodologies. They are proficient in using specific literacy strategies. SLPs know when, where, and how to use this information within their own schools and districts to promote change. As a district literacy coach, Susan Green is confident of her knowledge of literacy and her district's needs, is aware of her administrators' support, and knows the types of professional development offerings to provide for her coaches and teachers. She is aware of the pressures and needs that teachers have, and she uses this knowledge as well as her own understanding of her coaches' needs to assist both groups.

The *emotional* dimension refers to feelings and sensibilities that include an ability to acknowledge inner conflict and an ability to express feelings vividly and convincingly. Successful SLPs are confident in overseeing their job and have a balanced perspective about their roles as leaders. They recognize their own strengths and weaknesses and know when they can help and when they cannot. They are honest with themselves about their feelings of irritation with people, policies, and practices, yet they are able to set those feelings aside to have a positive

Figure 2.2. Four Dimensions of Leadership of Specialized Literacy Professionals

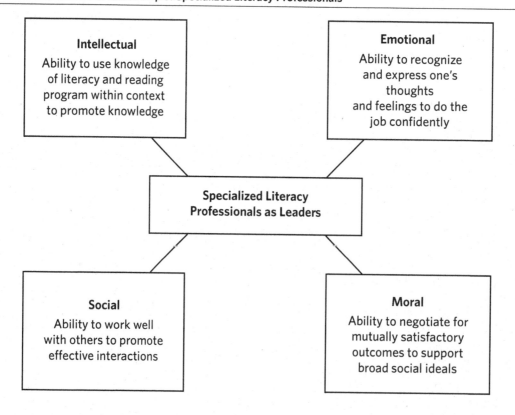

impact on their working environment. They also are comfortable in expressing their thoughts when people, policies, and practices inhibit learning or stifle teaching. They know that no matter how they feel, they must have patience and be flexible with their teachers so that they can support their teachers where they are. As a coach at the secondary level, Paula DiDomenico understands the need for flexibility very well. Because her teachers have many competing priorities, she is comfortable with taking a step back to figure out when to offer her coaching services and when to slow down. Even though she makes sure to learn about her teachers' areas of expertise, she fully appreciates that she does not have to be the expert. Rather, she is content to learn along with her teachers and is honest with herself in what she can do and cannot do.

The *social* dimension is about transactions with others, including societal and organizational relationships. Successful SLPs cope with conflict rather than ignore it, are tolerant and empathetic toward others, and respect individual differences. They listen, cooperate, collaborate, and encourage others to try new things. They work effectively with teachers, administrators, students, and parents on an individual and group basis. Their interactions with their constituencies promote positive responses to themselves and to their ideas. Susan Green knows that one of the most important parts of her position is to build relationships with the principals, coaches, and teachers. She works hard to keep the lines of communication open by listening first to the teachers because they know their students and then taking the information to the coaches and principals so that they understand what the teachers need to sharpen their instructional practices

The *moral* dimension has to do with a sense of conscience and accountability, and the desire to negotiate energetically for mutually satisfactory solutions to problems. SLPs who are successful know how to maintain confidentiality and believe strongly in working together with others to get the best possible outcome for both parties. They do what they say they are going to do. They are committed to doing the right thing as much as doing the thing right. In other words, short-term losses are seen as opportunities for long-term gains. We are aware of school districts that have engaged in questionable practices with their statewide assessments because

some students have great difficulty passing the test, no matter what is tried. As a former language arts teacher in a middle school, Joseph Franks knows that some of the school's students will have great difficulty passing the statewide tests. While he knows that his principal wants as many students as possible to pass, he will not compromise his values for a few better scores. Instead, he works closely with his teacher colleagues to provide them with test-taking strategies that may help the students to pass.

In summary, SLPs with characteristics in these four dimensions have qualities that help them to meet the demands of their roles. Committed to the ideal of developing students' literacy, they have the intellectual and emotional stamina to work well with all constituencies to get the most from them. SLPs know enough about their school or district to establish and communicate realistic expectations. They are able to suggest ideas and materials, conduct professional development workshops, model strategies or techniques, and conduct demonstration lessons that fit with their teachers' needs. Their steadfast belief in the purpose of their role gives them emotional license to find ways to be heard and respected. This respect is especially important as they work with all other stakeholders connected directly or indirectly to a school or district literacy program.

OTHER PERSONNEL AS PARTNERS WITH SPECIALIZED LITERACY PROFESSIONALS

The Principal

Principals, as instructional leaders, are in a unique position to support the schoolwide literacy program. They are responsible for establishing the conditions for success of the literacy program by developing a culture that engages and supports teachers as they help students learn (International Literacy Association, 2019). Principals set the tone for the way in which teachers incorporate new mandates and requirements into their teaching, work with all types of student learners, and continue to develop as professionals. The tone that principals take is usually revealed by the way in which they establish and use teacher observation and evaluation, conference with teachers, provide professional development opportunities, and create teachers' schedules. When principals create schedules that allow for common times for meetings to take place, they are communicating that they value collaborative work.

The active support of principals is essential for the success of SLPs. Principals must assume responsibility for defining and communicating SLPs' roles within their schools to strengthen literacy programming (Prezyna et al., 2017). As a supporter of the SLP, the school principal can make sure that teachers regard the SLP as a critical person for developing the literacy program. The principal can also help teachers understand the importance of collaborating with SLPs. A recent study of principals indicated that they believe that SLPs are essential for helping teachers use and understand data, whether serving as reading/literacy specialists or literacy coaches. Principals also shared that they think that SLPs have an influence on raising student achievement, improving instructional practice, and creating a culture of collaboration and improvement (Bean et al., 2018; Ferguson, 2014; Ippolito et al., 2019).

A principal in a local elementary school exemplifies this understanding of SLPs' value. When he realized that his reading/literacy specialist needed additional training so that she could support the teachers in their use of a variety of digital technological tools for literacy development, he used his school's professional development funds to pay for her graduate coursework and send her to a conference focused on this topic.

Another principal who does not have a literacy background worked with the school's literacy coach to develop a plan so that the teachers know how to use the reading assessment system that the district has adopted for all the K–5 schools to inform instruction. The literacy coach is spending time with each grade to explain the assessment system and help the teachers understand how to analyze student data in relation to instructional decision-making. She also goes into individual classrooms to model and support the teachers with the assessments.

If a principal does not have a reading background, it is even more essential that an SLP be available to guide teachers with the implementation of the schoolwide literacy program. The SLP can inform the principal about current research and best practice for literacy programs and involve the principal in professional development along with the classroom teachers. In her role as a district literacy coach, Susan Green takes great pride in the type of professional development that she has provided for principals. She has helped them to understand the best use of coaches' time and the importance of using data to inform decision-making. She and her team of literacy coaches have provided monthly professional development for principals in various areas of literacy instruction that they will be evaluating in their buildings; for example, the workshop model, interactive writing, close reading, and effective conferencing.

The Classroom Teacher

Now more than ever, classroom teachers are seen as partners with SLPs in helping with students' literacy development, especially with the expectation to reach all types of diverse learners and use evidence-based instruction and materials to develop students' language, speaking, viewing, and visual-representation skills (International Literacy Association, 2018).

Classroom teachers are still the ones with consistent, long-term experience with their students in all areas of the curriculum who navigate their environments to support literacy development (Jaeger, 1996; Kelly et al., 2019). They have in-depth information about their students' classroom performance, work habits, social and emotional patterns, and family background. Although elementary classroom teachers have more time to learn about the whole child, secondary classroom teachers have in-depth knowledge about their students' patterns with specific content learning.

Traditionally, when classroom teachers had difficulty with struggling readers, they referred the students to someone else (literacy specialist, Title I teacher, special educator) for some type of intervention that might or might not have been consistent with classroom instruction. Today, classroom teachers are expected to be part of professional learning communities that work collaboratively with SLPs to make evidence-based decisions about students' instructional needs (Bean & Lillenstein, 2012; International Literacy Association, 2015).

Multitiered, schoolwide reading programs and other school-based learning community initiatives have required that teachers leave behind the idea that they can close their doors and decide independently what and how they will teach. Classroom teachers benefit from working with SLPs to master instructional strategies, become more self-reflective about their instructional practices, and achieve positive student outcomes (Bean et al., 2018; Ferguson, 2014; Hathaway et al., 2016; Walker-Dalhouse et al., 2010).

To facilitate such collaborative work, classroom teachers need to have in-depth knowledge of general and discipline-specific literacy development and instruction and an ability to interpret and use students' performance across multiple measures to make decisions about instruction and intervention. Classroom teachers' collaborative work with their grade-level and content-area colleagues, SLPs, and other specialized personnel is an important source of professional development and an opportunity to share responsibility for their students as they use data to make instructional decisions and communicate with families about the way in which assessment data is being used (Bean & Lillenstein, 2012; International Literacy Association, 2018).

Other Stakeholders

Parents. The SLP can and should build positive home/school relationships and help classroom teachers do the same. SLPs can provide workshops for parents and guardians so that children can receive positive support at home in their efforts to become or develop as readers and writers. Parents, as the most critical role models for their children, should learn how to be engaged with their schools so that they can keep in close contact with their children's teachers and be supportive of the school literacy program. They can spend time listening to their children read or discuss learning events from school, read aloud to their children, talk about and review homework assignments, limit the amount of screen time in the home, and provide a positive attitude about school for their children. An SLP from a culturally and linguistically diverse suburban district in New York created Family Literacy Night. Parents and children come to school in the evening to participate in read-alouds, reading games, and reading stations to promote at-home literacy activities.

Local School Boards. Local school boards should be informed of all facets of the district's literacy program. It is their responsibility to endorse exemplary practice of school personnel. Local school boards should be knowledgeable of what teachers, principals, and specialized literacy professions are doing to further the district's goals for the literacy program. They should support the literacy program by making informed decisions regarding budget, personnel, and curriculum.

State Departments of Education. ILA's Standards (2017) delineate seven performance standards that state departments of education should consider when approving graduate teacher education programs for prospective specialized literacy professionals: (1) foundational knowledge; (2) curriculum and instruction; (3) assessment and evaluation; (4) diversity and equity; (5) learners and the literacy environment; (6) professional learning and leadership; and (7) practicum/clinical experiences. When state departments align their certification requirements to ILA standards, reading/literacy specialist candidates will be better prepared to support students' literacy development.

State Boards of Education. Specialized literacy professionals' participation in statewide professional organizations and statewide committees or task forces can influence decisions made by state boards of education. State boards are responsible for determining statewide regulations for pre-K–12 public schools, including state curriculum standards, high school graduation requirements, qualifications of professional education personnel, state accountability and assessment programs, and standards for accreditation of local school districts and teacher and leadership preparation programs. While the scope of board responsibility varies from state to state, school board members focus on the big picture and make policy based on the best interests of the public and America's youth (National Association of State Boards of Education, 2020). It is therefore important for specialized literacy professionals to work with other colleagues within and across their districts to advocate for state-level requirements that reflect the most current research on ways to promote literacy learning.

HOW SHOULD A SPECIALIZED LITERACY PROFESSIONAL BE PREPARED TO ASSUME THIS POSITION?

Specialized literacy professionals need to be knowledgeable about their three major roles (teaching, coaching, and leading), and have experiences that enable them to develop in these three roles. Graduate programs that prepare SLPs need to provide experiences that focus on all three roles. Practicum experiences call for experiences in diverse classrooms and schools that allow SLP candidates to engage with students experiencing difficulties with reading and writing, their families, and their teachers. This enables candidates to practice with appropriate planning, assessment, and instruction.

SLPs who will function as literacy coaches or literacy coordinators/supervisors should take more advanced coursework and engage in practicum experiences that help them lead professional development/learning with adults and collaborate with other stakeholders (e.g., administrators, colleagues, families, and community members) (International Literacy Association, 2015).

We recently surveyed literacy professors to find out their perceptions about the way they prepare specialized literacy professionals to serve as leaders of literacy. This was a follow-up study to a national survey that we had conducted 10 years ago to see if there were changes in their graduate programs since then (Wepner & Quatroche, 2011). Those who responded indicated that their graduate reading programs, which lead to reading/literacy specialist certification, require their candidates to shadow SLPs, engage in classroom observations, create professional development opportunities for teachers, coach a teacher or paraprofessional, analyze a school's literacy program and assessment plan, write literacy grants to seek funding for school needs, and develop a schoolwide literacy action plan. These experiences help them to coach and reflect on their own leadership practices.

As graduate literacy programs prepare to be reviewed by their state and national accrediting bodies, they would benefit from consulting ILA's *Standards for the Preparation of Literacy Professionals 2017*. These standards, developed by literacy experts across the United States, focus on the knowledge, skills, and dispositions that are essential for effective educational practice. At the same time, literacy experts need to continue to help states review and revise their standards for specialized literacy professionals so that they are more explicit about the leadership role. Such standards also need to be more consistent in general about requiring a master's degree in reading and teaching experience.

WHAT ARE FUTURE DIRECTIONS FOR SPECIALIZED LITERACY PROFESSIONALS?

Documentation of achievements with students and teachers will help SLPs get recognized for their work as leaders of literacy. Four types of documentation should include:

- Accomplishments with students' achievement that include pre/post informal and formal assessments.
- Evidence of teachers' growth as a result of coaching through pre/post assessment data.
- Records of changes in teachers' classrooms and the school environment with pre/post assessment instruments such as surveys, observations, and visual representations.
- Records of interactions and initiatives with parents such as workshops on at-home literacy practices or meetings about assessment data through online communication, printed programs, attendance lists, and evaluation forms.

These types of documentation help the local school district and educational community become aware of accomplishments that might not otherwise be evident. Of critical importance is the need for comparative achievement data of schools and school districts with and without SLPs to further document the importance of this position.

Also essential is the need to bring recognition to the work of the SLP by, for example, conducting case studies of exemplary SLPs, developing and presenting awards for outstanding SLPs, conducting webinars and special institutes about SLPs, publishing online studies about ways that SLPs are affecting teacher growth and student achievement, and creating press releases about SLPs' involvement with improved reading and writing scores.

Documenting and highlighting the significance of the SLP will help to ensure the position's solvency across schools, promote high standards for SLP licensure across states, and recognize the value of cultivating SLPs as leaders who encourage literacy across grades and disciplines.

CONCLUSION

As the roles and responsibilities of specialized literacy professionals continue to evolve, the leadership characteristics that contribute to creating a community of literacy advocates will be better understood. Every success story about the impact of SLPs on the literacy achievement of students helps others to acknowledge the need to have academically and professionally qualified literacy educators in such positions. SLPs should be expected to have the necessary credentials and should be able to help define their roles and responsibilities. If placed in leadership positions where much of what they do focuses on their work with teachers, administrators, and the community, they should be expected to function effectively in the four dimensions (intellectual, emotional, social, and moral) described above. They also should look for ways to highlight their accomplishments. As more schools and districts realize the importance of using qualified SLPs who can put into place the critical elements of literacy programs (see the chapters that follow), students' potential for learning will be realized.

REFLECTION QUESTIONS

1. In your new position as a specialized literacy professional for a K–5 school, you will be expected to work with students who are struggling readers and writers and to work with teachers to help them use and understand data so that there is instructional coordination. What strategies will you use to help your teachers work effectively with you?

2. Although all of your previous coaching experience has been at the elementary level, you have been hired as a literacy coach for a middle school to work with content-area teachers. What strategies will you use to develop credibility with these teachers?

3. What are some ways that you can encourage the teachers in your school to be collaborative?

PROJECT ASSIGNMENT

Conduct an assessment of teachers' professional development needs for teaching literacy for your grade level or school. Use the assessment results to develop a professional learning plan for one school year. If possible, actually deliver one topic from the plan as an interactive workshop to a group of teachers.

REFERENCES

Allington, R. L. (2006, February/March). Reading specialists, reading teachers, reading coaches: A question of credentials. *Reading Today, 23*(4), 16.

Allington, R. L., & Walmsley, S. (Eds.). (1995). *No quick fix: Rethinking literacy programs in America's elementary schools.* International Reading Association.

AASA The School Superintendents Association. (2019). *Secondary school reading.* https://www.aasa.org/SchoolAdministratorArticle.aspx?id=10592

Bean, R. M., Cassidy, J., Grumet, J. E., Shelton, D. S., & Wallis, S. R. (2002). What do reading specialists do? Results from a national survey. *The Reading Teacher, 55*(8), 736–745.

Bean, R. M., Swan Dagen, A., Ippolito, J., & Kern, D. (2018). Principals' perspectives on the roles of specialized literacy professionals. *Elementary School Journal, 119*(2), 327–350. https://doi.org/10.1086/700280

Bean, R. M., Dole, J. A., Nelson, K. L., Belcastro, E. G., & Zigmond, N. (2015). The sustainability of a national reading reform initiative in two states. *Reading & Writing Quarterly, 31*(1), 30–55. doi:10.1080/10573569 .2013.857947

Bean, R. M., & Kern, D. (2018). Multiple roles of specialized literacy professionals: The ILA 2017 standards. *The Reading Teacher, 71*(5), 615–621. https://doi.org/10.1002/trtr.1671

Bean, R. M., Kern, D., Goatley, V., Ortlieb, E., Shettel, J., Calo, K., Marinak, B., Sturtevant, E., Elish-Piper, L., L'Allier, S. K., Cox, M. A., Frost, S., Mason, P., Quatroche, D. J., & Cassidy, J. (2015). Specialized literacy professionals as literacy leaders: Results of a national survey. *Literacy Research and Instruction, 54*(2), 83–114.

Bean, R. M., & Lillenstein, J. (2012). Response to intervention and the changing roles of schoolwide personnel. *The Reading Teacher, 65*(7), 491–501.

Bean, R. M., Swan, A. L., & Knaub, R. (2003). Reading specialists in schools with exemplary reading programs: Functional, versatile, and prepared. *The Reading Teacher, 56*, 446–455.

Brownell, M. T., Yeager, E., Rennells, M. S., & Riley, T. (1997). Teachers working together: What teacher educators and researchers should know. *Teacher Education and Special Education, 20*(4), 340–359.

Carlson, C. L. (2011). Lowering the high school dropout rate in the United States: The need for secondary reading specialists and how scarce they really are. *International Journal of Humanities and Social Science, 1*(13), 20.

Edwards, T. (2015). *The tale of two middle school literacy coaches: Implications for building coaching capacity* [Doctoral dissertation]. National Louis University. https://digitalcommons.nl.edu/diss/126

Ferguson, K. (2014). How three schools view the success of literacy coaching: Teachers', principals' and literacy coaches' perceived indicators of success. *Reading Horizons: A Journal of Literacy and Language Arts, 53*(1), 24–48. https://scholarworks.wmich.edu/reading_horizons/vol53/iss1/9/

Galloway, E. P., & Lesaux, N. K. (2014). Leader, teacher, diagnostician, colleague, and change agent: A synthesis of the research on the role of the reading specialist in this era of RTI-based literacy reform. *The Reading Teacher, 67*(7), 517–526. doi:10.1002/trtr.1251

Guth, N. D., & Pettengill, S. S. (2005). *Leading a successful reading program: Administrators and reading specialists working together to make it happen.* International Reading Association.

Hathaway, J. I., Martin, C. S., & Mraz, M. (2016). Revisiting the roles of literacy coaches: Does reality match research? *Reading Psychology, 37*(2), 230–256.

International Reading Association. (2000). *Teaching all children to read: The roles of the reading specialist.*

International Reading Association. (2004). *The role and qualifications of the reading coach in the United States.*

International Reading Association. (2010). *Standards 2010: Reading specialist/literacy coach.* https://literacyworldwide.org/get-resources/standards/standards-for-reading-professionals/standards-2010-role-5

International Literacy Association. (2015). *The multiple roles of school-based specialized literacy professionals* [Research brief].

International Literacy Association. (2018). *Standards for the preparation of literacy professionals 2017.*

International Literacy Association. (2019). *Principals as literacy leaders.* https://literacyworldwide.org/docs/default-source/where-we-stand/ila-principals-as-literacy-leaders.pdf

Ippolito, J., Bean, R. M., Kern, D., & Swan Dagen, A. (2019). Specialists, coaches, coordinators, oh my! Looking back and looking forward on the roles and responsibilities of specialized literacy professionals. *Massachusetts Reading Association Primer, 47*(2), 19–28.

Ippolito, J., & Lieberman, J. (2012). Reading specialists and literacy coaches in secondary schools. In R. M. Bean & A. Swan Dagen (Eds.), *Best practices of literacy leaders: Keys to school improvement* (pp. 63–85). Guilford Press.

Jaeger, E. L. (1996). The reading specialist as collaborative consultant. *The Reading Teacher, 49*(8), 622–629.

Kelly, C. M., Miller, S. E., Kleppe Graham, K., Bahlmann Bollinger, C. M., Sanden, S., & McManus, M. (2019). Breaking through the noise: Literacy teachers in the face of accountability, evaluation, and reform. *Reading Horizons: A Journal of Literacy and Language Arts, 58*(2). https://scholarworks.wmich.edu/reading_horizons/

L'Allier, S. K., Elish-Piper, L., & Bean, R. M. (2010). What matters for elementary literacy coaching? Guiding principles for instructional improvement and student achievement. *The Reading Teacher, 63*(7), 544–554. *DOI*:10.1598/RT.63.7.2

Long, R. (1995, April). Preserving the role of the reading specialist. *Reading Today, 12*(5), 6.

McCabe, P. R. (2003). Enhancing self-efficacy for high-stakes reading tests. *The Reading Teacher, 57*(1), 12–20.

National Association of State Boards of Education. (2020). *About state boards of education.* http://www.nasbe.org/about-us/state-boards-of-education/

Pipes, G. (2004). *What are they really doing? A mixed methodology inquiry into the multi-faceted role of the elementary reading specialist* [Unpublished doctoral dissertation]. University of Alabama, Tuscaloosa.

Pletcher, B. C., Hudson, A. K., & Alison Scott, L. J. (2018) Coaching on borrowed time: Balancing the roles of the literacy professional. *The Reading Teacher, 72*(6), 689–699. https://doi.org/10.1002/trtr.1777

Prezyna, D. M., Garrison, M. J., Gold, C. P., & Lockte, H. A. (2017). Principal leadership and reading specialist role understanding in the era of test-based accountability policies. *International Journal of*

Education Policy & Leadership, 12(2), 1–16. https://doi.org/10.22230/ijepl.2017v12n2a686

Quatroche, D. J., Bean, R. M., & Hamilton, R. L. (2001). The role of the reading specialist: A review of research. *The Reading Teacher, 55*(3), 282–294.

Quatroche, D. J., & Wepner, S. B. (2008). Developing reading specialists/literacy coaches as leaders: New directions for program development. *Literacy Research and Instruction, 47*(2), 99–115.

Robinson, H. A., & Rauch, S. J. (1965). *Guiding the reading program: A reading consultant's handbook.* Science Research Associates.

Steinbacher-Reed, C., & Powers, E. A. (2011). Coaching without a coach. *Educational Leadership, 69*(4), 68–72.

Stover, K., Kissel, B., Haag, K., & Shoniker, R. (2011). Differentiated coaching: Fostering reflection with teachers. *The Reading Teacher, 64*(7), 498–509.

Toll, C. A. (2018). Progress in literacy coaching success—A dozen years on. *The Clearing House: A Journal of Educational Strategies, Issues, and Ideas, 91*(1), 14–20. https://doi.org/10.1080/00098655.2017.1348733

Vogt, M. E., & Shearer, B. A. (2003). *Reading specialists in the real world: A sociocultural view.* Allyn and Bacon.

Walker-Dalhouse, D., Risko, V. J., Lathrop, K., & Porter, S. (2010). Helping diverse struggling readers through reflective teaching and coaching. *The Reading Teacher, 64*(1), 70–72.

Wepner, S. B., D'Onofrio, A., & Wilhite, S. C., (2003). Understanding four dimensions of leadership as education dean. *Action in Teacher Education, 25*(3), 13–23.

Wepner, S. B., D'Onofrio, A., & Wilhite, S. C. (2008). The leadership dimensions of education deans. *Journal of Teacher Education, 59*(2), 153–169.

Wepner, S. B., & Quatroche, D. J. (2011). How are colleges and universities preparing reading specialist candidates for leadership positions in the schools? *Reading Horizons, 51*(2), 103–118.

Wepner, S. B., Wilhite, S. C., & D'Onofrio, A. (2011). Using vignettes to search for education deans. *Perspective: Policy and Practice in Higher Education, 15*(2), 59–68.

CHAPTER 3

Considering the Foreground and Background of Effective Literacy Coaching

Jacy Ippolito

- With strategic implementation, literacy coaching can be one of the most powerful ways for schools to support the continual improvement of literacy teaching and learning.
- Effective coaching requires more than just a knowledgeable and skilled coach—establishing and sustaining effective coaching requires attention to both the foreground of coaching (i.e., the knowledge, skills, and work of the coach) and the background of coaching (i.e., the support of school and district leaders, which sets the coaching context).
- Coaches and principals must collaborate to ensure that a cohesive portrait of effective coaching emerges, unifying foreground and background coaching work.

Over the past 4 decades of educational reform in the United States (1980s–2020s), literacy coaching has emerged as a powerful and prevalent lever for improving literacy teaching and learning in schools (Ippolito et al., 2019; Kraft et al., 2018). Coaching is routinely named as a key form of site-based, ongoing professional learning designed to support teachers in strengthening their instruction—particularly of reading, writing, and discussion across grade levels (Darling-Hammond et al., 2009, 2017; International Literacy Association [ILA], 2018). However, all too often, in both the research and practice literature focused on coaching, the coach is situated as the primary or even lone figure responsible for the success or failure of any specific literacy reform initiative. While coaching initiatives can be quite successful, resulting in refinement of literacy teaching and gains in student literacy outcomes, researchers have documented great variability in the efficacy of coaching initiatives across a wide variety of school contexts (Kraft et al., 2018).

Reflecting on my own work as a coach, research on coaching, and consulting with schools around coaching initiatives over the past decade (Bean & Ippolito, 2016; Ippolito, 2010; Ippolito et al., 2019; Ippolito & Bean, 2018), I have come to understand that part of the variability of coaching success rests on the ways in which coaching work is framed for school leaders, teachers, and coaches themselves. District and school leaders tend to frame coaching success as the result of the inherent skills and knowledge of specific individual coaches. This tacit theory of action suggests that if a coach is personable, hard-working, and knowledgeable about literacy instruction, then that coach will be effective in helping teachers to refine their instruction and support student learning. If coaching efforts do not produce intended results, well then, the problem must reside somewhere within the individual coach, right? Unfortunately, this frame undermines effective coaching, limits coaching at scale, and prevents talented individual coaches from achieving district and school goals for improving literacy teaching and learning.

In this chapter, I present a new frame for effective coaching that highlights the contextual nature of coaching success, based on existing research about coaching roles, responsibilities, and contexts.

Equipped with this new frame, coaches and school leaders might engage in productive conversations about how best to establish and sustain effective coaching initiatives in their schools. Let's begin with an arts-based metaphor in which both the coach and the principal collaborate in creating a successful coaching model.

COACH AS PAINTER AND PRINCIPAL AS PATRON: A METAPHOR TO SUPPORT EFFECTIVE COACHING

The coach–principal relationship is central to any successful coaching initiative (Ippolito & Bean, 2019). However, principals do not always view themselves as full partners in coaching work, nor do they necessarily have a full understanding of coaches' roles and responsibilities or familiarity with recent coaching knowledge and practice standards (Ippolito, 2009; Mahaffey et al., 2020). This is not surprising, as more is being asked of principals today than ever before, and rarely do principal-preparation programs focus on the ways in which building-based leaders can support and foster teacher leadership and coaching work. Consequently, to better support coach–principal pairs, it is useful to think of the coach–principal relationship as one not entirely different from the relationship of painter to patron, as a portrait of effective coaching in schools is created.

Imagine a successful coaching initiative as a classical Renaissance portrait (think: Leonardo's *Mona Lisa*). In the *foreground* is the noble coach, representing all of the highly visible knowledge, skills, and work that a coach shares with teachers on a daily basis. The foreground of the painting (i.e., the coach and their daily actions) is what many rightly focus on when considering coaching initiatives (see Figure 3.1). Foreground questions focus on the coach's knowledge of and experience with child development, curriculum and instruction, foundations of teaching literacy, assessment and evaluation, skills with facilitating adult learning, and many of the qualities highlighted in the recently published ILA *Standards for the Preparation of Literacy Professionals 2017* (2018). Critical foreground questions might include:

- Does the coach have a strong grasp of the school's literacy curriculum, and is the coach able to craft a plan for how to move teachers and students ever closer to the school's literacy achievement goals?
- Is the coach able to forge and maintain strong relationships with teachers and other specialists in the school?
- Is the coach working with teachers one-on-one, in small groups, and in large groups, facilitating adult learning and encouraging teacher leadership?

Positive answers to these questions are essential in crafting an effective coaching model. If properly supported, coaches can indeed guide a school's literacy teaching and learning efforts. Coaches and their knowledge, skills, and actions are rightly positioned as central figures, the *foreground*, in any portrait of successful coaching.

However, principals' explicit support of coaching initiatives, including their efforts to create collaborative cultures, form the necessary *background* in any portrait of successful coaching work. Research has repeatedly emphasized the critical roles that principals and school cultures play in promoting coaching success (Bean et al., 2018; Ippolito, 2009; Ippolito & Bean, 2019; Matsumura et al., 2009). The most celebrated Renaissance portraits would not be complete without a detailed background that both allows the painting's subject to shine and also adds detail and structure that enrich and enliven the entire work. In the case of a portrait of effective coaching, the background might include the following:

- A schoolwide vision for literacy teaching and learning
- A clearly articulated theory of action for the school's coaching model
- Clearly defined coach role descriptions that are regularly and widely shared with teachers and the school community
- A collaboratively crafted coaching schedule that helps all teachers, coaches, and administrators understand how coaches' time is best utilized
- Regularly scheduled meetings between coaches and principals

The importance of these background, supporting elements can sometimes be overlooked by schools and districts rushing to complete a portrait of an effective literacy program and focusing solely on the foreground—the characteristics of the coach.

The portrait of effective coaching is truly a self-portrait: the coach is both the painter and the subject/foreground of the final work. The coach is the local expert often best positioned to guide the development of a schoolwide vision for literacy teaching and learning. The coach can take charge of crafting an effective coaching schedule and guiding adult learning around literacy teaching and learning. The coach is the professional holding the brush and choosing the paint colors. However, the principal needs to be the engaged, collaborative patron. The principal (and district administration) creates the context in which coaches can do their best work. Without supportive patronage, the resulting portraits of coaching work will not be as brilliant or effective.

Figure 3.1. The Foreground and Background of Effective Literacy Coaching

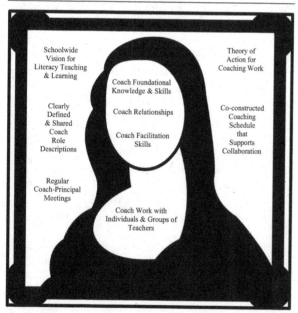

Note: Figure adapted from The Noun Project (June 15, 2016), Noun project - Mona Lisa - in frame.svg (June 15, 2016), CC BY 3.0 us. https://commons.wikimedia.org/wiki/File:Noun_project_-_Mona_Lisa_-_in_frame.svg

In the following sections of this chapter, I expand this metaphor by detailing which aspects of coaching work might fall into the *foreground* and which might fall into the *background* of a portrait of effective coaching, each supported by research and practice literature. These sections also highlight the ways in which coaches can take the lead (as painters) and how principals and other school leaders can support the work (as patrons). Together, coaches and principals can create a portrait of an effective coaching model that meets teachers' and students' needs now and over time.

THE FOREGROUND OF EFFECTIVE COACHING: WHEN COACHES TAKE THE LEAD

The foreground elements of effective coaching are those that educators and researchers associate with coaching work and with coaches themselves: coach knowledge and skills related to literacy instruction; strong coaching relationships; and facilitating adult learning one-on-one and in small and large groups. While not an exhaustive list, these elements are critical to the success of any coaching initiative, and they provide a starting place for coaches and principals to consider which elements of coaching work should be foregrounded in their school.

Foreground Element 1. Coach Foundational Knowledge and Skills

What is at the heart of this element? A coach's foundational knowledge of research-based literacy instructional practices is at the absolute heart of any effective coaching model. Frost and Bean (2006) describe the "gold standard" for literacy coach knowledge as graduate training in literacy (e.g., obtaining a master's degree in literacy before applying for licensure as a reading specialist) coupled with direct literacy teaching experience, all before taking on coaching work. Admittedly, this gold standard is not always possible to achieve in all contexts, and may sometimes be less necessary, as can be the case when coaching high school teachers, where content-focused teacher leaders might play important roles as coaches and facilitators (Charner-Laird et al., 2016). However, Frost and Bean's point still holds true. The more that a literacy coach knows about research-based literacy teaching and learning practices, the better. In fact, spreading research-based literacy practices far and wide in a school is arguably the most important role that each coach plays.

Foundational knowledge forms the core of the first standard for literacy coaches in the ILA *Standards 2017* (2018) for preparing future specialized literacy professionals. It is difficult (though not impossible) to coach what you have not taught and have not mastered. While every coach has different strengths and areas of growth related to foundational knowledge, a background in literacy teaching and learning coupled with knowledge about literacy development across the lifespan seems to be a reasonable starting place. Additional knowledge might include a rich theoretical and practical background in assessment methods, writing instruction, and working with a wide range of learners (diversity across grades, home languages, race, culture, and so on).

A coach's foundational knowledge is in the foreground of any portrait of effective coaching. Teachers and community members position coaches as experts regardless of how fervently coaches may reposition themselves as co-learners and co-facilitators of adult learning. If coaches do not have a broad familiarity with literacy instructional practices and children's literacy development, then teachers may quickly forego working with the coach. This element is also in the foreground because it is an element for which the coach is primarily responsible, either through professional preparation (i.e., a master's degree in literacy; a graduate certificate in coaching; licensure as a reading specialist) or through ongoing professional learning within or beyond the district. Ultimately, coaches are responsible for their own ever-growing foundational knowledge.

How can coaches strengthen this element? This element is always in need of strengthening, even for the most knowledgeable and credentialed of coaches. Standard 6 of the ILA *Standards 2017* (2018) explicitly names ongoing professional learning as a key to early and continued coaching success. It is recommended that coaches join local and national professional organizations that support learning about new literacy research and practices such as the International Literacy Association, the National Council of Teachers of English (NCTE), and perhaps one or more of the myriad content-focused organizations that support literacy in the disciplines. Furthermore, in this digital age, there are a large number of free or low-cost ways of increasing both literacy content and coaching knowledge. Coaches can participate in free Twitter chats focused on literacy research and practice (hosted by ILA, Learning Forward, NCTE, and so on); they can join Twitter coaching groups or follow coaching hashtags (e.g., follow gurus like Jim Knight [@jimknight99]; follow hashtags such as #educoach); or coaches can participate in webinars with national leaders focused on newly published literacy research. There are more ways for coaches to increase their foundational knowledge now than ever before.

What subverts or disrupts this element? Foundational knowledge and continual professional learning can be subverted in several ways that should be guarded against. First, schools and districts often position coaches as literacy experts who deliver professional learning but don't need to attend professional learning themselves. School leaders would be wise to consult their coaches and, together with them, craft individual professional learning plans. Coaches often know exactly what professional learning they need next (e.g., deeper knowledge about vocabulary or writing instruction; strengthening their understanding of biliteracy and dual language instruction). Principals can support coaches' professional learning without great expenditures of time or money, but the question "What do our coaches want and need to learn next?" should be asked and answered every year. Second, coaches themselves can become overwhelmed by all they are expected to know and be able to do. Again, understanding principals can allay coaches' fears that they should be experts in everything all at once. Instead, principals should collaboratively plan for coaches' professional learning in just one to three domains each year, so that coaches are not paralyzed. If coaches are overwhelmed, they will not be able to support teachers effectively.

What resources are recommended related to this element? The following resources may support the identification and bolstering of coaches' foundational knowledge:

- International Literacy Association. (2018). *Standards for the preparation of literacy professionals 2017.* This is a one-stop resource for coaches and principals considering which domains of content and pedagogical knowledge support effective coaching work.
- Walpole, S., & McKenna, M. C. (2013). *The literacy coach's handbook: A guide to research-based practice* (2nd ed.). Guilford Press. Years later, this still is one of the best guides to coach foundational knowledge.

Foreground Element 2. Strong Coaching Relationships

What is at the heart of this element? By definition, coaching is relational work. If a coach cannot quickly form strong, positive relationships with teachers, principals, and students, then little improvement may be seen in teaching and learning outcomes. Many have written about power and positionality in coach–teacher relationships (Gray & Myers, 2018; Hunt, 2018; Ippolito, 2010; Jones & Rainville, 2014; Rainville & Jones, 2008). Across studies, the key finding seems to be that strong relationships rest on clear communication and continual negotiation of the work. Coaching is not a simple matter of telling teachers what to do or merely modeling best practices; instead, it is a continually negotiated relationship among peer professionals. A comprehensive meta-analysis of the coaching relational literature suggests that coaching relationships are perhaps best framed as *coconstructions,* as a "dialogic flow between coach and teacher that assumes equity in knowledge, experience, and emotional exchange" (Robertson et al., 2020, p. 64). In other words, it may be best for all coaching work to be considered a coconstruction of knowledge and practice between coaches and teachers, and not as a one-way sharing of expertise from coach to teacher.

A coach's ability to forge and maintain strong relationships with teachers (first and foremost), as well as with specialists, school leaders, students, and parents is a critical factor in the success of any coaching initiative. How a coach balances responsive (teacher-focused) and directive (programmatic- or content-focused) approaches to their work with teachers can shape the ways in which teachers respond to and take up new instructional work (Ippolito, 2010). If a coach is inattentive to the relational work of the job or allows principals or other school personnel to subvert coaching relationships, then coaching success may suffer.

Relational work is in the foreground of effective coaching because it is highly visible, and without strong relationships, very little coaching work can proceed. Yet strong relationships alone also won't carry the day; they are merely a foundation. As Bean and Ippolito (2016) suggest in the "Levels of Intensity" (pp. 9–12) of coaching activities, relationship building is critical early in coaching work, but the work must proceed to focus on content and instructional practice quickly so as to deepen trusting relationships and produce intended outcomes. Coaches must not languish in a perpetual loop of trying to build relationships sans substantive work. No amount of small talk or snacks at meetings will change teacher practice.

How can coaches strengthen this element? While some might assume that strong coaching relationships are the result of each coach's naturally gregarious personality, there is a great deal that coaches (even introverts) can do to strengthen their relationships with teachers. Coaches can review the relational coaching literature (see Robertson et al., 2020, for an overview) and consider what kinds of relationships they want to foster. Coaches who position themselves as co-learners and co-experts with teachers in the joint enterprise of meeting students' literacy needs are more likely to find success. This is reminiscent of the balanced approach to coaching (Ippolito, 2010), in which coaches toggle between responding to teachers' questions and needs (responsive coaching) and inviting teachers to try new programmatic or curricular activities (directive coaching).

Coaches can also establish different channels through which teachers can communicate with them: email, phone, text, Google Docs, and so on. Being available to teachers when and how they need support is crucial. Coaches can publicly post their schedules and menu of services (more on these in Element 3), making it abundantly clear which services are available. Coaches can also use discussion-based protocols to support individual and group coaching sessions, creating structured holding environments in which all voices can be heard and trust can be systematically built (Pomerantz & Ippolito, 2015). Ultimately, strong and trusting relationships can be built when coaches give their word and follow up consistently. As Robert Evans suggests, strong relationships are built when leaders "preach what they believe and practice what they preach" (2007, p. 136).

What subverts or disrupts this element? Coaching relationships can sour for a number of reasons: teachers feeling overwhelmed by too many change initiatives all at once; a novice coach matched with a veteran teacher who does not see the value of coaching; coaches and principals pushing for instructional change too quickly; and garden-variety misunderstandings and miscommunications (Hunt & Handsfield, 2013; Jacobs et al., 2018). However, the most common way coaching relationships deteriorate is when a clear coaching model is not specified in a school. Then principals and/or coaches inadvertently promote an expert coach narrative, with coaches often being directed to work primarily or only with teachers identified to be struggling educators. When coaches are deployed in this manner, as flawless experts supporting failing teachers, then teachers understandably shy away from the work. Instead, if principals and coaches promote a coconstruction frame, in which all educators engage in professional learning and coaching regardless of years of experience or perceived success in the classroom, then a culture of ongoing learning is fostered, and coaching relationships may be more profitable.

What resources are recommended related to this element? The following resources may support coaches in deepening and strengthening their relationships in schools:

- Aguilar, E. (2013). *The art of coaching: Effective strategies for school transformation.* Jossey-Bass.
- Aguilar, E. (2016). *The art of coaching teams: Building resilient communities that transform schools.* Jossey-Bass.
- Aguilar, E. (2020). *Coaching for equity: Conversations that change practice.* Jossey-Bass. Aguilar's books put coaching relationships front and center, providing numerous suggestions for how to build and strengthen coach-teacher relations via clear planning and communication structures.
- Costa, A. L., & Garmston, R. J. (2002). *Cognitive coaching: A foundation for*

renaissance schools (2nd ed.). Christopher-Gordon. This book is a classic in the coaching literature and is the basis for the highly relational cognitive coaching work that forms the basis of much coaching today.

Foreground Element 3. Coach Facilitation Skills for Working with Individuals and Groups

What is at the heart of this element? Beyond foundational knowledge and an ability to forge and maintain strong relationships, coaching success depends greatly on facilitation skills. We have likely all met educational professionals who know a great deal about literacy teaching and learning, and who are very personable, and yet who still struggle to communicate their knowledge and facilitate adult learning in productive ways. It is this last piece—facilitation of adult learning—that is perhaps the most visible aspect of all foreground coaching work. The professional support that most coaches need is related to their facilitation of adult learning in a wide variety of interactive formats: individual, small-group, and large-group settings.

Breidenstein et al. (2012) argue that both formal school leaders (e.g., principals) and informal teacher leaders (e.g., coaches) must facilitate professional learning experiences for faculty with full awareness of how adults in schools fall along a developmental continuum of how they make meaning in the world. Based on the work of Robert Kegan (1998) and Ellie Drago-Severson (2009), Breidenstein et al. detail how leaders in schools (such as coaches) can meet various adult learners' needs by toggling between instrumental, socializing, and self-authoring learning experiences.

- *Instrumental* experiences are focused on the clear delivery of information, for example, the introduction of a new piece of technology or pedagogical strategy.
- *Socializing* experiences are focused on helping adult educators share experiences and practices, delve into each other's practices, and collaboratively refine their work.
- *Self-authoring* experiences are those in which colleagues are supported in challenging fundamental, deeply held assumptions about students, instruction, and the ways in which schools support or subvert learning for everyone.

Each of these notions is supported by specific facilitation structures, also referred to as discussion-based protocols, which help coaches to create holding environments (Kegan, 1998) in which educators might safely challenge one another and their own ways of thinking and working.

The notion of strategically facilitating adult learning, using proven structures and strategies, has been taken up by a number of authors and researchers over time (see the School Reform Initiative's review of this literature, https://www.schoolreforminitiative.org/research/). Many facilitation structures and protocols are available without cost for coaches to pick and choose based on their teachers' needs (see https://www.schoolreforminitiative.org/protocols/). However, it is useful to organize facilitation protocols and practices along a continuum of familiarity and trust, moving from early work where coaches are forging relationships with teachers to later work that pushes boundaries and challenges assumptions. A chart of protocols organized by degree of trust and amount of time educators have been collaborating can be found at the School Reform Initiative's site at https://www.schoolreforminitiative.org/download/continuum-of-discussion-based-protocols/ (Ippolito, 2017).

One way for a coach to begin to facilitate with developmental intent is to allow teachers some freedom in selecting the form that coaching work takes. Some coaches create a public menu of options that outline individual, small-group, and large-group coaching structures. In this way, teachers can select and take some ownership over the ways in which coaches meet with and support them (see Figure 3.2 for a sample menu). As Diane Sweeney (2011) points out in her book *Student-Centered Coaching*, a balance of one-on-one, small-group, and large-group coaching seems to be most effective in meeting all teachers' needs in a school. Sweeney outlines how a coach might meet with an individual teacher to conduct an in-depth coaching cycle over a period of weeks, in which the coach observes the teacher, helps the teacher identify a focal area of practice, collaboratively inquires into the target practice, supports the teacher in trying new pedagogical moves, and then observes again or co-teaches alongside the

Figure 3.2. Sample Coaching Menu for Elementary Schools in a Single District

Coaching Activities

As part of professional learning and coaching work in our district, all elementary teachers will participate in a combination of the coaching and professional learning structures listed below. The exact nature of individual and team participation will be collaboratively decided in conversation with individual coaches, building-based administrators, and teachers. Across a single school year, teachers and coaches will collaboratively choose an array of structures from those below that will best serve grade-level and building-based goals. Whenever possible, and where applicable according to grade level, these activities also may be strategically sequenced as part of deliberate coaching cycles, in which coaches will commit to focused work with one or more teachers for a brief period of time to investigate and refine a particular area of instructional practice.

Coaching cycles include:

- pre-observation meeting(s) where coaches and teachers choose an instructional focus
- co-planning, co-teaching, demonstration lessons, observational rounds, etc.
- post-observation debrief meeting(s) to reflect on collaborative work
- weekly connections for an agreed upon period of time, to refine practices

Coaching Menu of Services

Getting Started	Deepening the Work	Transforming Practice
• Resource gathering • Content presentations • Coach observation of classrooms • Co-observing with teachers in classrooms and then debriefing • Coach demonstration lessons • Brainstorming sessions • Listening and on-demand support	• Observation and debrief cycles • Co-planning • Coach-led study/book groups • Coach-supported peer coaching work • Data-based analysis and conversations • Looking at student work sessions • Facilitating professional learning community meetings	• Guided reflection opportunities • Coach-supported collaboration with other educators across grades/schools/districts • Coach-supported individual or collaborative inquiry cycles • Co-teaching

Note: Inspired by Bean & Ippolito's (2016) Levels of Intensity (pp. 9–12) and work with Wakefield Public School coaches and principals in Wakefield, MA.

teacher to support mastery. This same coach might also meet with a small group of grade-level teachers to facilitate an investigation into how to meet the needs of English learners in 3rd grade. Finally, the coach might also deliver monthly whole-school professional learning sessions on writing instruction.

A diversity of meeting structures is key for the coach to connect with a large number of teachers in ways that will support them best. Others, such as Moran (2007), have suggested frameworks for how coaches might move systematically from less intrusive coaching structures such as sharing resources and presenting information to groups, to more intrusive coaching structures such as co-planning, demonstrating lessons in classrooms, and even co-teaching. All of these notions point in the same direction: effective coaching for teachers is differentiated in structure and intensity, in response to teachers' needs. Yet all the work must be well facilitated to be successful.

How can coaches strengthen this element? Strengthening coaches' facilitation skills begins with experiencing strong facilitation themselves. Participating in a well-facilitated professional learning community and taking notes on what the facilitator does is a good starting place. If such opportunities are unavailable in a school or district, then organizations such as the School Reform Initiative (www.schoolreforminitiative.org) regularly offer in-person and virtual facilitation opportunities for coaches, teacher leaders, and principals. Participation can significantly improve a coach's facilitation work overnight. Reading widely across the literature on facilitation is also a great starting place, including how to establish group norms, how to select and facilitate different discussion-based protocols, and how to manage moments of tension that will inevitably arise. If possible, participating in a hands-on training or professional learning experience to improve facilitation is well worth the time and cost. In the best-case scenario, all teacher leaders, coaches, and principals in a district would undergo the same facilitative training so that a shared understanding of effective facilitation can be built.

What subverts or disrupts this element? One of the major pitfalls related to facilitating and leading adult learning occurs when coaches are locked into specific routines regardless of teachers' experience or preferences. One example might be if coaches were obliged to conduct coaching cycles during the introduction of new curriculum. This could be detrimental because teachers are just learning the new curriculum and may be less able to choose a specific aspect of practice to focus on, inquire into, and improve. The teachers are just getting their feet wet and likely need small- or large-group introductions to the materials and practices. Similarly, if coaching focuses for too long on instrumental information delivery in large-group professional learning settings and does not shift to smaller-group or one-on-one refinement of work over time, then opportunities can be lost for pinpointing and addressing areas of growth.

The key, once again, is offering a menu of services and varying the coaching methods over time to meet teachers' needs. However, it is important to note that coaches need a schoolwide schedule that supports a variety of coaching methods. If coaches are deployed in ways that limit their ability to toggle between modalities (i.e., if coaches are asked to cover lunch duties or assigned so many student intervention groups that they cannot meet with teachers one-on-one or in small groups), then the effects of coaching may be limited.

What resources are recommended related to this element? The following resources are recommended to help coaches and principals build facilitation skills with individuals and groups:

- Bean, R. M., & Ippolito, J. (2016). *Cultivating coaching mindsets: An action guide for literacy leaders.* Learning Sciences International. This book focuses on systems

and structures for coaches, the theories behind adult learning, and how to engage teachers individually and in groups using a wide variety of discussion-based protocols and coaching tools.

- Knight, J. (2017). *The impact cycle: What instructional coaches should do to foster powerful improvements in teaching.* Corwin Press. This new classic provides one of the clearest pictures available of how to facilitate a data-based, collaborative look at teachers' practice, putting teachers in the driver's seat.

THE BACKGROUND OF EFFECTIVE COACHING: PRINCIPAL PATRONAGE MAKES ALL THE DIFFERENCE

Many of the *background* elements in a portrait of effective coaching are not the sole responsibility of the coach. However, they remain critical to the successful coaching of teachers and the improvement of teaching and learning in a school building. Carefully consider what kinds of principal patronage might be required to bring each element to life.

Background Element 1. Schoolwide Vision for Literacy Teaching and Learning

First and foremost, a principal can support effective coaching by collaboratively crafting a schoolwide vision for literacy teaching and learning. While crafting a schoolwide vision for literacy teaching and learning may be a separate endeavor from coaching-specific work, it should include coaching work and be guided (at least in part) by coaches and perhaps a literacy leadership team. Without a schoolwide vision for what literacy teaching and learning should look like at each grade level, and in each discipline, it is difficult to define a target for coaching work. Bean and Ippolito (2016) explain in some detail how to establish a schoolwide vision for literacy; meanwhile, a freely available resource from the Massachusetts Department of Elementary and Secondary Education related to developing district and schoolwide literacy plans can be downloaded from https://www.publicconsultinggroup.com/media/1265/literacy-guidelines.pdf. This visioning work provides a rich context within which coaching can take root and flourish.

Background Element 2. Theory of Action for Coaching Work

After establishing a schoolwide vision for literacy teaching and learning, one of the next most important questions for any principal/coach pair to answer is: "What is our *theory of action* for how coaching works in our school?" While many principals and coaches hold tacit beliefs about the power of coaching to transform teaching and learning, very few take the time to collaboratively articulate their theory of action. How exactly do they see coach, principal, and teacher actions translating into shifts in instruction and gains in student learning? This is an explicit conversation that principals and coaches must have as they establish and sustain coaching work. Whiteboarding a theory of action or using a shared Google Doc is recommended so that the theory of action can then serve as a reference point for gauging later coaching success. A documented theory of action can also be tweaked over time, as principals and coaches shift the focus of coaching (e.g., from introducing new instructional practices to refining practices that are already in place).

Similar to the theory of action presented by Kraft et al. (2018, p. 552), my recommendation is that coach–principal pairs record their thoughts in several big columns that reflect the larger "if/then" proposition of a theory of action (see Figure 3.3 for a template to use). *If* coaches take particular actions (1st column), and are supported by principals and other school structures (2nd column), *then* what short- and long-term outcomes would be expected (columns 4 and 5)? The middle column (column 3) is a list of potential barriers that might prevent the realization of intended outcomes—these are to be watched for and mitigated. Once coaches and principals map a theory of action for coaching and literacy professional learning work, then they can collectively hold themselves accountable and tweak plans to achieve intended outcomes.

Background Element 3. Clearly Defined and Shared Coach Role Descriptions

Next is the need for a clearly defined role description for coaches in the district and each school. It is critical for principals (as coaching patrons) to introduce coaches as powerful supports for teachers (Matsumura et al., 2009), helping faculty to see them as supportive guides (and not evaluators or classroom spies). To do this, principals cannot simply introduce coaches once and then never mention them again. Coach–principal pairs should craft a one-page coach role description that the principal then introduces at the outset of each year when talking about professional learning arcs, reintroducing and reiterating the role periodically throughout the school year as a reminder of coaching work. Once crafted, a role description can be referenced when principals observe teachers, talk about growth opportunities, and suggest ways that coaches might assist. A role description can be referenced in principal newsletters about coaching work. The description should ideally be a living document that can be tweaked over time to best fit school and teacher needs. At a minimum, the role description should clearly state expectations of coaches' and teachers' participation in literacy professional learning work. A menu of coaching services (refer to Figure 3.2) should be included as part of the role description, clearly demonstrating

Figure 3.3. Template for Drafting a Theory of Action for Coaching Work

IF . . .			THEN . . .	
Coach Actions	Supports		Short-Term Outcomes	Long-Term Outcomes
What do coaches actually do? (List all coach routines, methods, work in this column)	What are principal, specialist, teacher actions and structural supports? (List all actions of other professionals & structures that support coaching work)	Potential Barriers & Obstacles to Minimize (List anything that might subvert coaching work here—these are to be mitigated)	If coach actions & supports are effective, what results might we anticipate in the short-term?	If coach actions & supports are effective, what results might we anticipate in the long-term?

the many ways that a coach can be an invaluable support.

Background Element 4. Coconstructed Coaching Schedule that Supports Collaboration

One of the common complaints of most coaches is that they do not have enough time, nor an efficient schedule that allows for the real-time coaching of teachers. While some principals leave a coach's schedule completely up to the coach to define, savvy principals sit with coaches and coconstruct a schedule that will allow for individual, small-group, and large-group coaching opportunities. If a principal takes part in crafting a coaching schedule, this also signals to all faculty that coaching is valuable and part of the schoolwide vision for continual improvement of literacy teaching and learning. A collaboratively crafted schedule can also pinpoint times when the principal can sit in on coaching and professional learning sessions—an important part of the soft accountability coaching initiatives need. Coaches support teachers; principals hold teachers and coaches accountable for their work. A collaboratively crafted schedule supports both principals and coaches in playing their parts, as well as ensuring plenty of collaborative adult professional learning time (e.g., professional learning community times blocked off, coaching cycles articulated, and large-group coaching sessions clearly noted).

Background Element 5. Regular Coach–Principal Meetings

Last, but certainly not least, the more regularly that coaches and principals meet, the closer they can collectively come to a shared understanding of coaching goals, actions, and outcomes. One recommendation is that coach–principal pairs meet at least monthly, and if possible, every two weeks or weekly. In these meetings between painter (coach) and patron (principal), the coaching theory of action can be referenced and refined. Coach–principal meetings should be held sacred and not cancelled when faced with other daily pressures. Both coaches and principals have many demands on their time, but regular meetings together must be considered part of the leadership work of the school. For suggested topics of conversation for coach–principal meetings, see Ippolito & Bean (2018, 2019).

CONCLUSION

While effective coaching has been divided into foreground and background elements in this chapter, it is the synthesis of these elements that truly makes a difference. The whole picture is greater than the sum of its individual parts. Moreover, while some elements fall more squarely on the coach to develop and maintain (e.g., relationships and facilitation skills), principals and coaches are encouraged to review the elements together to determine where each professional might explicitly support and bolster each element. For example, if during the era of COVID-19 and increased virtual coaching a coach determines that they need to improve their online adult-facilitation skills, then the coach might research professional-learning opportunities focused on online facilitation (perhaps from established groups such as the School Reform Initiative or Learning Forward). Meanwhile, the principal might play a role in securing funding, asking pertinent questions of the coach about professional learning goals and outcomes, and then asking the coach to share newly learned digital skills and resources with teacher leaders across the school. In this way, coaches and principals become mutually accountable to each other, taking collective ownership and supporting all elements of effective coaching.

A final caveat: there are several more elements of effective coaching that could be part of the portrait metaphor and yet are not emphasized in this chapter. For instance, the role that some coaches play as data managers and facilitators of data teams might be prominent in some schools. Instead of aiming for an exhaustive list, it is perhaps more important to consider which elements are most important in *your* school and district. Where would you place each element in your own portrait of effective coaching? Would you place them in the foreground as highly visible, prominent aspects of coaching work, or in the background, as less visible but equally essential elements bolstered by principals and the wider school community? Are these elements primarily the responsibility of the coach to develop and sustain (foreground territory)? Or are they primarily governed by the principal, or perhaps the coach and principal in conversation (background territory)?

Ultimately, it is less important whether an element of effective coaching is painted in the foreground or background of a specific portrait; instead, it is more important to open clear lines of communication among coaches, principals, and teachers around what constitutes effective coaching in each specific school and district. The portrait (foreground/background) metaphor in this chapter is shared as a way to foster those meaningful conversations. Like a painting from one of the Renaissance masters, effective coaching is a mixture of planning, strategy, artistry, and implementation. Whether you are the painter (coach) or the patron (principal), your role is vital in collaboratively creating a portrait of effective coaching that supports teachers and students.

REFLECTION QUESTIONS

1. Which of the foreground elements of effective coaching highlighted in this chapter are strongest in your school or district? Are any elements missing that you would add?
2. Which of the background elements of effective coaching highlighted in this chapter are strongest in your school or district? Are any elements missing that you would add?
3. What would need to happen in order to bolster elements that are not as strong, and how can coaches and principals work together to do so?

PROJECT ASSIGNMENT

As part of specifying and strengthening your school's theory of action around coaching work, come together in coach–principal pairs or as a literacy leadership team to craft your own portrait of effective coaching. Download or draw a blank coaching portrait template of your own and determine which elements of effective coaching are in the foreground and in the background in your setting. Reference the ILA *Standards 2017* (2018) as a resource. Which elements from the standards map onto elements highlighted in this chapter? Which elements would you add?

Consider coach, principal, and school strengths and areas of growth in each category (foreground/background) for your personal portrait. What might you, as a literacy leadership team, wish to try next or bolster? Don't try to bolster all elements at once; instead, choose one to three target elements (across the foreground/background) to focus on

each school year as you continually refine your specific coaching model.

Share your portraits of effective coaching across schools in your district, county, or state in order to promote a larger coaching network that can become a source of continued learning and growth for coaches and principals alike. Look for similarities and differences across portraits of effective coaching from different schools. Reflect, revise, and share again.

REFERENCES

Bean, R. M., & Ippolito, J. (2016). *Cultivating coaching mindsets: An action guide for literacy leaders.* Learning Sciences International.

Bean, R. M., Swan Dagen, A., Ippolito, J., & Kern, D. (2018). Principals' perspectives on the roles of specialized literacy professionals. *The Elementary School Journal, 119*(2), 327–350.

Breidenstein, A., Fahey, K., Glickman, C., & Hensley, F. (2012). *Leading for powerful learning: A guide for instructional leaders.* Teachers College Press.

Charner-Laird, M., Ippolito, J., & Dobbs, C. L. (2016). The roles of teacher leaders in guiding PLCs focused on disciplinary literacy. *Journal of School Leadership, 26*(6), 975–1001.

Darling-Hammond, L., Hyler, M. E., & Gardner, M. (2017). *Effective teacher professional development.* Learning Policy Institute.

Darling-Hammond, L., Wei, R. C., Andree, A., Richardson, N., & Orphanos, S. (2009). *Professional learning in the learning profession: A status report on teacher development in the United States and abroad.* National Staff Development Council and The School Redesign Network, Stanford University.

Drago-Severson, E. (2009). *Leading adult learning: Supporting adult development in our schools.* Corwin Press.

Evans, R. (2007). The authentic leader. In *The Jossey-Bass Reader on Educational Leadership* (2nd ed.). Jossey-Bass.

Frost, S., & Bean, R. (2006). Qualifications for literacy coaches: Achieving the gold standard. *Literacy Coaching Clearinghouse.* National Council of Teachers of English. https://eric.ed.gov/?id=ED530335

Gray, E. S., & Myers, J. (2018). Two types of coaching styles: Graduate and undergraduate students collaborate in a university reading clinic. *Mentoring & Tutoring: Partnership in Learning, 26*(3), 249–266.

Hunt, C. S. (2018). Toward dialogic professional learning: Negotiating authoritative discourses within literacy coaching interaction. *Research in the Teaching of English*, 52(3), 262–287.

Hunt, C. S., & Handsfield, L. J. (2013). The emotional landscapes of literacy coaching: Issues of identity, power, and positioning. *Journal of Literacy Research*, 45(1), 47-86.

Ippolito, J. (2009). Principals as partners with literacy coaches: Striking a balance between neglect and interference. *Literacy Coaching Clearinghouse*. National Council of Teachers of English. https://eric.ed.gov/?id=ED530261

Ippolito, J. (2010). Three ways that literacy coaches balance responsive and directive relationships with teachers. *The Elementary School Journal*, 111(1), 164-190.

Ippolito, J. (2017). *Continuum of discussion-based protocols*. School Reform Initiative. https://www.schoolreforminitiative.org/download/continuum-of-discussion-based-protocols/

Ippolito, J., & Bean, R. M. (2018). *Unpacking coaching mindsets: Collaboration between principals and coaches*. Learning Sciences International.

Ippolito, J., & Bean, R. M. (2019). A principal's guide to supporting instructional coaching. *Educational Leadership*, 77(3), 68–73.

Ippolito, J., Bean, R. M., Kern, D., & Swan Dagen, A. (2019). Specialists, coaches, coordinators, oh my! Looking back and looking forward on the roles and responsibilities of specialized literacy professionals. *Massachusetts Reading Association Primer*, 47(2), 19–28.

Jacobs, J., Boardman, A., Potvin, A., & Wang, C. (2018). Understanding teacher resistance to instructional coaching. *Professional Development in Education*, 44(5), 690–703.

Jones, S., & Rainville, K. N. (2014). Flowing toward understanding: Suffering, humility, and compassion in literacy coaching. *Reading & Writing Quarterly*, 30(3), 270–287.

Kegan, R. (1998). *In over our heads: The mental demands of modern life*. Harvard University Press.

Kraft, M.A., Blazar, D., & Hogan, D. (2018). The effect of teaching coaching on instruction and achievement: A meta-analysis of the causal evidence. *Review of Educational Research, 88*(4), 547–588.

Mahaffey, A., Wolfe, Z., & Ciampa, K. (2020). Elementary principals' knowledge of and expectations for specialized literacy professionals. *Journal of Organizational & Educational Leadership*, 5(2). https://digitalcommons.gardner-webb.edu/joel/vol5/iss2/6

Matsumura, L. C., Sartoris, M., Bickel, D. D., & Garnier, H. (2009). Leadership for literacy coaching: The principal's role in launching a new coaching program. *Educational Administration Quarterly*, 45(5), 655–693.

Moran, M. C. (2007). *Differentiated literacy coaching: Scaffolding for student and teacher success*. ASCD.

Pomerantz, F., & Ippolito, J. (2015). Power tools for talking: Custom protocols enrich coaching conversations. *Journal of Staff Development (JSD)*, 36(1), 40–43.

Rainville, K. N., & Jones, S. (2008). Situated identities: Power and positioning in the work of a literacy coach. *The Reading Teacher*, 61(6), 440–448.

Robertson, D. A., Padesky, L. B., Ford-Connors, E., & Paratore, J. R. (2020). What does it mean to say coaching is relational? *Journal of Literacy Research*, 52(1), 55–78.

Sweeney, D. (2011). *Student-centered coaching: A guide for K–8 coaches and principals*. Corwin Press.

Part II

PROGRAM DEVELOPMENT

Literacy development is both similar and different across grade levels and contexts. It is similar in that the basic principles of language and learning hold true throughout. It is different in that the application of these principles differs depending on what is developmentally appropriate at each level. Part II includes three chapters that focus on the various settings for which specialized literacy professionals must plan and implement literacy programs. It offers suggestions for responding to the differing instructional needs of students as they progress through the grades.

Chapter 4, written by D. Ray Reutzel and Parker C. Fawson, offers a leader's guide for early childhood education. The guide draws on data from national studies to provide a rationale for understanding the science of how young children learn to read and write. Multiple strategies are offered to incorporate into the early literacy curriculum, including an instructional routine framework. With a focus on addressing the needs of all young learners, this chapter offers research-based instructional and assessment policies and practices for literacy leaders to consider and use with their teachers to promote effective early literacy instruction.

A set of comprehensive guidelines for developing a successful elementary literacy program is the focus of Chapter 5, written by Timothy Rasinski, Chase Young, and Meghan Valerio. The authors explain in great detail the curricular and instructional components that a schoolwide Literacy Leadership Team needs to incorporate into an effective elementary literacy program. General and intervention instruction, assessment, parent and community reporting and outreach, and professional development are presented as key components of such a program. The authors emphasize that an effective literacy program must be based on scientific and evidence-based findings, responsive to students' needs, and open to teachers as artists.

In Chapter 6, William G. Brozo focuses on adolescent literacy. The complexities of serving as literacy leaders in middle and high schools to promote adolescent literacy reform are described. Five leadership principles are proposed for promoting sustainable secondary literacy reform. Examples of how these principles—the criticality of leadership from the top, relationship building, development of strategic vernacular, capacity for reform, and forums for teachers' professional learning—work are illustrated on a national and international scale through vignettes. The importance of collaboration between school leaders and teachers is stressed as a key contributor to literacy improvement.

Broadly interpreted, the principles and guidelines presented in each chapter may be applied to all the others. This is reassuring for specialized literacy professionals and administrators, since it means that the essence of sound, effective literacy practices remains the same for students at all levels.

CHAPTER 4

Understanding Literacy Learning in the Early Years

A Leader's Guide

D. Ray Reutzel and Parker C. Fawson

- Research shows that early literacy learning contributes to students' success throughout their schooling and on into later adult life.
- Literacy leaders need to understand the science of how young children learn to read and write.
- Literacy leaders should provide effective professional development and other support for teachers in the science of effective early literacy instruction.

Americans are increasingly concerned that young children are falling behind academically due to the impacts of the worldwide COVID-19 pandemic and a near-exclusive reliance on remote learning. The Pew Research Center reported in February 2021 that 61% of surveyed Americans are concerned that "students will fall behind academically without in-person instruction" (Horowitz, 2021). Falling behind academically can be a real-life disaster for millions for young children, especially if they fail to learn to read and write early and well.

It should go without saying that acquiring literacy is a vital skill that supports overall quality of life. Literacy gives people access to the written word, to powerful ideas, to debate and dissent, and more. If these are denied, then people lose many of the advantages associated with a learned society.

According to the National Assessment of Education Progress (NAEP) 2019 *Reading Report Card* (National Center for Education Statistics, 2019), only about one-third of 4th-graders in the United States are considered proficient readers. Results for students living in poverty and students of color show an even lower proportion of 4th-grade students achieving proficient reading levels. The NAEP results on students' writing progress are even less inspiring (National Center for Educational Statistics, 2011). The last NAEP *Writing Report Card* in 2011 showed that only about one-quarter of 8th-graders were proficient in writing.

Research in the science of early learning continues to confirm several foundational skills that young students need to be taught and learn to enable future reading and writing achievement and eventual school success (Castles et al., 2018; Deans for Impact, 2019). This chapter describes what school leaders and literacy supervisors need to know about current and ongoing early literacy research, knowledge-based curricula, and the science of early reading and offers evidence-based suggestions for policy and practice.

GOALS OF A COHESIVE LITERACY-LEARNING, KNOWLEDGE-BASED CURRICULUM, PRE-K–3

Educators, policymakers, and the general public have increasingly viewed support for early learning as a strategic investment in the future of children, particularly those considered at risk (Reutzel, 2013). The hope, of course, in doing so is to mitigate serious later learning gaps that are evidenced by grade 3 and often persist throughout the grades, leading to negative academic, social, and economic outcomes for older students. We identify five general goals of a literacy curriculum that, if met, can help keep young students on track for later success.

Achieve On-Grade Level Reading by Grade 3

Students need to read on grade level by 3rd grade to be ready to comprehend the text types and complex materials they will need to read in the middle grades and beyond. A couple of frequently cited studies on this topic—*Double Jeopardy: How Third-Grade Reading Skills and Poverty Influence High School Graduation* (Hernandez, 2012) and *Early Warning! Why Reading by the End of Third Grade Matters* (Annie E. Casey Foundation, 2010)—serve as stark reminders that the literacy achievement gap starts early and persists throughout the grades. What these statistics translate into later in life—greater struggles in high school, lower college attendance and graduation rates, a higher likelihood of incarceration, and generally bleaker economic and social futures—ought to concern everyone who is part of or served by the current educational system. What's worse, scores seem to be going in the wrong direction, with current scores *lower* than those from two years before.

Supportive policy and practice by school leaders and literacy supervisors will include greater availability of high-quality, knowledge-based prekindergarten programs especially for those students most at-risk; summer school and summer literacy programs; attention to the alignment and integration of reading curriculum, standards, and instruction across the prekindergarten through grade 3 levels; higher standards for the preparation of early childhood teachers accompanied by improved professional development; and improved school–family partnerships.

Build Knowledge of the World

The Common Core State ELA standards (CCSS) recognized the need to increase exposure to and reading of content-rich information texts when it recommended that elementary schools use a 50/50 mix of fiction and information books in early reading instruction.

The earlier we start building children's knowledge of the world, the better our chances will be of narrowing a pervasive and persistent knowledge gap and leveling the playing field in early literacy instruction. It turns out that deep and broad prior knowledge and experiences boost reading comprehension significantly in later years (Tyner & Kabourek, 2020). Consequently, we ought to be concerned that *all* students, but especially those who come to school with limited background knowledge and experiences, engage with meaty informational texts through read-alouds and in their early reading instruction. In addition, Mohr (2003) found that Hispanic and non-Hispanic 1st-grade students vastly preferred to read informational texts, even when given a chance to select a book from a wide array of books including those that mirrored the cultural, racial, and ethnic backgrounds of the students. Teachers and school leaders must understand and support the teaching of evidence-based early reading skills and strategies as well as the reading of information-rich texts as vital elements of an effective early reading instructional program (Reutzel et al., 2005).

School leaders might also consider complementing their early reading curriculum by adopting commercially produced knowledge-based curricula. Examples of commercially available knowledge-based curricula include Amplify's *Core Knowledge*® (https://amplify.com/programs/amplify-core-knowledge-language-arts/) and Great Minds's *Wit and Wisdom* (https://greatminds.org/english/teachers). An effective early childhood literacy curriculum should be designed with the essential elements of a knowledge-based curriculum in mind, should meet the goals found in national early literacy standards (Common Core State Standards Initiative, 2010), and should require the teaching of evidence-based literacy strategies and skills needed to effectively learn from complex texts. It is also helpful if school leaders work with school faculty to coordinate, align, and articulate the content of a knowledge-based curriculum both horizontally and vertically to support early literacy programs. This should not be a contest between opposing forces, but rather an exercise in integration that results in an inclusive and effective early childhood literacy program and curriculum.

Supportive policy and practice by school leaders and literacy supervisors will include greater coordination and articulation among educators at all levels across the prekindergarten–grade 3 spectrum to assure horizontal and vertical alignment of the curriculum. There will also be increased attention given to teaching literacy skills and strategies taught within a strong framework aimed at acquisition of coherent domains of knowledge to close the knowledge gap (Neuman & Celano, in press; Willingham, 2017).

Meet Common Core State Standards

Over the past decade, teachers of young children have refined their instructional supports and delivery methods to better align them toward achieving annual learning outcome expectations for their students as represented in the Common Core State Standards (CCSS). The CCSS are grounded in a desire to position each young child to be college and/or career ready by the time they exit high school (Common Core State Standards Initiative, 2010). Since literacy is identified as a critical skill that students must master to fully take advantage of life opportunities, the CCSS provides specific guidance on the English Language Arts (ELA) learning trajectory for children across grades as well as important end-of-year outcomes. ELA standards address Reading, Writing, Speaking, and Listening along with Language strands and are integrated across content fields throughout the CCSS and represent shared responsibilities by all in the school. ELA standards are intended to be integrated with one another and with content knowledge acquisition across the curriculum (Wexler, 2019).

Students should be supported in learning foundational language skills, strategies, and knowledge that will enable their development toward independence while also exposing them to a range of text types including narrative and informational text. Discussing texts of varying types, range, and challenge across the year will help to expand the quality of student discourse and thinking. Providing explicit instructional support on how to think about a story or informational text will assist students in developing and refining their own capacities to understand and express their understanding of complex texts in increasingly sophisticated ways. It is important to emphasize the independent reading of challenging and complex texts across content areas. This emphasis should include the teacher modeling cognitive processes used to successfully interact with challenging text and should be followed by opportunities to guide student practice in using similar cognitive processes in their reading of complex texts.

Supportive policy and practice for school leaders and literacy supervisors will emphasize the need to be aware of what learning and literacy standards are essential to ensure that each student is sufficiently prepared to navigate future learning opportunities successfully. Being able to design and deliver standards-based instruction to meet specific grade-level literacy outcomes in an integrated way is a critical skill every teacher should master and every school leader should be able to effectively evaluate.

Integrate Technology and Early Education

The past decade has produced a number of research and policy reports on the use of technology to enhance young student learning (Administration for Children and Families, Office of Planning, Research & Evaluation, 2015; National Association for the Education of Young Children, 2012; Office of Educational Technology, 2017). Historically, the physical school was where learning took place. We now see more clearly that opportunities for learning are all around young children, and technology can help to make this all-the-time learning accessible for every child no matter what their background. The COVID-19 pandemic has added urgency to this need when many physical schools globally and across the United States were closed to student access. Countless school systems were ill-equipped, in this virtual school setting, to continue scaffolding student learning. With this situation in mind, what are some important guiding principles school leaders and literacy supervisors may consider to more effectively implement supportive technology into their learning settings? The U.S. Department of Education and the U.S. Department of Health and Human Services (2016) address guidelines for early learning and education technology at https://tech.ed.gov/files/2016/10/Early-Learning-Tech-Policy-Brief.pdf. While these principles provide some guidance on how to make better decisions around technology use to support young children's learning, there is still much to learn about effective use of technology and how it impacts positive outcomes for all children. Ongoing research into these important learning supports will refine our abilities to introduce technologies that, when combined with the expertise of

knowledgeable leaders and teachers, have a proven impact on the learning growth of the young child.

Supportive policy and practice for school leaders and literacy supervisors will include a commitment to intensive, ongoing professional development that provides teachers with the information and resources to select appropriate technology and integrate its use into the curriculum and early childhood education literacy program.

Evaluate Teacher and Leader Effectiveness

Teachers matter more to student achievement than any other aspect of schooling (Opper, 2019). Moreover, teachers matter not only for tested outcomes; they matter also for non-tested school outcomes (Doan, 2019). Research indicates that a teacher's contribution to student learning matters more than any other single factor, including class size, school size, and the quality of after-school programs (Chetty et al., 2012; Opper, 2020). It is no surprise, then, that teacher and leader quality also matters greatly in child care and prekindergarten programs (Branch et al., 2019; Hanushek et al., 2019). Obviously, the ultimate goal of effectiveness evaluations, whether they focus on teachers, coaches, literacy supervisors, or school leaders, is to improve teaching and learning outcomes for children.

Supportive policy and practice for school leaders and literacy supervisors will include an environment in which teachers and school leaders view the evaluation process as a collaborative effort that is effective, supportive, and thoughtfully designed. Evaluation information is used to plan ongoing professional development to support teachers' abilities to demonstrate competence in the areas in which they are evaluated.

COMPONENTS OF AN EARLY LITERACY CURRICULUM AND SUPPORTING INSTRUCTIONAL STRATEGIES

Long before formal schooling begins, parents and caregivers help lay the foundation for the development of essential cognitive skills and attitudes toward learning (Strickland & Townsend, 2010).

Building on this foundation, early childhood education programs should include

1. A coherent, knowledge-based curriculum with clear curriculum goals
2. Evidence of intentional planning and implementation of evidence-based strategies that are embedded within the curriculum goals
3. A plan for ongoing student assessment
4. A plan for overall program evaluation

Achieving nearly every major educational objective—from improving reading comprehension to fostering critical thinking—is based in the acquisition and use of knowledge. Without a broad, solid foundation of knowledge and vocabulary built from the earliest years of schooling, better student outcomes may not be achievable in the long run. Yet, in many schools, the curriculum has narrowed to an overemphasis on teaching reading, writing, and math. We must also ensure that history, science, geography, art, music, and more are generously taught to all students in the earliest years of schooling, especially to those who are least likely to gain such knowledge outside school.

We also want to emphasize that play serves an essential role in an effective early childhood literacy curriculum (Morrow, 1990; Morrow et al., 2013; Neuman & Roskos, 1992, 1997). Instructional strategies that promote a playful environment in the classroom cultivate quite naturally a positive view toward reading and other literacy experiences that are essential for helping children learn to read and write *and* to want to read and write. Teachers should construct play environments amply supplied with cultural literacy tools for children's use and exploration that promote curiosity and imaginative play focused on literacy behaviors and literate language use.

Throughout the research literature, the terms *evidence-based* or *research-based* appear to be the operative words; in other words, make sure that literature guiding your decisions is based on reliable research and strong evidence. In what follows, we present a sampling of instructional strategies that have strong evidence for advancing high-quality literacy learning and teaching in the early years. Attention to spiraling of these strategies, as suggested by the Common Core State ELA Standards (Common Core State Standards Initiative, 2010),

clearly supports the research that has shown distributed practice to be most effective (Deans for Impact, 2019). This means that using similar standards with increasing complexity from grade to grade, year after year, will help to provide a cohesive and distributed review of literacy skills and strategies in the early language and literacy curriculum.

These strategies must be embedded in a strong, coherent, knowledge-based curriculum attached to reading complex and knowledge-rich texts, both narrative and informational, for disadvantaged students to have an equitable chance at accessing a store of background knowledge and experiences that will ensure significant learning advantages throughout the early childhood years and into later educational settings and life (Wexler, 2020; Willingham, 2017).

Below are descriptions of evidence-based early literacy curriculum components generally included in early childhood literacy programs. We also review research-based, effective strategies that literacy supervisors and school leaders should expect to observe when early childhood teachers are instructing young children.

Reading Aloud—With a Focus on Language Development

Lonigan and Whitehurst (1998) describe an evidence-based read-aloud technique called *dialogic reading*. In this style of reading aloud with young children, the teacher asks the child increasingly difficult questions about the book, the language, and the illustrations. After the child answers, the teacher either reiterates or expands on the child's response. Dialogic reading promotes a turn-taking style of interaction during reading aloud. For example, reading aloud the classic book *Corduroy* by Don Freeman (1968), the teacher might prompt a student to say something about the book by asking her to recall a detail of the story such as, "How did Corduroy get from the toy department to the big room with all the beds?" The student might answer, "He rode an elevator." The teacher might then gently correct this answer's misinformation and explain, "That was not an elevator. It's called an escalator." The teacher might also expand this response by clarifying, "An escalator is like stairs that move for you so you don't have to walk up them by yourself." To ensure that the student understands the new term and is able to use it correctly, the teacher might ask the student to tell her how Corduroy reached the second floor of the store. Hopefully, the student would reply, "He rode an escalator." Finally, the teacher could ask the student if she had ever ridden on an escalator and to relate the experience to the teacher.

Results of Lonigan and Whitehurst's (1998) research showed that after only six weeks, the children who participated in dialogic reading scored significantly higher on both receptive and expressive language skills than students in a control group who did not receive this dialogic reading. Full-day early childhood education programs should offer numerous read-aloud opportunities throughout the day as a means for expanding and developing language abilities in young children (McGee, 2013). Whenever possible, use volunteers to read one-to-one or to pairs of children, which has been shown for many decades to be effective (Morrow, 1988). Keep in mind that it is both the reading and the talking about the reading that help expand children's vocabularies and conceptual understandings. Figure 4.1 offers some dos and don'ts for reading aloud to young children based on the work of Jim Trelease (2013).

Awareness of Concepts About Print and the Functions of Print

Print concepts are arbitrary conventions such as spaces between words, directionality, and punctuation that govern written language production and processing (Reutzel & Cooter, 2019). Awareness of print in the environment is a significant first step, according to Clay (2000), toward developing an understanding of what it means to be a reader and writer.

Opportunities for teaching concepts about print abound during the day, but especially during shared reading. When teachers read aloud from enlarged print, children learn that it is the print, not the pictures, that represent spoken words. When teachers speak as they write when creating a Language Experience Chart or in interactive writing, children hear and see the words written. In these demonstrations of speech written down, children begin to develop an awareness of the importance of directionality, top to bottom and left to right, and the concept of a word as it appears in print.

Figure 4.1. Dos and Don'ts of Reading Aloud

DO

- Do begin reading to children as early in their lives as they can be supported to sit and listen.
- Do use rhymes, raps, songs, chants, poetry, and pictures to stimulate their oral language development, listening, and interaction with others.
- Do read aloud to children at least 10–15 minutes daily, more often if possible.
- Do set aside a time for daily reading aloud in your curriculum schedule and at home.
- Do read picture books to all ages, but also gradually move to reading longer books without pictures as well.
- Do vary the topics and genre of your read-aloud selections.
- Do read aloud books to children that stretch their intellectual and oral language development.
- Do allow plenty of time for interaction before, during, and after the reading.
- Do read aloud with expression and enthusiasm.
- Do add another dimension to your reading sometimes, such as using hand movements or puppets or dressing up in costume.
- Do carry a book with you at all times to model your love of books and reading.

DON'T

- Don't read aloud too fast.
- Don't read aloud books children that can read independently—give a "book talk" instead!
- Don't read aloud books and stories that you don't enjoy yourself.
- Don't read aloud books and stories that exceed the children's emotional development.
- Don't continue reading a book you don't like. Admit it and choose another.
- Don't impose your interpretations and preferences on children.
- Don't confuse quantity with quality.
- Don't use reading aloud as a reward or punishment.

Source: Adapted from *The Read Aloud Handbook* (7th ed.), by J. Trelease, 2013, Penguin Books.

Knowledge of how print is used for everyday purposes helps children view literacy learning as meaningful and useful. Common purposes for engaging in literacy include writing notes, blogs, social media posts, cards, and emails; reading print and electronic newspapers and magazines, and websites; making and using lists; and surfing the Internet and using a variety of online entertainment guides. Cultural artifacts and writing media such as food containers, menus, cookbooks, tickets, paper and writing utensils, e-tablets, and printed receipts may be included for exploration in literacy centers (Neuman & Roskos, 1997).

Familiarity with a Variety of Types of Texts and Text Structures

Children's understanding about the nature of stories and how they are constructed greatly influences their ability to comprehend and compose (National Early Literacy Panel, 2008). Although most of the material used to teach reading to young children in the past has been narratives or stories, teachers are encouraged nowadays, with the wide acceptance of the Common Core State ELA Standards (Common Core State Standards Initiative, 2010), to expose children to a wider variety of types of texts, including poetry, but most especially informational books and informational digital media. Fortunately, informational books and other informational media are available for young children on a wide variety of topics intended to grow their knowledge of the world around them (Wexler, 2020). The CCSSI calls for 50/50 attention to be given to reading narrative (literary) and informational texts to build young students' vocabulary and background knowledge and provide them with exposure to ideas presented in a variety of organizational (text) structures.

Teachers should use evidence-based prompts that follow the elements of story structure, such as the following:

1. Who were the main characters?
2. What happened to them?
3. What happened next?
4. How did things turn out?

Teachers might also help students by guiding them to make use of story maps or graphic organizers to anchor their reading in the prototypical structure of narrative texts or stories (Reutzel & Cooter, 2019, 2020).

The text structure of narratives differs from the text structures found in informational texts. Narrative texts typically follow a singular story grammar or structure, with characters, a setting (location and time), a problem, a plan or goal, attempts to solve the problem, and a resolution (Mandler & Johnson, 1977; Stein & Glenn, 1979). Informational texts, on the other hand, can use one or more text organization strategies individually or in combination, including description, compare-contrast, problem-solution, cause-effect, or sequential-procedural (Jones et al., 2016; Shanahan et al., 2010; Williams et al., 2007, 2009).

Listening Comprehension

Young children need many opportunities to listen and respond to books, stories, and various other types of texts in order to understand their content or to perform a task. In the simple view of reading (Gough & Tunmer, 1986), reading is thought to be composed of two key components—decoding ability + listening comprehension. Research has shown that listening comprehension and reading comprehension are two sides of the same coin (Duke & Pearson, 2002). Teachers need to pose questions during read-alouds that highlight key vocabulary, and ask children to make inferences about why a character behaved in a certain way. Children can also be asked to imagine what they might have done under similar circumstances based on their own experiences and backgrounds as well as information from the text. Questions of these types involve the ability to use information from various sources within and external to the text to form an answer (National Early Literacy Panel, 2008; National Reading Panel, 2000). Questions that focus students' attention on making local inferences such as location, agent, time, action, instrument, category, object, cause/effect, problem/solution, feelings/attitudes, sequence, and compare/contrast can be answered by having students highlight key vocabulary in the text that act as clues for making specific or local inferences while listening to stories read aloud (Reutzel & Hollingsworth, 1988). Doing so can also help to teach younger students that the number of types of local inferences that any text might require is a finite set (Johnson & Johnson, 1986).

Knowledge of Alphabet Letters, Phonological and Phonemic Awareness, and Phonics

Letter-name knowledge is a strong predictor of success in early reading (National Early Literacy Panel, 2008). Research in this area suggests that alphabet knowledge is a byproduct of extensive early literacy experiences. Thus, simply training children on the alphabet in isolation, devoid of rich literacy experiences, has proven unsuccessful (Burns et al., 1999). The alphabet should be conspicuously displayed in the classroom and regularly referenced during classroom literacy instruction. For the youngest students, pre-K and early K, students' given names are excellent vehicles for focusing on letters as components of words (Justice et al., 2006). Names should be displayed, read, and used for various purposes, such as taking attendance and identifying ownership of items. Teachers can demonstrate how names are constructed by cutting a young child's name into its individual letters and then reconstructing it. Children may be given the opportunity to do the same with their own names and the names of their peers.

Research indicates that *phonemic awareness*, the understanding that speech is composed of individual sounds, is a causal, not correlational, predictor of reading success (National Early Literacy Panel, 2008; National Reading Panel, 2000). There is reason to believe that phonemic awareness is best learned in connection with alphabet letter learning and phonics instruction (Piasta & Wagner, 2010).

Phonological awareness, the ability to recognize and manipulate the spoken parts of words, and phonemic awareness activities should be included as part of daily literacy instruction. Activities should be playful, game-like, and relatively brief, about five minutes. For example, when reading aloud, a teacher might pause after reading a word to stretch the word in order to count the number of sounds heard in the word. After reading a sentence, a teacher might invite children to clap the number of words they hear in a sentence or the number of syllables they hear in a word.

Phonics involves teaching young students that letters and spoken sounds map onto one another in written language. Knowledge of phonics is essential in developing blending and segmenting processes that are important to both reading and spelling (Reutzel, 2015; Reutzel & Cooter, 2019). Opportunities to point out patterns in written language constantly occur throughout the day in early childhood classrooms. Attention to sound/letter relationships is most effectively made through explicit phonics instruction in blending and segmenting as well as applying phonics knowledge during reading decodable books and pattern books, and writing dictated words and sentences. Teachers need to focus children's attention on learning the alphabetic principle and applying this knowledge in reading and writing, not on simply memorizing sounds that relate to letters.

Opportunities to Write

Reading and writing development go hand in hand (Fitzgerald & Shanahan, 2000). Children learn a great deal about the purposes for writing long before they attempt to write on their own (Clay, 1975). For young children, drawing and writing blend as a way to express what young children think and talk about. Young students' written expression should not be mistaken as handwriting practice. Early writing may range from scribbling to the use of letters and the beginnings of spelling. Children's initial attempts at spelling provide them opportunities to apply what they know about written language and develop new understandings about word structure, phonics, and how writing offers a means for communicating meaning (Reutzel & Cooter, 2019).

Teachers can and should provide time as well as resources for children to write every day. As a response to a shared or dialogic read-aloud session, teachers can engage younger students in shared or interactive writing. A writing area where all the materials for writing are available to children should be included in the classroom. Clipboards, stickers, alphabet at eye level, differing writing media, paper, binding or display supplies, and alphabet manipulatives may be included. Children should be encouraged to use the writing resources provided and to share what they have produced at the end of the day. Occasionally, teachers should offer students a prompt like a photo, picture, or object for drawing/writing about that is related to something of interest to the individual or to the group's activities. Figure 4.2 offers a basic structure for conducting shared writing activities with young children.

Figure 4.2. Tips for Engaging in Shared Writing

The teacher demonstrates and children participate in the process of writing during shared writing activities. Chart paper, a whiteboard, a document camera, or a computer or e-tablet and projector may be used. The text may be as brief as a single sentence or a few words. Simple pictures may be included to begin with—captioned pictures or photos can be a very simple beginning point for shared writing. Topics may encompass current events, including personal experiences and news, responses to stories or books read aloud, and recipes, notes, messages, or shopping or to-do lists.

A typical shared writing activity might include the following:

1. Children participate in a read-aloud experience, or simply respond to simple photo, video, picture, or object prompts. A discussion follows.
2. Teacher elicits comments to be written down. For example: What would you label or call this picture? What did you like best about the story?
3. Teacher writes what the children suggest and reads it aloud during the writing.
4. Teacher reads and discusses finished writing with children. They discuss ideas, language patterns, words, and letters. The focus is on what they know at their stage of written language development.
5. Group rereads the shared writing with the teacher.
6. Children are encouraged to draw/write their own words or drawings independently during the day.
7. Children are given an opportunity to share their independent writing.
8. Extensions: Teachers may save shared writing charts to be displayed for students to reread with a partner or alone later on. Students can find or match known words and letters on these charts, which serve to focus students' attention on both reading and writing.

ESTABLISHMENT OF A LITERACY INSTRUCTIONAL ROUTINE

The establishment of a literacy instructional routine is critical. Young children find instructional routines comforting and predictable. For the youngest learners, early literacy instructional routines can be planned for at least 30 and up to 60 minutes per day. The Daily Literacy Routine shown in Figure 4.3 is offered as an organizational guide for teachers to plan literacy experiences for the youngest children.

The three components included in Figure 4.3 are: (1) Teacher-directed literacy foundation activities, which generally take place at circle time "on the rug" and include teacher modeling and guided practice around concepts of print, letters, sounds, phonemic and phonological awareness, phonics, and spelling. (2) Teacher demonstrations of reading and thinking aloud about reading that use enlarged texts with child participation in dialogic reading and shared reading activities. Texts for reading aloud are selected intentionally to develop student knowledge around relevant domains in math, science, or social studies. (3) Teacher demonstrations of writing and thinking aloud about writing that include child participation during shared writing and interactive writing to produce group-authored, enlarged texts.

STRATEGIES FOR ACCOUNTABILITY AND ASSESSMENT

Assessment in early childhood classrooms should measure student literacy development and growth using what is known from the evidence base about how young children learn to read and write. These assessment tools should possess expected psychometric properties such as validity and reliability. A literacy assessment plan should gather information from a variety of sources, including real literacy learning experiences. The plan should be designed as an ongoing process, integral for informing instruction, and strive not to displace instruction with large amounts of time for assessment. School leaders and literacy supervisors should expect teachers to have a system in place for keeping track of children's literacy development and progress. Formative assessment results should be used as an ongoing source of information to make instructional decisions about the literacy performance of individual children and about instructional groups relative to the goals

Figure 4.3. Early Literacy Instructional Routine: Daily Engagement in Literacy Foundations, Reading, and Writing (60 Minutes)

Reading and Writing Foundational Skills (20 Minutes)

During this block of time the teacher guides students through short lessons on the following reading and writing foundational skills and concepts:

- Oral Language Development (5 minutes)
- Phonological and Phonemic Awareness (5 Minutes)
- Alphabetic Principle and Letter Name Learning (5 Minutes)
- Phonics (5 Minutes)

Applying Foundational Skills in Reading Texts (20 Minutes)

During this block of time the teacher guides students through dialogic read-aloud or shared reading of a variety of text types and genres while simultaneously teaching the following during text talks or discussions:

- Embedded concepts about print instruction using enlarged print
- Vocabulary—Discussion of word meanings and context clues
- Comprehension—Main Ideas, Details, Story Structure, Simple Informational Text Structures, and Local Inferences

Applying Writing Foundational Skills in Writing Texts (20 Minutes)

During this block of time the teacher guides students through interactive writing or shared writing of a variety of texts including words, sentences, stories, informational texts, and other specific simple genres:

- Phonics through spelling
- Writing words, sentences and short stories or informational texts
- Writing specific text genres—captioned pictures, stating opinions, description, etc.

of instruction. For example, assessment during shared reading could take the form of an informal observation of the overall progress of the group by using choral response techniques such as holding up a whiteboard to show the results of a dictation task. The items suggested in Figure 4.4 may be helpful in deciding upon a set of observational criteria.

At times a teacher might select an individual for special monitoring. For example, a teacher might want to assess the literacy development of a child who rarely participates in the group or take a closer look at the literacy knowledge of particularly advanced children in order to accelerate their progress. Evidence of oral language competence can also be gathered as teachers listen critically to children's talk over time. Figure 4.5 contains some criteria to keep in mind regarding oral language development based on the *Teacher Rating of Oral Language and Literacy* (TROLL) instrument (Dickinson et al., 2003).

CONCLUSION

One of the greatest frustrations that school leaders and literacy supervisors experience is the fact that they can never hope to be expert in all the disciplines, developmental levels, and areas of concern for which they are often held responsible. Everyone concedes that this is true. It is possible, however, for school leaders and literacy supervisors to become effective observers and relentless questioners. School leaders and literacy supervisors certainly may not have all the answers, but they should at least be able to ask well-informed questions!

Early literacy is a crucially important, issue-laden topic. It is an interest in which the public is increasingly involved and about which stakeholders are likely to have a variety of questions and opinions. For these reasons, it is essential that school leaders and literacy supervisors have sufficient background in early literacy to serve as active, informed participants in its discussion.

Figure 4.4. Observation Checklist for Use During Shared Reading and Writing Activities

Book Handling and Concepts About Print

Students demonstrate an understanding of the following:

- ☐ Right side up of reading material
- ☐ Front and back of book
- ☐ Front-to-back directionality
- ☐ Title
- ☐ Author
- ☐ Illustrator
- ☐ Print evokes meaning
- ☐ Pictures evoke and enhance meaning
- ☐ Left-to-right direction
- ☐ Sentence
- ☐ Words
- ☐ Letters
- ☐ Punctuation
- ☐ First, last ordinal concepts
- ☐ Reversals in words and letters

Comprehension and Composition

Students demonstrate understanding and production of text through the following:

- ☐ Discuss meanings related to narrative and informational text content
- ☐ Make and confirm reasonable predictions where possible—guessing is not predicting
- ☐ Infer words in cloze or maze-type activities
- ☐ Compare/contrast events/facts within and between texts
- ☐ Determine main idea(s)
- ☐ Determine supportive details
- ☐ Recognize and use narrative structure in recalling, retelling, and writing stories
- ☐ Recognize sequential and question-answer text structure in recalling, retelling, and writing simple informational text

Motivation and Engagement in Reading and Writing

Students demonstrate their interest in reading and writing through the following behaviors:

- ☐ Show interest in listening to stories
- ☐ Show interest in captioning pictures, writing sentences and stories
- ☐ Actively participate in shared and dialogic readings of both stories and informational texts
- ☐ Engage in talk about stories and informational texts
- ☐ Request favorite books to be read aloud
- ☐ View themselves as readers and writers

As follow-up to shared reading and writing, students:

- ☐ Voluntarily select books in the classroom library to read or listen to
- ☐ Engage in writing words, sentences, and simple stories or information books
- ☐ Show pleasure in reading and writing more independently

Figure 4.5. Oral Language Checklist

☐ The student starts conversations with others and continues trying to communicate when not initially understood.

☐ The student shares personal experiences in a clear and logical way.

☐ The student asks questions about topics of interest (e.g., why things happen, why people act the way they do).

☐ The student uses imaginative and context-related talk in play centers.

☐ The student uses varied vocabulary or tries out new words in speaking.

☐ The student can be understood when he or she speaks to adults and other children in the classroom.

Source: Based on Dickinson, McCabe, & Sprague (2003), *Teacher Rating of Oral Language and Literacy* (TROLL).

REFLECTION QUESTIONS

1. Discuss how the widely examined and debated "Science of Reading" has affected your work in terms of curriculum, instructional strategies, and assessment. What are the most significant changes you have observed?

2. Which, if any, of the current and ongoing early literacy programs, initiatives, or practices discussed in this chapter has been a focus in your school, district, or state? Share how that effort is progressing in terms of the challenges and successes you have observed.

3. Inappropriate use of assessment tools and data are a source of serious concern among educators. Discuss how this is being addressed in your district, including the involvement of teachers in the process and the preparation of supervisors and administrators to address the concerns around assessment.

PROJECT ASSIGNMENT

Consider the three questions offered above and complete an in-depth investigation and analysis of the implementation of a literacy-related initiative at your state, district, and school levels (as applicable). You may select the Common Core State Standards, an early-literacy-related initiative, or literacy assessment as it relates to early childhood teachers. Include interviews, related background materials, and examples of curriculum, instructional strategies, and materials. Provide a section that links the project you have selected with the current literature on that topic. Conclude with a section offering your opinion about how you think the policy and practice have evolved and how the linkage might be improved.

REFERENCES

Administration for Children and Families/Office of Planning, Research & Evaluation. (2015). *Uses of technology to support early childhood practice: Full Report.* https://www.acf.hhs.gov/opre/resource/uses-of-technology-to-support-early-childhood-practice-full-report

Annie E. Casey Foundation. (2010). *Early warning! Why reading by the end of third grade matters.* Kids Count. https://www.aecf.org/resources/early-warning-why-reading-by-the-end-of-third-grade-matters/

Branch, G. F., Hanushek, E. A., & Rivkin, S. G. (2019). School leaders matter: Measuring the impact of effective principals. *Education Next, 13*(1), 1–8. http://hanushek.stanford.edu/publications/school-leaders-matter-measuring-impact-effective-principals

Burns, M. S., Griffin, P., & Snow, C. E. (Eds.). (1999). *Starting out right: A guide to promoting children's reading success.* National Academy Press.

Castles, A., Rastle, K., & Nation, K. (2018). Ending the reading wars: Reading acquisition from novice to expert. *Psychological Science in the Public Interest, 19*(1), 5–51. doi: 10.1177/1529100618772271

Chetty, R., Friedman, J. N., & Rockoff, J. E. (2014). Measuring the impacts of teachers II: Teacher value-added and student outcomes in adulthood. *American Economic Review 104*(9), 2633–2679.

Clay, M. M. (1975). *What did I write: Beginning writing behavior.* Heinemann.

Clay, M. M. (2000). *Concepts about print: What have children learned about the way we print language?* Heinemann.

Common Core State Standards Initiative. (2010). *Common Core State Standards for English language arts and literacy in history, social studies, science and technical subjects.* Council of Chief State School Officers & National Governors Association. http://www.corestandards.org/ELA-Literacy/

Deans for Impact. (2019). *The science of learning.* https://deansforimpact.org/resources/the-science-of-learning/

Dickinson, D. K., McCabe, A., & Sprague, K. (2003). Teacher Rating of Oral Language and Literacy (TROLL): Individualizing early literacy instruction with a standards-based rating tool. *The Reading Teacher, 56*(6), 554–564.

Doan, S. (2019). *Beyond achievement: How teachers affect outcomes other than test scores.* Rand Corporation. https://www.rand.org/pubs/research_reports/RR4312z6.html

Duke, N. K., & Pearson, P. D. (2002). Effective practices for developing reading comprehension. In S. J. Samuels & A. Farstrup (Eds.), *What research has to say about reading instruction* (3rd edition, pp. 205–242). International Reading Association.

Fitzgerald, J., & Shanahan, T. (2000). Reading and writing relations and their development. *Educational Psychologist, 35*(1), 39–50.

Freeman, D. (1968). *Corduroy.* Viking Press.

Gough, P., & Tunmer, W. (1986). Decoding, reading, and reading disability. *Remedial and Special Education, 7*(1), 6–10.

Hanushek, E. A., Piopiunik, M., & Wiederhold, S. (2019). The value of smarter teachers: International evidence on teacher cognitive skills and student performance. *The Journal of Human Resources, 54*(4), 857–899.

Hernandez, D. J. (2012, January). *Double jeopardy: How third-grade reading skills and poverty influence high school graduation.* The Annie E. Casey Foundation. https://www.aecf.org/resources/double-jeopardy/

Horowitz, J. M. (2021). *More Americans now say academic concerns should be a top factor in deciding to reopen K–12 schools.* Pew Research Center. https://www.pewresearch.org/fact-tank/2021/02/24/more-americans-now-say-academic-concerns-should-be-a-top-factor-in-deciding-to-reopen-k-12-schools/

Johnson, R. T., & Johnson, D. W. (1986). Action research: Cooperative learning in the science classroom. *Science and Children, 24*(2), 31–32.

Jones, C. D., Clark, S. K., & Reutzel, D. R. (2016). Teaching text structure: Examining the affordances of children's informational texts. *The Elementary School Journal 117*(1), 143–169.

Justice, L. M., Pence, K., Bowles, R. B., & Wiggins, A. (2006). An investigation of four hypotheses concerning the order by which 4-year-old children learn the alphabet letters. *Early Childhood Research Quarterly 21*(3), 374–389.

Lonigan, C. J., & Whitehurst, G. J. (1998). Relative efficacy of parent and teacher involvement in a shared-reading intervention for preschool children from low-income backgrounds. *Early Childhood Research Quarterly, 13*(2), 263–290.

Mandler, J. M., & Johnson, N. S. (1977). Remembrance of things parsed: Story structure and recall. *Cognitive Psychology, 9*(1), 111–151. https://doi.org/10.1016/0010-0285(77)90006-8

McGee, L. M. (2013). Read me a story: Reaping the benefits of reading for young children. In D. R. Reutzel (Ed.), *The handbook of research-based practice in early education* (pp. 364–379). Guilford Press.

Mohr, K. A. J. (2003). Children's choices: A comparison of book preferences between Hispanic and Non-Hispanic first-graders. *Reading Psychology, 24*(2), 163–176.

Morrow, L. M. (1988). Young children's responses to one-to-one readings in school settings. *Reading Research Quarterly, 23*, 89–107.

Morrow, L. M. (1990). Preparing the classroom environment to promote literacy during play. *Early Childhood Research Quarterly, 5*, 537–554.

Morrow, L. M., Berkule, S. B., Mendelsohn, A. L., & Healey, K. M. (2013). Learning through play. In D. R. Reutzel (Ed.) *The handbook of research-based practice in early education* (pp. 100–118). Guilford Press.

National Association for the Education of Young Children. (2012). *Technology and interactive media as tools in early childhood programs serving children from birth through age 8* [Position statement]. https://www.naeyc.org/sites/default/files/globally-shared/downloads/PDFs/resources/topics/PS_technology_WEB.pdf

National Center for Education Statistics. (2011). *National Assessment of Educational Progress at Grades 8 & 12: Writing Report Card 2011.* U. S. Department of Education. https://nces.ed.gov/nationsreportcard/pdf/main2011/2012470.pdf

National Center for Education Statistics. (2019). *National Assessment of Educational Progress Reading Report Card 2019.* U.S. Department of Education. https://www.nationsreportcard.gov/reading?grade=4

National Early Literacy Panel (NELP). (2008). *Developing early literacy: Report of the National Early Literacy Panel*. National Institute for Literacy.

National Reading Panel. (2000). *Report of the National Reading Panel: Teaching children to read*. National Institute of Child Health and Human Development.

Neuman, S. B., & Celano, D. C. (in press). *The new science of reading*. Harvard Education Press.

Neuman, S. B., & Roskos, K. (1992). Literacy objects as cultural tools: Effects on children's literacy behaviors in play. *Reading Research Quarterly, 27*(3), 202–225.

Neuman, S. B., & Roskos, K. (1997). Literacy knowledge in practice: Contexts of participation for young writers and readers. *Reading Research Quarterly, 32*(1), 10–32.

Office of Educational Technology. (2017). *Reimagining the role of technology in education: 2017 National Education Technology Plan Update*. U.S. Department of Education. https://tech.ed.gov/files/2017/01/NETP17.pdf

Opper, I. M. (2019). Does helping John help Sue? Evidence of spillovers in education. *American Economic Review, 109*(3), 1080–1115.

Opper, I. M. (2020). *Teachers matter: Understanding teachers' impact on student achievement*. RAND Corporation. https://www.rand.org/pubs/research_reports/RR4312.html

Piasta, S. B., & Wagner, R. K. (2010). Developing early literacy skills: A meta-analysis of alphabet learning and instruction. *Reading Research Quarterly, 45*(1), 8–38.

Reutzel, D. R. (2013). *Handbook of research-based practice in early education*. Guilford Press.

Reutzel, D. R. (2015). The inside track: Early literacy research: Findings primary grade teachers will want to know! *The Reading Teacher 69*(1), 12–22.

Reutzel, D. R., & Cooter, R. B. (2019). *Teaching children to read: The teacher makes the difference* (8th ed.). Pearson Education.

Reutzel, D. R., & Cooter, R. B. (2020). *Strategies for reading assessment and instruction: Helping every child succeed* (6th ed.). Pearson Education.

Reutzel, D. R., & Hollingsworth, P. M. (1988). Highlighting key vocabulary: A generative reciprocal inference procedure for teaching selected inference types. *Reading Research Quarterly, 23*(3), 358–378.

Reutzel, D. R., Smith, J. A., & Fawson, P. C. (2005). An evaluation of two approaches for teaching reading comprehension strategies in the primary years using science information texts. *Early Childhood Research Quarterly, 20*(3), 276–305.

Shanahan, T., Callison, K., Carriere, C., Duke, N. K., Pearson, P. D., Schatschneider, C., & Torgesen, J. (2010). *Improving reading comprehension in kindergarten through 3rd grade: A practice guide* (NCEE 2010-4038). National Center for Education Evaluation and Regional Assistance, Institute of Education Sciences, U.S. Department of Education. https://ies.ed.gov/ncee/wwc/PracticeGuide/14

Stein, N., & Glenn, C. (1979). An analysis of story comprehension in elementary school children. In R. O. Freedle (Ed.), *New directions in discourse processing* (Vol. 2, pp. 53–120).

Strickland, D. S., & Townsend, D. (2010). The development of literacy in the elementary school. In D. L. Lapp & D. Fisher (Eds.), *Handbook of research on teaching the English language arts* (3rd ed.) (pp. 46–52). Routledge.

Trelease, J. (2013). *The read aloud handbook* (7th ed.). Penguin Books.

Tyner, A., & Kabourek, S. (2020). *Social studies instruction and reading comprehension: Evidence from the early childhood longitudinal study*. Thomas B. Fordham Institute. https://fordhaminstitute.org/national/resources/social-studies-instruction-and-reading-comprehension

U.S. Department of Education & U.S. Department of Human Services. (2016). *Early learning and educational technology brief*. https://tech.ed.gov/files/2016/10/Early-Learning-Tech-Policy-Brief.pdf

Wexler, N. (2019). Elementary education has gone terribly wrong. *The Atlantic*. https://www.theatlantic.com/magazine/archive/2019/08/the-radical-case-for-teaching-kids-stuff/592765/

Wexler, N. (2020, June 6). How "reading instruction" fails black and brown children. *Forbes*. https://www.forbes.com/sites/nataliewexler/2020/06/06/how-reading-instruction-fails-black-and-brown-children/#fe471384ebe8

Williams, J. P., Nubla-Kung, A. M., Pollini, S., Stafford, K. B., Garcia, A., & Snyder, A. E. (2007). Teaching cause-effect text structure through social studies content to at-risk second graders. *Journal of Learning Disabilities, 40*(2), 111–120.

Williams, J. P., Stafford, K. B., Lauer, K. D., Hall, K. M., & Pollini, S. (2009). Embedding reading comprehension training in content-area instruction. *Journal of Educational Psychology, 101*(1), 1–20.

Willingham, D. T. (2017). *The reading mind: A cognitive approach to understanding how the mind reads*. Jossey-Bass.

CHAPTER 5

Improving Literacy Achievement in the Elementary Grades

Timothy Rasinski, Chase Young, and Meghan Valerio

- The improvement of literacy achievement must be a schoolwide, coordinated effort that is horizontal, vertical, and across the home–school divide.
- An effective literacy curriculum requires a plan and a leadership team made up of all constituent groups in the school.
- An effective literacy program (both curriculum and instruction) should be based on scientific and evidence-based findings, responsive to students' needs, and open to teachers as artists.

The report *A Nation at Risk* (National Commission on Excellence in Education, 1983) alerted Americans to the need for educational reform. Since that time scholars, policymakers, and practitioners have given particular emphasis to improving reading achievement in students, as reading is the foundation for all academic learning. Over the last several years reports and programs such as the National Reading Panel's report *Teaching Children to Read* (2000), *Reading First* (No Child Left Behind Act, 2002), the Common Core State Standards Initiative (2016) at the national level, and state-level initiatives such as California's *English Language Arts Framework* (California Department of Education, 2014) have all been designed and implemented with the intention of improving students' reading achievement.

Despite these significant initiatives, reading achievement has barely budged over the past 25+ years. According to the 2019 National Assessment of Educational Progress (National Center for Education Statistics, 2019), 34% of American 4th-grade students read at a level considered "below basic," while only 35% are considered "proficient" or higher. At the 8th-grade level 27% of students are "below basic" and only 33% read at a level of "proficient" or higher. Moreover, these results are not substantively different from the results of previous years' reports. Clearly, as a nation, we are not making the kinds of progress in literacy achievement that we aspire to. What is to be done?

In the mainstream media, there seem to be regular calls for the application of the science of reading in developing effective reading curricula and instruction (e.g., Hanford, 2018). These reports tend to focus almost exclusively on the need to provide systematic and explicit instruction in phonics in the primary grades.

Reading instruction should certainly be guided by the scientific research on how children best learn to read. However, a scientific approach to reading instruction is not sufficient to achieve the ultimate goal of literacy instruction: proficient, engaged, and lifelong readers. To truly change the course of reading outcomes for students, a schoolwide horizontal and vertical approach to literacy instruction, based on the science of reading and responsive to the school culture, is needed. This chapter explores the development of schoolwide approaches to effective literacy programs for students, including features that are essential to success. These recommendations are guidelines, and in some cases starting points, for true literacy success is also about responding to the individual needs of a student that a guideline may not have considered.

THE LITERACY LEADERSHIP TEAM

A schoolwide literacy program needs leadership—knowledgeable colleagues who are willing to create a schoolwide plan for success and ensure that the plan is maintained in all grade levels. Clearly, a lead person for such a team is the school principal. The dual usage of the word "principal" suggests this person's essential role. "Principal" can be used both as a noun and as an adjective that modifies the noun "teacher." In its truest sense, an effective school principal is a teacher, or instructional leader. Therefore, it is imperative that the principal be well-versed in effective literacy instruction.

Of course, a team is made up of more than one person. Who else should be part of a Literacy Leadership Team (LLT)? We suggest including the school literacy specialist(s), the literacy teaching staff of different grade levels and experiences, the special education staff, the media center staff, arts and physical education staff, and parents. Even community members such as a representative from the local community library should be considered for membership. The LLT should not be so large as to be unwieldy in its ability to make decisions but should represent various stakeholders in teaching children to read. Eight to twelve members is a good range.

The LLT's responsibility is to provide direction for the schoolwide literacy effort. The team should consider overarching questions that cross grade levels and stakeholders to address the specific literacy needs of the school. Here are initiatives that an LLT might pursue:

- Analyze data from literacy assessments, surveys, and so on to identify areas of success and areas of weakness in literacy for the school.
- Develop schoolwide goals for literacy achievement that build on existing successes.
- Define what counts as effective literacy instruction that will address the goals for schoolwide literacy achievement.
- Evaluate materials to be used in the schoolwide literacy curriculum.

- Develop a systematic plan for assessment of the overall literacy program that determines and monitors literacy concerns.
- Develop a systematic plan for professional development for teachers and parents aligned with schoolwide literacy goals.
- Develop strategic partnerships with local universities, libraries, and other resources.
- Develop and implement methods of communication with stakeholders, including parents and community members.
- Identify and implement literacy initiatives outside of regular classroom instruction (e.g., arts and physical education, summer and vacation reading programs, and parent-involvement programs) and across subject areas.
- Create a shared understanding of desired outcomes.

With such an ambitious set of goals, the LLT must meet on a regular and scheduled basis. At the very least, monthly meetings should be scheduled with the possibility for subgroup meetings more often.

CURRICULUM AND INSTRUCTIONAL COMPONENTS

Several key considerations for literacy instruction are offered in this section. Although the LLT will be responsible for identifying grade levels and specific classrooms that would benefit from instruction in each of these areas, a common schoolwide understanding of literacy instruction is essential for successful implementation at the classroom, school, home, and community levels.

What Counts as Literacy Instruction, and How Much Time Should be Devoted to It?

A central question that needs to be addressed by any program that focuses on literacy instruction is what actually constitutes such instruction. In other words, before moving forward with any literacy initiative, there needs to be a consensus on what literacy instruction is. While literacy (i.e., listening, speaking, reading, and writing) happens all through the instructional day, literacy *instruction* occurs when the teacher is actively and intentionally interacting with

students for the purpose of improving some aspect of their literacy development. This could involve reading aloud to students, reading chorally with students, and listening to students read and conferencing with them about the content of their reading; providing instruction in decoding, spelling, and understanding words; demonstrating how to write the letters of the alphabet; and assessing individual or small groups of students in their reading and writing development.

Literacy activities that do not involve active involvement of the teacher may include whole-class seatwork, independent reading or writing, and independent time at centers, computers, or other workstations. While these learning opportunities are also critical for development, they are not counted as actual instruction, since students are working independently without the teacher. They are necessary components of a literacy curriculum, when done with intention and supported by instruction that prepares students to be successful independently.

How much time, then, should be devoted to actual literacy instruction? There is no scientifically agreed-upon ideal time for literacy instruction (U.S. Department of Education, Institute of Education Sciences, National Center for Education Evaluation and Regional Assistance, Regional Educational Laboratory Northwest, 2014), and there are relatively wide differences in the amount of time teachers give to literacy instruction (Rasinski et al., 2020). There is evidence that time for instruction is highly correlated with achievement (Furry & Domaradzki, 2010; Snow et al., 1998). That is, more time spent on literacy instruction means higher levels of literacy achievement among students.

We recommend that actual literacy instruction should average between 120 and 150 minutes per day (Shanahan, 2019). During this period, the teacher should be involved with students in the instructional activities mentioned above. Figure 5.1 provides general guidelines for the allocation of time for daily literacy instruction. There should be variations of whole-group and small-group instruction. The amount of time devoted to specific instructional activities may vary depending on the grade level and instructional needs of students. For example, as students move from word recognition to fluency development, less time can be devoted to phonics while more time is allotted for fluency.

Figure 5.1. General Guidelines for Allocation of Time for Daily Literacy Instruction

Literacy Activity	Duration	Recommended Integrated Components (as needed)
Word Study	15–20 minutes	phonemic awareness, phonics, vocabulary, spelling
Read-Aloud	15–20 minutes	phonics, vocabulary, comprehension, fluency, strategy instruction, whole-group lesson based on the text
Writing Instruction	15–20 minutes	explicit writing instruction in brainstorming, planning, drafting, revising, editing in various genres, conferring with students
Shared Reading	15–20 minutes	shared reading of a text with explicit teaching and modeling of specific literacy skills within the text (phonemic awareness, phonics, fluency, vocabulary, comprehension, writing)
Guided Practice	40 minutes	phonemic awareness, phonics, fluency, vocabulary, comprehension, guided reading, writing
Independent Work	20–30 minutes	independent reading, independent word study, fluency development, comprehension strategy application, writing
Total	120–150 minutes	

Note: At each grade level, times allotted to different literacy activities may vary. For instance, kindergartners may participate in shared reading for a total of 5–10 minutes before moving into guided practice, while 5th-graders may participate for 15–20 minutes.

A portion of literacy instruction should be dedicated to whole-group instruction, specifically *shared reading*. Shared reading is the act of sharing the responsibility of reading between teacher and student (Parkes, 2000). At each grade level, the time spent in shared reading can vary. In kindergarten and 1st grade, the teacher may lead students through choral and echo reading of big books and poems. These young students have opportunities to engage in repeated readings of the same text, first reading for meaning, pleasure, and experience of the text, and then (usually the next day) with a targeted skill or comprehension strategy in mind to dive deeper into the text. When kindergarten and 1st-grade students are ready, they receive their own copy of the text and engage in multiple readings over several days. This repeated reading strategy also applies to grades 2 and above for students who have not achieved sufficient fluency in their reading. The teacher should use combinations and variations of independent reading of the text before reading it aloud and engaging in partner reading. Round-robin reading, or one child reading at a time (sometimes disguised as popcorn reading), has been shown to be a harmful practice that impedes fluency and comprehension, and should be avoided (Opitz & Rasinski, 2008).

Moving into small-group rotations is a way for teachers to meet the needs of students while providing opportunities for them to engage in independent reading and writing, which are essential components of an effective literacy curriculum (e.g., Samuels & Wu, 2003). During this time, the teacher should meet with small groups of students to teach mini-lessons to meet specific needs, lead literature circles where students are reading and discussing a text, or use guided reading. Guided reading occurs when the teacher, meeting with students grouped by skill level, who are using a text on their level, provides instruction that meets their needs to understand the text (Fountas & Pinnell, 1996). While the teacher is meeting with small groups of students, other students are engaged in independent reading (Clay, 2017), independent writing, or work at learning centers.

The LLT for each school needs to determine the appropriate amount of time during the school day to be devoted to literacy instruction. There sometimes are requirements beyond the control of some LLTs, including district guidelines to follow. However, the LLT should be as generous as possible in the allocation of time, particularly in the K–3 grades where children need to develop proficiency in the foundational reading areas—phonemic awareness, phonics, and fluency—in order to get to the ultimate goal of comprehending the text. Intermediate grades need time for bolstering their reading comprehension and engaging in authentic "adult-like" reading activities such as literature circles or book clubs. The LLT often has the difficult task of generating or reallocating time to literacy instruction. Finding time requires creativity, flexibility, integration, and perseverance.

Where to Focus Instruction?

The original work of the National Reading Panel (2000) reported that certain competencies are critical for developing proficiency in reading. More recent research and scholarly thought have supported these initial recommendations, and developed them even further (Duke & Block, 2012; Reutzel & Cooter, 2016). The initial guidelines and recent research are used as a framework for the suggestions that follow for designing literacy instruction.

Word decoding/encoding: phonemic awareness, phonics, and spelling. Becoming proficient in decoding words is essential to reading success. Readers cannot understand a text if they are unable to decode (sound out) too many of the words in the text. It is clear that a significant amount of instructional time should be devoted to word decoding and spelling (encoding) until students master and apply these skills independently, especially in the primary grades (K–3).

Phonemic awareness refers to the ability of students to isolate, blend, and manipulate the sounds of language (phonemes). Phonics, the ability to use the sound-symbol relationships in words to decode the words, requires proficiency in phonemic awareness. In kindergarten and 1st grade, daily explicit instruction and practice in developing phonemic awareness are essential. There are many ways to develop students' phonemic awareness, including reading aloud, playing word/sound games, engaging students in rhyming activities, and singing songs.

With phonics instruction, students develop proficiency in letter identification and the sounds associated with letters and letter combinations. Research has shown that many students struggle in developing proficiency with this competency (Torgesen et al., 1999). The importance of daily explicit and systematic instruction in phonics for students' reading proficiency cannot be overstated (Duke & Mesmer, 2018; Stahl et al., 1998). To help students move toward fluent reading, 20–30 minutes per day should be devoted to phonics instruction based on assessment of children's needs, so that time is not taken away from other essential literacy instruction (Duke & Mesmer, 2018).

Although there are many commercial print and digital programs available for guiding phonics instruction, teachers can also employ their own systematic instructional approaches (National Reading Panel, 2000). This gives teachers ownership of their curriculum as they design their own instruction for students. For example, the use of a word-building activity in which students are guided by the teacher to manipulate a limited set of letters (and sounds) to make words has been shown to be quite effective in developing students' ability to decode and spell words (Beck & Beck, 2013; Cunningham & Cunningham, 1992). Additionally, helping students recognize larger letter patterns such as word families (rimes) can be another approach that teachers use. Mastery of one word family (e.g., -*ack*) can lead students to decoding (and encoding) multiple words (e.g., *back, Jack, lack, pack, sack,* and *stack*). Since word families rhyme, word family instruction can be combined with students learning and reciting poetry.

Spelling instruction should be considered part of the phonics program (Bowers & Bowers, 2017). Encoding, or learning to spell words (going from sound to written letters), is the other side of learning to decode words (going from written letters to the sounding-out of words). As teachers develop lessons aimed at word decoding, simultaneous instructional emphasis should be placed on word encoding. Spelling should not be considered a subject area separate from the reading curriculum. Selecting an effective spelling program or approach requires extensive research and discussion with the LLT so that there is a shared understanding of the complex cognitive processes involved in learning how to spell (Bear et al., 2012). Once a program or approach is selected, high-quality and continuous professional development for teachers is recommended.

Vocabulary instruction. Vocabulary involves understanding the meaning of words. Readers cannot fully understand a text if they are not familiar with the meanings of the words. Since vocabulary instruction deals with words, a focus on word meanings should be included with phonics and spelling instruction. While vocabulary instruction is embedded within other literacy instruction (i.e., phonics and spelling, shared reading, guided reading), there may be times when explicit instruction is needed. In these instances, 15–30 minutes of the 120–150 minutes should be used daily for vocabulary instruction.

Instructional activities that help students understand meaningful patterns within words are essential to building vocabulary. Knowledge about meaningful units called morphemes (which include base words, prefixes, and suffixes) and of the patterns in which they are assembled can be used to aid understanding of new words. For example, if students know that the morpheme *sub-* means "under," they will have a better understanding of words such as *subway, subtract, subterranean, submarine, submit, substitute,* and *subordinate.* Regular instruction with one to two morphemes per week has been shown to be a successful way to improve students' vocabularies and reading comprehension (Baumann et al., 2002).

Other teacher-initiated approaches to vocabulary instruction might include synonym and antonym awareness activities such as vocabulary ladders, concept maps in which students are guided in constructing definitions of words, figurative language exploration, phrase meanings, word games such as Wordo or Word Bingo, and word histories (etymologies) (Rasinski & Zutell, 2010). Teachers can weave these and other generic vocabulary activities into a vocabulary curriculum so that students will not only expand their vocabularies for reading and writing but will also learn to take ownership in learning about words.

Reading fluency. Fluency has been called the neglected goal of the reading curriculum (Allington, 1983). Indeed, research has shown that students who struggle in reading often manifest difficulties in fluency (Buly & Valencia, 2002; Valencia & Buly, 2004). Moreover, research has shown that fluency is often given secondary status in the reading curriculum. Fluency must be given the same priority as the other building blocks of the reading curriculum—20–30 minutes of the 120 minutes per day allotted for reading instruction (Rasinski, 2010). This may be a focused goal during shared reading or perhaps a target during small-group instruction, either in a mini-lesson or guided reading.

Fluency is the ability to decode words automatically or effortlessly. Students who are fluent readers do not have to put much cognitive effort or energy into decoding the words they encounter when reading. That cognitive energy can thus be devoted to reading comprehension (LaBerge & Samuels, 1974). Fluency also includes the ability of readers to read texts with a level of expression that reflects and elaborates on the meaning of the passage.

Fluency in reading, like fluency in any human activity, is developed through practice. Two kinds of practice are particularly important—assisted reading and repeated reading (Kuhn & Stahl, 2003). Assisted reading involves students reading a text silently or orally while simultaneously hearing a fluent reading of the same text. Assisted reading can be done with either shared reading or choral reading, but it can also be done individually with one student working with one partner (a more fluent classmate or adult). It can also occur when reading a text and listening to a fluent recorded version of the text during center or learning station time.

Many students who struggle in reading do not read a text fluently during their initial reading. Repeated reading involves reading a text multiple times until it can be read fluently. Research has shown that repeated reading of one text leads to improvements in fluency and comprehension of new texts that have not previously been read (Therrien, 2004); that is, the practice on one text generalizes to new texts (Rasinski et al., 2011). Students should be exposed to a variety of genres that are read repeatedly both in shared reading and small-group instruction.

Fluency instruction can be made an authentic part of the reading curriculum through regular performance activities (Young & Nageldinger, 2014). That is, when students know that they will be performing a poem, singing a song, or reading a portion of a script in a reader's theater activity, they have a natural motivation to engage in assisted and repeated readings (Tyler & Chard, 2000). This practice enables students to learn to read the text automatically and with good oral expression. A weekly routine in which students rehearse a text throughout the week in order to perform it at the end of the week has been found to be an effective and engaging approach to fluency instruction (Young et al., 2019).

Reading comprehension. The goal of reading is to comprehend the message intended by the author of a text (Palinscar & Duke, 2004). To become good comprehenders of texts, readers must accurately and automatically decode and understand the words in a text. They must also be able to read texts with appropriate expression. However, these abilities are not sufficient to guarantee good comprehension. Readers must also engage in actively constructing meaning from the text. Comprehension is a not a passive process. Good readers are constantly relating texts to their own background knowledge, making predictions or inferences about the meaning of a passage, and comparing and contrasting information in a text with other sources of information. These comprehension processes need to be taught to students (Coyne et al., 2009; Duke & Pearson, 2002). This should be the heart of any reading curriculum, which means that 30 to 60 minutes of the 120 minutes per day should be focused on comprehension during shared reading and small-group instruction, with opportunities for students to practice independently.

Since comprehension involves the construction of meaning from a text, the essential element for comprehension instruction is a text from which students can make meaning. Comprehension instruction, then, begins with a text that students either read on their own, read with teacher assistance, or listen to the teacher read to them.

Comprehension has been described as a process of the reader bridging known information and new information in the text. This simple definition suggests two key ingredients for comprehension instruction: (1) readers having a solid base of information about the topic, and (2) readers having active strategies for integrating the new information in the text into their known information (Fisher & Frey, 2009).

Building background knowledge is critical, especially for children who may not have deep reservoirs of knowledge about topics they are reading about. Indeed, the very nature of being a child means that background knowledge and experience are limited by the child's age, and some children may have missed early opportunities that would build literacy opportunities (Reutzel & Cooter, 2016). Teachers need to be reminded of the need to provide students with background knowledge prior to students' reading. This information can be provided through teacher read-alouds of related materials, multimedia resources such as videos and other resources, and guest speakers in the classroom.

Teachers should also be aware of the need to teach various strategies for comprehension so that students employ them in their reading (Coyne et al., 2009). Strategies include the teacher encouraging students to make predictions or hypotheses about what they will be reading, comparing and contrasting information in the text being read with other information sources (e.g., other readings and current events), creating and sharing images that represent and reflect what students are reading, and having students transform the text they have read into another form (e.g., story into a script for reader's theater or informational text summarized as a rhyming poem). In all these activities, students are asked to respond actively in some way to what they have read. The act of responding allows readers to consider and integrate the textual information into their own cognitive structures. Other appropriate comprehension strategies include engaging students in discussion about what they have read (the strategies mentioned above can all be enacted within the context of a discussion), engaging students in literature circles, having students write about what they have read in a response journal, or doing something with the information in the text such as writing a letter to a public official or engaging in a science experiment. The LLT should reflect with teachers on what counts as reading comprehension instruction. For example, it may be assumed that having a child read and then asking questions might constitute reading comprehension instruction, but this is better viewed as assessment. A teacher's modeling of higher-level thinking through a think-aloud is a good example of instruction, as students are taught how to think about text rather than being asked if they understood. The LLT needs to be very clear on what, indeed, counts as reading comprehension instruction.

Comprehension instruction needs to occur daily in all elementary classrooms, in both whole-group and small-group settings; and comprehension is more than having students read texts passively. Teachers need to be reminded and encouraged regularly, by the LLT, of the importance of active engagement in the processing of information in texts.

Writing. Reading and writing go hand in hand. Students improve their reading by writing, and, of course, writing is often inspired and modeled by what students read (Applebee & Langer, 1983). Students need to be engaged in writing and writing instruction daily. The amount of time can vary from as little as 15 minutes at the kindergarten level to 30 minutes in the upper elementary grades. What happens during writing instruction can differ greatly. Certainly, mini-lessons on various topics related to writing should be a common and regular feature. Topics can range from topic selection to editing.

The major portion of the time for writing should involve students actually writing. In kindergarten and 1st grade, students will likely need the mechanical aspects of handwriting instruction, while building toward independently writing complete sentences through strategies like sharing the pen, reading together and writing morning messages, and practicing with dictated sentences (Morrow, 2020). As students progress through the upper elementary grades, teachers should confer/meet frequently with students about their writing. The teacher should provide specific, individualized feedback about the student's strengths and support their needs (Fletcher & Portalupi, 2001). A good writing program should engage students in a variety of writing genres—stories, poems, informational texts, persuasive essays, scripts for performance, and more. The LLT should provide ongoing guidance and support for teachers to ensure that writing is an integral part of the schoolwide literacy curriculum.

Reading aloud. One of most important arts of any literacy curriculum is the daily opportunity for teachers to read to students. Teachers at all grade levels should be expected to spend time (15–20 minutes of the 120–150 minutes) reading to students daily. Even teachers across content areas should be encouraged to find ways to read aloud to students.

The benefits of reading aloud to students are many. Through read-alouds, teachers can introduce students to writing styles, other genres, and authors that may not be familiar. Teachers can read materials above students' own reading ability, thus improving comprehension through tackling more sophisticated texts and ideas that students would not normally read on their own. By reading aloud more sophisticated material to students, teachers can help students to expand their vocabularies, particularly of literary and academic words (Massaro, 2015). Fluent reading is modeled through the expressive oral reading done by the teacher (Farrell, 1966). Read-alouds provide teachers with opportunities to build background knowledge and inspiration for students' future readings, writings, and further explorations. And perhaps, best of all, the read-aloud allows students to experience the pleasure and enjoyment of reading. The fondest memory of elementary school for many adults was the regular time that a special teacher read to the class. Just as with the other areas of the literacy curriculum described previously,

read-aloud should be a nonnegotiable, daily, and integral part at all grade levels.

LITERACY INSTRUCTION BEYOND THE REGULAR CLASSROOM

Involving Other School Staff

Literacy instruction should not occur only in students' regular classrooms. The LLT should explore and suggest ways for the art, music, physical education, media specialist, and other specialist teachers and staff to include literacy-related activities in their own work with students. Learning to read and write is a cumulative process that has no beginning and end. Students do not read just during Reading Time, and it is not the regular classroom teacher's job alone to establish literacy behaviors. When special-area teachers see themselves as literacy teachers, they help their students to become better readers and writers.

Literacy in the special areas can take a variety of forms. In music, students can sing and read lyrics of songs; in art, students can read about various forms of art; and in physical education, students can read about the cardiovascular system and famous athletes, or listen to a teacher read short vignettes from the current sports scene. Schoolwide literacy activities can involve the principal who shares a special word or poem of the day. Creating a print-rich environment that includes posters, poems, or other informative texts throughout the school can allow for all opportunities to be literacy ones, even a class trip to the restroom. The key is to get words and texts in front of students as much as possible so that reading is taking place. In schools with populations who speak more than one language, including bilingual labels is a way not only to promote reading for all, but also to give consideration to more than one culture. The LLT and the full school staff should be encouraged to find ways to make this happen.

Reaching Out to Parents

An effective literacy program does not end at the school door. Students spend more time at home than in school. The LLT, as well as individual teachers, must develop ways to include parents and other family members in the literacy development of their children. Communication with the home is vital. The LLT should develop schoolwide methods for communicating with parents. Regular newsletters are one way to inform parents of schoolwide and classroom specific literacy instruction and communicate ways that parents can support these instructional strategies at home.

Paired reading (Topping, 1987), a simple ten-minute activity in which parents and children read together, has been found to accelerate students' reading progress. Similarly, *Fast Start* (Rasinski & Stevenson, 2005), a home reading program for primary-grade children and their parents reading short rhymes together, was found to be particularly effective in helping 1st-grade students most at risk for reading difficulties. Both paired reading and *Fast Start*, as well as other proven parent-involvement programs in reading, should be presented to parents as possible schoolwide, gradewide, or individual classroom initiatives. The LLT should address how parent involvement can help to meet schoolwide literacy goals.

Studies show that, in general, students do not read much at home, typically averaging 10–12 minutes per day (Anderson et al., 1988). What would happen if students were to increase their home reading to 20 minutes per day? Certainly, we could expect reading achievement to improve, at least with some students. A simple schoolwide approach to increase reading at home would be to create a schoolwide challenge: Determine the total number of minutes that it would take for every student in the school to read for 20 minutes per day, every day of the school year (e.g., 200 students x 20 minutes x 270 days = 1,080,000 minutes), and then have every student in every home work toward the total for the entire school year. An effective literacy initiative requires active linkages to parents and homes, both at the schoolwide and individual classroom level (McCarthy, 2000).

ASSESSMENT

Goals for literacy are established by evaluating existing assessment data, designing effective instruction to meet student needs, and selecting ways to measure success and determine additional instructional changes through ongoing progress monitoring. The LLT needs to consider whether the assessments selected match the content taught. Through assessment, the LLT and individual teachers can determine if literacy goals are being achieved, identify students who may be experiencing difficulties in literacy, and identify areas for improvement of the curriculum. Assessment is essential. The challenge with any assessment in a school setting is that the time given to assessment is time taken away from instruction. The LLT should consider the following:

- What sort of assessments should be given schoolwide?
- Who should administer the assessments?
- How often should the assessments be administered?
- How will data be analyzed?

Forms of Assessment

Many school systems must use reading achievement tests such as the Partnership for Assessment of Readiness for College and Careers (PARCC) assessment, also known as criterion-referenced assessments (Reutzel & Cooter, 2016), as mandated by individual states. While these assessments may provide annual school performance data and reveal overall school system trends, they do not provide timely, specific information that can help guide student instruction.

Formative assessments are a way for teachers to assess a student's strengths and weaknesses, as well as gather information on students' learning after daily instruction. Formative assessments can take the form of progress monitoring, or a way to assess a child periodically to see if certain goals, objectives, or other benchmarks are met (Reutzel & Cooter, 2016). There are a number of formative assessments that can be used (Rasinski & Padak, 2005). The LLT should establish a way to measure student progress three times a year, preferably using an informal reading inventory (IRI). Informal reading inventories are valid and reliable assessments that can act as a foundation for the school's reading program because they provide feedback to the LLT on the progress of individual students and areas of concern for individuals or groups of students who may be struggling in reading. They can offer teachers insights on how best to help students improve their reading. Teachers can use an IRI to monitor students' progress during the school year and determine any potential loss of achievement over the summer by comparing spring results from one school year to the fall results of the following.

In addition to IRIs, running records can track students' progress in reading on an informal and frequent basis (Clay, 2017). With running records, individual students read a grade- level passage and either respond to questions about the passage or do a retelling of the passage while a teacher takes anecdotal notes, marking words read correctly and noting errors. From this reading, the teacher is able to determine a student's word recognition accuracy (percentage of words read accurately), word recognition automaticity (reading rate or words read correctly per minute), prosody (teacher rating of expression based on a rubric), and reading comprehension from a retelling of the text. The teacher is then able to analyze the child's errors. The teacher can also determine the independent level, or level when a child can read 96% or more of the text correctly and with ease; the instructional level, or the level where 90–95% of the text is read with accuracy; and the frustration level, or when 89% of the text or less is read with accuracy (Clay, 2017).

A running record can help teachers adjust groups and help students choose appropriate texts for independent reading and at-home reading without carrying out a full IRI, which can be time-consuming. In addition, students who perform at a level above, at, or near grade-level expectations can be assumed to be on track for continued growth in their reading. Students who perform significantly below grade-level expectations in one or more areas can be referred for additional and more in-depth assessment and possible placement in an intervention program.

Running records are fairly simple and time-efficient, but they do require some degree of expertise on the part of the teacher. Although it may be tempting to recommend that other school staff administer the IRI or running records, it does give the teacher the opportunity to observe and analyze each student's reading behaviors individually. Another adult or school staff member could teach the whole class while the teacher pulls students out of class for this assessment.

Regular professional development that supports teachers and staff on the administration, scoring, and interpretation and understanding of the IRI, running record, and other research-based assessments should be led by the LLT. Teachers should be meeting within

grade levels, above and below grade levels they teach, and with literacy specialists so that the teachers have meaningful conversations about data findings and instructional decisions. Moreover, the simple formats of IRIs and running records allow parents, with support from teachers who help review assessment results, to better understand their own child's reading development and how they may be able to assist their child's continued growth in reading.

Obviously, children in kindergarten are likely not to be reading in a conventional sense. Thus, the use of an IRI or running records would not be useful. There are the other critical reading-related competencies that can be assessed in young children to determine their readiness for reading. Areas for which assessments could be fairly easily developed or procured include letter identification (recognition and sound representation), phonemic awareness (sound isolation, manipulation, and blending), concepts of print, receptive vocabulary, and listening comprehension.

A data management system developed by the LLT would allow IRI, running records, and other assessment data to be recorded in a spreadsheet format for each elementary school student. This system could track individual and school progress and identify possible schoolwide or grade-level areas of concern for which professional development could be provided.

Identifying Struggling Readers for Intervention

One of the major purposes of regular assessment is to identify students who are struggling in reading. After an initial assessment, these students will need further assessment to determine the nature of their difficulties and the level at which they are reading. Then, based on the results of an in-depth assessment, the students should be assigned to work with an intervention specialist who will address their instructional needs. The U.S. Department of Education (Connor et al., 2014) has cautioned that students are often overidentified as having a reading disability, and therefore has suggested Response to Intervention (RTI) to differentiate instruction to meet the needs of all students and prevent unnecessary labels when students may just need targeted instruction (Reutzel & Cooter, 2016). With RTI and Multi-Tiered Systems of Support (MTSS; see Chapter 14), literacy instruction is divided into three levels or tiers (Hughes & Dexter, 2011; Reutzel & Cooter, 2016). Tier 1 is regular classroom instruction for all children. Tier 2 is for students who are experiencing a moderate level of difficulty in reading and would benefit from supplemental support. Tier 3 is for students who are experiencing significant difficulties and need intense intervention. Most students fit into Tier 1, with fewer children in Tier 2, and the fewest in Tier 3.

The LLT should develop a systematic plan for assessment and establish guidelines and responsibilities for the school reading intervention program. Among the decisions to be made by the LLT are the following:

- Performance criteria for those students who need additional assessments and the types of assessments to use
- Criteria for inclusion into Tier 2 and Tier 3 interventions
- General nature of instruction for Tier 2 and Tier 3 (How much time should be allocated for instruction? Does instruction take place in the classroom or in a separate location? Does Tier 2 and Tier 3 instruction supplement or supplant regular classroom instruction? How often should students be reassessed?)
- Qualifications for teachers in Tier 2 and Tier 3 interventions
- Communication strategies between parents and teachers for students involved in Tier 2 and Tier 3 interventions
- Professional development support for Tier 2 and Tier 3 teachers

Interventions for struggling readers are guided to some extent by the rules established by states and other local education agencies. However, because of the unique nature of every individual school, it is critical that the LLT have a role in making instruction for struggling readers as effective and productive as possible.

PROFESSIONAL DEVELOPMENT

One of the most important roles of a school's LLT is to guide the professional development of teachers and school staff. A well-planned professional development program is essential to ensure that all

teachers are highly qualified in the teaching of reading. Professional development should:

- Focus on scientifically validated areas of the reading curriculum (e.g., phonemic awareness, phonics, fluency, vocabulary, and comprehension) as well as clearly crucial needs (e.g., motivation for reading, assessment, and parental involvement)
- Be responsive to the needs of the school, based on assessment data
- Be an ongoing process that focuses on one topic in depth over a period of time rather than single sessions on a variety of topics
- Involve presentations by professional developers, professional readings and collegial discussions, observations of exemplary instruction, grade level and cross-grade level planning, and team building
- Include, if possible, graduate-level reading education coursework that is brought to the school to be taken by teams of teachers and school administrators

CONCLUSION

The administration and supervision of an elementary school's literacy program is no simple task. As described in this chapter, there is much that is involved in developing an effective and seamless program for students. This work cannot be done by one person alone. It requires a team effort of representatives from all constituent groups in a school community—administrators, teachers, staff, parents, and community members—striving together to maximize literacy success for all students. The team should be knowledgeable about the science of reading and aware of the needs within the school. The LLT's key responsibilities focus on the school's literacy curriculum, general and intervention instruction, assessment, parent and community reporting and outreach, and professional development.

The key to success in developing a successful literacy program is the LLT. If you are in a position of leadership in an elementary school, the first action you should take is to form the LLT that will guide and support you and your school to achieve the critical goal of proficient literacy for all students.

REFLECTION QUESTIONS

1. To what extent does your school have a Literacy Leadership Team? Are all members of the school community represented? What have been the positive results of your school's LLT? What does your school's LLT still need to do?
2. To what extent is there vertical coordination (K–5) of literacy instruction in your school? How is such coordination achieved?
3. How does your school ensure positive and productive school–home connections related to student literacy learning? What else might be done?

PROJECT ASSIGNMENT

You have been hired as a consultant to a school that has requested your assistance in developing a schoolwide literacy plan. Over the course of the next three months, how would you go about your work?

- How would you learn about the school's culture and literacy curriculum?
- How would you organize the school's LLT? How many members and from which constituent groups? How would you invite members to join?
- What would be your nonnegotiables in the school's mission statement?
- How would you address the need for the school literacy curriculum to be scientifically and evidence based?

REFERENCES

Allington, R. (1983). Fluency: The neglected reading goal. *The Reading Teacher, 36*(6), 556–561.

Anderson, R. C., Wilson, P. T., & Fielding, L. G. (1988). Growth in reading and how children spend their time outside of school. *Reading Research Quarterly, 23*(3), 285–303.

Applebee, A. N., & Langer, J. (1983). Instructional scaffolding: Reading and writing as natural language activities. *Language Arts, 60*(2), 168–175.

Baumann, J. F., Edwards, E. C., Font, G., Tereshinski, C. A., Kame'enui, E. J., & Olejnik, S. F. (2002). Teaching morphemic and contextual analysis to fifth-grade students. *Reading Research Quarterly, 37*(2), 150–176.

Bear, D. R., Invernizzi, M., Templeton, S., & Johnston, F. (2012). *Words their way: Word study for phonics, vocabulary, and spelling instruction* (5th ed.). Pearson.

Beck, I. L., & Beck, M. E. (2013). *Making sense of phonics: The hows and why* (2nd ed.). Guilford Press.

Bowers, J. S., & Bowers, P. (2017). Beyond phonics: The case for teaching children the logic of the English spelling system. *Educational Psychologist, 52*(2), 124–141.

Buly, M. R., & Valencia, S. W. (2002). Below the bar: Profiles of students who fail state reading assessments. *Educational Evaluation and Policy Analysis, 24*(3), 219–239.

California Department of Education. (2014). *English Language Arts/English Language Development Framework.* California Department of Education.

Clay, M. (2017). *Running records for classroom teachers* (2nd ed.). Heinemann.

Common Core State Standards Initiative. (2016). *Common Core State Standards Initiative: English Language Arts Standards.* http://www.corestandards.org/ELA-Literacy/

Connor, C. M., Alberto, P. A., Compton, D. L., & O'Connor, R. E. (2014). *Improving reading outcomes for students with or at risk for reading disabilities: A synthesis of the contributions from the Institute of Education Sciences Research Centers* (NCSER 2014-3000). National Center for Special Education Research, Institute of Education Sciences, U.S. Department of Education.

Coyne, M. D., Zipoli, R. P., Jr., Chard, D. J., Faggella-Luby, M., Ruby, M., Santoro, L. E., & Baker, S. (2009). Direct instruction of comprehension: Instructional examples from intervention research on listening and reading comprehension. *Reading & Writing Quarterly, 25*(2–3), 221–245.

Cunningham, P. M., & Cunningham, J. W. (1992). Making Words: Enhancing the invented spelling-decoding connection. *The Reading Teacher, 46*(2), 106–115.

Duke, N. K., & Block, M. K. (2012). Improving reading in the primary grades. *Future of Children, 22*(2), 55–72.

Duke, N. K., & Mesmer, H. A. E. (2018). Phonics faux pas: Avoiding instructional missteps in teaching letter-sound relationships. *American Educator, 42*(4), 12–16.

Duke, N. K., & Pearson, P. D. (2002). Effective practices for developing reading comprehension. In A. E. Farstrup & S. J. Samuels (Eds.), *What research has to say about reading instruction* (3rd ed., pp. 205–242). International Reading Association.

Farrell, E. (1966). Listen, my children, and you shall read . . . . *The English Journal, 55*(1), 39–68.

Fisher, D., & Frey, N. (2009). *Background knowledge: The missing piece of the comprehension puzzle.* Heinemann.

Fletcher, R., & Portalupi, J. (2001). *Writing workshop: The essential guide.* Heinemann.

Fountas, I. C., & Pinnell, G. S. (1996). *Guided Reading: Good first teaching for all children.* Heinemann.

Furry, A., & Domaradzki, L. (2010). *The value of instructional time and pacing schedules for K–3 reading.* National Reading Technical Assistance Center (NRTAC), RMC Research Corporation.

Hanford, E. (2018, Sept 10). *Hard words: Why aren't kids being taught to read?* American Public Media Reports. https://www.apmreports.org/story/2018/09/10/hard-words-why-american-kids-arent-being-taught-to-read

Hughes, C. A., & Dexter, D. D. (2011). Response to intervention: A research-based summary. *Theory into Practice, 50*(1), 4–11.

Kuhn, M. R., & Stahl, S. A. (2003). Fluency: A review of developmental and remedial practices. *Journal of Educational Psychology, 95*(1), 3–21.

LaBerge, D., & Samuels, S. J. (1974). Toward a theory of automatic information processing in reading. *Cognitive Psychology, 6*(2), 293–323.

Massaro, D. W. (2015). Two different communication genres and implications for vocabulary development and learning to read. *Journal of Literacy Research, 47*(4), 505–527.

McCarthy, S. (2000). Home school connections: A review of the literature. *Journal of Educational Research, 93*(3), 145–153.

Morrow, L. M. (2020). *Literacy development in the early years: Helping children read and write* (9th ed.). Allyn & Bacon/Pearson.

National Center for Education Statistics. (2019). *The Nation's Report Card: Reading: 2019 NAEP Reading Assessment.* https://www.nationsreportcard.gov/reading?grade=4

National Commission on Excellence in Education. (1983). *A nation at risk: The imperative for educational reform.*

National Reading Panel. (2000). *Report of the National Reading Panel: Teaching children to read. Report of the subgroups.* U.S. Department of Health and Human Services, National Institutes of Health.

No Child Left Behind Act of 2001, Pub. L. No. 107-110, § 101, Stat. 1425 (2002).

Opitz, M. F., & Rasinski, T. V. (2008). *Good-bye round robin.* Heinemann.

Palincsar, A. S., & Duke, N. K. (2004). The role of text and text-reader interactions in young children's reading development and achievement. *Elementary School Journal, 105*(2), 183–196.

Parkes, B. (2000). *Read it again! Revisiting shared reading.* Stenhouse Publishers.

Rasinski, T. V. (2010). *The fluent reader: Oral and silent reading strategies for building word recognition, fluency, and comprehension* (2nd ed.). Scholastic.

Rasinski, T. V., & Padak, N. (2005). *Three minute reading assessments: Word recognition, fluency, and comprehension for grades 1–4.* Scholastic.

Rasinski, T. V., Reutzel, C. R., Chard, D., & Linan-Thompson, S. (2011). Reading fluency. In M. L. Kamil, P. D. Pearson, B. Moje, & P. Afflerbach (Eds.), *Handbook of reading research, volume IV* (pp. 286–319). Routledge.

Rasinski, T., & Stevenson, B. (2005). The effects of fast start reading, a fluency based home involvement reading program, on the reading achievement of beginning readers. *Reading Psychology: An International Quarterly, 26*(2), 109–125.

Rasinski, T., Tschantz, B., Austin, J., Evans, K., Lowers, J., Papa, J., & Spear-Hoffman, E. (2020). Time for reading instruction: How much time should schools and teachers devote to reading instruction in grades K–2? *World Journal of Educational Research, 7*(1). https://core.ac.uk/reader/287182890

Rasinski, T., & Zutell, J. (2010). *Essential strategies for word study.* Scholastic.

Reutzel, D. R., & Cooter, R. B. (2016). *Strategies for reading assessment and instruction in an era of common core standards: Helping every child succeed.* Pearson.

Samuels, S. J., & Wu, Y. C. (2003). *How the amount of time spent on reading effects reading achievement: A response to the National Reading Panel.* University of Minnesota.

Shanahan, T. (2019). How would you schedule the reading instruction? *Shanahan on Literacy Blog.* http://www.shanahanonliteracy.com/blog/how-would-you-schedule-the-reading-instruction#sthash.TGiHZKfJ.dpbs

Snow, C. E., Burns, M. S., & Griffin, P. (Eds.). (1998). *Preventing reading difficulties in young children.* Report of the Committee on the Prevention of Reading

Difficulties in Young Children, National Research Council. National Academies Press.

Stahl, S. A., Duffy-Hester, A. M., & Stahl, K. A. D. (1998). Everything you wanted to know about phonics (but were afraid to ask). *Reading Research Quarterly, 33*(3), 338–355.

Therrien, W. J. (2004). Fluency and comprehension gains as a result of repeated reading: A meta-analysis. *Remedial and Special Education, 25*(4), 252–261.

Topping, K. (1987). Paired reading: A powerful technique for parent use. *The Reading Teacher, 40*(7), 608–614.

Torgesen, J., Wagner, R., Rashotte, C., Rose, E., Lindamood, P., Conway, T., & Garvan, C. (1999). Preventing reading failure in young children with phonological processing disabilities: Group and individual responses to instruction. *Journal of Educational Psychology, 91*, 579–593.

Tyler, B.-J., & Chard, D. J. (2000). Using readers theater to foster fluency in struggling readers: A twist on the repeated reading strategy. *Reading and Writing Quarterly, 16*(2), 163–168.

U.S. Department of Education, Institute of Education Sciences, National Center for Education Evaluation and Regional Assistance, Regional Educational Laboratory Northwest. (2014, June 4). *Ask-A-REL request: Does research support the move to a 90-minute literacy block at the elementary level?*

Valencia, S. W., & Buly, M. R. (2004). Behind test scores: What struggling readers really need. *The Reading Teacher, 57*(6), 520–531.

Young, C., Durham, P., Miller, M., Rasinski, T., & Lane, F. (2019). Improving reading comprehension with readers theater. *Journal of Educational Research, 112*(5), 615–626.

Young, C., & Nageldinger, J. (2017). Considering the context and texts for fluency: Performance, readers theater, and poetry. *International Electronic Journal of Elementary Education, 7*(1), 47–56.

CHAPTER 6

The Role of Leadership in Secondary Literacy Reform

William G. Brozo

- Leadership of adolescent literacy reform is complex due to issues of secondary school structure and culture, teacher efficacy, and disciplinary boundaries.
- Effective secondary literacy reform is a process of collaborative effort by a community of dedicated system administrators, school leaders, professional developers, and teachers.
- Five principles of literacy leadership can provide guidance to meaningful and sustainable secondary literacy reform.

In August 2005 the state of Louisiana was slammed by a hurricane of historic proportions. Katrina wreaked particular havoc on New Orleans and surrounding parishes, where floodwaters deluged the homes and businesses of countless citizens and nearly 2,000 lives were lost. Though financial relief was slow to arrive, eventually billions of federal dollars flowed to the state in support of its recovery. Like many organizations and agencies, the Louisiana Department of Education took advantage of this new source of revenue to enact needed reforms statewide. I was honored to be called upon to contribute the literacy piece to this massive effort and spent the next few years working with a team from Baton Rouge as well as administrators and teachers from every corner of the Bayou State on an overhaul of its Comprehensive Curriculum—the master plan that established content standards and guided instruction from kindergarten through grade 12 Advanced Placement courses (Robken, 2016).

This experience taught me about leadership, teacher professional learning, managing expectations for students' literacy improvement, and administrative support for initiating reforms, sustaining effort, and building teacher capacity. These insights have found their way into this chapter in the form of five principles of effective secondary literacy leadership and professional learning. I have also included vignettes, both national and international, of responsive practices by supervisors, administrators, and professional consultants that promote middle and high school students' literacy development.

THE CHALLENGES OF SECONDARY LITERACY REFORM

Literacy improvement in any context does not just happen. To use a seasoned cliché, it takes a village, or at least a community of dedicated teachers, administrators, and others, to bring about meaningful and sustainable literacy reform, particularly at the secondary level (Campbell & Kmiecik, 2004; Patterson et al., 2010; Witte et al., 2010). Those of us with decades of experience advocating for and working with schools and systems to bring about responsive literacy programs for middle and high school students are familiar enough with the tribulations and triumphs that accompany such efforts (Brozo & Hargis, 2003). Changes in teaching practices, unless integral to systemic and structural changes and regularly invigorated by engaged leadership, rarely outlast the consultants' or professional developers' direct involvement with a project. Moreover, without sustained engagement in the reforms by teachers themselves, which could mean multiple years of commitment (Timperley, 2008), positive student outcomes are less likely to be realized.

For a multitude of reasons, adolescent literacy appears to be unusually resistant to reform efforts. Twenty-five years ago, O'Brien, Stewart, and Moje (1995) identified some of the complexities involved in bringing about changes in teaching practices for content literacy. Perplexed by the hard sell of "every teacher a teacher of reading"—a notion that has become deeply embedded in the content-area literacy community's vernacular (Fisher & Ivey, 2005; Spencer et al., 2008)—these authors explored pedagogical, curricular, and school cultural factors influencing secondary teacher resistance to content literacy. They argued that delivering a set of reading techniques and strategies to secondary content teachers would be largely ineffective if detached from an appreciation of their existing skills and knowledge, insensitive to the curricular exigencies they must negotiate, and without regard to norms, relationships, and power dynamics in particular schools.

Along with these critical considerations for leaders of reform of middle and high school literacy instructional practices and programs are issues of teacher efficacy and agency (Cantrell et al., 2009; Hall, 2005), which relate closely at the secondary school level to disciplinary instruction (Gilles et al., 2013; Jenkins, 2011). Disciplinary instruction involves teaching students how the disciplines are different from one another and how to develop the critical literacy skills necessary to understand the ways knowledge is produced and obtained in each discipline (Brozo et al., 2013; Moje, 2015). From this perspective, each discipline functions as its own unique domain with its own unique literacy practices (Brozo, 2017a; Brozo et al., 2018).

For a disciplinary literacy curriculum to be meaningful, secondary teachers should have firsthand knowledge and experience with expert practices of science, history, English language arts, or math (Brozo et al., 2018). What is more typical, however, is that secondary teachers are able to show enthusiasm for their subject and have command of the content but are not fluent in the literacy-related practices of disciplinary insiders. This situation presents at least two problems for teacher leaders. The first is that secondary subject-area teachers are likely to view themselves as content experts. Those of us experienced in professional development (PD) for adolescent literacy have all heard the common complaint: "You know nothing about math so don't tell me how to teach" or "I teach science, not reading." These refrains remind us that for many secondary teachers, their sense of efficacy is tied to what they know. Challenging this expertise by asking them to develop discipline-specific literacy pedagogy skills in addition to their content knowledge is often perceived as a core threat to their sense of competency and agency (Hall, 2005; Wilson et al., 2009). Thus, although disciplinary expertise is an essential attribute of a quality secondary-level teacher, it can be an impediment to the realization of effective literacy reform at that level, which requires all teachers, regardless of what they teach and the context of instruction, to contribute to the leavening of students' literacy competencies. The second related problem is that to expect students to be active participants in the disciplinary practices of a subject area means that secondary teachers need to be authentic models of these practices, including the critical languaging skills inherent to each discipline. Changing secondary teachers' perceptions of their own expertise, then, will largely depend on responsive professional development (Darling-Hammond et al., 2009) and sustained administrative commitment (Giles & Hargreaves, 2006; Robinson, 2008).

On a nuts-and-bolts level, the fate of secondary literacy reform initiatives may turn on whether adequate time can be found in a typical school day for reform activity. For example, one of the stiffest barriers to implementing a Response to Intervention (RTI) program in traditional U.S. high schools is logistics (Brozo, 2011). The most ardent RTI supporters must overcome "rigid departmentalization of programs and courses as well as complex scheduling schemes to accommodate large numbers of students in both regular curriculum and extracurricular activities" (Brozo, 2011, p. 28). In one documented case, a principal's enthusiasm for RTI was blunted by the reality of trying to organize an effective tiered literacy intervention system at his traditionally structured high school. As the school year progressed, administrative injunctions concerning RTI became increasingly muffled, drowned out by the exigencies of running a complex institution. And as faculty and student routines took hold, any serious attempt at RTI-like reforms grew increasingly unlikely, until finally at midyear the principal and his staff decided an RTI system, as characterized by the original workshop advocates who conducted whole-school PD, was too ambitious and needed much more advance planning and ongoing technical support.

All of these challenges to adolescent literacy reform—ways to honor teacher agency while stretching comfort zones, threats to administrative focus and staying power, and ever-present logistical barriers—are well-documented in the school reform literature. Based on what the literature says about leadership practices as well as my own long history as a professional developer and supporter of literacy reform, the five principles of effective leadership that are presented below start with the broad leadership context of literacy reform and move toward the details of supporting reform in the school and the individual classroom.

PRINCIPLES OF EFFECTIVE LITERACY LEADERSHIP

Principle 1. Leadership from the Top Is Critical for Starting a Reform Movement

Within any discussion of leadership for literacy reform, it is important to remind ourselves that the ultimate beneficiaries of this activity should be students (Brozo, 2006). And though we tend to focus on individual schools as the sites of reform, where reform activity of principals and teachers can be observed, in reality these reform efforts often begin with visionaries at the highest tiers of educational leadership (Goertz et al., 1995; Lykins & Heyneman, 2008; National Policy Board for Educational Administration, 2015). At the state level this could include directors of education departments or ministries, superintendents, senior curriculum staff, and heads of teacher professional learning. These are the system leaders individually and collectively responsible for starting movements of educational change (Fullan, 2013; Tucker, 2011). Their articulation of a vision for reform helps to establish a standard of expectation for all other stakeholders, and when their vision is bolstered by commitments of necessary resources, it can be transformed into genuine change (Layland, 2019; Louis et al., 2010).

This is not to say grassroots reform movements cannot instigate meaningful change in local educational policies and practices (Ferman, 2017) or that top-down champions of reform are always impelled by evidence and vision instead of politics and financial gain (Finnigan & Daly, 2014; Office of Inspector General of the United States, 2006). By dint of enthusiasm and charisma, a lone teacher or reading specialist who embraces innovative literacy practices may expand individual influence beyond a single classroom or school that creates a pocket of reform (International Literacy Association,

2016; Lewis-Spector & Jay, 2011). And the scandals uncovered in investigations of Reading First remind us that politics cloaked in science may thwart the best-intentioned reformers (Bailey, 2013). Nonetheless, because of the inertia of teacher folkways and school cultures (Hall, 2005; Hargreaves, 1994; Hinde, 2004), durable, capacity-building change in education needs a visionary impetus from system leaders (Hargreaves et al., 2009).

Macedonia, Europe

As the Balkan Wars finally ended earlier this century, the last republic of the former Yugoslavia to experience ethnic bloodshed was Macedonia (known formally today as the Republic of North Macedonia). Although the warring between Slavic Christians and Albanian Muslims in Macedonia was not as catastrophic or protracted as the carnage in Bosnia or Kosovo, the degradation of infrastructure and institutions of civil society caused by the strife left a yawning need for redevelopment.

In the rebuilding process, visionaries at the federal level in the Ministry of Education in Skopje seized on international grant opportunities to reform their education system from one mired in the traditions of the former Soviet sphere of influence to a progressive future-oriented model with the goal of better positioning Macedonian youth for a post-socialist, free-market competitive world. Focusing on secondary vocational schools across the country, ministry officials with the assistance of in-country consultants were successful in procuring several millions in funding from the United States Agency for International Development (USAID).

In collaboration with USAID project staff and Ministry of Education personnel, a team of literacy volunteers transformed a broad vision of educational reform into a series of professional development workshops for secondary teachers from virtually every discipline. Graduates of this workshop series were then given the opportunity to become teacher leaders of the innovative instructional practices in their own schools, ultimately expanding the reach of the reforms to every secondary vocational school in Macedonia.

Known as the Secondary Education Activity or SEA, the project helped teachers rethink the front-of-room transmission approach to instruction and come to embrace the classroom as an interactive, student-centered learning environment. To imbue students with a sense of empowerment and agency, the literacy and learning practices promoted in SEA were designed to foster a kind of cognitive flexibility, or intellectual entrepreneurism (Brozo, 2017b), so that students could create their own niche in the new labor market. This sea change in thinking and practice among Macedonians was critical, since once the socialist system in the former republics of Yugoslavia capitulated, graduates from secondary and postsecondary schools could no longer assume that a guaranteed position awaited them in state-run factories and businesses.

The Macedonian government sustained their commitment to SEA for the five-year grant life of the USAID educational reform project (2003–2008), all the more impressive as there were three different heads of state representing two opposing political parties during that period. The impact of this commitment was established in the final report compiled by the American Institutes for Research and the International Reading Association (2009), which found that a statistically significant majority of teachers welcomed and regularly employed the innovative literacy and learning instructional practices. Furthermore, those teachers who after initial training became literacy coaches in their own schools also reported a significant change in attitude about interactive teaching and learning as well as their ability to positively influence their colleagues (Sturtevant & Linek, 2007).

Principle 2. Relationship Building Must Occur Between Key State, District, and School Personnel

It is understood that collective leadership at several levels is needed to influence student learning (Wahlstrom et al., 2010). This means state-level personnel initiating reforms need to ensure that district-level stakeholders feel invested in the process of planning and implementing reforms (Supovitz, 2006). Otherwise, state-level bureaucratic allocation of responsibility will not necessarily result in the transfer or development of district-level influence for needed changes in policy and practice (Firestone, 2009; Waters & Marzano, 2006).

Relationship building by state-level individuals associated with the reforms may necessitate hands-on involvement with district personnel as demonstration of their commitment to the changes they advocate. Ideally, known and respected reform leaders engage in detailed planning with district-level stakeholders to gain their buy-in to the reform agenda, since they are the ones who will extend the reform vision to school-level teacher-leaders. Cooter (2004) refers to these key leaders of educational reform as "warm demanders," who, with tact and respect for the dignity of those lower on the administrative ladder, make expectations for reform clear.

Evidence suggests systematic and ongoing engagement between these key stakeholders is essential for strengthening the design of and fostering broad support for ambitious educational reforms (Bae & Stosich, 2018). This form of collective leadership can increase input and participation, leading to more responsive district-level enactments of reform that are better matched to local needs and aspirations (Darling-Hammond et al., 2016; Louis et al., 2008).

Relationship building for shared leadership should reach ultimately to school-level leaders, who along with teachers will be the ones translating reforms into action (Fullan, 2002; Knapp et al., 2014; Rowland, 2017). If these frontline professionals do not become enthusiastic advocates of the reform agenda, its chances for success are greatly diminished (Cuban, 2011; Zimmerman, 2006). When school administrators and teachers give less than full support to a new literacy initiative, there are documented adverse effects on students' reading achievement and motivation (Brozo, 2006). Thus, to promote change readiness at the district and school levels, leaders of innovative educational policy, curriculum, and practice must forge connections with system stakeholders based on trust and a feeling of partnership in the reform effort (DuFour & Marzano, 2011; Ikemoto et al., 2014; Supovitz, 2006).

Louisiana, USA

Two individuals at the Department of Education in Louisiana had principal responsibility for spearheading the revision of the state's Comprehensive Curriculum. Beth and Dorothy were ideal advocates for the reforms, as they were already well-known and respected career teachers and teacher leaders in the Bayou State. Because of their prior experience in school and district leadership roles, they knew instinctively that to build support for integrating literacy practices into the state's instructional master plan they would first need to bring superintendents, curriculum and literacy coordinators, principals, and other school-level leaders on board. Without enthusiastic backing of the reform initiative by these key personnel, teachers were less likely to see the importance of literacy-strategy instruction or expend the effort needed to employ the strategies effectively.

Beth and Dorothy exploited their deft interpersonal skills to convince district and school leaders to participate in many of the same professional learning activities the project offered their K–12 teachers. In this way, these leaders could learn about and experience these new practices alongside teachers and debrief with them afterwards. This created an atmosphere of collaboration and contextual problem solving, where challenges with implementation could be discussed and the literacy innovations incorporated into district and school improvement plans. In addition, to promote the rollout of the revised Comprehensive Curriculum, professional learning sessions designed exclusively for district and school leaders were held at various locations across Louisiana, from the Recovery School District of New Orleans to a high school in Bossier City. For all of these PD sessions, Beth and Dorothy made certain one or both of them attended and participated in order to reinforce the personal connection from the Department of Education to the district, school, and classroom.

It is worth noting that several school principals who participated in these workshops were so inspired by them that they went on to pursue university coursework in reading literacy to become more knowledgeable and better mentors of their teachers' efforts to implement the new practices in the Comprehensive Curriculum. They often commented about how privileged they felt by their inclusion in the state-sponsored effort and credited Beth and Dorothy for these opportunities to further solidify collective commitment to the literacy reforms.

Principle 3. Building a Strategic Vernacular Reinforces the Systemic Nature of the Reforms

There are quite literally hundreds of literacy strategies and instructional routines available to secondary teachers (Fisher et al., 2015; Stahl, 1983).

Traditional approaches to elevating middle and high school literacy programs have typically included professional developers and/or teacher leaders introducing a few or many of these strategies to instructional staff with the expectation that everyone will either adopt a small common set, implement those of their choosing, or some combination of both. Regardless of the specific expectations for adopting particular literacy strategies, what seems to be crucial is ensuring that teachers develop an understanding of the cognitive processing involved in the new instructional routines and the language to describe, as well as labels to identify, the routines. In this way, teachers participating in literacy reform activities will be capable of communicating among their colleagues using a strategic vernacular and, moreover, of making explicit for students ways of enacting the textual practices.

Washington, DC, USA

In the Reading Across the Curriculum project, a citywide literacy reform initiative for all middle and high schools in the District of Columbia, teachers acquired knowledge of an array of reading and writing strategies through a 10-session PD series. The central planning office delegated consultants to lead the summer writing of the curriculum, which involved university literacy consultants together with district teachers and literacy leaders. Late in the summer, secondary school groups and universities were paired into clusters. Principals were brought on board, and logistical plans made for the coordination of twice-monthly, half-day workshops. In the fall and winter of that school year a series of 10 workshops for each of the content-area groups within each of the university clusters was offered during the school day, and later as a Saturday option. These workshops utilized literacy and content-area resources, the instructor's subject-matter expertise, and a structure that was designed to allow for reflection, research-based strategy instruction, demonstration, discussion, and one hour of collaborative planning. Selected content literacy texts, along with a curriculum notebook, were given to each participant and used throughout the series. At the end of the series and during the following summer months, each of the universities offered extension opportunities for the cluster schools in its partnership.

The year-long partnership with seven secondary schools came as part of a larger coordinated effort involving multiple local universities; a private, central planning office working directly with the district's leaders; and nearly all the district's secondary schools.

Ultimately, participants in the PD series were provided instructional experiences around numerous literacy strategies. Because teachers were encouraged to implement in their classrooms what was learned in the workshop setting and to reflect on the affordances for themselves and their students by debriefing with colleagues, a common language of literacy spread across the district. This strategic vernacular was reinforced in the monthly PD sessions, where further opportunities were created for teachers to discuss specific strategies with colleagues from different schools in the clusters.

Although it was hoped participants would be able to adapt the strategies to their classrooms that they had learned in the Reading Across the Curriculum project, the decisions around this issue were left ultimately to principals and literacy coaches in the individual schools. The overarching goal of, for example, Franklin Middle School's literacy improvement plan was to ensure every teacher was taking equal responsibility for the literacy growth of all students. Franklin's principal and her team knew that if their teachers were overwhelmed by a large number of new adolescent literacy strategies, they might find it easier to stick with the status quo than try to decide which strategies to apply. Franklin's approach garnered a great deal of attention across the district as school leaders and teachers decided to adopt just a few new literacy instructional routines but to embrace them through a total school commitment. Every teacher at this middle school, regardless of subject area, became deeply knowledgeable of and skillful with three effective strategies, known as the "Franklin 3," acquired through the workshop series. So devoted was Franklin to this approach that teachers and staff helped students and parents internalize the strategies and even featured the strategy names on the school marquee.

Louisiana. USA

In Louisiana, creating a strategic vernacular for the literacy strategies of the reform program was accomplished by embedding a range of strategies into the Comprehensive Curriculum. The genius of the state-level curriculum leaders was to ensure broad scale support of the initiative by (a) providing extensive professional learning experiences for teachers and teacher leaders throughout the state; (b) identifying in these sessions exceptionally responsive and enthusiastic teacher participants from all the disciplines; and (c) bringing these teachers together to form a writing team to try out and then describe application of the literacy strategies in the most influential statewide curriculum guide. The strategy descriptions and examples had immediate credibility with teachers throughout the state because they were taught and written by fellow teachers. The examples came from authentic classroom and textual practices in English/language arts, science, social studies, and math. These 18 literacy/learning strategies are outlined in a document I prepared for the Louisiana Comprehensive Curriculum, available at https://www.lpssonline.com/uploads/MicrosoftWordLitStrategiesDescriptions.pdf. They formed the basis of this statewide effort to reform the ways teachers engaged students in reading, writing, and classroom talk.

The language of literacy strategies and practices had become a kind of lingua franca, so much so that in schools from St. Bernard to Shreveport and Lake Charles to Monroe, teachers could talk with one another about anticipation guides or split-page note-taking based on a common understanding of the processes and applications of these useful strategies (Howe et al., 2012), even if their own adaptations were unique. This common instructional language was further reinforced with the production of videos showcasing teachers from across Louisiana in their actual content classrooms conducting lessons with strategies from the Comprehensive Curriculum.

Principle 4. Pilot Schools of Committed Professionals Build Capacity for Reforms

As noted, secondary teachers may resist literacy innovations for a range of reasons (Hall, 2005; Siebert & Draper, 2008; Wilson et al., 2009). And yet, if literacy reforms are to gain traction, capacity must be built among enough teachers in a school to fully implement the new instructional practices, document their impact on student literacy growth and achievement, and continue to refine the practices to make them more responsive to students' needs (Aumen, 2017; Bamford, 2011).

Reform leaders know one of the best ways to promote systemic change is to produce demonstrable evidence of an innovation's effectiveness (Desimone & Garet, 2015; Finnigan & Daly, 2014; Guskey, 2002). This evidence is more likely to be produced in schools with engaged leadership and by high-quality, motivated teachers who have made a commitment to a reform agenda (Timperley, 2008). To establish sites of success, therefore, literacy leaders should begin by working in individual secondary schools with those who are most eager to be innovative, while creating opportunities for all to learn and grow together (Brozo & Fisher, 2010).

A secondary literacy coach serves as a teacher leader who builds professional learning communities, engages teachers in ongoing collaborative professional development, and is dedicated to improving the overall literate culture of a school (Taylor et al., 2013). School principals are instrumental to a literacy coach's effectiveness in advancing a reform plan by establishing the context for reform, including setting role expectations for coaches and allotting time for coaching activity (Helman & Pekel, 2020; Moxley & Taylor, 2006).

A major role teacher leaders and literacy coaches can play in a systemic reform initiative is to transform their school into a model site where everyone works collaboratively on behalf of students' literacy development, where literacy innovations are delivered responsively and with enthusiasm, and where student growth linked to the reforms is documented. A pilot school that showcases the advantages of the reform program can serve as a clearinghouse of effective practices for other schools in a system. A model site can open its doors to teachers in other system schools to visit, observe, and learn from those who have developed expertise with literacy strategies and practices in the reform program. Technology can allow viewing of classroom teachers enacting the literacy practices and literacy leaders providing forums of support to teachers.

Northern Virginia, USA

County High School, a large suburban school in Northern Virginia, participated in a districtwide literacy initiative. County's social studies faculty took ownership of several new instructional routines and not only expanded their influence among their colleagues in other disciplines but also produced a video of best practices with the strategies for dissemination throughout the district and beyond. The district's secondary literacy coordinator approached each school guided by a philosophy she summed up with the expression, "Don't water the rocks," meaning if some faculty are resistant to change, shift energy and attention to those teachers who are interested in adopting new literacy practices. Her idea was to build critical mass for reform with highly engaged and effective teachers who would gradually influence their initially reluctant peers to take up the literacy innovations.

After a series of late-summer workshops for teachers across the district, school-based follow-up sessions were conducted and classroom technical support provided by the literacy consultant and a team of district and school leaders. In County High it became immediately apparent teachers in the social studies department were enthusiastic about gaining expertise with several of the literacy strategies from the workshops. The support team focused its attention on these teachers, building rapport by conducting demonstration lessons, co-teaching, and debriefing with them. Before long, the social studies teachers were implementing adaptations of instructional routines tailored to their texts and their students' needs.

In one highly successful case, the teachers embraced the SQPL strategy, making it their own with responsive modifications. The letters in this strategy stand for Student Questioning for Purposeful Learning. It typically begins with a thought-provoking statement or injunction supplied by the teacher related to the content about to be read and studied. With this statement, students generate questions they want answered and then are supported in finding answers to their questions as they progress through the lesson. The social studies teachers found students were not keen on the name of the strategy, which requires saying each of the four letters individually, so together they rebranded it as "Squipple." The County High students in various history and civics courses engaged in the Squipple process frequently, learning to ask questions about content at various levels of thinking, such as factual, interpretive, critical, and applied. They became more independent gatherers of information and ideas as a result, working in pairs and small groups to maximize understanding of texts, as well as more engaged in class discussion activities.

Before long, teachers in English, science, and math were expressing curiosity about Squipple and other literacy strategies, having heard about them from their students, who preferred these strategies over typical classroom activities. Based on this growing interest within County High, the social studies faculty were invited to provide short workshops focused on their experiences, successes, and challenges with the strategies. They encouraged their colleagues in other disciplines to adapt the strategies to their unique reading, writing, and discussion requirements, and to take advantage of the in-class technical assistance available from the lead consultant and other support team members.

To expand the reach of the excellent work of the teachers, the support team helped them produce a video of the strategies being conducted in their classes along with student responses. Video examples of strategies like Squipple were put on the district website for teachers in the other secondary schools to access. These video resources were then used by lead teachers in the other district middle and high schools as well as by the literacy consultant to demonstrate approaches to adapting, conducting, and evaluating the effectiveness of the new strategies.

Principle 5. Establishing Forums for Teachers to Plan, Reflect On, and Refine Professional Learning Improves Adoption of New Instructional Practices

One of the most important, though often neglected, considerations when planning professional learning opportunities is input from the individuals for whom the new innovative practices are intended—classroom teachers. The least successful PD is the one-size-fits-all, one-shot workshop, as confirmed by teacher-change experts (Cooter, 2004; Guskey, 2002; O'Brien, 2011) and secondary literacy reform research (Dillon et al., 2010; Leko & Mundy, 2012; Lillge, 2015; Reed, 2009). While schools and districts will continue to offer these traditional approaches to PD, it is important that teacher leaders and professional developers listen to teachers about how to structure and deliver PD that is responsive to their needs and genuinely furthers the goal of improving student learning. Listening to the voices of teachers who arguably occupy the most critical link in the chain of educational reform can result in PD leaders and designers modifying and improving professional learning experiences to better meet the learning needs of teachers. The reality is that "policy makers can enact the laws, administrators can supply the pressure, staff developers can present the innovative strategies, but teachers make the decision to change or not to change the ways they teach" (Brozo & Simpson, 2003, p. 446).

Professional development that allows teachers to share experiences and knowledge and interact with one another as they negotiate a reform agenda fosters a sense of shared responsibility for the success of the initiative (Ronfeldt et al., 2015; Thibodeau, 2008). To achieve this goal means dealing with teachers as trusted change agents (Evers & Kneyber, 2016). Netolicky (2020) argues that "policy and research would benefit from honouring teachers' and leaders' voices, addressing the multidimensionality of work in schools, and acknowledging its situatedness and complexity. Education reforms would benefit from engaging with how teachers and school leaders perceive and describe themselves, their lives, and their work" (p. 16).

Europe

BaCuLit (Basic Curriculum for Teachers' In-service Training in Content Area Literacy in Secondary Schools) was a large pan-European teacher development project (2010–2013). Funded by the European Union, BaCuLit partner institutions were from Germany, Hungary, the Netherlands, Norway, Portugal, Romania, and Sweden. In this far-reaching and impactful initiative, lead teachers established supportive collaborative forums in their schools as classroom teachers tried out, reflected on, revised, and implemented again practices from the BaCuLit modules. Like professional learning communities in the United States, these school-based support teams offered teachers opportunities to (a) co-teach literacy strategies, (b) observe colleagues implementing strategies, (c) debrief with colleagues after observing strategy implementation, (d) collaborate on refining and contextualizing strategies, and (e) evaluate the strategies relative to student achievement and motivation.

One of the strategies in the BaCuLit modules was the content area reading inventory, or CARI (Brozo, 2014). The process involves creating a reading assessment from a disciplinary textbook to determine individual student strengths and areas of concern,

as well as patterns of need among a whole class. As was the case with all module content, lead teachers were the first to receive exposure and experience with this strategy in a PD context. Afterward, they used the training support materials from the project to redeliver PD on the CARI to teachers in their schools. In a secondary school outside of Berlin, Germany, the project lead teacher and her colleagues worked together on the construction of a CARI to maximize its assessment power. After rounds of implementation, individual and group reflection, and collaborative redesign of this textbook reading tool, the project teachers had crafted a highly useful and informative reading assessment that determined students' prior knowledge, understanding of key terms, comprehension of passages, and ability to design study aids and write summaries and responses using textbooks from social studies and science. Because the CARI leaves open to teachers the decision about which aspects of reading to emphasize, colleagues from this German school studied the issue collaboratively and adapted the tool in ways that met their needs as disciplinary classroom teachers.

East Tennessee, USA

At Mountain View High, in the shadows of the Great Smokies, two lead literacy consultants led a yearlong, schoolwide reform initiative to elevate the literacy achievement of students and the literate culture of the school.

The initiative began in August with pretesting of reading for all students to establish a baseline of performance. Once testing was completed, the consultants met regularly with all classroom teachers, the curriculum coordinator, principal and his assistants, counselor, and director of special education to develop a literacy-reform plan. Three initiatives were endorsed by the administration and a majority of the faculty: sustained silent reading, reading young adult novels in the content classroom, and making alternatives to the textbook available for struggling students and superior readers. The Mountain View faculty and administrative staff wanted to add one additional support option for students who had very low scores on the achievement test but were not receiving special education services. This evolved into a "Reading

Buddy" program arranged during the second half of one class block for qualifying students. After launching these initiatives, the lead literacy consultants held frequent formal and informal sessions with individuals, small groups, and the whole staff to share concerns and successes. These frank and open conversations proved invaluable for nurturing commitment to the literacy reforms.

Teachers were also asked to gather in focus groups to discuss and propose literacy priorities for their students. Emerging from these conversations, initiatives such as daily independent reading with regular teacher-student conferences and block scheduling were put into practice. These two reforms were later highlighted by teachers as contributing to the positive changes in student reading scores (Brozo & Hargis, 2003).

In addition to the structural reforms emerging from the feedback and recommendations by teacher focus groups, a staff development committee was formed to identify reading-across-the-curriculum strategies that all teachers were expected to incorporate into their lessons. After extensive teacher input and research, the committee set the literacy agenda for the school with strategies such as writing to learn, K-W-L charts, concept mapping, reciprocal teaching, vocabulary instruction, note-taking techniques, and read-alouds (Fisher et al., 2015). The committee and school administrators provided additional monthly meetings to allow teachers to discuss their challenges and successes in implementing the selected strategies. These meetings were held during the day to ensure maximum attendance and participation as well as to embed professional development into the school day.

In addition, teachers demonstrated their use of these strategies in front of their peers during their prep period professional development sessions. Teachers formed study groups and used 1:1 peer coaching to facilitate the schoolwide implementation of these instructional strategies.

CONCLUSION

Leadership for secondary literacy reform begins with a vision (Kurland et al., 2010) of how the status quo can be disrupted in ways to achieve the goal of higher literacy achievement for students. The Ministry of Education in Macedonia and the State Department of Education in Baton Rouge, Louisiana, exemplify visionary planning. Successful leaders of secondary literacy reform create a culture of shared responsibility for crafting and implementing an agenda that strengthens the literacy abilities of students (Graham, 2014; Leithwood & Louis, 2012; Witte et al., 2010). The Reading Across the Curriculum project in the District of Columbia enlisted the effort of all stakeholders in elevating students' literacy achievement. Leaders of effective literacy reform initiatives and programs know that teachers and schools require ongoing professional learning to build capacity for sustaining the reforms (Darling-Hammond, 2010; Gallucci et al., 2010; Imbarlina, 2014; Smylie, 2010). The leadership teams in Europe, Northern Virginia, and East Tennessee built capacity through their ongoing support of teachers' adaptations of innovative literacy practices.

Above all, developing proficient adolescent readers requires an organizational approach in which system and school leaders form relationships and create structures that allow teachers to acquire the necessary knowledge and practices of effective literacy instruction. Developing advanced literacy skills for secondary students happens when professional development efforts, teacher collaboration, systemic commitment, and leadership engagement all work in tandem.

REFLECTION QUESTIONS

1. While acknowledging the value of bottom-up, teacher-led change, a strong case is made in this chapter for the importance of top-down advocacy of literacy reform; in what ways is this consistent with your own experiences and philosophy?

2. In your role as a leader of literacy reform, how have you ensured that PD supports your colleagues in ways that are sensitive to the challenges of the change process while expanding skills and instructional boundaries?

3. As asserted in this chapter, the path to achieving improved literacy for students must be travelled by a number of stakeholders. What have you done to include the expertise and talents of all those with a stake in furthering the goals of secondary literacy reform?

PROJECT ASSIGNMENT

Craft a proposal for programmatic reform of adolescent literacy: (1) include any potential barriers to effective implementation as well as successful practices of previous reform initiatives, (2) identify the outcomes of reform in terms of teacher and student expectations, and (3) specify the roles each stakeholder, such as state and district administration, school-based personnel, literacy coaches, and external experts, might play in the reform activity. Discuss the proposal with your colleagues.

REFERENCES

American Institutes for Research. (2009). *Secondary education activity: Final report: September 5, 2003–September 4, 2008.* https://www.air.org/sites/default/files/downloads/report/EQUIP1-Secondary_Ed_Activity-Macedonia-Final_report_0.pdf

Aumen, J. T. (2017). *Supporting teacher learning about disciplinary literacy: An exploration of professional development, social studies teachers' thinking, and inherent challenges* [Unpublished doctoral dissertation]. University of Michigan.

Bae, S., & Stosich, E.L. (2018). *Redesigning state policy for meaningful and equitable learning: Lessons from California, Iowa, New Hampshire, and Vermont.* Stanford Center for Opportunity Policy in Education.

Bailey, N. E. (2013). *Misguided education reform: Debating the impacts.* Rowan & Littlefield.

Bamford, B. J. D. (2011). *Instructional coaching and disciplinary literacy: An examination of the engagement of secondary content-area teachers in professional development* [Unpublished doctoral dissertation]. Oregon State University.

Brozo, W. G. (2006). Tales out of school: Accounting for adolescents in a literacy reform community. *Journal of Adolescent & Adult Literacy, 49*(5), 410–418.

Brozo, W. G. (2011). *RTI and the adolescent reader: Responsive literacy instruction in secondary schools.* Teachers College Press.

Brozo, W. G. (2014). Assessment for responsive adolescent literacy instruction. In K. Hinchman & H. Sheridan-Thomas (Eds.), *Best practices in adolescent literacy instruction* (2nd ed.) (pp. 348–364). Guilford Press.

Brozo, W. G. (2017a). *Disciplinary and content literacy for today's adolescents: Honoring diversity and building competence* (6th ed.). Guilford Press.

Brozo, W. G. (2017b, December). *Global learning outcomes: Designs and metrics for the 21st century.* Paper presented at the 2nd International Conference on Assessment, Riyadh, Saudi Arabia.

Brozo, W. G., & Fisher, D. (2010). Literacy starts with the teachers. *Educational Leadership, 67*(6), 74–77.

Brozo, W. G., & Hargis, C. H. (2003). Taking seriously the idea of reform: One high school's efforts to make reading more responsive to all students. *Journal of Adolescent & Adult Literacy, 47*(1), 14–23.

Brozo, W. G., Moorman, G., Meyer, C., & Stewart, T. (2013). Content area reading and disciplinary literacy: A case for the radical center. *Journal of Adolescent & Adult Literacy, 56*(5), 353–357.

Brozo, W. G., & Simpson, M. L. (2003). *Readers, teachers, learners: Expanding literacy across the content areas.* Merrill/Prentice Hall.

Brozo, W. G., Sulkunen, S., & Veijola, A. (2018). Participation as a pathway to content knowledge: Engaging all students in disciplinary literacy practices. *International Journal of Education and Social Science, 5*(7), 21–29.

Campbell, M. B., & Kmiecik, M. M. (2004). The greatest literacy challenges facing contemporary high school teachers: Implications for secondary teacher preparation. *Reading Horizons: A Journal of Literacy and Language Arts, 45*(1), 1–25.

Cantrell, S., Burns, L., & Callaway, P. (2009). Middle- and high-school content area teachers' perceptions about literacy teaching and learning. *Literacy Research and Instruction, 48*(1), 76–94.

Cooter, R. B. (2004). Deep training + coaching: A capacity-building model for teacher development. In R. B. Cooter (Ed.), *Perspectives on rescuing urban literacy education: Spies, saboteurs & saints* (pp. 83–94). Lawrence Erlbaum Associates.

Cuban, L. (2011). Teacher resistance and reform failure. *Larry Cuban on school reform and classroom practice.* http://larrycuban.wordpress.com/2011/04/30/teacher-resistance-and-reform-failure/

Darling-Hammond, L. (2010). *Preparing principals for a changing world: Lessons from effective school leadership programs.* Jossey-Bass.

Darling-Hammond, L., Bae, S., Cook-Harvey, C., Lam, L., Mercer, C., Podolsky, A., & Stosich, E. L. (2016). *Pathways to new accountability through the Every Student Succeeds Act.* Learning Policy Institute.

Darling-Hammond, L., Wei, R. C., Andree, A., Richardson, N., & Orphanos, S. (2009). *Professional learning in the learning profession: A status report on teacher development in the United States and abroad.* National Staff Development Council.

Desimone, L. M., & Garet, M. S. (2015). Best practices in teachers' professional development in the United States. *Psychology, Society and Education, 7*(3), 252–263.

Dillon, D., O'Brien, D., Sato, M., & Kelly, C. M. (2010). Professional development/teacher education for reading instruction. In M. L. Kamil, P. D. Pearson, E. B. Moje, & P. Afflerbach (Eds.), *Handbook of reading research* (Vol. IV, pp. 629–660). Routledge.

DuFour, R., & Marzano, R. (2011). *Leaders of learning: How district, school, and classroom leaders improve student achievement*. Solution Tree.

Evers, J., & Kneyber, R. (2016). *Flip the system: Changing education from the ground up*. Routledge.

Ferman, B. (2017). *The fight for America's schools: Grassroots organizing in education*. Harvard Education Press.

Finnigan, K. S., & Daly, A. J. (2014). *Using research evidence in education: From the schoolhouse door to Capitol Hill*. Springer.

Firestone, W. (2009). Culture and process in effective school districts. In W. Hoy & M. DiPaola (Eds.), *Studies in school improvement* (pp. 177–203). IAP Publishing.

Fisher, D., Brozo, W. G., Frey, N., & Ivey, G. (2015). *50 instructional routines to develop content literacy* (3rd ed.). Pearson.

Fisher, D., & Ivey, G. (2005). Literacy and language as learning in content-area classes: A departure from "every teacher a teacher of reading". *Action in Teacher Education*, *27*(2), 3–11.

Fullan, M. (2002). The change leader. *Educational Leadership*, *59*(8), 16–21.

Fullan, M. (2013). *Great to excellent: Launching the next stage of Ontario's education reform*. http://michaelfullan.ca/wp-content/uploads/2016/06/13599974110.pdf

Gallucci, C., Lare, M., Yoon, I., & Boatwright, B. (2010). Instructional coaching: Building theory about the role and organizational support for professional learning. *American Educational Research Journal*, *47*(4), 919–963.

Giles, C., & Hargreaves, A. (2006). The sustainability of innovative schools as learning organizations and professional learning communities during standardized reform. *Educational Administration Quarterly*, *42*(1), 124–156.

Gilles, C., Wang, Y., Smith, J., & Johnson, D. (2013). "I'm no longer just teaching history." Professional development for teaching Common Core State Standards for literacy in social studies. *Middle School Journal*, *44*(3), 34–43.

Goertz, M. E., Floden, R. E., & O'Day, J. (1995). *Studies of education reform: Systemic reform volume I: Findings and conclusions*. U.S. Department of Education, Office of Educational Research and Improvement.

Graham, D. (2014). Collegial administrative support: Reflections from a principal at an at-risk public high school. *Delta Kappa Gamma Bulletin*, *81*(1), 40–44.

Guskey, T. R. (2002). Professional development and teacher change. *Teachers and Teaching: Theory and Practice*, *8*(3), 381–391.

Hall, L. (2005). Teachers and content area reading: Attitudes, beliefs and change. *Teaching & Teacher Education*, *21*(4), 403–414.

Hargreaves, A. (1994). *Changing teachers: Changing times*. Cassell.

Hargreaves, A., Lieberman, A., Fullan, M., & Hopkins, D. (2009). *Second international handbook of educational change*. Springer.

Helman, L., & Pekel, K. (2020). The principal's role in literacy leadership. In A. Swan Dagan & R. M. Bean (Eds.), *Best practices of literacy leaders: Keys to school improvement* (2nd ed.) (pp. 92–110). Guilford Press.

Hinde, E. R. (2004). School culture and change: An examination of the effects of school culture on the process of change. *Essays in Education*, *12*, 1–12.

Howe, M. E., Mundy, M. A., Kupczynski, L., & Cummins, C. (2012). Louisiana teachers' familiarity, usefulness and recommendation of content literacy strategies. *Journal of Instructional Pedagogies*, *8*, 1–18.

Ikemoto, G., Taliaferro, L., Fenton, B., & Davis, J. (2014). *Great principals at scale: Creating district conditions that enable all principals to be effective*. The George W. Bush Institute and New Leaders. https://files.eric.ed.gov/fulltext/ED556346.pdf

Imbarlina, M. (2014). *An analysis of secondary schools and principals' needs to implement literacy instruction across the content areas* [Unpublished doctoral dissertation]. University of Pittsburgh.

International Literacy Association. (2016). *Frameworks for literacy education reform*.

Jenkins, K. D. (2011). *Examining secondary school reform through discipline specific literacy instruction* [Unpublished doctoral dissertation]. University of Pittsburgh.

Knapp, M. S., Honig, M. I., Plecki, M. L., Portin, B. S., & Copland, M. A. (2014). *Learning-focused leadership in action: Improving instruction in schools and districts*. Routledge.

Kurland, H., Peretz, H., & Hertz-Lazarowitz, R. (2010). Leadership style and organizational learning: The mediate effect of school vision. *Journal of Educational Administration*, *48*(1), 7–30.

Layland, A. (2019). *Connecting commitments, principles, and practices to strategically address equity and improvement*. Council of Chief State School Officers.

Leko, M., & Mundy, C. (2012). Preparing secondary educators to support adolescent struggling readers. *Preventing School Failure, 56*(2), 137–147.

Leithwood, K., & Louis, K. S. (2012). *Linking leadership to student learning*. Jossey-Bass.

Lewis-Spector, J., & Jay, A. B. (2011). *Leadership for literacy in the 21st century*. Association of Literacy Educators and Researchers. https://cdn.ymaws.com/www.aleronline.org/resource/resmgr/files/aler_white_paper_on_literacy.pdf

Lillge, D. M. (2015). *When does literacy professional development work? Understanding how instructors learn to teach writing in their disciplinary classrooms* [Unpublished doctoral dissertation]. University of Michigan. https://deepblue.lib.umich.edu/bitstream/handle/2027.42/111474/lillged_1.pdf?sequence=1

Louis, K. S., Leithwood, K., Wahlstrom, K. L., & Anderson, S. E. (2010). *Investigating the links to improved student learning: Final report of research findings*. Learning from Leadership Project, University of Minnesota. https://www.wallacefoundation.org/knowledge-center/Documents/Investigating-the-Links-to-Improved-Student-Learning.pdf

Louis, K. S., Thomas, E., Gordon, M. F., & Febey, K. S. (2008). State leadership for school improvement: An analysis of three states. *Educational Administration Quarterly, 44*(4), 562–592.

Lykins, C., & Heyneman, S. (2008). *The federal role in education: Lessons from Australia, Germany, and Canada*. Center on Education Policy.

Moje, E. B. (2015). Doing and teaching disciplinary literacy with adolescent learners: A social and cultural enterprise. *Harvard Educational Review, 85*(2), 254–279.

Moxley, D. E., & Taylor, R. T. (2006). *Literacy coaching: A handbook for school leaders*. Corwin Press/NASSP.

National Policy Board for Educational Administration. (2015). *Professional standards for educational leaders 2015*.

Netolicky, D. M. (2020). *Transformational professional learning: Making a difference in schools*. Routledge.

O'Brien, J. (2011). The system is broken and it's failing these kids: High school social studies teachers' attitudes towards training for ELLs. *Journal of Social Studies Research, 35*(1), 22–38.

O'Brien, D. G., Stewart, R. A., & Moje, E. B. (1995). Why content literacy is difficult to infuse into the secondary school: Complexities of curriculum, pedagogy, and school culture. *Reading Research Quarterly, 30*(3), 442–463.

Office of Inspector General of the United States. (2006). *The Reading First program's grant application process: Final inspection report*. U.S Department of Education Office of Inspector General.

Patterson, J. A., Eubank, H., Rathbun, S. E., & Noble, S. (2010). Making sense of an urban district's adolescent literacy reform. *NASSP Bulletin, 94*(3), 227–246.

Reed, D. K. (2009). A synthesis of professional development on the implementation of literacy strategies for middle school content area teachers. *Research in Middle Level Education, 32*(10), 1–12.

Robinson, J. A. (2008). *Principals' perspectives on adolescent literacy implementation and support in secondary schools: Views through a sociocultural lens* [Unpublished doctoral dissertation]. Utah State University.

Robken, S. R. (2016). *The effect of a district-wide literacy initiative on English/ Language Arts standardized test scores* [Unpublished doctoral dissertation]. Louisiana Tech University.

Ronfeldt, M., Farmer, S. O, McQueen, K., & Grissom, J. A. (2015). Teacher collaboration in instructional teams and student achievement. *American Educational Research Journal, 52*(3), 475–514.

Rowland, C. (2017). *Principal professional development: New opportunities for a renewed state focus*. American Institutes for Research. https://www.air.org/sites/default/files/downloads/report/Principal-Professional-Development-New-Opportunities-State-Focus-February-2017.pdf

Siebert, D., & Draper, R. J. (2008). Why content-area literacy messages do not speak to mathematics teachers: A critical content analysis. *Literacy Research and Instruction, 47*(4), 229–245.

Smylie, M. A. (2010). *Continuous school improvement*. Thousand Oaks, CA: Corwin.

Spencer, V. G., Carter, B. B., Boon, R. T., & Simpson-Garcia, C. (2008). If you teach—you teach reading. *International Journal of Special Education, 23*(2), 1–7.

Stahl, N. A. (1983). *A historical analysis of textbook-study systems* [Unpublished doctoral dissertation]. University of Pittsburgh.

Sturtevant, E. G., & Linek, W. M. (2007). Secondary literacy coaching: A Macedonian perspective. *Journal of Adolescent & Adult Literacy, 51*(3), 240–250.

Supovitz, J. A. (2006). *The case for district-based reform: Leading, building, and sustaining school improvement*. Harvard Education Press.

Taylor, R. T., Zugelder, B. S., & Bowman, P. (2013). Literacy coach effectiveness: The need for measurement. *International Journal of Mentoring and Coaching in Education, 2*(1), 34–46.

Thibodeau, G. M. (2008). A content literacy collaborative study group: High school teachers take charge of their professional learning. *Journal of Adolescent & Adult Literacy, 52*(1), 54–64.

Timperley, H. (2008). *Teacher professional learning and development*. International Academy of Education.

Tucker, M. (2011). *Standing on the shoulders of giants: An American agenda for education reform*. National Center on Education and the Economy. http://www.ncee.org/wp-content/uploads/2011/05/Standing-on-the-Shoulders-of-Giants-An-American-Agenda-for-Education-Reform.pdf

Wahlstrom, K. L., Louis, K. S., Leithwood, K., & Anderson, S. E. (2010). *Investigating the links to improved student learning*. https://www.wallacefoundation.org/knowledge-center/Documents/Investigating-the-Links-to-Improved-Student-Learning-Executive-Summary.pdf

Waters, T., & Marzano, R. J. (2006). *School district leadership that works: The effect of superintendent leadership on student achievement*. Mid-continent Research for Education and Learning (McREL).

Wilson, N., Grisham, D., & Smetana, L. (2009). Investigating content area teachers' understanding of a content literacy framework: A yearlong professional development initiative. *Journal of Adolescent & Adult Literacy, 52*(8), 708–718.

Witte, S., Beemer, J., & Arjona, C. (2010). "Re-vision": Our journey in developing a secondary literacy plan. *American Secondary Education, 39*(1), 15–26.

Zimmerman, J. (2006). Why some teachers resist change and what principals can do about it. *NASSP Bulletin, 90*(3), 238–249.

PROGRAM IMPLEMENTATION AND EVALUATION

Part III includes five chapters about program implementation and evaluation. These chapters discuss, in depth, factors that contribute to effective literacy program development: materials selection, evaluation of teachers' instructional and assessment practices, participation in professional development, assessment of students' progress with instruction, and assessment of the overall school- and districtwide literacy program

Chapter 7, written by Alejandro Gonzalez Ojeda, Toni Faddis, and Diane Lapp, presents ideas for selecting quality materials that foster instructional equity. In discussing the need for a culturally relevant curriculum to address the needs of diverse student populations, the authors set forth criteria for literacy leaders, school administrators, and teachers to use as they choose a wide array of literacy materials. An equity lens—diverse students are represented in texts, unbiased instruction prevails, and all language arts are promoted—is used as the focal point for making decisions. Specific guidelines are offered for the selection, purchase, and implementation of literacy materials.

A brief review of teacher evaluation systems and related policies that have influenced them are discussed in Chapter 8 by Nancy Frey and Douglas Fisher. Current trends that move away from adherence to federal mandates, including the use of value-added models, in favor of using locally developed teacher evaluation systems are explained. Examples of growth-producing teacher evaluation systems that involve teachers as drivers of the observation and evaluation process are presented. These new models, which build on the history of teacher evaluation, are based on specific criteria and student learning outcomes.

Chapter 9, written by Maryann Mraz, Jean Payne Vintinner, and Miranda S. Fitzgerald, addresses current professional development initiatives and their impact on the practices of those involved in literacy instruction. Characteristics of high-quality professional development and the role of administrators in promoting professional development are discussed. Examples of strategies to support change are described: university–school collaborations such as professional development schools, professional learning communities, data-driven instruction, and the National Board for Professional Teaching Standards certification.

In Chapter 10, Peter Afflerbach, Hyoju Ahn, and Moonyoung Park provide an overview of how assessment is evolving to account for students' reading development and reading achievement. They promote the idea of developing an inventory of reading assessments to ensure that reading assessment programs account for appropriate audiences and purposes. Such an inventory should include a balance of formative and summative assessments, develop students' self-assessment routines, and take into account students' diverse cognitive, affective, and conative factors. The authors describe the dynamic and evolving nature of online assessment and digital reading, with a look ahead to the potential of augmented, virtual, and mixed reality-based assessment.

Chapter 11, written by Misty Sailors and James V. Hoffman with Jimmie Walker and Yadira Palacios, focuses on ways that leaders of literacy can facilitate the assessment of the school literacy program to improve the quality of support for students. They demonstrate how one district used the PASS (Purposes, Actions, Students, and Standards) evaluation model to identify strengths and areas in need of improvement for writing instruction. Specific survey, interviewing, and observational techniques are described that can bring the school community together, establishing and sustaining improved instructional and assessment processes. Woven throughout this chapter is a focus on the culture of change within a district to help innovations to take root.

This part of the book helps leaders of literacy provide the best possible instructional literacy programs by focusing on five critical areas of implementation and evaluation: selection of materials, teacher evaluation, professional development, assessment of students, and evaluation of programs.

CHAPTER 7

Selecting Materials for Literacy Programs That Foster Instructional Equity

Alejandro Gonzalez Ojeda, Toni Faddis, and Diane Lapp

- Instructional materials should be comprehensive and promote differentiated and equitable instruction and learning.
- Instructional materials should allow students to see themselves represented, promote unbiased instruction, and ensure that all four language arts strands are emphasized.
- Literacy leaders should develop and implement practices and processes, including the selection of instructional materials, to help close a school's achievement gap.

The selection of literacy materials has been, and continues to be, a complex and often highly charged and political process (National Council of Teachers of English, 2014). While procedures for viewing, piloting, and purchasing materials vary in schools and across systems, literacy leaders' input and guidance are crucial during this process. A case can be made that there is not another function more important in the school than ensuring a sound literacy program that results in high levels of student engagement and strong academic performance (Wallace Foundation, 2013). For this reason, literacy leaders must understand relevant policy, local and state standards, and the use and value of formative and summative assessments that provide feedback about student learning. Without this understanding, literacy leaders may not be equipped to collaborate with teachers to select literacy materials that benefit individual learners and groups of learners.

Principals and literacy leaders continuously receive solicitations to consider reading apps, literacy programs, and educational websites that promise silver bullet solutions to students' reading achievement needs. Leaders should have a process in place to vet these resources to ensure that selected literacy materials are comprehensive and inclusive, align with state standards, and address identified student needs.

In addition to selecting new materials, principals and literacy leaders must also be aware of existing materials that teachers incorporate into lessons and units year after year, such as trade books, magazines, and other old favorites. Many of these resources remain relevant over time, but there is a growing recognition that some classics contain language and themes that are offensive to today's multicultural learners. While some teachers may be unaware of messages that students find hurtful, others are asking for help to be more equitable by providing sensitive, inclusive curriculum and instruction in their classrooms. Selected materials should not merely avoid offense; they should speak directly to students' lives. In a recent study, 1,143 literacy professionals reported that the number-one area in which they wanted support was in addressing the disconnects between the school curriculum and students' actual needs (International Literacy Association, 2020).

In this chapter we address this call for support through the voices of school principals recognized for closing achievement gaps at their schools. They offer guidance for selecting materials and leading literacy efforts with equity in mind. Their explanations and the tools we share will assist literacy leaders in collaboration with teachers to investigate, select, and purchase quality materials that are responsive to the needs of all students.

CONSIDERATIONS FOR SELECTING INSTRUCTIONAL MATERIALS

The stakes are high in selecting literacy materials. Students who do not read proficiently by 3rd grade are "four times more likely to leave school without a diploma than proficient readers" (Henderson, 2011, p.1). Students must have excellent teachers and access to excellent materials in order to meet minimum thresholds to be successful in school and in life. All students, but especially students of color (whose home cultures may be considerably different from their mostly White teachers') need a wide range of literacy materials.

Whether they choose literacy adoption programs or commercially available trade books for novel study and literature circles, the decisions of district leaders, principals, literacy leaders, and school staffs have long-term ramifications for the children in their care (National Council of Teachers of English, 2014). Teachers need training and empowerment to make decisions about how best to teach their students (Duncan-Owens, 2009) and the best curricula and materials to do so. Absent culturally relevant curricula, students from diverse backgrounds may be less likely to engage in learning and therefore not perform to optimal levels or reach their potential. Without attention to a careful process to investigate, select, and purchase materials, unchecked implicit bias may also play a role in dampening student achievement if teachers, principals, and district leaders rely on past practices that unintentionally advantage some students while underserving others.

Realities of Inequalities

There often are issues with the types of literacy materials that are available for instruction, particularly for struggling readers, English learners, and hard-to-reach students, which further widens existing achievement, opportunity, and equity gaps. The National Education Association (NEA, 2019) indicates that the four ethnic groups of students that are more likely to experience achievement gaps with White students are:

- Blacks
- Hispanics
- American Indian/Alaskan Natives
- Asian Americans and Pacific Islanders

The NEA indicates other student groups also likely to experience achievement gaps in educational settings include:

- Students with disabilities
- English learners
- Students from low-income families
- Gay, lesbian, bisexual, and transgender students

It is not surprising that 61% of teachers report that their top challenge is "addressing inequity in education and instruction" (International Literacy Association, 2020, p. 18). While a wide array of curriculum materials may be available, stock teacher's editions (TE) rarely, if ever, provide sufficient guidance for teachers to reference when planning and implementing literacy units and lessons for the range of learners in their classrooms (Duncan-Owens, 2009). It is little wonder that many teachers say that bridging the disconnects between students' needs and available school curriculum is at the top of their list of concerns (International Literacy Association, 2020). It is crucial that curriculum and related materials be carefully vetted using lenses that promote equity. Teachers need to be mindful of pictures, characters, or text in curricular resources that portray people of color negatively, with little or no mention of a particular group's positive contributions to society. Instead of strengthening a student's identity, racial microaggressions in the program may significantly harm a child's sense of self, thereby diminishing learning opportunities (Pérez Huber et al., 2020). Literacy materials play a critical role in shaping students' perceptions and understanding of racism, sexism, classism, ableism, and other forms of oppression.

Previous Priorities and Processes for Selecting Literacy Materials

Much research describes typical processes districts and schools utilize when selecting programmatic literacy materials, such as trade books, workbooks, and adoption kits that contain core and ancillary materials (Flood & Lapp, 1986, 1987; Lapp, Fisher, & Flood, 2008). This process, often influenced by new or bright and shiny features, may or may not begin with an understanding of students' current performance in literacy.

Historically, principals relied on teachers to choose adoption kits, texts, and other resources to plan and present literacy programs. Principals often considered their role to be that of a facilitator, leaving teachers to choose the materials they thought best for the learners in their classrooms. Without oversight, the literacy program implemented by the teacher in one 1st-grade class could be vastly different from the program implemented by the 1st-grade teacher in the adjacent classroom. Similarly, students in secondary schools often received an uncoordinated literacy experience as they ascended to the upper grade levels. Principals who considered themselves to be facilitators rather than instructional leaders faced a harsh reality when the mismatch between teachers' text selections and standardized test results became evident with the adoption of the Common Core State Standards (CCSS) in the mid-2010s (Clifford & Mason, 2013).

Prior to the adoption of the CCSS, many literacy materials were purchased because of the quality of literature selections and the vast array of resources that purportedly addressed students' language and knowledge differences. The literature selections, however, did not necessarily reflect students' diversity. One wonders if the program with the most boxes of resources for the teachers was the one selected, purchased, and adopted. This mindset of *more is better* extended with the integration of digital media and technology components that accompany many adoption kits to this day.

The *more is better* approach to selecting literacy materials is problematic for several reasons, though only three will be discussed here to provide context and suggestions for less experienced literacy leaders. The materials, chosen by the teachers without the backing of a plan made in collaboration with leaders, arrive in daunting quantity. Professional development to train the teachers how best to use and connect the materials is scanty. Without help from a team of literacy leaders who understand the program, teachers fall back on the material they already have ideas about and miss out on the material that would promote language development, knowledge acquisition, and the range of other skills needed by their students.

A second problem of the *more is better* approach is that relying solely on a TE makes teaching complicated. Publishers provide scripts, models, and references to a mountain of other resources throughout the margins of a TE. Most educators find that attending to all pieces described in the TE takes most of the instructional day, and often confines students to whole-group instruction that is oriented towards a minimum standard, often considered *basic*. Ironically, the teacher edition, which is supposed to simplify the teacher's task, actually complicates it and takes over the school day with all its directions and suggestions. Literacy leaders need to partner with teachers and teacher teams to identify, through diagnostic assessment, the skills and concepts each student needs to engage successfully with the materials. Collaborating to design a literacy experience based upon identified student needs is likely to yield greater student engagement and performance.

The third issue of *more is better* may seem counterintuitive: When teachers teach exclusively from the TE, limited viewpoints and perspectives of authors, characters, and subjects are presented to students. Given that most publishing companies, as well as many teachers, have a Eurocentric orientation, diverse students may not see their culture or racial groups represented in literature or informational text. Literacy leaders should collaborate with teachers to design literacy experiences that are inclusive of all races and cultures in the classroom.

The *more is better* approach to the selection, purchase, and implementation of adoption kits and literacy materials is faulty. The availability of electronic resources in recent years, however, has helped to invite greater student engagement in learning because of the inclusion of broader perspectives. As literacy leaders move forward to select materials and monitor instruction, it is important that there be a commitment to equity.

CURRENT PRIORITIES AND PROCESSES FOR SELECTING LITERACY MATERIALS

Leadership matters, and perhaps nowhere else is this more evident than in turnaround schools (Leithwood et al., 2004). Turnaround schools are those where achievement gaps have been closed as a result of a number of coordinated strategies. Schools that transform from low-performing to high-performing typically have literacy leaders who collaborate with teachers across school topics, including the selection of materials.

In a study conducted in the summer of 2020, 10 literacy leaders from California, New York, and Texas shared their insights on their priorities and processes for selecting materials. Additionally, a representative from an educational publishing company provided insights about the trends observed with the development of instructional materials. In the following section we present a summary of the insights shared by these literacy leaders.

Leaders' Top Priorities for Closing the Achievement Gap

Be an instructional leader. The leaders overwhelmingly spoke to the value they place on being instructional leaders. They recognize the instructional program as their top priority and interpret their leadership decisions as having a direct impact on the instructional practices of teachers, the learning experiences of students at their schools, and the materials purchased to support learning.

Focus on standards. The second priority identified by these leaders is that instructional materials and strategies must align with the expectations of state grade-level standards. Because of differing student needs, educators must continually monitor instruction to ensure that rigorous literacy content is aligned with state standards while addressing identified gaps in student learning.

Collaborate with teachers. The third most noted priority identified by leaders in this study was conferencing with teachers. They believe that face-to-face or online communication is a vital function to affirm teachers' instructional efforts. Whether conferencing with teachers about procedures or providing social and emotional support, leaders value connecting with teachers as a fundamental practice of instructional leadership.

Select curricular materials. Leaders view their decisions about the selection of literacy materials as being critical in the process of closing the achievement gap. In fact, the majority of these leaders identified seeking and selecting materials for their site as a key responsibility of their leadership. They noted that they collaborate with teachers to identify standards-aligned content and effective instructional practices contained within adoption kits, trade books, or other literacy materials.

Work within budgets. Managing a school's budget is another important priority for leaders. As stewards of public funds, these leaders understand that they are responsible for fiscal oversight when purchasing curricular materials. They think about maximizing resources to ensure that teachers and students have access to materials for in-person and online learning. They understand that investments in static, hard-copy materials may pose challenges, particularly around distribution and access.

Publishers' Priorities for Developing Literacy Materials

While we recognize that publishers use for-profit models to make decisions about product development, they also attend to the educational market needs. The following insights were shared by a representative of a publishing company about developing products based on market research.

Access. Publishers' first priority is to provide flexible and dynamic formats such as e-books and digital resources that are fast and easy for teachers and students to use. Publishers are working to provide integration with existing systems that schools have in place to make materials accessible. This ease of integration is made possible with online tools that are compatible with student information systems (SIS) for rostering and automatic grading. Interoperability platforms have become popular ways for publishers and school systems to integrate student data and provide access to online tools. Tools such as ClassLink (https://www.classlink.com) and Clever (https://www.clever.com) provide a platform that helps publishers and a school's SIS connect for the purpose of implementing digital resources. Such integration is an important part of the selection process for leaders. Leaders should consider the logistical components of adoption for implementing these types of digital tools (i.e., student rosters, logins, and resource access) to help inform expectations for timelines and use of existing resources. Patrick Keeley, a principal at a rural high school in Pine Valley, California, shared how open-resource texts are often first considered because of the ease of access to these types of materials, versus the process required to seek, propose, evaluate, and adopt proprietary or boxed materials.

Formative data. Frequent review of students' performance helps teachers to know where students are in their learning progression and how to best support their growth. Data tell only part of a student's story, though it is an important part that is needed to help teachers have a more complete understanding of a student's needs. Publishers can help with systems that facilitate collection, analysis, and reporting of data. These systems can support teachers to accommodate a wider diversity of students through screening tests, diagnostic assessments, the grouping of resources, and materials for responsive instruction. Hard and soft data offer opportunities for conversations about common trends and gaps. Shared visions and decisions on ways to strategize require that school communities look at data together to identify needs. Leaders pointed to discussions around data sources that raised awareness about gaps and unifying efforts to address them.

Capacity building. Professional development that is targeted and based on best practices helps to address school demands and needs (Joyce & Showers, 2002). Leaders and publishers understand that they must consider teachers' professional needs, particularly when designing learning opportunities that address both content and practice. As Precious Jackson Hubbard, a principal at a middle school in San Diego, California, shared, "Listen to the voices of the teachers to hear their strengths, struggles, and needs. They will tell you if they know you are listening." Valuing teacher voice is a practice that the leaders indicated was key to building trust within their schools. Lisa Trevino-Forehand, an elementary principal in Chula Vista, California, has a deliberate approach to "coach not catch" when making observations during professional development cycles.

To further extend efforts around capacity, trust, and transparency, publishers are also working to provide educational webinars for parents. While there has always been a benefit to having parents as co-educators in students' homes, now more than ever it is important to empower parents with knowledge and skills about the materials their children are using.

Pedagogical support. Publishers are working to create materials that help support rigorous instruction with embedded scaffolds for differentiation. Publishers are providing professional development for educators centered on increasing their capacity to understand and use their materials. Instruction should be rigorous, and leaders are focused on this in selecting materials, building capacity, and supporting teachers. Principal Trevino-Forehand's key goal for each student is to make a year's worth of growth, regardless of where they started.

Relevancy. It is critical that publishers develop materials that provide a meaningful scope and sequence and include related assessments and identifiable outcomes. Such materials need to be supportive of a range of teacher knowledge, provide appropriate grade-level content, offer techniques for differentiation, provide scaffolds to support all students, and be sensitive to students' social and emotional health. Publishers have to consider how to best structure materials, supports, and features to give schools options on how to accommodate students' learning trajectories and individuality. School leaders are using relationship-building opportunities with teachers to understand relevant ways of aligning materials and instructional practices. Principal Hubbard asks of her staff: "Let's get to know each other. What do we know about our kids?"

USING EQUITY LENSES TO CHOOSE MATERIALS THAT CORRELATE WITH STATE STANDARDS

While each state has its own standards, one of the commonalities among the standards is a commitment to a rigorous education that results in students being college and career ready upon high school graduation. Rigorous learning experiences include students persisting through challenges, demonstrating flexible thinking, and being actively involved in their academic journeys. For many students to master the standards, particularly students of color, there must be a conscious and deliberate effort by educators to provide a literacy program that is culturally responsive and affirming to each student's developing self-concept. This means that literacy leaders and teachers must approach instruction using four lenses for equity.

Equity Lens 1. Ensure That Students See Themselves Represented in Text

Equity in education begins with an educator's understanding that each student is unique and arrives at school with a particular set of assets that are shaped by family structure and values, race, cultural orientation, and religious background, among many other factors (San Diego State University, 2021). Since students' sense of self is often impacted by racism and bias, it is important that educators reject color blindness and truly *see* each student for who they are as an individual. Further, students must see themselves represented in literature and nonfiction texts that are presented in classes. Teachers act in culturally responsive ways when they select materials that are relevant to students' lives. This often requires training for teachers to understand practices that may unintentionally offend individual students and groups of students. For example, English teachers have used Harper Lee's *To Kill a Mockingbird* (1960) for decades, but this novel may be offensive to students of color because of the disrespectful vocabulary and racial slurs that appear in the text. There is also an implication that the narrator, Scout, provides readers with a singular and *correct* perspective, which may rub against the experiences of students of color. Classics should not be eliminated from the curriculum, but educators should teach students to interrogate them with a critical eye toward issues of fairness, humanity, and systemic racism.

Numerous opportunities for awareness of social topics and affirmation of students' own personal identities develop from exposure to famous American and world figures through biographies, fictionalized accounts, and nonfiction texts. When students think critically, they interact with a text by analyzing the author's message and perspective in skillful ways (Lapp et al., 2015a, b). Efforts toward developing students' critical thinking skills often correlate to increased academic achievement on mandated tests (Smith & Szymanski, 2013).

Equity Lens 2. Work to Alleviate Biased Instruction

In addition to being aware of the frequency of Eurocentric viewpoints in education, it is also important that educators ensure that a range of authors, perspectives, and texts are presented to students. Since students' experiences may be moderated by teachers' perspectives and through text choices, an array of multicultural text selections mitigates these occurrences. Multicultural texts also foster critical thinking and discussion, and provide opportunities for students to examine the ways an author's opinion can influence an audience—skills that meet state standards.

Teachers, as well as literacy leaders, must also be adept at guiding student discussions around racially and ethnically charged topics, both inside the English Language Arts (ELA) classroom as well as other content areas. For example, copies of Mark Twain's *The Adventures of Huckleberry Finn* (1884) can be located on school campuses throughout the United States. The book's themes of friendship and coming of age are often appealing to teachers, so they continue to require students to read and discuss this text. This may be because the book is considered to be a classic, it was required reading in teachers' personal high school experiences, or there are copies of the book available for each student. However, the book also portrays anti-Black attitudes and uses racialized language that schools would not accept from students today.

Classics with racist themes could be grouped together to allow students to trace the portrayal of systemic racism across texts. With the support of the school or a local librarian, collections of books containing examples of systemic racism or cultural insensitivity could become a unit of study. Scharf (2014) notes that when students "read against the grain" (p. 3), they challenge the default positionality of privileged texts as they uncover the experiences of minoritized individuals and communities in the textual discourse. When teachers use traditional, but

unexamined, resources and deliver instruction based upon long-held beliefs about particular texts and people, students of all races lose out on rich learning opportunities that have the potential to expand their thinking and develop empathy for others.

Equity Lens 3. Promote Reading, Writing, Speaking, and Listening Expressions

The third equity lens recommended for educators is to provide students with experiences that develop all four language arts strands. Listening and speaking are important aspects of communication and are critical life skills, but often take a back seat to reading and writing on standardized tests. As a result, many teachers give less attention to these skills and instead focus on reading and writing skills and facts so that students are successful with the standardized tests. This is unfortunate, because some cultures use storytelling as a means of transmitting familial and cultural information from generation to generation; these skills may be lost due to modern testing mandates.

All students can benefit from curricular materials and instructional practices that emphasize speaking and listening skills alongside reading and writing skills. For example, in *Teammates* (Golenbach & Bacon, 1990), children learn of the friendship that existed between Jackie Robinson and Pee Wee Reese, two players on the Brooklyn Dodgers in 1947. The text also reveals that Jackie Robinson was the first Black player to play baseball in the Major Leagues, effectively breaking the color barrier. Teachers might consider arranging students into groups to have one student retell the story while the others listen for and record important details from the first student's account. Critical literacy, perspective, and thinking skills are fostered when teachers guide students to honor an example of teamwork with all four language arts skills while also demonstrating an understanding of a socially relevant topic.

Equity Lens 4. Build Multicultural Classroom Libraries

It is evident that the selection of literacy materials and instructional practices must be purposeful, as both contribute to students' knowledge base and their developing sense of self. Further, selecting literature and nonfiction text can become a "method of gatekeeping and censoring whose voices, stories, and histories are valued and whose are not" (Zapata et al., 2018, p. 2). Traditionally, reading materials at both the elementary and secondary levels have contained far more texts authored by people of European descent than texts authored by Black, Indigenous, and other people of color. This misalignment "constitutes a hidden curriculum that perpetuates Whiteness as normal and neutral" (Borsheim-Black, 2015, p. 408). Purposeful selection of texts should be representative of the diversity of cultures, histories, and languages that comprise today's increasingly global society (Zapata et al., 2018).

The practice of building school and classroom libraries that contain multicultural titles is not only affirming to students but gives teachers and librarians opportunities to see worlds and viewpoints that may be different from their own. A stance toward multicultural texts does not mean that the classics that many teachers have used must be discarded. Rather, a more expansive approach to text selections may redefine existing narratives and empower students to recognize themselves in the books that are presented in class as well as what they self-select. When students feel stronger connections to texts, their personal engagement increases, which in turn drives deeper literacy (Zapata et al., 2018).

WHAT ROLE SHOULD LITERACY LEADERS PLAY IN SELECTING INSTRUCTIONAL MATERIALS?

Literacy leaders have multifaceted roles in the materials selection process. Leaders start the process and help keep it on track. They oversee others involved in the material selection process, serve as consultants securing information and reviewing resources, and often become the final decision-makers for material selection. Literacy leaders, along with their building and district administrators, play a significant role in the outcome of the selection process. Simply providing teachers with a plethora of materials and instructional tools is not an effective approach to empower them and ensure students a strong education. Leaders have many roles—but overall they must lead planning.

The best processes for selecting materials begin with established procedures and identified criteria by which to view materials. Components may include, but are not limited to:

- quality of topics and inclusiveness of characters in a wide range of literature
- range of topics contained in nonfiction text
- culturally responsive text selections and relevant activities
- perspectives presented from a range of authors from multiple ethnicities, cultures, and genders
- ancillary materials for gifted learners and high achievers
- differentiated support systems for remediation and acceleration
- home language connections

In addition to these criteria, literacy leaders should use a process for selecting literacy materials that builds upon and adds to practitioner priorities from previous eras. While an eye for equity was not typically a concern of prior selection processes, many critical components are still relevant and should be considered as literacy leaders engage in this process.

Although publishers provide opportunities for professional development, it is important that literacy leaders respond to local needs and not fall back into the one-size-fits-all trap. Thoughtful planning, materials selection, and professional learning experiences will empower principals and teachers to implement a literacy program that is rich in text selections, standards-aligned, and responsive to the identified needs of the school community. Figure 7.1 offers tips and guidelines to approach the selection, purchase, and implementation of literacy materials.

CONCLUSION

Over the years, educators' priorities and processes for selecting literacy materials have not necessarily focused on students' diversity. It has become imperative to take deliberate actions to understand students as individuals, design instruction to address their needs, and select curriculum materials that support their skills and backgrounds; in other words, to take an equity-oriented approach. Literacy leaders who understand this imperative help teachers select and use materials that support a culturally responsive curriculum. Such leaders can apply the equity-oriented approaches shared in this chapter as a framework for promoting literacy instruction.

Figure 7.1. Action Steps and Considerations for Selection of Literacy Materials

1. Determine the Lens, Budget, and Timeline

When making materials selections, the first step is to consider the parameters for the process. It is important that principals have an idea of the type and price of materials that will be approved by local Boards of Education, district leaders, and other stakeholders.

- ☐ Determine the school and/or district lens, budget, and timeline.
- ☐ Consider existing systems (Student Information Systems, Learning Management Systems) and the need for compatibility with these to determine expectations during adoption and implementation of new materials.

2. Analyze Formative and Summative Data and Gather Community Input

Purchases should be driven by current student needs that have been identified by qualitative and quantitative data, rather than fads and price tags. Begin by asking questions of the teachers and the school community to hear their opinions. Then examine existing formative and summative data to draw conclusions and make recommendations.

- ☐ Ask teachers and the school community for their input about the literacy program. What are their concerns? What are their hopes?
- ☐ Examine current ELA data by disaggregated student groups. List and discuss key findings and implications.

3. Examine ELA Materials

There are many sources and types of books, literature, informational texts, digital media, and adoption kits to examine. Investigate what your state or district has approved for purchase. Note that materials approved for purchase in one state may not be approved in another.

- ☐ Investigate the integration of the four ELA strands: reading, writing, speaking, and listening.
- ☐ Probe the foundational literacy components (phonics, phonological awareness, vocabulary, oral comprehension, fluency, and writing).
- ☐ Study and determine if instructional routines and engagement strategies will meet the needs of a range of learners.
- ☐ Examine the integration of collaborative activities for students to engage in peer conversations that develop literacy and language.
- ☐ Ensure that texts provide a balance of fiction and nonfiction.
- ☐ Determine if complementary writing materials and activities include narrative, opinion, and informative writing.
- ☐ Inspect the conceptual themes for their degree of research and inquiry.
- ☐ Determine the degrees of alignment of ELA and English Language Development components.
- ☐ Identify technological tools that assist, enhance, and/or accelerate student learning.
- ☐ Inspect technological tools for ease of teacher use, including group organizational and learning designs, student monitoring, and scoring.
- ☐ Assess TEs for ease of instructional planning and location of rubrics, writing samples, and other supporting materials.
- ☐ Consider if, and to what extent, all phases of the Gradual Release of Responsibility framework for moving students toward independence (focused instruction, guided instruction, collaborative learning, and independent learning) are integrated into lessons and units.
- ☐ Determine cross-curricular connections.

4. Ensure Rigorous Content

Explore the degree of rigor in literacy materials. This is important because students must be expected to master grade-level standards in all content areas. This means that English learners, students with disabilities, and others may need additional intervention to reach grade-level goals. Educators can determine levels of rigor by utilizing these guiding questions:

(continued)

Figure 7.1. Action Steps and Considerations for Selection of Literacy Materials (continued)

☐ How are reading, questioning, and writing tasks integrated and connected within lessons and throughout units?

☐ How are speaking and listening opportunities purposefully aligned to reading and writing goals?

☐ How is language instruction (grammar, conventions, language, and vocabulary) meaningfully connected to reading, writing, speaking, and listening instruction?

☐ How is writing instruction delivered, and are there opportunities for listening, speaking, and collaboration?

☐ In what ways do lesson and unit goals align to state and/or national standards?

5. Investigate Assessment Opportunities

Assessment opportunities are crucial for teachers to plan whole-group, small-group, and individualized lessons for students. Being responsive to students needs means that each teacher must be afforded the flexibility to make professional judgments as to when and how to modify lessons based on student needs. Formative assessment can take many forms; all can serve to affirm a teacher's planning or provide the evidence for adjustments.

☐ Determine identified opportunities for formative assessment that teachers might utilize to further individual- and group-guided instruction.

☐ Inspect for a range of assessment types, including selected response, short answer, performance tasks, and technology-embedded tools.

☐ Detect how auxiliary materials for frontloading and reteaching reinforce the core curriculum and grade-level standards.

☐ Learn how opportunities for summative assessment are embedded so teachers may gauge student progress towards mastery of standards.

6. Consider Culturally Responsive Curriculum

Meeting students' needs requires a wide range of texts and perspectives written by diverse authors. Students must be able to see themselves within texts and find relevance in lessons and units. To determine the degree of culturally responsive curriculum and related instruction, ask yourself these questions:

☐ How is new knowledge built upon students' primary languages, cultures, and prior knowledge?

☐ Are appropriate scaffolds provided for all learners to access grade-level content?

☐ How are lessons and units sequenced to strategically build knowledge and language proficiency?

REFLECTION QUESTIONS

1. How have your priorities changed for selecting materials as a result of thinking about the principals' ideas presented in this chapter for closing the achievement gap?

2. How will you ensure that equity is a driver in your materials selection process? Consider the three equity lenses presented in this chapter as a framework for your response.

3. What steps do you need to take as a literacy leader to promote an equitable materials selection process?

PROJECT ASSIGNMENT

Evaluate your school's or district's current process for materials selection in relation to the action steps provided in Figure 7.1. Identify the areas that need to improve and develop a plan of action for such improvement.

REFERENCES

Borsheim-Black, C. (2015). "It's pretty much white": Challenges and opportunities of an antiracist approach to literature instruction in a multilayered white context. *Research in the Teaching of English, 49*(4), 407–429.

Clifford, M. & Mason, C. (2013). *Leadership for the Common Core: More than one thousand school principals respond.* National Association of Elementary School Principals. http://www.nysed.gov/common/nysed/files/principal-project-leadership-for-the-common-core.pdf

Duncan-Owens, D. (2009). Scripted reading programs: Fishing for success. *Principal, 88*(3), 26–29.

Flood, J., & Lapp, D. (1986). Types of writing in basal readers: The match between texts and tests. *Reading Research Quarterly, 21*(3), 284–297.

Flood, J., & Lapp, D. (1987). Forms of discourse in basal readers. *Elementary School Journal, 87*(3), 229–306.

Golenbock, P., & Bacon, P. (1990). *Teammates.* Harcourt.

Henderson, D. J. (2011). *Double jeopardy: How third-grade reading skills and poverty influence high school graduation.* The Annie E. Casey Foundation. https://www.aecf.org/resources/double-jeopardy/

International Literacy Association. (2020, February). *What's hot in literacy.* https://literacyworldwide.org/get-resources/whats-hot-report

Joyce, B., & Showers, B. (2002). *Student achievement through staff development.* ASCD.

Lapp, D., Fisher, D., & Flood, J. (2008). Selecting instructional materials for the literacy program. In S. B. Wepner & D. S. Strickland (Eds.). *The administration and supervision of reading programs* (4th ed., pp. 104–117). Teachers College Press.

Lapp, D., Moss, B., Grant, M., & Johnson, K. (2015a). *A close look at close reading: Teaching students to analyze complex texts (K–5).* ASCD.

Lapp, D., Moss, B., Grant, M., & Johnson, K. (2015b, June 16). Creating close reading lessons in grades K–5. *ASCD Inservice.* http://inservice.ascd.org/creating-close-reading-lessons-in-grades-k-5/

Lee, H. (1960). *To kill a mockingbird.* Lippincott.

Leithwood, K., Louis, K. S., Anderson, S., & Wahlstrom, K. (2004). *Review of research: How leadership influences student learning.* Wallace Foundation. www.wallacefoundation.org/knowledge-center/school-leadership/key-research/documents/how-leadership-influences-student-learning.pdf

National Council of Teachers of English. (2014). *Guidelines for selection of materials in English Language Arts programs.* https://ncte.org/statement/material-selection-ela/

National Education Association. (2019). *Students affected by achievement gaps.* http://web.archive.org/web/20200701074924/http://www.nea.org/home/20380.htm

Pérez Huber, L., Gonzalez, L. C., & Solórzano, D. G. (2020). Theorizing a critical race content analysis for children's literature about People of Color. *Urban Education.* https://doi.org/10.1177/0042085920963713

San Diego State University. (2021). *Preliminary administrative services credential student handbook.* https://education.sdsu.edu/edl/current-students/edl-student-2021-handbook.pdf

Scharf, A. (2014). *Critical practices for anti-bias education. Perspectives for a diverse America.* Teaching Tolerance Program, Southern Poverty Law Center. https://www.learningforjustice.org/sites/default/files/general/PDA%20Critical%20Practices.pdf

Smith, V. G., & Szymanski, A. (2013). Critical thinking: More than test scores. *NCPEA International Journal of Educational Leadership Preparation, 8*(2), 16–25. https://files.eric.ed.gov/fulltext/EJ1016160.pdf

Twain, M. (1884). *The adventures of Huckleberry Finn.* Charles L. Webster and Company.

Wallace Foundation. (2013). *Five key responsibilities: The school principal as leader.* https://www.wallacefoundation.org/knowledge-center/pages/key-responsibilities-the-school-principal-as-leader.aspx

Zapata, A., Kleekamp, M., & King, C. (2018). *Expanding the canon: How diverse literature can transform literacy learning.* International Literacy Association. https://www.literacyworldwide.org/docs/default-source/where-we-stand/ila-expanding-the-canon.pdf

CHAPTER 8

Teacher Evaluation

Nancy Frey and Douglas Fisher

- Although teachers have been evaluated for decades, the tools used to evaluate them have changed.
- Agreeing on expectations, and then providing teachers with feedback based on those expectations, is an effective way of making the evaluation process useful.
- New models of evaluations, based on specific criteria and student learning outcomes, are building on the history of teacher evaluation, and balancing process and product.

What are the characteristics of an effective teacher? This question is at the heart of teacher evaluation systems, and the answer continues to prove to be elusive. A meta-analysis of 27 studies on teachers' cognitive ability, as measured by college entrance exam scores or basic skills tests, and student achievement found little relationship between the two (Bardach & Klassen, 2020). Other meta-analyses focusing on studies of teachers' verbal ability (Aloe & Becker, 2009) and personality (Klassen & Tze, 2014) showed a small positive effect size on student learning. However, teacher dispositions do have a larger effect size. The expectations teachers hold for their students has a distinct influence on learning (Liu et al., 2016). The interactions between the teacher and the student reveal a meaningful pattern of teacher behaviors related to emotional, instructional, and organizational support (Hamre et al., 2007).

Teachers theoretically draw from two major knowledge domains to inform their teaching. The first is content knowledge, which is knowledge of the subject matter, and the second is pedagogical content knowledge, which is knowing how to teach the subject matter (Shulman, 1986). These two knowledge domains are influenced in part, although not entirely, by the amount and quality of the experiences the teacher has had (Jordan et al., 2018). Simply assuming expertise based on years of experience and advanced degrees is not sufficient. In practice, what constitutes "knowledge and skills" of a reading teacher are not easily untangled from the context of the school, administrators' decisions, and the professional development offered. Wijekumar et al. (2019) studied the knowledge domains of 280 reading teachers and their administrators. They found that 11 of the 12 principals in the study were not able to provide accurate feedback about three recorded reading lessons they viewed, despite the fact that most of them had once been reading teachers themselves.

A skilled teacher can have a profound impact on students in both the short and long term. In the short term, effective teachers increase student understanding and performance (Stronge et al., 2011). In the long term, effective teachers impact college achievement and lifelong earnings. For example, in a large-scale longitudinal study of the economic repercussions of access to quality teaching, three public economists (not educators) drew from two sources of data—federal income tax records and standardized test scores—from the years 1988 to 2009. Investigating the economic impact of a high-value teacher (top 5%) on the lifetime earnings of a student, their analysis revealed that having such a teacher for 1 year correlated with a $50,000 lifetime earnings increase for that student (Chetty et al., 2012). Their data suggested that students educated by skilled teachers were more likely to go to college and, for girls, less likely to become teenage mothers. They also noted that replacing a low-value teacher

(bottom 5%) with an average one equated to increasing overall lifetime earnings for students that approached $1.4 million per class.

If you paused at that last paragraph and found yourself wondering about the wisdom of using standardized test scores to identify "high-value and low-value teachers," you are not alone. The value-added model (VAM) of teacher evaluation has drawn criticism as being unreliable and unstable. Close, Amrein-Beardsley, and Collins (2020) noted in their review of state teacher evaluation plans that "current research suggests that teachers classified as 'effective' one year will have a 25%–59% chance of being classified as 'ineffective' the next year" (p. 7). Others have criticized the unintended consequences of such policies on the teaching force, including demoralization and teachers leaving schools that teach vulnerable children for those with higher reported test scores (Gottfried & Conchas, 2016).

In this chapter, we provide a brief review of teacher evaluation systems and related policies that have influenced them. We then discuss classroom observation processes and the increasing role of teachers as drivers of the observation and evaluation process. We conclude the chapter with an innovative model for teacher evaluation that holds promise as being growth-producing at the individual and school levels.

EVOLVING PRACTICES IN TEACHER EVALUATION

Teacher evaluation has been part and parcel of a measure of job performance. In the mid-20th century, teacher evaluation focused on teachers' individual and unique development. As an example, Coleman (1945) suggested that the supervisory visit focus on the uniqueness of each teacher and learning context, noting, "The first fundamental in understanding the teacher is . . . that the teacher is a person, different from every other person, living in an environment which affects and in turn is affected by that person" (p. 165).

This emphasis on the individual, combined with the need to improve instruction, resulted in the Clinical Supervision Model, first developed in the 1950s and popularized in the 1960s and 1970s. Goldhammer's (1969) five-phase model of clinical supervision was designed to allow for collaborative conversations between the teacher and supervisor. These phases included:

- *Phase 1—Pre-observation Conference:* This phase was designed to provide a conceptual framework for the observation. During this phase, the teacher and supervisor planned the specifics of the observation.
- *Phase 2—Classroom Observation:* During this phase, the supervisor observed the teacher using the framework articulated in Phase 1.
- *Phase 3—Analysis:* Data from the observation were organized by the supervisor with the intent of helping teachers participate "in developing evaluations of their own teaching" (p. 63).
- *Phase 4—A Supervision Conference:* The teacher and supervisor engaged in a dialogue about the data. The teacher was asked to reflect upon and explain his or her professional practice. This stage also could include providing "didactic assistance" (p. 70) to the teacher.
- *Phase 5—Analysis of the Analysis:* The supervisor's "practice was examined with all of the rigor and for basically the same purposes that teacher's professional behavior was analyzed theretofore" (p. 71).

Clinical supervision is still popular today despite evidence that many of these reflective conversations are not specific enough to create change in teachers' practices. A study by RAND suggests that teachers appreciate and expect feedback based on clear expectations and standard procedures. "In their [teachers'] view, narrative evaluation provided insufficient information about the standards and criteria against which teachers were evaluated and resulted in inconsistent ratings among schools" (Wise et al., 1984, p. 16).

FEDERAL POLICY INFLUENCES IN TEACHER EVALUATION

While in the past teacher evaluation fell distinctly under the purview of individual school districts, increasing federal oversight, beginning with the No Child Left Behind (NCLB) Act in 2002, made teacher evaluation part of educational accountability policies. Despite an accountability model that included punitive consequences, NCLB did not deliver on the promise that all students would achieve at mastery levels by 2014 (Harman et al., 2016).

The next major federal policy initiative came later in the decade when the federal government introduced its Race to the Top (RTTT) initiative in 2009. A major component required that states accepting RTTT funding reform their teacher evaluation systems to include student test scores as part of holding teachers accountable (Onosco, 2011). In response, 40 states as well as the District of Columbia implemented some version of a value-added model as a component to quantify the impact of a teacher on their students' academic achievement on state test scores (Collins & Amrein-Beardsley, 2014). However, these too have proven to be problematic, and in some cases have been the subject of litigation (Hazi, 2017).

Value-Added Propositions for Teacher Evaluation

Sanders and Horn (1994) proposed using a value-added model to measure teacher effectiveness through examination of their students' state test scores. The intent was to be able to determine which teachers contributed additional value to a student's learning, and which teachers had a detrimental effect. Scherrer (2012) noted shortcomings in the use of student achievement data in teachers' evaluations. He noted that there were unintended incentives to cheat on reporting student scores, a focus on high-achieving students, and a narrowing of the curriculum to only those things on the test.

VAM seems intuitively simple. Just subtract the student's score at the end of the year from that same student's score from the previous year. Of course, there are a number of issues that would have to be addressed to accomplish this. First of all, teachers and administrators would have to agree on what students should learn. Standards-based reform tries to meet this need, though imperfectly. Second, the school would have to select and use reliable assessments that measure the content expected to be taught. Third, the process depends upon the assumption that teachers possess a set of skills they carry from one year to the next regardless of the context. These assumptions are imperfectly realized in practice yet are linked to high-stakes decisions about employment (Amrein-Beardsley & Holloway, 2019).

A complicating factor that affects value-added models is that allocation of students does not occur in a vacuum. There are many decisions that impact where students attend school. Rivkin (2007) indicates that school choice is a factor that influences VAM. "Families choose a community and school, possibly trading off school quality with other housing amenities. Given preferences, additional income is used in part to send children to a more expensive school" (p. 2).

Even if these major stumbling blocks are solved and the school agrees on what should be taught and how to assess that knowledge, there are challenges to overcome. If two schools make equal levels of progress but one school started off much lower than the other, performance gaps exist and will continue to exist year after year, despite the fact that progress has been made and achievement has been monitored.

The biggest criticism of VAM is that it can lead to the misuse of student achievement data as a means to measure teacher effectiveness. Partly, achievement data that emanate from test scores have been contested due to measurement error. As Hanushek and Rivkin (2010) indicate, "Another testing issue involves measurement error, a complication that takes on added importance in residual-based estimates of variance of teacher quality" (p. 2). When using student achievement data that come from large-scale tests, measurement errors factor in a number of ways. Errors, rather than teacher performance, can be the result of such aspects as the manner in which questions are formatted, the test-taking skills of students, or even their motivation and engagement with the test itself. And at the heart of this argument lies an incontrovertible truth: achievement tests were designed to measure student knowledge, not teacher effects (Popham, 2013). In other words, these instruments are only sensitive to what students know, and are insensitive to any instruction that might have occurred to build that knowledge.

Both the questions of allocation of students, and the complicated pathway through which a student is in a particular classroom, in a particular school, with a particular teacher, and the question of measurement error highlight areas that need attention in any value-added model. Value-added models acknowledge the important difference a quality teacher can have on a student's academic achievement; however, there are many complicating factors that influence academic achievement. Nearly two decades of problems with VAM have likely contributed to the

move away from this method with the passage of the Every Student Succeeds Act (ESSA) in 2015.

Every Student Succeeds Act

The passage of ESSA is the latest permutation of the Elementary and Secondary Education Act of 1965. This renewal replaced NCLB, and with it came a de-emphasis on teacher evaluation. Further, it "signaled an end of a period of heightened federal activity" that NCLB and RTTT embodied (Ross & Walsh, 2019, p. 3). In the years since, a number of states have retreated from VAM as part of their teacher evaluation system. Close and colleagues (2020) performed a 50-state analysis of ESSA plans for teacher evaluation and compared them to the plans in 2011 (NCLB) and 2014 (RTTT). By 2018, the number of states using VAMs decreased from 21 to 15, marking a 29% decline. In addition, only 1 of the 18 states who were in development for using VAM continued to do so. Interestingly, three states are now using VAM for formative purposes, primarily to inform professional learning, rather than for accountability. This is a rise from zero states doing so in 2014. Clearly, shifting federal policies in the last two decades have had a strong influence on teacher evaluation systems.

With the retreat of federal guidelines requiring teacher evaluation systems, states are returning to a level of local control on the matter not seen since the passage of NCLB. As states have retreated from the use of VAMs as a sole source of information, more of them are shifting to a multiple-measures approach to teacher evaluation (Steinberg & Donaldson, 2016). However, experiences with VAM have led many to retain some element of value-added modeling alongside other measures. The purpose is to yield a composite rating that includes classroom observations and student surveys in addition to VAM. A criticism of this approach, however, is methodological in nature. Cronbach and colleagues (1997) noted that aggregating measures does not cancel out measurement errors. A simulation of composite scores using New Mexico's TEACH evaluation system, which includes VAM in addition to observations and surveys, showed "decreases in rating consistency associated with value-added score weight" (Doan et al., 2019, p. 2144). Doan et al. further reported that somewhere between 25% and 40% of New Mexico teachers in the 2015–2016 school year would have received different composite ratings depending on the VAM weight assigned in two different statistical models. They found classroom observations and student surveys to be more stable.

CLASSROOM OBSERVATION FOR TEACHER EVALUATION

Pianta and Hamre (2009) argue that classroom observations using a structured protocol yield stable data that can be utilized by teachers and schools. Further, the reliability and validity of these observations increase significantly when they are utilized at several points during the school year. An analysis of large data sets generated using three classroom observation instruments found that reliability improved significantly on the fourth lesson observed (MET Project, 2013).

The number of observations conducted as part of the teacher-evaluation process varies widely. Hill et al. (2012) draw upon a 2011 NCTE report and Louisiana Act 54 of 2010 and find that Tennessee planned four observations per year for tenured teachers while Louisiana would require only one, commenting, "In neither case is there evidence that states generated these numbers via scientific study" (p. 57). Four is more than one observation, but is four the right number? For example, should new reading teachers be evaluated more frequently or less frequently than veteran reading teachers? Should those who have previously been evaluated as highly effective be observed more or less frequently? An argument can be made in either direction. Certainly, there is much to be learned from highly effective teachers, and these observations may validate and extend their practices. For teachers who are struggling, resources in the form of instructional coaching and personalized professional development should be redirected.

The Content of the Observation Instrument

The 50-state analysis of state teacher evaluation plans revealed that 36 states use either Danielson's Framework for Teaching, the Marzano Casual Teacher Evaluation Model (Marzano & Toth, 2013), or a derivative of one or both (Close et al., 2020). Content of the observations has been as problematic as the number of times a teacher is observed.

The number of items on an observational tool reflect the complexity and difficulty raters can experience. For example, Danielson's Framework for Teaching, a commonly used observational instrument, has 76 indicators grouped into 22 actual items for observers to track (Danielson Group, 2013). In both the Danielson and Marzano models, training is required for observers to master the instruments.

The Tennessee observation framework (Tennessee Department of Education, 2011) contains 14 indicators organized into 6 items, whereas the Boston teacher evaluation instrument (Boston Public Schools [BPS] Office of Human Capital, 2017) has 33 indicators grouped into 16 areas. In the case of BPS, these are contained in the form of an interactive rubric that includes "look-fors" for observers and teachers. As Hill et al. (2012) note, "Despite such variability, we found no studies of how the quantity of items on an instrument might affect raters' performance and consequently the characteristics of the resulting teacher scores" (p. 58). In other words, as with the frequency of observation, there is a lack of consensus about what is being evaluated.

Specific to literacy learning, Henk et al. (2000) developed and validated an observation tool for reading that includes classroom climate, prereading phase, guided reading phase, postreading phase, skill and strategy instruction, materials and tasks of the lesson, and teacher practice. In the classroom climate area, they ask evaluators to comment on whether each component was: (1) observed and satisfactory; (2) observed and of high quality; (3) not observed or of unsatisfactory quality; or (4) not applicable for the lesson. The specific components of classroom climate include:

A. Many different types of authentic reading materials such as magazines, newspapers, novels, and nonfiction works are displayed and available for children to read independently.

B. The classroom has a reading area such as a corner or classroom library where children are encouraged to read for enjoyment.

C. An area is available for small-group reading instruction.

D. Active participation and social interaction are integral parts of reading instruction in this classroom.

E. The classroom environment indicates that reading and writing are valued and actively promoted (e.g., purposeful writing is displayed, journals are maintained, word walls are used, book talks and read-alouds by teacher occur regularly). (p. 360)

A more technical observation tool for primary grades reading instruction is the Classroom Observation of Student–Teacher Interactions (COSTI), which examines four aspects of instruction: explicit teacher demonstrations, student independent practice, student errors, and teacher corrective feedback (Smolkowski & Gunn, 2012). These interactions commonly occur in effective beginning reading instructional delivery. Rather than the broader scope of the previous tool, which includes elements of the classroom environment, this instrument focuses exclusively on the instructional moves made by the teacher. The authors provide an example:

In a demonstration the teacher would show students what the skill looks and sounds like: "Listen, the first sound in *ran* is /rrr/," or the teacher does what she wants the students to do "Watch me write the letter capital letter *J*." In student independent practice, the teacher asks students to provide some information that demonstrates their understanding of the activity: "Why did the children in this story get wet?" or "What sound does *r* make?" (p. 320)

The overall purpose on this observational tool is not for teacher evaluation, but rather for providing feedback to the teacher. In fact, the tool includes supplemental materials for use in instructional coaching. In sum, these observational instruments highlight the process aspects of teaching events rather than the outcomes of those events.

Infusing Teacher Evaluation with Instructional Growth

Teacher evaluations should result in teacher growth. A narrow emphasis on categorizing "high-value" and "low-value" teachers does not serve the professional well. If the intention of an evaluation process is to improve and deepen skills and knowledge, then the process must include instructional growth as a desired outcome. Both the Danielson and Marzano instruments require that the teacher be an active participant in the process. However, another teacher

evaluation instrument requires more active collaboration from the administrator. The 5D+ Rubric for Instructional Growth and Teacher Evaluation was developed by the Center for Educational Leadership (2019) at the University of Washington in 2007. The instrument has 30 indicators distributed across five dimensions tied to classroom observations:

- Purpose
- Student Engagement
- Curriculum and Pedagogy
- Assessment for Student Learning
- Classroom Environment and Culture

An additional dimension, Professional Collaboration and Communication, is not tied to classroom observations, but rather focuses on the ways the teacher communicates with peers, students, administrators, and families. The 5D+ evaluation system includes other nonteaching elements such as keeping accurate records and supporting school, district, and state policies and initiatives. Performance in each of the six dimensions is described across four levels of attainment: Ineffective, partially effective, effective, and highly effective.

The 5D+ evaluation system uses teacher-driven cycles that begin with (1) a self-assessment to determine a focus, followed by (2) collaboration with an administrator to examine evidence and finalize the focus of the observation, and (3) extended inquiry. Interestingly, the third step is perhaps the most important, as the teacher and the principal together spend several weeks or months learning about the selected focus area. The intention is for this to be a growth-oriented process with both educators working side by side (Maxfield & Williams, 2014). This stage of the process may include professional learning, readings and discussions, and observations of other classes. The final step in the cycle is an analysis of the impact of the teacher's inquiry on teaching, including observational data and feedback. By involving the administrator directly in the process, that school leader is better able to identify needs in the school and design professional learning for school improvement.

Classroom observation tools, whether be they from Danielson, Marzano, COSTI, or 5D+, operate on the exchange of perspectives between the teacher being observed and the person doing the observing. In other words, they are not intended to be a one-way transaction where a score is provided with little participation from the teacher. In this way, this component of teacher evaluation maintains the reflective nature of the teacher–supervisor interaction described by Coleman (1945) while including specific criteria for success. This brings us to our major recommendation: *Regardless of the system chosen, make teacher expectations clear.*

FOCUS ON TEACHER EXPECTATIONS IN ADVANCE OF TEACHER EVALUATION

People want to know what is expected of them; they want to know what defines quality work. At Disneyland, employees know what makes "good show" versus "bad show." They are shown pictures and illustrations of each, down to hairstyles, facial hair, and fingernail polish. The organization is very clear about its expectations, including the interactions cast members have with guests, the way questions are answered, and the overall look of the facility and those who work there.

However, in too many school systems, the expectations are vague and may be interpreted differently by different administrators. This recalls the findings of the study of teachers and administrators earlier in this chapter, where teacher behaviors were variable due to administrators' largely inaccurate feedback about reading instruction (Wijekumar et al., 2019). A characteristic of high-performing schools is that teachers know what is expected, and they have a chance to discuss the expectations before they are evaluated against those expectations. The process for identifying expectations is also important. It is not sufficient to simply tell teachers what is expected of them. Instead, they need to have time to coconstruct expectations, to reflect on the expectations, and to ask questions about the expectations.

Consider the expectations for faculty at Health Sciences High in San Diego (see Figure 8.1). Discussed and revised each year, these expectations clearly communicate the values of the organization. These expectations might not work, or work well, in another school. It is not as simple as copying the expectations another school has set. Instead, these expectations need to be developed and owned by each school's teachers and revisited annually to refine them. This process and the expectations that are coconstructed

by teachers are an example of the return to a greater degree of local control in the ESSA era.

Once these expectations are owned, they can be used in evaluations. For example, in the area of instruction, an English teacher received the following comments about her instructional performance:

> Ms. X's instruction employs a gradual-release-of-responsibility instructional framework that is anchored by daily use of learning intentions and success criteria. These learning intentions include content, language, and social objectives, which are vital for supporting English learners, while infusing social and emotional learning into content. Ms. X has increased both the amount and the quality of small group instruction over the course of this school year. Early observations did not include teacher-directed small group learning. However, by January classroom observations revealed that she was using this format both to remediate students who were struggling, as well as to provide extensions for those who are accelerating. The teacher makes these decisions based on the regular use of exit tickets to gain formative feedback on next steps in instruction.

This teacher knew what to focus on instructionally because the expectations were communicated in advance and the feedback she received after each formative observation was consistent with those expectations. It is important to note that these summary comments were made following five formal observations following the clinical supervision cycle. But in this case, the supervision cycle focused on specific behaviors that had been agreed upon in advance of the observations, which underscores the importance of evaluators spending time in classrooms observing teaching events.

CONCLUSION

Evaluation of teachers is not new, and dates to the colonial era in the United States. Indeed, many of the issues we wrestle with today were present even at that time. Who should evaluate, and by what means? In the 1700s the task was left to religious leaders; by the 20th century it had become an important part of the principal's job.

Figure 8.1. Teacher Expectations at the Best School in the Universe

Records	Supervision
• Attendance each period is accurate and timely. • Grade books updated at least twice weekly. • Student work is returned within one week. • Routine paperwork and substitute plans are completed on time.	• Lunchtime supervision during non-office hours is maintained. • Attendance at extracurricular activities occurs regularly. • Hallway supervision during passing periods for non-instructional personnel is ongoing. • Student behavior is monitored, and feedback about their citizenship is provided.

Instruction	Curriculum
• Daily content, language, and social purposes are posted, and lessons are relevant and interesting. • Teacher modeling occurs in each lesson. • Application and productive group work is extensive, and collaboration occurs daily. • Formal and informal assessments are used formatively to guide instruction. • Small group instruction and intervention occurs regularly. • Students read, write, and speak daily in every class. • Targeted instruction and language supports are provided to English learners. • Homework is used formatively (review, fluency, application, extension).	• Lessons, both live and blended, are rigorous, systematic, and planned, and based on state content and language development standards. • Units are appropriately interdisciplinary, blended, and linked to essential questions and/or health topics. • Assessments and grading are competency-based. • Honors contracts are offered and executed. • Feature-length films are used minimally, judiciously, and are pre-approved. Short films include vocabulary and/or writing activities.

Communication	Professional Learning
• Choice words and nonverbal cues are used to build each student's agency and identity. • Parents, students, and colleagues receive responses within 1 workday. • Departments, grade levels, and student-support staff members interact regularly using affective statements and growth-producing approaches. • Restorative practices are used to resolve conflict and repair harm. Follow-up is used to build students' agency.	• Every adult is a learner and a teacher. • Coaching is essential to learning, and everyone is coached. • Professional development is essential to continuous improvement and takes priority over other professional obligations. • Classrooms and hallways are welcoming of visitors, who also help us to learn more about ourselves.

Student Support	Peer Support
• Teachers are available for office hours weekly. • Proactive engagement with students about their attendance, performance, language development, and recovery needs is ongoing. • Attendance at, and participation in, IEP meetings occurs regularly. • Students are spotlighted for positive accomplishments and areas of concern. • Appropriate interventions are implemented.	• Honest, humane, and growth-producing conversations occur regularly. • Choice words are used to build agency and identity between and among staff. • Mentoring and coaching relationships are supportive and ongoing. • Each adult does whatever it takes to ensure the success of others. • Successes and achievements are celebrated. • Asking for help is a sign of strength, not weakness.

The introduction of value-added assessments has been a source of controversy, and many have argued about the algorithms involved in their calculation. However, it should not be lost that this represents a fundamental change in *who* is doing the evaluation. A number of states and districts are using student achievement measures of progress as a factor in teacher evaluation. Despite changes in federal policies that have shifted away from teacher evaluation, the lasting impact of VAM has resulted in many states still retaining some dimension of student test scores, even when other measures are used. The inclusion of these data brings another observer to the table: The public's accountability system. The resultant conversations about improvement take on a different dimension when another unseen observer is a participant in the discourse.

In an effort to ensure that local measures are made more robust, newer instruments are being used. While some schools and districts define quality instruction through negotiation and ongoing revisions, others are turning to those instruments that have been crafted for use in a wider range of contexts. Both of these approaches have merits and drawbacks. On the one hand, local measures have the potential to reflect the unique features of a school or district, but they can fall victim to instrument design errors that can obscure the subsequent dialogue between teacher and principal. In contrast, commercially prepared instruments may reduce the measurement errors but cannot account for local context. Also, any instrument, regardless of its origin, runs the risk of becoming cumbersome in the hands of an inexperienced observer.

In the face of the sweeping changes we are experiencing in education today, it is advisable that teachers, administrators, policymakers, and the public approach teacher evaluation with respect. The rapid pivot to distance learning as a result of a global pandemic has created new questions about teacher evaluation. At the time of this writing in March 2021, there were no published studies on K–12 teacher evaluation in distance learning situations. The few studies that had been done were in higher education and focused primarily on course design rather than teaching (Thomas & Graham, 2019). Teacher evaluation, whether in face-to-face or virtual environments, should be seen as an iterative process, and one that continues to inform how we work together as adults to reach a common goal: the education of children.

REFLECTION QUESTIONS

1. What evaluation system is used in your state? Does it include student achievement data? How has this system changed over the past several years?
2. Do you see history repeating itself in terms of teacher evaluation? What might be different this time as school systems revise their teacher evaluation procedures?
3. There are several teacher evaluation models profiled in this chapter. What do you believe are the relative strengths of each? What recommendations would you make for other measures to be used?

PROJECT ASSIGNMENT

Conduct a classroom observation using the clinical supervision cycle and clear expectations. What role does feedback play in this experience? How responsive was the person to your feedback? What did you learn from the experience?

REFERENCES

Aloe, A. M., & Becker, B. J. (2009). Teacher verbal ability and school outcomes: Where is the evidence? *Educational Researcher, 38*(8), 612–624. https://doi.org/10.3102/0013189X09353939

Amrein-Beardsley, A., & Holloway, J. (2019). Value-Added Models for teacher evaluation and accountability: Commonsense assumptions. *Educational Policy, 33*(3), 516–542. https://doi.org/10.1177/0895904817719519

Bardach, L., & Klassen, R. M. (2020). Smart teachers, successful students? A systematic review of the literature on teachers' cognitive abilities and teacher effectiveness. *Educational Research Review, 30.* https://doi.org/10.1016/j.edurev.2020.100312

Boston Public Schools Office of Human Capital. (2017). *Interactive rubric overview.* https://www.bostonpublicschools.org/Page/416

Center for Educational Leadership. (2019). *5D+ rubric for instructional growth and teacher evaluation.* University of Washington. http://info.k-12leadership.org/5d-teacher-evaluation-rubric

Chetty, R., Friedman, J. N., & Rockoff, J. E. (2012). *The long-term impacts of teachers: Teacher value-added and student outcomes in adulthood* (Working paper no. 17699, Executive summary). National Bureau of Economic Research. http://obs.rc.fas.harvard.edu/chetty/value_added.html

Close, K., Amrein-Beardsley, A., & Collins, C. (2020). Putting teacher evaluation systems on the map: An overview of states' teacher evaluation systems post–Every Student Succeeds Act. *Education Policy Analysis Archives, 28*(58), 1–27.

Coleman, E. (1945). The "supervisory visit." *Educational Leadership, 2*(4), 164–167.

Collins, C., & Amrein-Beardsley, A. (2014). Putting growth and value-added models on the map: A national overview. *Teachers College Record, 16*(1). http://www.nysed.gov/common/nysed/files/beardsley puttinggrowthandvalueaddedmodel.pdf

Cronbach, L. J., Linn, R. L., Brennan, R. L., & Haertel, E. H. (1997). Generalizability analysis for performance assessments of student achievement or school effectiveness. *Educational & Psychological Measurement, 57*(3), 373–399. https://doi.org/10.1177/0013164497057003001

Danielson Group. (2013). *Framework for teaching evaluation instrument.* https://danielsongroup.org/downloads/framework-clusters

Doan, S., Schweig, J. D., & Mihaly, K. (2019). The consistency of composite ratings of teacher effectiveness: Evidence from New Mexico. *American Educational Research Journal, 56*(6), 2116–2146. https://doi.org/10.3102/0002831219841369

Goldhammer, R. (1969). *Clinical supervision: Special methods for the supervision of teachers.* Holt, Rinehart & Winston.

Gottfried, M. A., & Conchas, G. Q. (2016). *When school policies backfire: How well-intentioned measures can harm our most vulnerable students.* Harvard Education Press.

Hamre, B. K., Pianta, R. C., Mashburn, A. J., & Downer, J. T. (2007). *Building a science of classrooms: Application of the CLASS framework in over 4,000 US early childhood and elementary classrooms.* Foundation for Child Development.

Hanushek, E. A., & Rivkin, S. G. (2010). *Using value-added measures of teacher quality* (Brief 9). The Urban Institute.

Harman, W. G., Boden, C., Karpenski, J., & Muchowicz, N. (2016). No Child Left Behind: A postmortem for Illinois. *Education Policy Analysis Archives, 24*(47/48), 1–24. https://doi.org/10.14507/epaa.24.2186

Hazi, H. M. (2017). VAM under scrutiny: Teacher evaluation litigation in the states. *The Clearing House: A Journal of Educational Strategies, Issues and Ideas, 90*(5–6), 184–190. https://doi.org/10.1080/00098655.2017.1366803

Henk, W. A., Moore, J. C., Marinak, B. A., & Tomasetti, B. W. (2000). A reading lesson observation framework for elementary teachers, principals, and literacy supervisors. *The Reading Teacher, 53*(5), 358–369.

Hill, H., Charalambous, C., & Kraft, M. (2012). When rater reliability is not enough: Teacher observation systems and a case for the generalizability study. *Educational Researcher, 41*(2), 56–64.

Jordan, R. L. P., Bratsch-Hines, M., & Vernon-Feagans, L. (2018). Kindergarten and first grade teachers' content and pedagogical content knowledge of reading and associations with teacher characteristics at rural low-wealth schools. *Teaching & Teacher Education, 74*, 190–204. https://doi.org/10.1016/j.tate.2018.05.002

Klassen, R. M., & Tze, V. M. C. (2014). Teachers' self-efficacy, personality, and teaching effectiveness: A meta-analysis. *Educational Research Review, 12*, 59–76. https://doi.org/10.1016/j.edurev.2014.06.001

Liu, S., Hallinger, P., & Feng, D. (2016). Supporting the professional learning of teachers in China: Does principal leadership make a difference? *Teaching & Teacher Education, 59*, 79–91. https://doi.org/10.1016/j.tate.2016.05.023

Louisiana Act 54. (2010). http://www.act54.org/about.html

Marzano, R. J., & Toth, M. D. (2013). *Teacher evaluation that makes a difference: A new model for teacher growth and student achievement.* ASCD.

Maxfield, P., & Williams, S. (2014). Learning side-by-side: Teachers and principals work together to strengthen instruction. *Journal of Staff Development, 35*(4), 18–24.

MET Project. (2013). *Ensuring fair and reliable measures of effective teaching: Culminating findings from the MET Project's three-year study.*

National Center for Teacher Effectiveness. (2011). *Online poll of states engaged in reform of teacher evaluation systems.*

Onosco, J. (2011). Race to the Top leaves children and future citizens behind: The devastating effects of centralization, standardization, and high stakes accountability. *Democracy and Education, 19*(2), 1–11.

Pianta, R. C., & Hamre, B. K. (2009). Conceptualization, measurement, and improvement of classroom processes: Standardized observation can leverage capacity. *Educational Researcher, 38*(2), 109–119. https://doi.org/10.3102/0013189X09332374

Popham, W. J. (2013). *Evaluating America's teachers: Mission possible?* Corwin.

Rivkin, S. G. (2007). *Value-added analysis and education policy* (Brief 1). The Urban Institute.

Ross, E., & Walsh, K. (2019). *State of the states 2019: Teacher and principal evaluation policy.* National Council on Teacher Quality.

Sanders, W. L., & Horn, S. (1994). The Tennessee Value-Added Assessment System (TVAAS): Mixed-model methodology in educational assessment. *Journal of Personnel Evaluation in Education, 8*(3), 299–311. https://doi.org/10.1007/bf00973726

Scherrer, J. (2012). What's the value of VAM (value-added modeling)? *Phi Delta Kappan, 93*(8), 58–60.

Shulman, L. (1986). Those who understand: Knowledge growth in teaching. *Educational Researcher, 15*(2), 4–14. https://doi.org/10.3102/0013189X015002004

Smolkowski, K., & Gunn, B. (2012). Reliability and validity of the Classroom Observations of Student–Teacher Interactions (COSTI) for kindergarten reading instruction. *Early Childhood Research Quarterly, 27*(2), 316–328. https://doi.org/10.1016/j.ecresq.2011.09.004

Steinberg, M. P., & Donaldson, M. L. (2016). The new educational accountability: Teacher evaluation in the post-NCLB era. *Education Finance and Policy, 11,* 340–359.

Stronge, J. H., Ward, T. J., & Grant, L. W. (2011). What makes good teachers good? A cross-case analysis of the connection between teacher effectiveness and student achievement. *Journal of Teacher Education, 62,* 339–355.

Tennessee Department of Education. *About Tennessee Educator Acceleration Model (TEAM).* https://team-tn.org/

Thomas, J. E., & Graham, C. R. (2019). Online teaching competencies in observational rubrics: What are institutions evaluating? *Distance Education, 40*(1), 114–132. https://doi.org/10.1080/01587919.2018.1553564

Wijekumar, K., Beerwinkle, A. L., Harris, K. R., & Graham, S. (2019). Etiology of teacher knowledge and instructional skills for literacy at the upper elementary grades. *Annals of Dyslexia, 69*(1), 5–20. https://doi.org/10.1007/s11881-018-00170-6

Wise, A. E., Darling-Hammond, L., McLaughlin, M. W., & Bernstein, H. T. (1984). *Teacher evaluation: A study of effective practices.* RAND Corporation.

CHAPTER 9

Professional Development

Maryann Mraz, Jean Payne Vintinner, and Miranda S. Fitzgerald

- Administrators have an important role to play in supporting teachers' professional development and participating in professional development opportunities.
- Strategies that support effective professional development include university-school collaborations such as Professional Development Schools; Professional Learning Communities; data-driven instruction; and certification by the National Board for Professional Teaching Standards.
- Site-based professional development requires collaboration and reflection on the part of both teachers and administrators.

In order for students to achieve desired learning outcomes, continuous, supportive learning opportunities must be available to teachers (Claxton et al., 2016). Professional development can provide strategic and systematic support to teachers as they seek to continuously improve their instructional practices. Changes in federal and state policies, curriculum standards, assessment mandates, technology innovations, and funding can all impact professional development needs. Those responsible for overseeing literacy programs must deliver professional development programs that support teachers in effectively responding to changing expectations. This chapter discusses several different aspects of professional development.

CHARACTERISTICS OF HIGH-QUALITY PROFESSIONAL DEVELOPMENT

The National Council on Teacher Quality (McGannon, 2016) acknowledges that effective teachers are an important factor in student success. When students have access to effective teachers in the classroom, literacy learning can be approached with purpose and enthusiasm, and opportunity gaps can be narrowed (Vacca et al., 2017). In today's educational and political climate, teacher effectiveness continues to be closely tied to student achievement. While the Every Student Succeeds Act (2015) offers a shift away from federal intervention to more state and local control (Beachum, 2018), it maintains state-level accountability testing as a measure of student achievements and, in turn, teacher effectiveness. Researchers offer a broader definition of effective teaching that extends beyond standardized test scores. Darling-Hammond (2009) expands the notion of teacher quality to include traits and characteristics such as:

- strong verbal ability
- ability to observe and think diagnostically
- strong content knowledge
- knowledge of how to develop higher-order thinking skills
- ability to assess and scaffold learning to support students who have learning differences

In addition to mandating state-level testing, ESSA requires that educators develop evidence-based plans for measuring student learning and for addressing the needs of struggling learners. ESSA promotes the use of personalized interventions to meet the diverse learning needs of students (Weiss & McGuinn, 2016). The legislation also recognizes the importance of effective, ongoing professional development, tailored to meet the individual needs of teachers and principals, as an essential component in

meeting student learning goals. Title II funds within ESSA are designated for improvement of instruction and professional development support (Herman et al., 2017).

Researchers (Bellanca, 2009; Darling-Hammond et al., 2009; Duncan, 2010; Kindall et al., 2018; Knight, 2009; Liston et al., 2006; Webster-Wright, 2009) have identified the following characteristics as evident in successful professional development initiatives. Professional development was most successful when it

- was a sustained, intensive process;
- focused on appropriate content;
- provided teachers with opportunities for active learning;
- provided support to teachers on how to transfer professional development content to their teaching practices;
- gave teachers a voice in both the content and the process of professional development;
- provided supportive follow-up through observation, feedback, faculty dialogues, or study groups;
- encouraged collegiality;
- sought consensus among participants on goals;
- received support from administrators;
- received adequate funding for materials, consultants, and staffing;
- acknowledged participants' existing beliefs and instructional practices.

Professional development that supports effective teaching cannot simply be an isolated activity; rather, it must be an ethos that supports teachers throughout their professional lives as they strive to be thoughtful, pragmatic, and responsive practitioners (Pearson & Hoffman, 2011).

THE ROLE OF THE ADMINISTRATOR

As they prepare to make decisions about professional development, administrators must consider issues related to content, process, and context. What content-area knowledge and content-specific instructional methods should be addressed? How can professional development be implemented so that teachers build self-efficacy and develop a sense of ownership of their professional growth process? How do scheduling and funding support, or constrain, professional development options (Tallerico, 2014)? At different stages in their careers, teachers possess different levels of expertise in their craft. They need professional development that responds to their differing levels of development. Teachers undergo a continuum of development through both their teacher preparation programs and through their ongoing work in the field. Preservice teachers, for example, acquire general pedagogical and subject-matter knowledge. Their knowledge becomes strengthened through their coursework and field experiences. Next the candidate works under the supervision of an experienced teacher or mentor and obtains a professional license. Through continued growth in the field, specialization can be achieved (National Council for the Accreditation of Teacher Education, 2009).

Sustained professional development is essential for progressing through the more advanced levels of this continuum. The primary role of administrators (principals, academic coordinators, or literacy coordinators/supervisors) in the professional development process is one of enabling teachers to talk about teaching and to build upon their existing knowledge of teaching and learning in order to improve their own instructional practices.

All too often, traditional professional development programs require only passive involvement on the part of teachers. Teachers may, for example, listen to a single lecture and demonstration of a new strategy. Following such a program, more often than not, teachers return to their classroom routines, applying little if any of the in-service information to their own instructional practice (Kent, 2004; Steyn, 2005). Professional development should be a collaboration between school leaders and teachers. Administrators must support teachers in being active participants in their own professional development, and the administrators must be active and informed participants on the professional development team.

The principal's role is that of "lead learner" (International Literacy Association, 2019)—one who sets high expectations for literacy learning and fosters a learning community where shared learning opportunities are valued. For example,

in one district, principals participated not only in the reading program selection process, but also in the professional development programs that were designed to teach teachers how to implement the new reading program. By attending these sessions, administrators gained an understanding of how the reading program operated and how its implementation could be effectively monitored. As a result, when teachers had questions about how to use the new materials, principals were able to assist. In such an environment, the principal's role is that of instructional leader, rather than program manager (Kindall et al., 2018).

Administrators can be supportive of professional development in other ways as well. One resource that is often in short supply for teachers is time. Teachers need time during the school day to discuss the needs of their students, as well as their visions of the broader needs of their school, and to collaborate on ways in which those needs can be effectively addressed (Paez, 2003). Careful arrangement of planning times may facilitate the formation of professional learning communities or study groups among the faculty.

Today's technological innovations bring a wealth of online resources to teachers, including websites for school districts, state and federal education departments, and professional organizations. These resources provide updates on standards, research, assessments, and instructional strategies, as well as forums that invite teachers to engage in discussions with colleagues on topics relevant to teaching and learning. A systemwide commitment to change must be demonstrated by support for release time, reimbursement for conferences, and establishment of local workshops, either face-to-face or virtual. By incorporating paid curriculum days into the summer and school-year calendars, time can be allotted for teachers to discuss issues and develop collaborative solutions. When high-quality, face-to-face professional development is cost-prohibitive, digital options such as webinars, remote coaching, and online courses can facilitate professional-development opportunities (Snell et al., 2019). The administrator's commitment to change is demonstrated by providing materials to support literacy teaching and learning and access to technology resources, such as video examples of model lessons for teacher study of literacy issues.

STRATEGIES TO SUPPORT CHANGE

General Strategies to Support Change

Change can be uncomfortable and demanding, and the rate of change can vary depending on the nature of the change required and the willingness of participants to undertake it. Professional development to support change should focus on content that is relevant to teachers and that aligns with goals that they have had a voice in establishing. Sustained professional development is most effective when it focuses more on active learning through activities such as mentoring relationships and study groups, and less on passive presentations (Tallerico, 2014). A number of strategies are useful for supporting teachers as they navigate change and continue to develop professionally (DeMonte, 2013; Hall, 2005; Hirsh, 2005; Levy & Murnane, 2004; Youngs, 2013):

- observations in each other's classroom in one's own or another building;
- mentoring programs for new teachers and for experienced teachers who are new to a grade level;
- book clubs that provide a face-to-face or electronic forum for discussing professional literature with colleagues;
- peer support teams where peers share questions, concerns, and ideas for solutions as they seek to implement changes in their teaching and literacy programs;
- lesson demonstrations and guided practice of new instructional strategies;
- threaded discussions and forums via email or an online platform;
- availability of technology resources, such as podcasts and websites, where teachers can share resources, ideas for lesson plans, and relevant data.

In addition to the general strategies for supporting change, there are a number of more expansive strategies that can be used to support teacher growth and student achievement. In the following sections we discuss university–school collaboration, Professional Learning Communities, data-driven instruction, and the process of the National Board for Professional Teaching Standards.

University–School Collaboration

Professional Development Partnerships. When pre-K–12 and university educators and organizations develop collaborative and sustained relationships, their collective advocacy provides strong support for teacher growth, allowing teachers to address the needs of the children, families, and communities they serve (Darling-Hammond et al., 2017). One university-school collaboration effort in Michigan was launched in 2015 by an Early Literacy Task Force (ELTF), a subcommittee of the General Education Leadership Network (GELN) that is part of the Michigan Association of Intermediate School Administrators (MAISA). This collaboration was created to support statewide professional development and coaching focused on research-supported instructional practices in literacy. The task force included representatives from Intermediate School Districts, the Michigan Department of Education, Michigan State University, and the University of Michigan, among others.

The initial work of the task force and its partners, including university faculty, was supported by state funding and grants, and focused on developing a suite of foundational documents that identified research-supported practices in literacy instruction and coaching across pre-K–12 to guide professional learning throughout the state (Duke, 2016). Since the publication of the *Essential Instructional Practices in Early Literacy: Grades K–3* and the *Essential Coaching Practices for Elementary Literacy* documents in 2016 (MAISA GELN ELTF, 2016a, 2016b), hundreds of district literacy coaches, school leaders, and other school-team representatives (e.g., lead teachers and English Learner practitioners) have participated in professional learning sessions and received ongoing support provided by university literacy faculty partners focused on these practices (MAISA GELN ELTF, n.d.).

The Essential Instructional Practices initiative implemented a blended model of professional development for literacy coaches that include a combination of face-to-face and online experiences to provide professional learning and aligned wraparound supports focused on the instructional and coaching practices. The comprehensive professional development system included: (a) statewide professional learning sessions; (b) regional and local professional learning sessions; and (c) a suite of online videos, modules, and resources to support coaches and the teachers they serve. As an example, university literacy faculty partners have led multiday summer institutes focused on supporting literacy coaches and school administrators to plan their school's literacy professional learning for the year. This planning includes examining the instructional practices and supporting research, both for areas affirmed (i.e., practices teachers are already using well) and areas for improvement (i.e., practices teachers are not yet using and/or using consistently). The learning and planning that coaches accomplish during the institute are then sustained through yearlong supports, such as regular webinars.

Supported by their participation in multiday institutes and other face-to-face professional learning sessions and webinars led by university faculty, literacy coaches and administrators design and lead their own site-based professional learning sessions and coaching in their local schools and districts. These sessions are supported by the Essential Instructional Practices documents, an extensive library of videos that illustrate the instructional practices, and free online modules that serve as resources for teachers' professional learning. Michigan's Essential Instructional Practices initiative, which initiated and sustains professional development partnerships statewide, exemplifies several features of effective professional development. For example, professional learning sessions and ongoing support

- Focus on foundational documents that outline research-supported instructional practices in literacy
- Model what the instructional practices look like through face-to-face sessions, webinars, and an extensive suite of classroom video resources
- Provide both coaching and expert support from university literacy faculty
- Provide sustained wraparound support through a statewide literacy mentors' network and follow-up webinars that extend learning beyond face-to-face institutes within and across years (Darling-Hammond et al., 2017)

In the context of professional development partnerships, as elsewhere in K–12 education, the COVID-19 pandemic necessitated shifts in resources and supports provided to school. Many teachers across the nation were required to deliver their reading instruction remotely. To address the needs of teachers in response to these unprecedented changes in instruction, and to support the use of research-supported practices in early literacy when teaching remotely, the Essential Instructional Practices initiative provided learning resources online for elementary-grade teachers so that they could bring *Essential Instructional Practices in Early Literacy* to life in remote learning contexts (Remote Learning Resources, n.d.). These resources included a series of videos created by university faculty partners that illustrated how to provide, for example, small-group literacy, word work, and vocabulary instruction remotely.

Professional Development Schools. The Professional Development School (PDS) model is a vehicle for achieving collaboration between universities and school districts. PDSs seek to improve the preparation of new teachers, provide ongoing faculty development for experienced teachers, direct inquiry at the improvement of teaching practice, and enhance student achievement (National Association for Professional Development Schools, 2021; National Council for Accreditation of Teacher Education, 2009). These PDS partnerships support teachers in becoming knowledgeable practitioners who are able to reflect on their teaching practice and implement responsive instructional practices. Teachers participate in professional learning sessions provided by university faculty, serve as supervising teachers for teacher candidates, and co-teach site-based methods courses with teacher educators (Polly et al., 2019; Reischl et al., 2017). PDSs have been found to enhance teachers' opportunities to become leaders within their schools, to push teachers to think more deeply about their teaching practices, and to strengthen teachers' efficacy by empowering them to take ownership of supporting their colleagues and advocating for their students and profession (Carpenter & Sherretz, 2012; Rosenthal et al., 2017).

In PDS partnerships, one or more university faculty members serves as a liaison for a school. The school administrator appoints a school representative or team of representatives to serve as on-site coordinators. A team of faculty and administrators from both the university and the school establishes goals for the partnership and formulates plans, including assessment measures, to meet those goals.

Reischl et al. (2017) described three tools as key to ensuring the success of PDS partnerships:

1. Annual K–12 school improvement plans that outline school goals and plans for meeting those goals
2. University documents that outline research-based teaching practices that guide teacher education
3. Design principles for the PDS partnership

These types of tools can support both institutions to balance school and university interests, summarize goals and priorities, and communicate the partnership's aims to all stakeholders.

The breadth and depth of initiatives implemented through the PDS partnerships vary depending on the needs of each school. For example, some partnerships are focused on instructional projects, such as training teachers to conduct writing workshops with their students, establishing tutoring opportunities for students, integrating digital technologies into English Language Arts instruction (Hunter et al., 2018), or providing professional learning sessions focused on genre-based writing strategy instruction (Philippakos et al., 2018). Through other partnerships, methods courses, which are part of a preservice teacher education sequence, are conducted by university faculty at the school site. Classroom teachers are involved in the training of preservice teachers through observations, co-teaching, and shared professional development opportunities. Graduate-level classes are offered at some PDS sites for teachers who are pursuing advanced degrees through university programs. Opportunities to attend workshops and in-service programs can be offered to teachers who are not enrolled in a degree program.

Professional development beyond the school site is also available to teachers through PDS partnerships. For example, teachers can collaborate with university faculty to present the findings of studies conducted at the PDS school as well as experiences with PDS initiatives at regional, state, and national conferences, such as the annual National PDS Conference. Additionally, by hosting student teacher candidates in yearlong internship programs, the PDS partnership can serve as a valuable recruitment tool for school administrators who are seeking to hire new faculty members.

Professional Learning Communities

The use of Professional Learning Communities (PLCs) is an increasingly popular approach to professional development for K–12 teachers. When well-designed and well-implemented, PLCs can support improvement in teachers' instructional practices and student achievement (Darling-Hammond et al., 2017). Stoll et al. (2006) defined a PLC as "a group of people sharing and critically interrogating their practice in an ongoing, reflective, collaborative, inclusive, learning-oriented, growth-promoting way" (p. 223). Effective PLCs function as inquiry-oriented teams, in which groups of teachers work collaboratively toward common goals aimed at continuous improvements in teaching and learning.

PLCs can be organized in multiple ways. Many PLCs are made up of grade-level or content-area teams within a single school, while other PLCs are made up of teachers across schools, districts, or states. PLCs may also convene on different timelines, during different times of day, and in different formats, such as in-person or virtually. For example, depending on the specific goals of the PLC, teams may meet weekly, or once or twice a month. Some schools designate common planning times for grade-level or content-area PLC meetings during the school day, while others hold PLC meetings after school. Increasingly, and especially in response to the COVID-19 pandemic, PLCs may be conducted in online or blended (a combination of face-to-face and synchronous or asynchronous online activities) formats, which can provide team members with opportunities to connect in meaningful ways between face-to-face meetings, such as through asynchronous text-based discussions (Bates et al., 2016; Katz et al., 2019). Virtual activities, necessary during the COVID-19 pandemic, will likely remain an important format for PLCs moving forward due to the flexibility online and blended sessions offer.

PLCs focus on building the individual and collective capacity of teachers to enhance student learning. While the specific structure and aims of PLCs vary based on contextual factors, goals, and students' needs, they share common characteristics. These characteristics include establishing a common vision and goals, keeping student learning at the center of the PLC's collective work, trying out and reflecting on instructional practices and student learning in particular content areas, participating in reflective dialogue, and providing feedback on one another's instruction (Vescio et al., 2008). DuFour (2004) proposed three questions that are critical for driving PLCs' work:

1. What do we want students to learn?
2. How will we know when students have learned it?
3. How will we respond when students experience learning challenges?

Core foci that cut across PLCs include ensuring that students learn specific skills or content, creating and sustaining a culture of collaboration, and concentrating on student outcomes through continuous analysis of formative and summative assessment data (DuFour, 2004). The specific focus of a PLC team can be on any of a variety of aspects of literacy instruction, such as creating lessons for struggling readers (D'Ardenne et al., 2013), comprehension instruction (Stahl, 2015), integrating technology into literacy instruction (Thoma et al., 2017), or particular instructional approaches, such as Guided Reading or Reading Apprenticeship (Bates et al., 2016; Katz et al., 2019).

To launch PLCs within individual school sites, a school administrator may guide the initial construction of PLCs through providing school- or districtwide professional learning sessions that are aligned to the school vision and goals. Regardless of the specific instructional focus determined, effective PLCs typically dedicate time to collective analysis of student work samples to develop consensus around what high-quality student work looks like, common areas of learning strengths and needs among students, and the effectiveness of teachers' instructional practices (Darling-Hammond et al., 2017). Many PLCs also read and discuss professional texts that help them to address a particular problem of practice. PLC team members then work to translate what they have read into classroom practice. After classroom implementation, some PLCs engage in video sharing, in which teachers video-record their teaching, receive feedback from team members, and reflect on their practice. As a final example, some PLCs create products, such as instructional or assessment materials shared among team members or with other teachers in their school or district. The specific activities in which PLCs engage are often collaboratively negotiated as team members develop

group norms, set goals for the PLC, and identify materials—such as texts—that will guide their work.

Data-Driven Instruction

With ever-increasing levels of accountability for all stakeholders, from individual students and teachers to larger groups within education, many states and districts have adopted strict policies and resources to guide and support teachers as they try to plan appropriate and effective instruction (Gullo, 2013). With the recent resurgence of the science of reading influencing classroom practices, teachers are using student performance data to justify instructional decisions (Castles et al., 2018). *A Blueprint for Reform* (U.S. Department of Education Office of Planning, Evaluation and Policy Development, 2010) acknowledged the need for authentic assessments that allow educators to determine students' ability and growth as the first step in planning effective instruction. Race to the Top (U.S. Department of Education, 2009) recognized the value of data-driven instruction and built criteria into the grant applications that asked participants to explain how they would (1) fully implement a statewide longitudinal data system, (2) ensure that information from that data system is disseminated to all stakeholders, and (3) use data to make instructional decisions in the classroom and beyond. Data from these systems need to be disaggregated to determine instructional impact on student performance, special populations, school climate, student mobility, and student well-being.

Such directives are not exclusive to national agencies or formal policy initiatives. Many teachers and schools have decided to take a grassroots approach and conduct site-based action research to determine what works for their students. In cases such as this, teachers and administrators develop their own ideas for classroom change and scientifically study the effects on student learning (Gilles et al., 2010; Darling-Hammond et al., 2017). This type of research may be conducted through school-based action research procedures, or it may be guided by district-level personnel or university faculty, but it should always be governed by effective research practices to have the greatest impact on student success (Gullo, 2013). When teachers have a voice in evaluating students' needs and abilities, and determining types of professional development opportunities they require, engagement is high, and participants are more likely to implement effective strategies learned as the result of such endeavors.

National Board for Professional Teaching Standards

An independent, nonprofit organization for the voluntary certification of highly accomplished teachers, the National Board for Professional Teaching Standards (NBPTS, n.d.) reports that maintaining high standards for teaching performance enhances student learning and allows teachers to improve their instructional practice while demonstrating their commitment to excellence in their profession. Research has shown that Board-certified teachers have a positive impact on student learning and achievement, especially for students from traditionally underserved groups (Cowan & Goldhaber, 2015; NBPTS, n.d.). Participating in the NBPTS process is a way for teachers to engage in a series of professional development experiences that require them to assess and reflect on their own teaching practices.

The NBPTS process focuses on four key components: content knowledge; differentiation of instruction; teaching practice and the learning environment; and effective and reflective teaching practices. Content knowledge is assessed through a computer-based assessment of a candidate's responses to questions pertaining to content knowledge and classroom pedagogy. The remaining three components are assessed through a series of portfolios that include elements such as evidence of a candidate's ability to analyze assessment data and implement instruction to meet students' needs, videotaped interactions between the teacher and students, and self-reflections of one's teaching.

Portfolio evaluators are classroom teachers who have been trained in understanding the standards, the directions to candidates, and the scoring guides. Scoring is based on the collection of a candidate's responses: videotapes, student work samples, and the candidate's written analysis and reflection. Each of these pieces of evidence helps evaluators, who must all be practicing teachers, to assess a candidate's work in light of the conscious, deliberate, analytical, and reflective criteria the National Board standards endorse.

Administrators are not required to be involved in the NBPTS process. However, as teachers compile evidence of leadership and collaborative accomplishments within their educational community, most choose to include their administrator as a reference. Many schools have developed support groups for teachers within their district as they engage in the NBPTS process, and districts have district-level coordinators to coordinate resources and support teachers. Candidates have described such groups, as well as mentoring from teachers who have successfully completed the process, as invaluable. Guidance and mentoring can help candidates to better understand the process and its requirements.

GUIDELINES FOR SITE-BASED PROFESSIONAL DEVELOPMENT PROGRAMS

The successful planning and implementation of a professional development program at an individual school is a collaborative effort. It requires reflection, on the part of both teachers and administrators, about the current needs and strengths of the school's program. Together, the members of the school team can then co-produce a systematic plan for meeting those mutually agreed-upon needs. This section offers guidelines for generating and implementing such a plan.

Before making any consequential decisions, administrators need data-based information. Next, they need to work with participants in goal-setting. When teachers and administrators have a say in targeting goals for improvement, a balance across individual, instructional, school, and school district priorities is more achievable.

One of the most efficient and effective ways to engage in professional development planning is to follow a model that is both systematic and participatory. It should be orderly and flexible and depend on input from those most directly involved. Above all, a cyclical design is conducive to collaboration among teachers, administrators, coordinators, and committees. A plan such as this virtually assures that professional development will be tailored to meet participants' needs.

One of the challenges of site-based professional development is determining which practices will best meet the needs of students while still meeting state and district goals for curriculum. When preparing professional development, teams of teachers and administrators are tasked with wading through professional literature to determine which strategies are best supported by research. Documents that synthesize information about research-supported instructional practices, such as the What Works Clearinghouse Practice Guides from the Department of Education's Institute of Education Sciences (https://ies.ed.gov/ncee/wwc/PracticeGuides), can support this work. These teams must then develop materials to facilitate workshops to deliver these resources to teachers.

Incorporating technological resources into planning and implementing professional development can streamline the process. One example of facilitating site-based professional development with technology is the Classroom Education Plan (CEP) produced by the company Pathways for Learning (www.pathwaysforlearning.com). The Classroom Education Plan offers several pieces to access in creating a customized plan for professional development. First, CEP maintains a collection of strategies supported by up-to-date research and includes detailed directions for implementation and differentiation. Second, CEP gathers data through surveys administered to both teachers and students on the academic and nonacademic indicators that research shows to have the greatest impact on achievement. The results of these surveys determine which of the strategies will best meet the needs of students and align with curricular goals; these strategies become the focus of site-based professional development. This creates easy access to research-based practices for teachers to quickly implement and monitor in classrooms. The same software that analyzes the results of the surveys and aligns them with recommended strategies also tracks teachers' usage of strategies and gives teachers an opportunity to share success and feedback about strategies within a supported teacher-learning community. The conversation within this teacher community helps to inform both the process and the content of the strategies, strengthening the efficacy of the overall program. In this growing field of technologically supported professional development, a wealth of programs similar to CEP, such as Panorama Education (https://www.panoramaed.com/), also use programs to gather data, plan, and implement professional development to meet the needs of today's schools.

As a rule, for any site-based professional development, planning proceeds in phases, beginning with a proposal, often based on assessment data

or revised national or district standards, to initiate change in the school's reading program. This phase of planning relies on information and ideas from several sources, particularly the group for whom professional development is intended. A needs assessment enables the administrator and planning committee to identify needs, attitudes, interests, and potential resources. An example of a needs assessment survey designed to collect information from the faculty, in this case from elementary teachers, is shown in Figure 9.1. At this point in the planning process, basic goals and objectives can be set. The next phase—the actual implementation of content and process—is soon under way.

The implementation of professional development centers on delivery of the program. It should occur over a series of planned activities with appropriate follow-up, lasting anywhere from a month to a year or two depending on the goals and needs of the school or team. To work effectively with teachers, administrators need to be open to new ideas and demonstrate strategies and techniques for improving instruction. Interpersonal skills, as well as one's basic delivery and knowledge base, are important whether conducting a workshop or assisting in an action research project. The following are some personal characteristics that are associated with effective presenters at professional development sessions (Vacca et al., 2017):

- demonstrates enthusiasm and interest in the topic
- stimulates excitement
- relates in an open, honest, and friendly manner
- answers questions patiently
- doesn't talk down to participants
- displays a sense of humor

As literacy coaches are more frequently called upon to take on the role of staff developer, they, too, need to be confident and collaborate with teachers on ways to work effectively together toward shared goals. Professional development leaders need a tolerance for ambiguity and a realization that participants are involved in a learning effort.

One of the most practical ways to implement a professional development project is to incorporate the process of change with the best principles of adult learning. Essentially, adults go through a

Figure 9.1. Survey of Literacy Needs and Concerns for Elementary Teachers

Students require assistance with:	Strongly Disagree	Disagree	Agree	Strongly Agree
Phonological Awareness: broad term that includes phonemic awareness. In addition to phonemes, phonological awareness activities can involve work with rhymes, words, syllables, and onsets and rimes				
• Rhyming words: identifying and making oral rhymes				
• Syllabication: identifying and working with syllables in spoken words				
• Onset-Rime: parts of spoken language that are smaller than syllables but larger than phonemes. An onset is the initial consonant(s) sound of a syllable (the onset of bag is b-; of swim, sw-). A rime is the part of a syllable that contains the vowel and all that follows it (the rime of bag is -ag; of swim, -im).				
• Phonemes: identifying and working with individual phonemes in spoken words				
Phonemic Awareness: the ability to notice, think about, and work with the individual sounds in spoken words				
• Phoneme isolation: recognizing individual sounds in a word				
• Phoneme identity: recognizing the same sounds in different words				
• Phoneme categorization: recognizing the word in a set of three or four words that has the "odd" sound				
• Phoneme blending: listening to a sequence of separately spoken phonemes, and then combining the phonemes to form a word				
• Phoneme segmentation: breaking a word into its separate sounds, saying each sound as they tap out or count it				
• Phoneme deletion: recognizing the word that remains when a phoneme is removed from another word				
• Phoneme addition: making a new word by adding a phoneme to an existing word				
• Phoneme substitution: substituting one phoneme for another to make a new word				
Phonics: the understanding that there is a predictable relationship between phonemes (the sounds of spoken language) and graphemes (the letters and spellings that represent those sounds in written language)				
• Alphabetic principle: the systematic and predictable relationships between written letters and spoken sounds				
Orthography: spelling				
Fluency: the ability to read a text accurately and quickly				
• Accuracy: word recognition				
• Rate				
• Expression/prosody: reading so that it sounds natural, as if speaking. Pausing appropriately within and at the ends of sentences and knowing when to change emphasis and tone				
Vocabulary				

(continued)

Figure 9.1. Survey of Literacy Needs and Concerns for Elementary Teachers (continued)

• Using word parts (morphology): knowing some common prefixes and suffixes (affixes), base words, and root words to help learn the meanings of many new words				
• Context clues: hints about the meaning of an unknown word that are provided in the words, phrases, and sentences that surround the word. Context clues include definitions, restatements, examples, or descriptions				
Comprehension				
• Metacognition: monitoring their comprehension so that they know when they understand what they read and when they do not.				
• Asking/answering questions: learning to answer questions better and, therefore, learning more as they read				
• Recognizing text structure: the way the content and events of a story are organized into a plot, which helps with greater appreciation, understanding, and memory for stories				
• Summarizing: synthesis of the important ideas in a text to determine what is important, condense information, and put it into their own words				

All definitions adapted from *Put Reading First: The Research Building Blocks of Reading Instruction: Kindergarten Through Grade 3* (3rd ed.), by B. B. Armbruster, F. Lehr, J. Osborn, & C. R. Adler, 2009, National Institute for Literacy.

change process beginning with unfreezing or readiness for change, next moving forward and gaining experience, then refreezing, and finally incorporating changes into the environment or routine. Implementing professional development with this process in mind allows reading coordinators/supervisors and literacy coaches to introduce a range of action-oriented instructional options to participating teachers. The key to effective delivery is involvement through hands-on activities such as role-playing, demonstration teaching, observations, interviewing, and problem-solving groups. When teachers are involved, they have opportunities to experience how theoretical information can be applied to their own classroom practice.

Frequent and informal evaluation of participants helps to keep their professional development on track. Leaders can use simple rating scales to find out the perceived value and usefulness of sessions, and determine modifications that will enhance the planned implementation of subsequent professional development sessions. Feedback at the end of each session might be a two-way street, with both the staff developer and teachers exchanging suggestions for future directions. Evaluation in this context, then, becomes an integral and responsive part of the professional development implementation.

CONCLUSION

Technological advances and a policy emphasis on data-driven instruction has changed the form and focus of many professional development initiatives. One constant remains: Professional development seeks to support teachers in being active participants in the continuous refinement of teaching theory and practice. Administrators have the potential to play a pivotal role in actualizing professional development programs that will support the advancement of teachers as professionals and, in turn, the quality of educational opportunities offered to students.

REFLECTION QUESTIONS

1. The chapter supports the idea that professional development needs to be ongoing to be successful. What initiatives could be instituted at your school to provide continual support for teachers? Consider ideas such as use of online modules or video libraries, professional book or journal clubs, mentoring programs, Professional Learning Communities, and other online support, such as webinars or remote coaching.
2. What community resources, such as professional development partnerships with organizations or PDS opportunities with universities, could support teachers in your area to advance students' reading growth?
3. For professional development to have a positive impact on student learning, it must align with students' learning strengths and needs. What assessment resources are available to identify students' needs? Are there any gaps in the information provided by these assessments? How can you help educators get a complete picture of what students can already do and are ready to learn next?

PROJECT ASSIGNMENT

Consider the local, state, or national instructional and assessment reading requirements for K–12 students with whom you work. Analyze available student reading and teacher observation data to identify areas of strengths and needs related to their reading instruction. Invite teachers into this process by working with them to create a needs assessment for the grade level they teach. Use these data sources and collaborative conversations to identify research-based instructional practices around which to develop ongoing and effective professional development.

REFERENCES

Armbruster, B. B., Lehr, F., Osborn, J., & Adler, C. R. (2009). *Put reading first: The research building blocks of reading instruction kindergarten through grade 3* (3rd ed.). National Institute for Literacy.

Bates, C. C., Huber, R., & McClure, E. (2016). Stay connected: Using technology to enhance professional learning communities. *The Reading Teacher, 70*(1), 99–102.

Beachum, F. (2018). The Every Student Succeeds Act and multicultural education: A critical race theory analysis. *Teachers College Record, 120*(13), 1–18. http://search.proquest.com/docview/2162745302/.

Bellanca, J. (2009). *Designing professional development for change* (2nd ed.). Corwin Press.

Carpenter, B. D., & Sherretz, C. E. (2012). Professional development school partnerships: An instrument for teacher leadership. *School-University Partnerships, 5*(1), 89–101.

Castles, A., Rastle, K., & Nation, K. (2018). Ending the reading wars: Reading acquisition from novice to expert. *Psychological Science in the Public Interest, 19*, 5–51. doi:10.1177/1529100618772271

Claxton, G., Costa, A., & Kallick, B. (2016). Hard thinking about soft skills. *Educational Leadership, 73*(6), 60–64. http://search.proquest.com/docreview/1772086760/

Cowan, J., & Goldhaber, D. (2015). *National board certification and teacher effectiveness: Evidence from Washington.* The Center for Education Data & Research.

D'Ardenne, C., Barnes, D. G., Hightower, E. S., Lamason, P. R., Mason, M., Patterson, P. C., Stephens, N., Wilson, C. E., Smith, V. H., & Erickson, K. A. (2013). PLCs in action: Innovating teaching for struggling grade 3–5 readers. *The Reading Teacher, 67*(2), 143–151.

Darling-Hammond, L. (2009). Recognizing and enhancing teacher effectiveness. *International Journal of Education and Psychology Assessment, 3*, 1–24.

Darling-Hammond, L., Hyler, M. E., & Gardner, M. (2017). *Effective teacher professional development.* Learning Policy Institute.

Darling-Hammond, L., Wei, R. C., Andree, A., Richardson, N., & Orphanos, S. (2009). *Professional learning in the learning profession: A status report on teacher development in the United States and abroad.* National Staff Development Council.

DeMonte, J. (2013, July 15). *High quality professional development for teachers: Supporting teacher training to improve student learning.* Center for American Progress. http://www.americanprogress.org/issues /education/report/2013/07/15/69592/high-quality -professional-development-for-teachers

DuFour, R. (2004). What is a "professional learning community"? *Educational Leadership, 61*(8), 6–11.

Duke, N. K. (2016, April 28). Getting on the same page about reading by third grade in Michigan. *Literacy Now.* https://literacyworldwide.org/blog/literacy -now/2016/04/28/getting-on-the-same-page-about -reading-by-third-grade-in-michigan

Duncan, S. (2010). Intentional and embedded professional development: Four steps to success. *Exchange Magazine, 191*, 70–72.

Every Student Succeeds Act, 20 U.S.C. § 6301 (2015). https://www.congress.gov/bill/114th-congress /senate-bill/1177

Gilles, C., Wilson, J., & Elias, M. (2010). Sustaining teachers' growth and renewal through action research, induction programs, and collaboration. *Teacher Education Quarterly, 37*(1), 91–108.

Gullo, D. F. (2013). Improving instructional practices, policies, and student outcomes for early childhood language and literacy through data-driven decision making. *Early Childhood Education Journal, 41*(6), 413–421.

Hall, P. (2005). A school reclaims itself. *Educational Leadership, 62*(5), 70–73.

Herman, R., Gates, S., Chavez-Herrerias, E., & Harris, M. (2017). *School leadership interventions under the Every Student Succeeds Act.* RAND Corporation. https:// www.rand.org/pubs/research_reports/RR1550-3.html

Hirsh, S. (2005). Professional development and closing the achievement gap. *Theory into Practice, 44*, 38–44.

Hunter, J. D., Silvestri, K. N., & Ackerman, M. L. (2018). "Feeling like a different kind of smart": Twitter as digital literacy mediates learning for urban youth and literacy specialist candidates. *School-University Partnerships, 11*(1), 36–45.

International Literacy Association (2019). *Principals as literacy leaders* [Literacy Leadership Brief].

Katz, M., Stump, M., Charney-Sirott, I., & Howlett, H. (2019). Traveling with integrity: Translating face-to-face teacher professional learning to online and blended spaces. *Journal of Adolescent & Adult Literacy, 63*(2), 217–223.

Kent, A. M. (2004). Improving teacher quality through professional development. *Education, 124*, 427–535.

Kindall, H. D., Crowe, T., & Elsass, A. (2018). The principal's influence on the novice teacher's professional development in literacy instruction. *Professional Development in Education, 44*(2), 307–31. https://doi .org/10.1080/19415257.2017.1299031

Knight, J. (2009). Coaching. *Journal of Staff Development, 30*(1), 18–22.

Levy, F., & Murnane, R. J. (2004). A role for technology in professional development? Lessons from IBM. *Phi Delta Kappan, 85*, 728–734.

Liston, D., Whitcomb, J., & Borko, H. (2006). Too little or too much: Teacher preparation and the first years of teaching. *Journal of Teacher Education, 57*(4), 351–358.

McGannon, C. (2016). A glimmer of hope on the bleak PD front. *TQB: Teacher Quality Bulletin.* https:// www.nctq.org/blog/A-glimmer-of-hope-on-the -bleak-PD-front

Michigan Association of Intermediate School Administrators General Education Leadership Network Early Literacy Task Force (MAISA GELN ELTF). (2016a). *Essential instructional practices in early literacy. K to 3.* Authors.

Michigan Association of Intermediate School Administrators General Education Leadership Network Early Literacy Task Force (MAISA GELN ELTF). (2016b). *Essential coaching practices for elementary literacy.*

Michigan Association of Intermediate School Administrators General Education Leadership Network Early Literacy Task Force (MAISA GELN ELTF). (n.d.). *Michigan literacy: From lagging to leading.* Authors. https://www.gomaisa.org/downloads/gelndocs /laggingleading.pdf

National Association for Professional Development Schools. (2021). *What it means to be a professional development school: The nine essentials* (2nd ed.). https://napds.org/nine-essentials/

National Board for Professional Teaching Standards. (n.d.). *Research.* http://www.nbpts.org/research/

National Council for the Accreditation of Teacher Education. (2009). *Standards for professional development schools.*

Paez, M. (2003). Gimme that school where everything's scripted! One teacher's journey toward effective literacy instruction. *Phi Delta Kappan, 84*, 757–763.

Pearson, P. D., & Hoffman, J. V. (2011). Principles of practice for the teaching of reading. In T. V. Rasinski (Ed.), *Rebuilding the foundation: Effective reading instruction for 21st century learning* (pp. 9–40). Solution Tree Press.

Philippakos, Z. T., Overly, M., Riches, C., Grace, L., & Johns, W. (2018). Supporting professional development on writing strategy instruction: Listening to the voices of collaborators as carriers of change. *School-University Partnerships, 11*(4), 64–77.

Polly, D., Reinke, L. T., & Putman, S. M. (2019). Examining school-university partnerships: Synthesizing the work of Googlad, AACTE, and NAPDS. *School-University Partnerships, 12*(3), 1–17.

Reischl, C. H., Khasnabis, D., & Karr, K. (2017). Cultivating a school-university partnership for teacher learning: A partnership between a research university and two schools in its community shows the power of collaboration to address achievement gaps while also preparing future teachers. *Phi Delta Kappan, 98*(8), 48–53.

Remote learning resources. (n.d.). Literacy Essentials. https://literacyessentials.org/literacy-essentials/new-remote-learning/

Rosenthal, J. L., Donnantuono, M., Lebron, M., & Flynn, C. (2017). Children's literacy growth, and candidates' and teachers' professional development resulting from a PDS-based initial certification literacy course. *School-University Partnerships, 10*(1), 57–65.

Snell, E. K., Hindman, A. H., & Wasik, B. (2019). A review of research on technology-mediated language and literacy professional development models. *Journal of Early Childhood Teacher Education, 40*(3), 205–220. https://doi.org/10.1080/10901027.2018.1539794

Stahl, K. A. D. (2015). Using professional learning communities to bolster comprehension instruction. *The Reading Teacher, 68*(5), 327–333.

Steyn, G. M. (2005). Exploring factors that influence the effective implementation of professional development programmes on invitational education. *Journal of Invitational Theory and Practice, 11*, 7–34.

Stoll, L., Bolam, R., McMahon, A., Wallace, M., & Thomas, S. (2006). Professional learning communities: A review of the literature. *Journal of Educational Change, 7*, 221–258.

Tallerico, M. (2014). District issues: Administrators at all levels involved in teachers' professional development. In L. E. Martin, S. Kragler, D. Quatroche, & K. L. Bauserman (Eds.), *Handbook of professional development in education: Successful models and practices, PreK–12* (pp. 125–144). Guilford Press.

Thoma, J., Hutchinson, A., Johnson, D., Johnson, K., & Stromer, E. (2017). Planning for technology integration in a professional learning community. *The Reading Teacher, 71*(2), 167–175.

U.S. Department of Education. (2009). *Race to the Top program executive summary.* www.ed.gov/programs/racetothetop/executive-summary.pdf

U.S. Department of Education Office of Planning, Evaluation and Policy Development. (2010). *A blueprint for reform.*

Vacca, R. T., Vacca, J. L., & Mraz, M. (2017). *Content area reading: Literacy and learning across the subject areas.* Pearson.

Vescio, V., Ross, D., & Adams, A. (2008). A review of research on the impact of professional learning communities on teaching practice and student learning. *Teaching and Teacher Education, 24*(1), 80–91.

Webster-Wright, A. (2009). Reframing professional development through understanding authentic professional learning. *Review of Educational Research, 79*(2), 702–739.

Weiss, J., & McGuinn, P. (2016). States as change agents under ESSA. *Phi Delta Kappan, 97*(8), 28–33.

Youngs, P. (2013). *Using teacher evaluation reform and professional development to support Common Core assessments.* Center for American Progress.

CHAPTER 10

Assessing Students' Reading Development and Reading Achievement

Peter Afflerbach, Hyoju Ahn, and Moonyoung Park

- Reading assessment programs can be created to serve diverse audiences and purposes.
- There are many formative and summative assessments that provide optimal information about students' reading development and achievement.
- There are promising and ongoing developments in reading assessment that measure cognitive, affective, and conative growth, and help students learn to "do assessment" for themselves.

This is an exciting time for reading assessment. Ideas about reading—how it works and how to best help student readers develop—are evolving, just as are ideas about reading assessment. That the two are changing creates an inflection point that is marked by both challenge and promise. In this chapter we examine these challenges and promises related to effective reading assessment practices and programs. We review the different audiences and purposes of assessment. We consider how assessment can be used to help students develop metacognition and self-assessment routines. We explore assessment that helps educators understand the diverse cognitive, affective, and conative (the inclination to act purposefully) factors that influence students' reading growth and achievement. We conclude our chapter with an examination of students' online reading and scenario-based reading assessment.

ASSESSMENT AUDIENCES AND PURPOSES

Effective assessment programs equitably address the different purposes and audiences for assessment (Afflerbach, 2017). Effective reading assessment provides teachers with information that guides instruction and leads to accurate evaluation of all students' classroom performance. Students and their families receive information that helps them link home, community, and school efforts to support literacy and that motivates students to read further. It also means that schools, districts, and states receive assessment information that describes the effectiveness of teaching, success of reading programs, and attainment of reading standards. Meeting the assessment needs of this broad roster of audiences and purposes and providing sufficient resources to do so is often a challenge, as indicated by the skewing of many schools' resources to summative assessments, high-stakes testing, and test preparation. To best understand the breadth and depth of a reading assessment program—and how well it may serve diverse audiences and purposes—an assessment inventory is recommended. This starts with an accounting of all reading assessments that are used in a classroom, school, district, and state. Conducting an inventory to optimize a reading assessment program allows programs to match assessments with audiences and purposes, and to address important questions such as:

- Is there an appropriate ratio of formative and summative assessment conducted across the school year so that programs learn about students' ongoing development as well as their ultimate achievements?
- Are teacher and student needs well-served by the current roster of assessments?
- Do the assessments help in understanding students' motivation and engagement, and their self-efficacy?
- Are there assessments that can be used to model assessment so that students develop

the ability to self-assess and be successful at independent reading?

In addition to understanding how well audience and purpose are served, an inventory can illustrate how (and if) all aspects of reading development are addressed. Over time, many districts, schools, and classrooms may accumulate assessments that sum to less than optimal matches with audience and purpose, and that have gaps or redundancies in what is measured. As to the latter, there may be areas of students' reading development adequately sampled by assessment while at the same time key aspects of development are thinly assessed, or not assessed at all. For example, an inventory of assessments may indicate that phonics is overassessed, while motivation and self-efficacy are underassessed. Fluency may be assessed frequently, while higher-order reading strategies are not. In summary, the results of conducting an assessment inventory are invaluable in determining whether existing assessments serve all audiences and purposes, and if they cover the full range of how student readers develop. Inventory results indicate areas of assessment strength and need, and thus place schools and programs in a good position to advocate for needed assessments.

FORMATIVE AND SUMMATIVE READING ASSESSMENTS

Balancing formative and summative assessment is a further hallmark of effective reading assessment programs. Each type of assessment provides important information and achieving balance between the two is crucial. Successful reading assessment helps teachers construct meaning about their students. Teachers strive to best understand each of their student readers and work toward the goals of knowing their strengths and needs. They want to know how instruction connects with student learning, and the ultimate influence of that instruction. Operating from this base of knowing students, teachers are in the best position to provide instruction that meets their specific needs.

At the heart of effective reading instruction is the classroom teacher's detailed knowledge of each student. Consider the zone of proximal development. According to Vygotsky (1978), optimal teaching and learning occur when teachers are able to specify a student's current level of understanding or development, and then provide instruction that meets the student at this level. How do teachers come to know these levels, or zones in which their teaching can be most effective? This knowledge is constructed through ongoing, formative assessments, conducted across the school day and the school year. Formative assessment is conducted with the goal of informing instruction and improving student learning. Formative reading assessment information gathered through observing and listening, and the use of valid and reliable instruments such as reading inventories, help fill in the details of both the current status of student learning and related needs. The value of formative assessments is that they help form an understanding of students as they learn and grow, and provide a basis for making real-time teaching decisions to address individual student needs.

In contrast, summative assessment is conducted after the fact of teaching, providing a summary of student learning. Students, teachers, and schools are evaluated by an annual series of tests, or summative reading assessments. Tests are summative assessments that provide information about students' reading, reporting achievement as a percentile rank, raw score, or grade-level equivalent. A particular value of such summative assessment is signaling if students have attained grade-level benchmarks and standards. Despite their popularity among the general public and their high costs, summative-assessment results are quite limited in terms of their ability to inform instruction and foster students' reading development. The data are often too old and distant and are often insufficiently specific to prove useful for instruction.

Summative assessment is also conducted to determine students' learning of course content. These assessments are done after learning is assumed to have taken place and can include quizzes and tests given at the end of marking periods, units of learning, or lessons. In this sense, the summative assessment does inform instruction, describing what a student has yet to learn related to hoped-for outcomes. High-quality assessments allow for valid inferences about the nature of students' reading development. As such, summative assessment can inform an understanding of student attainment of lesson and unit goals, end-of-year learning outcomes, and reading standards. The key is balancing formative assessment—the assessment that helps best to know students and guide instruction—with summative assessment, which tells a story of student achievement and instructional effectiveness.

USING ASSESSMENTS TO ENCOURAGE STUDENTS' SELF-ASSESSMENT

An underappreciated purpose of reading assessment is to help students learn to do assessment on their own, as they become metacognitive and independent. As noted by David Whitebread and colleagues (2005): "The aim of a good teacher should, of course, be to make themselves redundant. If we are to properly educate others, we must enable them to become independent learners" (p. 40). Student readers thrive when they are provided with timely formative feedback to influence their learning and development. As they develop, the expectation is that students will become independent readers and gradually assume the ability to self-assess themselves. Self-assessment allows students to provide their own formative feedback. This key aspect of metacognition grows as a result of teaching reading assessment. A relatively straightforward path for students to develop self-assessment is to encourage reflective mindsets and metacognitive routines.

In many classrooms, students have assessment done to them, or for them. Assessment is a "black box" (Black & Wiliam, 2010), and students understand little of how it works. Part of the work in reading classrooms should focus on uncovering the "black box" and familiarizing students with the ways and means of assessment. When conducting reading assessment, it is important to ask, "What can students learn about reading assessment that contributes to their ability to 'do assessment' on their own?" When assessment is regularly shared and discussed with students, their initial use of assessment can be scaffolded, and then they can be helped to construct increasingly elaborate self-assessment routines. When teachers ask questions in class, and then explain why these questions were asked, this shows students how their responses are evaluated. When scoring rubrics are used with clear and comprehensible descriptions of how grades and scores are earned, students are helped to better understand how reading is evaluated. This is part of the "uncovering" of the mystique of assessment.

Comprehension monitoring, an essential aspect of self-assessment, helps students determine if their reading is creating meaning. This monitoring is guided by questions like, "Does that make sense?" "Is there a problem?" and "What is the problem?" that are posed as students read. Over time and with experience, students can internalize these questions, developing self-assessment independence. Also, these seemingly simple comprehension-monitoring questions can evolve into complex self-assessment routines. Imagine the 1st-grade reader who consistently asks the three above questions moving through middle school and high school, regularly elaborating on the self-assessment process. Over the school year, and over the student's entire elementary school career, the rudimentary self-assessment checklist evolves into more detailed and sophisticated metacognitive routines. For example, a subsequent checklist could include the following:

- ☐ I remind myself why I am reading.
- ☐ I check to see if what I read makes sense.
- ☐ I focus on the goal of my reading while I read.
- ☐ I check to see if I can summarize sentences and paragraphs.
- ☐ If reading gets hard, I ask myself if there are any problems.
- ☐ I try to identify the problem.
- ☐ I try to fix the problem.
- ☐ When the problem is fixed, I get back to my reading, making sure I understand what I've read so far.

Teachers also model the use of the checklist by asking related questions of themselves when reading aloud to the students and thinking aloud about why they ask the questions and their answers to the questions. This predictable presentation of self-assessment routines can help set developing readers on a healthy path to self-assessment. Teachers do not give up their responsibility to conduct classroom-based reading assessments when they promote student self-assessment. Rather, they look for opportunities when using assessments to help students learn to do assessment themselves. Promoting self-assessment is imperative, for if in all the teaching related to reading, students do not begin to learn how to do self-assessment, they will not become truly independent readers.

ASSESSING AFFECTIVE AND CONATIVE FACTORS INFLUENCING READING ACHIEVEMENT

Accomplished student reading is the result of the complex interaction of diverse abilities and characteristics. Traditionally, reading assessment focuses on cognitive factors that are central to students' reading success: we assess readers' phonemic awareness and phonics development, as well as their fluency, listening comprehension, vocabulary development, and reading comprehension. As students grow as readers, assessments increasingly focus on what students understand from their reading and how they use this understanding in related tasks (National Assessment Governing Board, 2020). Representative assessments for measuring this cognitive development include Running Records, informal reading inventories, teacher questioning, end-of-unit quizzes, and any number of commercially published standardized reading tests. That these assessments focus on cognition is all well and good. However, when assessment is limited to evaluating only cognitive strategies and skills, it fails to describe students' reading development in full, and opportunities to further support students' reading growth are missed. Specifically, readers' metacognition, which helps students set goals, monitor progress, and manage reading, is necessary for independent and successful reading. Also, affective reader characteristics including motivation and attitude, and conative characteristics including self-efficacy and agency, are worthy of the attention provided by assessment.

Motivation and Engagement

Research describes that the effect of reading instruction on reading achievement is mediated by students' reading motivation (Guthrie, Wigfield, & You, 2012)—motivation matters. Cummins (2016) determined that the negative effects of socioeconomic disadvantage can be "pushed back" in schools and classrooms where students have access to a rich print environment and become actively engaged with literacy. Further, international assessments have determined that "engagement in reading can be a consequence, as well as a cause, of higher reading skill, but the evidence suggests that these two factors are mutually reinforcing" (Organisation for Economic Co-operation and Development, 2004, p. 8). In essence, reading research describes what insightful classroom teachers have long known: motivation and engagement strongly influence student readers' development. Irwin, Meltzer, and Dukes (2007) put it this way: "Motivation and engagement do not constitute a 'warm and fuzzy' extra component of efforts to improve literacy. These interrelated elements are a primary vehicle for improving literacy" (p. 31).

It is not a question of whether motivation and engagement should be assessed; rather, it is a matter of choosing from the no less than 16 scales and questionnaires that are available for assessing students' motivation and engagement (Davis et al., 2018).

Following are sample items from the Motivation to Read Profile-Revised (MRP-R) (Malloy et al., 2013) and the Elementary Reading Attitude Survey (ERAS) (McKenna et al., 1995). The MRP-R includes the following items:

> I think spending time reading is:
> Really boring
> Boring
> Great
> Really great
>
> Reading is:
> Very easy for me
> Kind of easy for me
> Kind of hard for me
> Very hard for me

The ERAS presents questions and statements such as "How do you feel when the teacher asks you questions about what you read?" and "How do you feel about reading for fun at home?," followed by four expressions of the cartoon cat character Garfield. Students circle the appropriate emotional image over a range from enthusiastic to uninterested. These assessments are psychometrically sound and provide valid and reliable data that describe the nature of students' reading motivation, along with exposing situational details that can enhance or detract from reading experiences.

Readers of this chapter are encouraged to scrutinize both the MRP-R and ERAS to judge their value in helping to understand students' reading motivations. Note that each of these assessments demands time that is often at a premium in classrooms, and that using these assessments may require advocating for "room" to do so in an already crowded assessment arena. However, use of an entire survey or

profile—or use of items that teachers select based on the item's ability to provide key information—should complement the information gathered from observing and listening to students. Indeed, assessing motivation with such formalized approaches is most often initiated because interactions with particular students indicate a potential lack of motivation.

Self-Efficacy

A second influence on reading development and achievement is self-efficacy. Like motivation and engagement, self-efficacy is deserving of assessment attention. Do student readers expect to succeed? Do they believe in themselves as readers? Students' self-efficacy determines the answers to these questions, and as Pajares (2005) reminds us: "Clearly, it is not simply a matter of how capable you are; it is also a matter of how capable you believe you are" (p. 343).

Talented readers read with the assurance that self-efficacy brings—they believe that they can succeed (Solheim, 2011). Self-efficacy is born of a history of succeeding as a reader, as past experiences greatly influence willingness and belief related to reading. While assessment related to readers' self-efficacy is not as developed as that of motivation and engagement, there are recent and compelling developments in the field. The Reading Self-Efficacy Questionnaire (Carroll & Fox, 2017) focuses on children's beliefs about their capabilities as readers when they are presented with common classroom situations. For example, students are asked to rate themselves (and thereby indicate the nature of their self-efficacy) on a scale of 1 ("Very certain I cannot do") to 7 ("Very certain I can do") in relation to the following:

- Reading out loud in front of the class
- Continuing to read even when I find it difficult
- Sounding out a word that I find hard to read
- Reading on my own without an adult's help

Like motivation and engagement, self-efficacy shows itself in relation to students' enthusiasm for reading, belief in self as a reader, and confidence when reading. The observant teacher's knowledge of a student's indicated self-efficacy challenges can be complemented by the Reading Self-Efficacy

Questionnaire, in full form or with particular items selected by the teacher. The information yielded can help the teacher pinpoint self-efficacy challenges and then design reading instruction and environments that support the indicated need.

Metacognition

A third aspect of students' reading development that deserves assessment attention is metacognition, which is closely related to the idea of student self-assessment discussed above. All accomplished readers know the power of metacognition because it lies at the heart of success. Decades of research describe metacognition as it promotes academic learning (Paris & Winograd, 1990) and improves reading comprehension (Borkowski & Turner, 1990). Further, even struggling readers can learn and use comprehension monitoring strategies (Palincsar & Brown, 1984). Earlier in this chapter, we proposed that a powerful and innovative use of reading assessment lies in teaching students to "do assessment" on their own. Focused assessment that describes students' metacognitive strengths and needs can expedite the process of learning to do assessment and becoming an independent reader. To investigate students' metacognitive development, the Metacognitive Awareness of Reading Strategies Inventory-Revised (MARSI) (Mokhtari, Dimitrov, & Reichard, 2018), which focuses on students' strategy and situation-specific metacognition, can be used. For example, using the MARSI, teachers learn about students' metacognition in relation to specific reading behaviors such as:

- I preview the text to see what it's about before reading it.
- I check my understanding when I come across conflicting information.
- When text becomes difficult, I pay closer attention to what I'm reading.
- When text becomes difficult, I re-read to increase my understanding.

What successful student readers need, beyond cognitive strategies and skills and sufficient background knowledge, is well researched. As research describes how various factors influence reading development and achievement, assessment must evolve to measure these influences. It is fortunate that ongoing efforts have yielded assessments that describe motivation and engagement, self-efficacy, and metacognition, and how they operate in all students' reading. Effective reading assessment programs will include a focus on these powerful factors using or guided by such questions and items as those reviewed above.

ASSESSING ONLINE READING: NAVIGATION, HYPERTEXT, AND MULTIMODAL READING STRATEGIES

The very nature of reading, in school and out, is changing (Leu et al., 2004; New London Group, 1996). Online reading is increasingly featured, as students construct, communicate, and negotiate meanings with digital texts (Lankshear & Knobel, 2011). There are seeming advantages to reading online: Users have access to vast amounts of information, and information is presented in multimodal forms, using images, written words, audio, and videos that support readers' comprehension. However, online reading is often complex (Afflerbach & Cho, 2009; Fabos, 2008), and this has important implications for assessment. Above and beyond comprehending texts, savvy Internet readers must determine the provenance of text and the accuracy of claims and statements contained in text. They must investigate the trustworthiness of authors. Student readers must also strategically manage the vast universe of texts yielded by Internet searches and keep track of their click-throughs and prior moves. Therefore, it is imperative for teachers to both teach and assess relevant online reading strategies as students comprehend and use the information on the Internet to accomplish their reading goals. While traditional and digital reading share many strategies (Afflerbach & Cho, 2009), the latter requires students who are adept at *navigation*, *hypertext reading*, and *multimodal reading* strategies.

Navigation refers to searching and finding information on the Internet. It is often conceptualized as a gate-opening skill, as it is required for locating the information or texts with which students construct understanding (Leu et al., 2013). Online navigation strategies include

- Determining the appropriate search terms and routes to access the information (Salmerón, Kintsch, & Cañas, 2006)

- Searching for goal-relevant information spaces (Cho, 2014)
- Modifying search terms or using different search functions (Rasmusson & Eklund, 2013)
- Using prior knowledge of website structure, hyperlink, or the topic

During the navigation process of realizing and constructing potential texts to read, strategic readers also work to reduce the levels of uncertainty while maintaining focus on the task (Afflerbach & Cho, 2009).

Hypertext refers to "a digital document that includes links to related documents, creating a network of information" (Bråten et al., 2016, p. 89). In accordance with navigation strategies, students must know how to read and use hyperlinks to ably navigate Internet information spaces. Readers need to know how hyperlinks work, how intertextual connections are made (Cho et al., 2018), how to infer and anticipate where the link might send them (Coiro & Dobler, 2007), and how to strategically select the order of reading (Salmerón et al., 2006).

Multimodal reading reflects the evolving nature of digital texts on the Internet, with information presented in different modes (Daly & Unsworth, 2011; Støle et al., 2020), including written language images, videos, audios, and diagrams (Kress, 2003). While multimodality can help student readers construct meaning, they need specific strategies for gathering information from and across modes (Fitzgerald & Palincsar, 2017), finding relationships between modes to construct meanings (Casey, 2012), or moving within and between multiple webpages or revisiting modes to synthesize and understand meanings (Cho & Afflerbach, 2015). Because digital Internet reading demands new strategies, teachers need new assessments to inform instruction. Fortunately, performance assessments allow a focus on the array of digital reading strategies used to construct meaning, the product—or comprehension—that results from using strategies, and the utilization of knowledge that student readers gain from reading.

Digital reading on the Internet often focuses on problem-based inquiry (Leu et al., 2013; Omerbašić, 2015). Readers search the Internet and use reading strategies to find information and construct meaning; assessing online reading strategies in these contexts helps describe our student readers' development

(Alexander, 2006; Cho, 2014). Performance assessments are well-suited for this purpose because they take readers beyond multiple-choice and short constructed response items to detailed alignment of the assessment with complex texts and tasks (Shavelson et al., 1991). Further, performance assessment of online reading allows for comparison of students with detailed, expected outcomes. Performance assessments can also describe *what* students understand from reading and *how* they use what is understood (Afflerbach, 2017; Baxter & Glaser, 1998). Performance assessments offer authenticity—especially compared to multiple-choice reading tests—as reading text and task combinations involve students in authentic contexts and problem-solving situations (Frey & Schmitt, 2007).

For example, the Online Reading Comprehension Assessment (ORCA) (Castek et al., 2015) is a performance-based assessment that examines students' online reading strategies, including searching, locating, evaluating, synthesizing, and communicating online information. Cho et al. (2018) assessed students' open (that is, without imposed parameters) strategic Internet reading, focusing on the strategies of information location, meaning-making, source evaluation, and self-monitoring. These studies demonstrated that, if properly used, performance assessments provide a valid venue for evaluating students' online reading strategies.

In addition, multimodal reading strategies can also be assessed using performance assessments. Rubrics for multimodal reading may include categories that record comprehension of various modes and design features in the multimodal text as well as written language comprehension (Serafini et al., 2020). Teachers can keep track of the modes students focus on and note how they gather and synthesize meanings from modes to accomplish the task. Students can explain what navigation, hypertext, or multimodal reading strategies they used while using learning logs. Assessment with such a process orientation can complement the product orientation of performance assessments and tests. This reflective process can also help teachers evaluate how familiar each student is with the concept of online reading strategies and so inform their online reading strategy instructions. In sum, rubrics, observations, and students' products (e.g., short answers, questions, reflections) jointly show the use of strategies and its result throughout the performance assessment. (For further information on performance-based assessment, see Chapter 15 in this book.)

SCENARIO-BASED ASSESSMENT

The performance assessments described in the previous section are an important precursor to scenario-based assessments (SBA) (Zhang et al., 2019). This approach to reading assessment delivers a set of tasks and items that provide a platform for measuring a range of often demanding reading skills, while simultaneously affording the potential to increase the instructional relevance of the assessment. SBAs in reading typically include principles and techniques that distinguish them from other types of assessments. For example, SBAs:

- provide an authentic purpose for reading
- place reading in context for completing a set of interrelated activities that may move from more guided to independent performance
- often require the integration and evaluation of a wide range of diverse reading sources
- can provide scaffolds (e.g., a graphic organizer for an analysis of text structures) and guidelines (e.g., tips for summary writing) to help students better understand and operate in accord with the target performance in the assessment (O'Reilly & Sabatini, 2013; Sabatini et al., 2018; Sabatini et al., 2020).

Due to their flexible nature, SBAs can have at their core the texts, tasks, and items that reflect the social aspects of literacy and learning, such as engaging with peers to clarify an understanding of text or reviewing and evaluating peer writing. As such, SBAs have the goal of situating reading assessment in authentic literacy contexts, thereby enhancing the validity of the outcome of reading assessment. Using these principles, SBAs may broaden the range of interactions, perspectives, and information used by student readers as they are assessed. Ultimately, the key aims of scenario-based reading assessments are to measure 21st-century reading ability as situated in authentic contexts while simultaneously supporting reading development and instructional usefulness (Song & Sparks, 2019).

An example of scenario-based assessment that focuses on reading is the Global Integrated Scenario-Based Assessment (GISA; Educational Testing Service, 2015). GISA has primary emphasis on reading related to benchmark performances (e.g., a complex state standard in reading/language arts), and frequently is designed using computer delivery and cognitive science concepts from kindergarten through 12th grade. GISA is intended to provide a detailed account of students' reading performance and is designed primarily to assess higher-order reading skills (e.g., the synthesis, assessment, and application of information that is gained from comprehending text). Although not considered as a direct part of the reading construct, performance moderators that impact reading (e.g., students' background knowledge, metacognition, self-regulation, motivation, and reading strategies) are also applied to GISA (Shore et al., 2017).

As highlighted in Shore et al. (2017), in GISA, test takers are presented with a purpose, such as determining if a community garden is feasible and beneficial for their neighborhood, in relation to reading a set of related sources (e.g., a plant and seed catalog, monthly temperature charts, narrative accounts of creating bountiful gardens, and a written inventory of "must-have" gardening implements and materials). These sources involve traditional print such as the narratives of creating gardens, and digital print related to temperatures, emails, and comments related to commercial gardening supplies. To assess test takers' performance, they are first asked to write a synopsis of the assigned readings. After the test takers write their synopses, simulated peers or avatars share their written samples of text synopses and highlight areas of the assessed students' writing that can be improved. The students being assessed then analyze and use the feedback provided by their avatar peers to further revise their thinking and writing. Lastly, the test takers are asked to correct any errors noted. Such methods of sequencing and scaffolding help to collect more information about students' reading competencies and model strategic reading behaviors. In this way, the SBA can serve as a tool for learning (Bennett & Gitomer, 2009).

ARTIFICIAL INTELLIGENCE-BASED ASSESSMENT

Artificial intelligence (AI) is an ability of automated systems to perform tasks that until recently required and revolved around human information processing.

Detailed, valid, and reliable reading assessment is demanding of time, resources, and effort, and teachers often face a tradeoff between offering instruction and devoting time to evaluating student skills (Bernstein et al., 2020). For example, complex performance assessments, accompanied by lengthy and detailed scoring rubrics, can yield extremely valuable information to inform instruction and student grading. However, the costs in terms of teacher time and development of assessment expertise may be prohibitive. Thus, any opportunity to reduce the costs (in terms of the time, resources, and effort spent on assessment) is worthy of consideration. AI has the potential to improve assessment-related grading and decision-making and to relieve the burden of time-consuming human tasks. Careful and reliable assessment of students' reading is one of these tasks.

Given the early stage of artificial intelligence (AI)-based literacy assessment, few empirical findings related to AI-based literacy assessment have been reported. However, narrative accounts indicate that initial efforts to coordinate AI technology with literacy assessment are promising. Bernstein et al. (2020) illustrate how machine learning is applied to build AI into an automated oral reading fluency (ORF) test, Moby.Read®. The Moby.Read® assessment from Analytic Measures Incorporated (https://www.analyticmeasures.com/moby-read) was developed to provide teachers with an easy way to get accurate ORF measures for children in grades 1 through 5. It measures four components of reading skill (comprehension, accuracy, reading rate, and expression) on leveled text. Another attempt at AI-based assessment is Lexplore (https://www.lexplore.com/), a web app that is powered by eye-tracking and artificial intelligence technologies. According to its promotion webpage, this unique high-tech process provides teachers with real-time data for intervention that directly correlates to a student's reading capability. The app is designed to help teachers quickly identify a student's reading level. Moreover, it is designed to quickly identify students with reading challenges so teachers can act immediately to get them on track to reading at or above grade level. The long-term success of these and other applications is not yet clear, but undoubtedly there will be more entrants in the field. For more discussion of literacy assessment via AI, Jiao's and Lissitz's (2020) edited book, *Application of Artificial Intelligence to Assessment*, treats this in several chapters.

AUGMENTED, VIRTUAL, AND MIXED REALITY-BASED ASSESSMENT: LOOKING AHEAD

Recent technological developments are changing the ways people experience physical and virtual environments. Specifically, virtual reality (VR) is likely to play a key role in numerous industries, including education (Merchant et al., 2014). Recent reports show that sales of VR head-mounted displays (HMD) have, for the first time, exceeded one million in a quarter (Alto, 2017); the value of VR devices sold is expected to have increased from $1.5 billion in 2017 to $9.1 billion by 2021 (CCSInsight, 2017); importantly, younger generations are the most interested in VR technology (Greenlight Insights, 2015). In addition to VR, augmented reality (AR) and mixed reality (MR) were ranked in the top 10 strategic trends for 2018, and the sales of these technologies in 2020 were forecasted to be 21 times higher than in 2016 (from $2.9 billion to $61.3 billion) (Superdata Research, 2017).

Despite their potential, the use of augmented, virtual, and mixed reality (AVMR) in literacy assessment is still at an early stage. Rosen (2020) highlights some significant potential applications for VR technologies in assessing and teaching adult learners' basic and advanced 21st-century digital literacy skills by facilitating more complicated and contextualized problem-solving tasks. McLauchlan and Farley (2019) reported an interesting use of VR technology and tablets for a low-level literacy and numeracy program targeting prisoners engaged in vocational education in New Zealand. This pilot project demonstrated that these technologies were engaging to learners. They developed their digital literacies while significantly improving their numeracy and literacy levels. Sample (2020) demonstrated the potential of AVMR technologies to reduce international students' library anxiety while enhancing their information literacy. Al-Megren and Almutairi (2018) introduced a mobile AR application to support the literacy development of Arabic children with hearing impairments. Developed mobile AR application includes Word and Sign, fingerspelling, and pictures. A series of tasks were conducted to assess the literacy development of children. The findings showed that participants who were taught spelling and vocabulary via the AR application completed significantly more tasks successfully and with significantly fewer errors compared to participants who were taught the new words via a traditional approach.

CONCLUSION

This chapter was begun with the claim that assessment is at an inflection point. Beyond the usual valid and reliable measures of phonemic awareness, phonics, fluency, vocabulary, and comprehension, there are many assessment opportunities and challenges. Reading assessments should not be limited to the measure of cognitive strategy and skill—although these foci of assessment will always be needed to judge reading achievement—and an inventory of assessments helps to determine coverage, gaps, and redundancies in an entire reading assessment program. High-quality reading programs include an optimal mix of formative and summative reading assessment. Further, assessment has additional critical roles. Assessment should be used to help teach students to "do assessment" for themselves, as self-assessment is a mandatory hallmark of successful, independent student readers. Reading development is not only about cognition. Powerful factors including motivation and engagement, self-efficacy, and metacognition all influence students' reading development and performance, and evaluating them should be a priority.

The dynamic and evolving nature of assessing online and digital reading was described. Some reading strategies and skills (e.g., reading critically) remain essential as student readers transition from traditional to digital print environments, while new strategies (e.g., managing the universe of reading information on the Internet; vetting texts found on the Internet for accuracy) demand new approaches to assessment. The performance assessments and scenario-based assessments described in this chapter offer a glimpse of this new generation of reading assessment. Going forward, superior reading assessment programs will sample from across the array of assessment goals and means described in this chapter. These assessment programs will focus first and foremost on the different audiences and purposes for assessment, and gain guidance from this focus.

REFLECTION QUESTIONS

1. Many reading assessment programs focus exclusively on cognitive aspects of student development. How might this exclusive focus shortchange students and teachers?
2. How can we use reading assessment to help students become metacognitive?
3. What are the benefits of conducting an inventory of the reading assessments used in your classroom, school, or district?

PROJECT ASSIGNMENT

Develop a reading assessment program that describes students' reading development and achievement; measures cognitive, affective and conative growth; and helps students learn to "do assessment" for themselves.

REFERENCES

Afflerbach, P. (2017). *Understanding and using reading assessment, K–12.* ASCD.

Afflerbach, P., & Cho, B. Y. (2009). Identifying and describing constructively responsive comprehension strategies in new and traditional forms of reading. In S. Israel & G. Duffy (Eds.), *Handbook of research on reading comprehension* (pp. 69–90). Routledge.

Alexander, P. A. (2006). *Psychology in learning and instruction.* Prentice-Hall.

Al-Megren, S., & Almutairi, A. (2018). Assessing the effectiveness of an augmented reality application for the literacy development of Arabic children with hearing impairments. In P.-L. P. Rau (Ed.), *Cross-cultural design: Applications in cultural heritage, creativity and social development* (pp. 3–18). Springer.

Alto, P. (2017). *Media alert: Virtual reality headset shipments top 1 million for the first time.* Canalys. https://www.canalys.com/newsroom/media-alert-virtual-reality-headset-shipmentstop-1-million-first-time

Baxter, G. P., & Glaser, R. (1998). Investigating the cognitive complexity of science assessments. *Educational Measurement: Issues and Practice, 17*(3), 37–45.

Bennett, R. E., & Gitomer, D. H. (2009). Transforming K–12 assessment: Integrating accountability testing, formative assessment and professional support. In C. Wyatt-Smith & J. J. Cumming (Eds.), *Educational assessment in the 21st century* (pp. 43–62). Springer.

Bernstein, J., Cheng, J., Balogh, J., & Downey, R. (2020). Artificial intelligence for scoring oral reading fluency. In H. Jiao & R. W. Lissitz (Eds.), *Application of artificial intelligence to assessment* (pp. 51–76). Information Age Publishing.

Black, P., & Wiliam, D. (2010). Inside the black box: Raising standards through classroom assessment. *Phi Delta Kappan, 92*(1), 81–90.

Borkowski, J. G., & Turner, L. A. (1990). Transsituational characteristics of metacognition. In W. Schneider & F. E. Weinert (Eds.), *Interactions among aptitudes, strategies, and knowledge in cognitive performance* (pp. 159–176). Springer-Verlag.

Bråten, I., Braasch, J. L., & Salmerón, L. (2016). Reading multiple and non-traditional texts: New opportunities and new challenges. In E. Moje, P. Afflerbach, P. Enciso, & N. Lesaux (Eds.), *Handbook of reading research* (5th ed., pp.79–98). Routledge.

Carroll, J., & Fox, A. (2017). Reading self-efficacy predicts word reading but not comprehension in both girls and boys. *Frontiers in Psychology, 7*, 1–9.

Casey, H. (2012). Multimodal learning clubs: Students in multimodal learning clubs use a variety of texts to learn important content. *Middle School Journal, 44*(2), 39–48.

Castek, J., Coiro, J., Henry, L. A., Leu, D. J., & Hartman, D. K. (2015). Research on instruction and assessment in the new literacies of online research and comprehension. In S. R. Parris & K. Headley (Eds.), *Comprehension instruction: Research-based best practices* (3rd ed., pp. 324–344). Guilford Press.

CCSInsight. (2017, February 23). *Clear potential for virtual reality headsets after a slow start.* https://www.ccsinsight.com/press/company-news/2919-clear-potential-for-virtual-reality-headsets-after-a-slow-start/

Cho, B. Y. (2014). Competent adolescent readers' use of Internet reading strategies: A think-aloud study. *Cognition and Instruction, 32*(3), 253–289.

Cho, B. Y., & Afflerbach, P. (2015). Reading on the Internet: Realizing and constructing potential texts. *Journal of Adolescent & Adult Literacy, 58*(6), 504–517.

Cho, B. Y., Afflerbach, P., & Han, H. (2018). Strategic processing in accessing, comprehending, and using multiple sources online. In J. L. G. Braasch, I. Bråten, & M. T. McCrudden (Eds.), *Handbook of multiple source use* (pp. 133–150). Routledge.

Coiro, J., & Dobler, E. (2007). Exploring the online reading comprehension strategies used by sixth-grade skilled readers to search for and locate information on the Internet. *Reading Research Quarterly, 42*(2), 214–257.

Cummins, J. (2016). Language differences that influence reading development. In P. Afflerbach (Ed.), *Handbook of individual differences in reading: Reader, text, and context* (pp. 233–244). Routledge.

Daly, A., & Unsworth, L. (2011). Analysis and comprehension of multimodal texts. *Australian Journal of Language and Literacy, 34*(1), 61.

Davis, M., Tonks, S., Hock, M., Wang, W., & Rodriguez, A. (2018). A review of reading motivation scales. *Reading Psychology, 39*(2), 121–187.

Educational Testing Service. (2015). *Reading for understanding.* http://www.ets.org/research/topics/reading_for_understanding/

Fabos, B. (2008). The price of information. In C. Lankshear, D. J. Leu, J. Coiro., & M. Knobel (Eds.), *Handbook of research on new literacies* (pp. 839–870). Lawrence Erlbaum Associates.

Fitzgerald, M. S., & Palincsar, A. S. (2017). Peer-mediated reading and writing in a digital, multimodal environment. *Reading & Writing Quarterly, 33*(4), 309–326.

Frey, B. B., & Schmitt, V. L. (2007). Coming to terms with classroom assessment. *Journal of Advanced Academics, 18*(3), 402–423.

Greenlight Insights. (2015, December 4). *Virtual reality consumer report.* https://greenlightinsights.com/2015-vr-consumer-report-infographic/

Guthrie, J. T., Wigfield, A., & You, W. (2012). Instructional contexts for engagement and achievement in reading. In S. L. Christenson, A. L. Reschly, & C. Wylie (Eds.), *Handbook of research on student engagement* (pp. 601–634). Springer Science + Business Media.

Irwin, J., Meltzer, J., & Dukes, M. (2007). *Taking action on adolescent literacy: An implementation guide for school leaders.* ASCD.

Jiao, H., & Lissitz, R. W. (Eds.). (2020). *Application of artificial intelligence to assessment.* Information Age Publishing.

Kress, G. (2003). *Literacy in the new media age.* Psychology Press.

Lankshear, C., & Knobel, M. (2011). *New literacies.* McGraw-Hill Education.

Leu, D. J., Kinzer, C. K., Coiro, J. L., & Cammack, D. W. (2004). Toward a theory of new literacies emerging from the Internet and other information and communication technologies. In R. B. Ruddell & N. Unrau (Eds.), *Theoretical models and processes of reading* (5th ed., pp. 1570–1613). Routledge.

Leu, D. J., Kinzer, C. K., Coiro, J., Castek, J., & Henry, L. A. (2013). New literacies and the new literacies of online reading comprehension: A dual level theory. In D. Alvermann, N. J. Unrau, & R. B. Ruddell (Eds.), *Theoretical models and processes of reading* (6th ed., pp. 1150–1181). Routledge.

Malloy, J., Marinak, B., Gambrell, L. & Mazzoni, S. (2013). Assessing motivation to read: The Motivation to Read Profile-Revised. *The Reading Teacher, 67*(4), 273–282.

McKenna, M., Kear, D., & Ellsworth, R. (1995). Children's attitudes toward reading: A national survey. *Reading Research Quarterly, 30*(4), 934–956.

McLauchlan, J., & Farley, H. (2019). Fast cars and fast learning: Using virtual reality to learn literacy and numeracy in prison. *Journal for Virtual Worlds Research, 12*(3), 1–11.

Merchant, Z., Goetz, E. T., Cifuentes, L., Keeney-Kennicutt, W., & Davis, T. J. (2014). Effectiveness of virtual reality-based instruction on students' learning outcomes in K–12 and higher education: A meta-analysis. *Computers & Education, 70,* 29–40.

Mokhtari, K., Dimitrov, D. M., & Reichard, C. A. (2018). Revising the Metacognitive Awareness of Reading Strategies Inventory (MARSI) and testing for factorial invariance. *Studies in Second Language Learning and Teaching, 8*(2), 219–246. https://doi.org/10.14746/ssllt.2018.8.2.3

National Assessment Governing Board. (2020). *Framework of the National Assessment of Educational Progress.*

The New London Group. (1996). A pedagogy of multiliteracies: Designing social futures. *Harvard Educational Review, 66,* 60–93.

Omerbašić, D. (2015). Literacy as a translocal practice: Digital multimodal literacy practices among girls resettled as refugees. *Journal of Adolescent & Adult Literacy, 58*(6), 472–481.

O'Reilly, T., & Sabatini, J. (2013). Reading for understanding: How performance moderators and scenarios impact assessment design. *ETS Research Report Series, 2013*(2), i–47.

Organisation for Economic Co-operation and Development. (2004). *Messages from PISA* 2000.

Pajares, F. (2005). Self-efficacy during childhood and adolescence: Implications for teachers and parents. In F. Pajares & T. Urdan (Eds.), *Self-efficacy beliefs of adolescents* (pp. 339–367). Information Age.

Palincsar, A., & Brown, A. (1984). Reciprocal teaching of comprehension-fostering and comprehension-monitoring activities. *Cognition and Instruction, 1*(2), 117–175.

Paris, S., & Winograd, P. (1990). Promoting metacognition and motivation of exceptional children. *Remedial and Special Education, 11*(6), 7–15.

Rasmusson, M., & Eklund, M. (2013). It's easier to read on the Internet—you just click on what you want to read . . . . *Education and Information Technologies, 18*(3), 401–419.

Rosen, D. J. (2020). Assessing and teaching adult learners' basic and advanced 21st century digital literacy skills. *Adult Literacy Education, 2*(1), 73–75.

Sabatini, J., O'Reilly, T., Wang, Z., & Dreier, K. (2018). Scenario-based assessment of multiple source use.

In J. L. G. Braasch, I. Bråten, & M. T. McCrudden (Eds.), *Handbook of multiple use source* (pp. 447–466). Routledge.

Sabatini, J., O'Reilly, T., Weeks, J., & Wang, Z. (2020). Engineering a twenty-first century reading comprehension assessment system utilizing scenario-based assessment techniques. *International Journal of Testing, 20*(1), 1–23.

Salmerón, L., Kintsch, W., & Cañas, J. (2006). Coherence or interest as basis for improving hypertext comprehension. *Information Design Journal, 14*(1), 45–55.

Sample, A. (2020). Using augmented and virtual reality in information literacy instruction to reduce library anxiety in non-traditional and international students. *Information Technology and Libraries, 39*(1). https://doi.org/10.6017/ital.v39i1.11723

Serafini, F., Moses, L., Kachorsky, D., & Rylak, D. (2020). Incorporating multimodal literacies into classroom-based reading assessment. *The Reading Teacher, 74*(3), 285–296.

Shavelson, R. J., Baxter, G. P., & Pine, J. (1991). Performance assessment in science. *Applied Measurement in Education, 4*(4), 347–362.

Shore, J. R., Wolf, M. K., O'Reilly, T., & Sabatini, J. P. (2017). Measuring 21st-century reading comprehension through scenario-based assessments. In M. K. Wolf & Y. G. Butler (Eds.), *English language proficiency assessments for young learners* (pp. 234–252). Routledge.

Solheim, O. J. (2011). The impact of reading self-efficacy and task value on reading comprehension scores in different item formats. *Reading Psychology, 32*(1), 1–27. doi:10.1080/02702710903256601

Song, Y., & Sparks, J. R. (2019). Measuring argumentation skills through a game-enhanced scenario-based assessment. *Journal of Educational Computing Research, 56*(8), 1324–1344.

Støle, H., Mangen, A., & Schwippert, K. (2020). Assessing children's reading comprehension on paper and screen: A mode-effect study. *Computers & Education, 151,* 103861.

Superdata Research. (2017). *Virtual reality market and consumers.* https://strivesponsorship.com/2018/02/03/superdata-2017-year-in-review-digital-games-and-interactive-media/

Vygotsky, L. (1978). *Mind in society.* Cambridge University Press.

Whitebread, D., Anderson, H., Coltman, P., Page, C., Pasternam, D., & Mehta, S. (2005). Developing independent learning in the early years. *Education, 33*(1), 40–50. doi: 10.1080/03004270585200081

Zhang, M., van Rijn, P. W., Deane, P., & Bennett, R. E. (2019). Scenario-based assessments in writing: An experimental study. *Educational Assessment, 24*(2), 73–90.

CHAPTER 11

Evaluation and Change in Literacy Programs

Using the PASS Model for School and District Improvement

Misty Sailors and James V. Hoffman, with Jimmie Walker and Yadira Palacios

- Evaluations of schoolwide literacy programs can be organized around guiding principles that are centered on data-driven evaluation.
- All school stakeholders must be involved in the evaluation process, and the process must build on the strengths of existing programs.
- A culture of change within a district is imperative for innovations to take root and be effective.

Alamo Heights Independent School District (AHISD) is one of the most innovative districts in the San Antonio metropolitan area. As one of the smallest school districts in the state, it is made up of one early childhood center, two elementary schools, one junior school, one high school, and one alternative high school. It supports nearly 5,000 students, of whom 2% are African American, 40% Hispanic, 52% White, 3% Asian, and 2% other. Although the community has historically been one of the wealthier ones in the metropolitan area, a growing number of students in the district are "economically disadvantaged" (20%). Six percent of the students are English Learners, 8% are bilingual, 9% receive special education services, and 8% receive gifted and talented services. In addition, the district has a low (7%) mobility rate.

Teachers in the district average 14.1 years of experience, and 53% of teachers in the district have an advanced degree. Although all schools in the district meet the expectations of the state on its accountability measures, AHISD struggles with a discrepancy between scores on the reading and writing assessments for 4th- and 7th-graders. Reading scores typically are higher than writing scores. AHISD administrators and teachers saw district-wide evaluation as a means to understand these discrepancies and to create leverage for using local expertise and resources to support change. The Purposes, Actions, Students, and Standards (PASS) model (Hoffman & Sailors, 2014) was adopted as one evaluation tool. This chapter outlines the principles of that model and details the ways in which one district, AHISD, implemented the model as part of its evaluation process, with the support of the authors of the model.

DEVELOP RELATIONSHIPS TO SUPPORT CHANGE

Principle: Evaluation and change are highly personal. No claims of "objectivity" or "data-driven decision-making" can circumvent the reality that significant change is never easy. People change first, then programs. School leaders and change facilitators cannot rush evaluation, but rather have to take time to develop a positive relationship with faculty and the rest of the school community. Initial efforts by school leaders should include taking time to talk to, interact with, and observe teachers, and to help teachers develop an understanding of the strengths that they bring to the school community. Leaders should value teachers' differences and create opportunities for them to build relationships of trust and respect through shared experiences. This may be accomplished through, for example, professional book clubs, the exploration of new children's literature, or attendance together at local or regional conferences. These experiences help to establish the understanding that program change is not about creating sameness, but rather about being responsive to learners' needs in a context where both students and teachers have individual differences.

Communities are also important. Effective schools are part of the community, and connections with parents can become a strong support for change. Communication can be established through both formal structures and informal exchanges. For example, mini-workshops for parents and responses to parents' feedback about community needs will build important relationships with families.

At AHISD, the literacy reform initiative focused on writing, grew quickly because of the trust that already had been established in the 12-member leadership team. Initiated by a senior academic leader at one of the AHISD schools, the reform effort attracted teachers and administrators from across the campuses who shared an interest in the initiative, were willing to take on a leadership role, and were considered exemplary teachers. Several were associated with the local affiliate of the National Writing Project, others were workshop presenters and consultants in the metropolitan area, and one teacher was a professional writer. They became the Literacy Leadership team for this initiative.

BUILD CAPACITY FOR CHANGE

Principle: The more those who are expected to change are involved in shaping the change process, the more sustainable the change effort will be. There is a tension described in the research literature on change that contrasts the benefits of top-down and bottom-up approaches. *Top-down* change tends to rely on mandates and is usually quite specific in terms of the kinds of changes that are to be made. These are the kinds of changes that are often observed in schools. For example, a school district adopts a commercial program that all schools are expected to implement; a school district wants to target specific changes in the reading curriculum to raise performance on state-mandated, high-stakes tests; a federal grant requires the use of certain materials and teaching strategies; or a state mandates the inclusion of common standards. *Bottom-up* change tends to focus on individual, small-group, or schoolwide initiatives that grow out of the immediate school context. For example, a group of teachers might work to introduce book clubs into their daily teaching routine; the school has committed to increasing the amount of time devoted to writing; or parents and teachers develop a plan for coordinating volunteer work in classrooms to support struggling readers. All of these changes are important, and facilitators need to be responsive to both kinds of change efforts.

Bottom-up change efforts are about building capacity. The teaching community is invested in the process and develops a sense of ownership of the change effort. Bottom-up change efforts are effective because they reflect the needs and the strengths of the immediate context. Further, the teaching community develops the capacity to take control over the top-down mandates and shape them in strategic ways to the needs of the school. The victimized mentality of "What do I have to do now?" or "Here we go again!" is replaced with an attitude of "How can we make this work for us?" The school community becomes self-renewing.

Capacity building toward change is a process that requires patience and a view toward the long term. School leaders can spend their time trying to convince teachers that they should adopt outside priorities ("Just look at our test scores"), or they can start with something more modest as a goal that grows out of listening to teachers as they talk about perceived needs. Setting shared goals, establishing a plan, and working together in order to achieve a positive outcome are important for changes and capacity building. As a result, the capacity of the system to solve problems will grow.

SURVEY THE LITERACY PROGRAM

Principle: Begin program evaluations with rich descriptions of what is, not what should be. The best place to start a literacy program evaluation is with a survey. The literacy specialist facilitates the school survey but works closely with the Literacy Leadership Team to organize the survey. The entire faculty should be invested in the process. A school survey might focus on the entire literacy program in a school (expanded to include the other language arts), just a few grade levels, or some specific component of the program. A survey seeks to describe the Purposes, Actions, Students, and Standards (PASS):

> **Purposes:** What are the purposes and goals that guide the literacy program?
> **Actions:** What are the teachers and students doing and with what as a way of promoting students' progress toward the purposes of the program? What assessments are used to inform teaching?

> **Students:** What are the students learning (short-term and long-term)? What data are being gathered to document the learning? How is progress being documented?
> **Standards:** Do the goals, actions, and student assessments meet the expectations of stakeholders and professional organizations?

The processes for gathering the survey data will vary as a function of the area of focus. In the section that follows, the ways the Literacy Leadership Team at AHISD gathered data for their program are illustrated. While the team could have started with only the primary/elementary schools, work was done across all campuses.

Purposes: What Are the Goals for Literacy Instruction?

A description of purposes and goals is focused on uncovering the goals of the teachers, not of the materials (e.g., the basal goals), the district (the curriculum), or the state (the standards). The purposes may be stated in terms of broad learning outcomes, operationalized as performance standards, or some combination. The identification of the purposes for literacy instruction (here, specifically writing instruction) can be thought of as a process of consensus-building.

The survey was organized into questions related to (1) overarching goals for writing instruction and (2) aspects of instruction that supported the goals. Teachers were also asked to identify the ways in which their school, district, and community supported meeting the goals. Figure 11.1 lists the questions. Upon the completion of the survey, teachers were asked for their demographic information (i.e., name, school, position, subject taught, and language program).

Fifty-four teachers from all schools completed the open-ended, online Purposes Survey. Eleven overarching categories of purposes emerged from teachers' responses (see Figure 11.2). Because there were so many individual purposes and because the team wanted to build those individual purposes into something that simulated a consensus across the district, collapsed results of the Purposes Survey were used to create a Delphi Survey. Used often in educational research, the Delphi technique produces a "group view" by capturing the contributions of community members (Green, 2014). The Delphi Survey invited teachers to affirm, reject, and modify the purposes identified through the coding process (see Figure 11.3). In Part I, the Delphi

Figure 11.1. Questions on the Survey

Overarching question:

- What is your overarching goal for literacy instruction?

Specific to writing instruction:

- More specifically, what is your first goal for writing instruction?
- What is your second goal for writing instruction?
- What is your third goal for writing instruction?
- Do you have more goals? If so, note them here.

Instruction to support those goals:

- What is one aspect of your instruction that is supportive of the goals you listed above?
- What is another aspect of your instruction that is supportive of the goals you listed above?
- What is a third aspect of your instruction that is supportive of the goals you listed above?

Support systems to help you meet your goals:

- What are some ways your SCHOOL supports you in meeting the goals you listed?
- What are some ways in which your DISTRICT supports you in meeting the goals you listed?
- What are some additional supports you'd like to see?
- What are some ways your community supports you in meeting the goals you listed?
- What are some ways you'd like to see the community support you in addition to what they are currently doing?

Figure 11.2. Categories of "Purposes" and Examples from the Data

Category	Sample teacher statement
Identity	I want my students to view themselves as passionate, lifelong writers and readers who write for themselves and others on a regular basis.
Purpose	I want my students to write for various purposes in and out of school (e.g., communicate their ideas, their beliefs, and their learning).
Self-efficacy	I want my students to have self-efficacy and be knowledgeable, confident, empathetic, critical writers and readers.
Community	I want my students to participate in a community of writers who take risks together.
Clarity	I want my students to be able to elaborate, write with clarity, and use discipline-specific vocabulary.
Process	I want my students to value writing as a process (e.g., selecting a topic, drafting, revising, editing, and publishing).
Literacy processes	I want my students to value the connections between writing, reading, listening, speaking, and thinking.
Skills and strategies	I want my students to use the necessary skills, conventions, and strategies to be successful writers and readers.
Perception of writing	I want my students to perceive writing as a purposeful, meaningful, pleasurable, and rewarding act.
Growth mindset	I want my students to talk about their growth as writers and readers.
Engage socially and globally	I want my students to use writing for the transformation of their world.

Figure 11.3. Statements on the Delphi Survey

Part I: Essential Goals for Writing

Below are 11 goal statements condensed from the districtwide survey on writing. Please provide feedback on the statements to help prioritize the goals for student writing across the district by marking "yes" or "no" based on your purposes for your writing instruction.

Goal Statement	Yes, this is an essential goal for my instruction.	No, this is not an essential goal for my writing instruction.
1. **Purpose:** I want my students to write for various purposes in and out of school (e.g., communicate their ideas, their beliefs, and their learning).		
2. **Identity:** I want my students to view themselves as passionate, lifelong writers and readers who write for themselves and others on a regular basis.		
3. **Self-efficacy:** I want my students to have self-efficacy and be knowledgeable, confident, empathetic, critical writers and readers.		
4. **Community:** I want my students to participate in a community of writers who take risks together.		
5. **Clarity:** I want my students to be able to elaborate, write with clarity, and use discipline-specific vocabulary.		
6. **Process:** I want my students to value writing as a process (e.g., selecting a topic, drafting, revising, editing, and publishing).		
7. **Literacy Processes:** I want my students to value the connections between writing, reading, listening, speaking, and thinking.		
8. **Skills and Strategies:** I want my students to use the necessary skills, conventions, and strategies to be successful readers and writers.		
9. **Perception of Writing:** I want my students to perceive writing as a purposeful, meaningful, pleasurable, and rewarding act.		
10. **Growth Mindset:** I want my students to talk about their growth as writers and readers.		
11. **Engage Socially and Globally:** I want my students to use writing for the transformation of their world.		

Part II: Top Priorities for Student Writing

Please select your top 5 goals.

Goal Statement	First Priority	Second Priority	Third Priority	Fourth Priority	Fifth Priority
1. **Purpose:** I want my students to write for various purposes in and out school (e.g., communicate their ideas, their beliefs, and their learning).					
2. **Identity:** I want my students to view themselves as passionate, lifelong writers and readers who write for themselves and others on a regular basis.					
3. **Self-efficacy:** I want my students to have self-efficacy and be knowledgeable, confident, empathetic, critical writers and readers.					

(continued)

Figure 11.3. Statements on the Delphi Survey *(continued)*

Goal Statement	First Priority	Second Priority	Third Priority	Fourth Priority	Fifth Priority
4. **Community:** I want my students to participate in a community of writers who take risks together.					
5. **Clarity:** I want my students to be able to elaborate, write with clarity, and use discipline-specific vocabulary.					
6. **Process:** I want my students to value writing as a process (e.g., selecting a topic, drafting, revising, editing, and publishing).					
7. **Literacy Processes:** I want my students to value the connections between writing, connections between writing, reading, listening, speaking, and thinking.					
8. **Skills and Strategies:** I want my students to use the necessary skills, conventions, and strategies to be successful readers and writers.					
9. **Perception of Writing:** I want my students to perceive writing as a purposeful, meaningful, pleasurable, and rewarding act.					
10. **Growth Mindset:** I want my students to talk about their growth as writers and readers.					
11. **Engage Socially and Globally:** I want my students to use writing for the transformation of their world.					

Part III: Tell us more . . .

On which campus do you teach: _____

Your Role on Campus, Grade Level, Subjects, and Language Program: _____

If you feel that any of the goal statements need to be reworded, please make suggestions below.

_____

_____

survey asked teachers to state whether the identified 11 goals were "essential" to writing instruction (responses were "yes" or "no"). In Part II, the survey asked teachers to prioritize their top 5 goals (we discuss the outcomes later in the chapter) and to identify how these five broad goals were supported by classroom instruction.

In total, 212 teachers completed the survey. The responses to the surveys included all campuses and subject area teachers.

Actions: What Are the Actors Doing and With What?

The next component in the PASS model is a critical look at what the people inside classrooms are doing and the tools being used. The "Actions" component of the model allows for the documentation of the realities of the classroom lives of teachers and students as a way of thinking about the role of the daily instruction that takes place in classrooms and how those daily routines are or are not supportive of meeting the goals and purposes described in the surveys. This stage involved a set of interviews, observations, and materials analysis. A protocol was developed that would capture a macro view of the classroom and a micro view of instruction.

For the macro view, the team documented elements of the classroom environment, including the climate of and texts located within the classroom. The micro view was documented through a careful look at the literacy events (and the interactions within them) that were taking place during the observation. The team documented those events using the following questions:

- What text is being used?
- Which students are participating in the event?
- What is the role of the teacher?
- What is the nature of dialogue between those participating in the event?

Each member of the Literacy Leadership team visited two or three classrooms and enacted the protocols. Each visit lasted about 45 minutes. In total, 40 observations were completed that spanned schools, grade levels, and subject areas.

Students: What Are the Students Learning?

The next component in the PASS model was a critical look at what the students inside classrooms were learning and why they thought they were learning it. The team was interested in hearing from the students themselves, as well as seeing formative and summative data (via informal and formal measures). Talking to the students would also yield data to complement the classroom observations (to help fully understand the purposes and intentions that surrounded the observed events). Each team member scheduled interviews with the teachers they observed and at least one student from the observed classroom. These interviews took place within 24 hours of the classroom visit. In addition to understanding the goals and purposes of the observed events, the team was interested in whether the commonplace events represented routines. The questions used for these interviews appear in Figures 11.4 and 11.5. All observations and interviews were completed in two months. In total, the team completed 28 student interviews and 40 teacher interviews.

Figure 11.4. Guiding Interview Questions: Teachers

Observed event: "Yesterday when I visited your classroom, I watched you _____ <name one of the events you observed>"

1. Talk to me about your goals/purposes for that event. <If the teacher doesn't mention a literacy goal, ask . . . Did you have a literacy goal in mind?>
2. What did you value about it?
3. What do you think your students valued about it?

4. Would you say that event was representative of your instruction?

Commonplace event: "Are there other lessons that you would have LIKED for me to have seen?"

5. Talk to me about your goals/purposes for that event. <If the teacher doesn't mention a literacy goal, ask . . . >
6. What do you value about it?
7. What do you think your students valued about it?
8. Would you say that event was representative of your instruction?

Desired event: "Is there something you would like to be doing in your classroom that you're not?"

9. Talk to me about your goals/purposes for that event. <If the teacher doesn't mention a literacy goal, ask . . . >
10. What do you value about it?
11. What do you think your students would value about it?
12. What do you need to make that happen?

Figure 11.5. Guiding Interview Questions: Students

Observed event: "Yesterday when I visited your classroom, I watched you _____ <name one of the events you observed>"

1. Talk to me about why you think your teacher had you do that. <If the student doesn't mention a literacy goal, ask . . . Do you think your teacher had a goal for literacy in mind?>
2. What did you value <or like> about it?
3. Is this something you do often in your classroom?

Commonplace event: "Are there other things that you do that you would have LIKED for me to have seen?"

4. Talk to me about why you think your teacher has you do that. <If the student doesn't mention a literacy goal, ask . . . Do you think your teacher has a goal for literacy in mind?>
5. What do you value <or like> about it?
6. Is this something you do often in your classroom?

Desired event: "Is there something you would like to be doing in your classroom that you're not?"

7. Talk to me about why you'd like to do that. <If the student doesn't mention a literacy goal, ask . . . >
8. What would you value about it?
9. What do you think your teacher would value about it?

Standards: How Does Classroom Practice Map Onto Standards of Professional Organizations?

Standards relate to the expectations for learning. There are different groups with different standards that schools must be aware of and accountable to. The team was curious as to how teachers' purposes for literacy instruction were aligned with the district expectations and professional standards. To be clear, standards do not tell teachers how to teach, but rather identify clear goals for learning and suggest a path for assessing progress toward these goals. Both district documents (*Profile of a Learner* and *Blueprint for Learning*) and the revised standards for literacy professionals by the International Literacy Association (ILA; 2018) were consulted. Questions that were asked by the team as they pored over ILA's standards were: "Is this what we believe?" "Is this what we do?" "Is this the best evidence we have to document student growth?"

ANALYZE THE DATA

Principle: Effective evaluation rests on the identification of coherence within the program as well as identification of the inconsistencies and contradictions within a program. Discrepancy analysis is at the heart of most evaluation models (see Stake, 2000; Steinmetz, 2000). A program survey sets the stage for the process of looking at what *is* and shifting the focus to what *should be*. The PASS framework described above invites this kind of analysis. There are potential discontinuities at any juncture across the program matrix. In a perfect world, a purpose would be identified for the development of decoding; there would be instructional actions, plans, materials, and assessments that nurture this purpose; students would be learning at the targeted levels; and expectations would meet or exceed all the standards. The reality is never so clean. Purposes (e.g., promote out-of-school reading or reading habits) might have no actions to support them and no data on how well the students are doing. Levels of performance that are below standards might be discovered. Outcomes might be measured for areas that have no articulated goals. The possibilities are numerous.

A coherent program is one that has the Purposes, Actions, Students, and Standards fully aligned. A good evaluation should lead to the identification of aspects of the program (these might be levels of components) that are in full alignment. These may be regarded as the strengths of the program. A good evaluation should also lead to the identification of aspects of the program that are out of alignment. For example, when reviewing the data from the AHISD evaluation surveys, we looked for discrepancies among purposes, actions, products, or standards within the writing program. In the sections that follow, we outline our findings after our analyses of the various components of the PASS evaluation.

Purposes

The Delphi survey revealed five overarching goals for writing and writing instruction in the district. These five goals were representative of those listed in Figure 11.3, Part II; in some cases, we collapsed across goals, as that made sense to the literacy team. The five most important goals of the teachers, presented in order of saliency, included the following:

Goal 1: Building Identity and Self-Efficacy. I want my students to have self-efficacy and be knowledgeable, confident, empathetic, critical writers and readers. I want my students to view themselves as passionate, lifelong writers and readers who write for themselves and others on a regular basis. These goals received the highest number of "yeses" by teachers (99%); they appeared in the top five rank-ordered goals of 158 teachers and were the top choice of 59 teachers. Analysis of observations and interviews indicated that teachers engaged students in building identity and self-efficacy. For many classrooms, choice played an important role in achieving this goal. In one primary-grade classroom, pages of the children's journals have an open space at the top for illustrations and a bottom space for writing. The children filled their journals with both illustrations and writing; the writing appears to have been self-generated versus driven by a prompt.

Similarly, it was important to teachers that students were confident in their abilities to write. This was most evident in primary-grade classrooms. One primary teacher told her children, "You really see yourself as a writer." One child said, "I like this and I would draw all day. I'd draw lots of stuff that's good."

Evidence of students' empathy and knowledge in primary and junior school English Language Arts

(ELA) classrooms was observed. One junior school ELA teacher stated, "Peer review creates a community of writers who value each other and get to know each other better and form a greater bond together." Evidence of the role of students' passion in building identity and self-efficacy was documented in two different schools. One very young child said, "Sometimes I save pages because I like to draw so much."

Evidence of the role of students' reflection in building identity and self-efficacy across grade levels was documented. One teacher developed independence in her very young children by instructing, "If you still need to talk about your ideas, you can stay on the carpet, but if you are ready to write, I want you writing." Another teacher supported young children writing their own goals: "We also change goals. I'm [going to write] my goal." In an upper elementary classroom, there was a prominently displayed "Student Activity Wall" where students set their goals and declared what skill they would be working on.

Routine seemed to play an important role in the building of identity and self-efficacy as writers; evidence of this was found across the campuses. Young children were engaged in portfolios, writing centers, monthly journals, and writing routines. As one student from the junior school said, "Well, we did it for book clubs, too, in groups of four. He takes us out of doors and talks to us so we can discuss quotes, chapters, and thought logs." Additionally, there was evidence of routines in one non-ELA classroom at the junior school: The students engaged in their Google classroom with documents and videos related to the lesson. Because of these routines, teachers reported that their students like writing and that they would often "beg for more [writing time]."

Goal 2: Writing with Clarity. I want my students to be able to elaborate, write with clarity, and use discipline-specific vocabulary.

This goal received the second highest number of "yeses" (98%). This goal appeared in the top five rank-ordered goals of 128 teachers and was the top choice of 27 teachers. Evidence of this goal was found across grade levels and campuses. Most teachers centered on details in writing as a form of elaboration. For example, one elementary teacher encouraged her student to add a name for the character in the story the child was describing. One 3rd-grade teacher complimented her students because "we worked hard to add details."

There was evidence of writing with clarity across the content areas. One junior school non-ELA teacher requested that class products "should be written clearly and concisely." In an early childhood classroom, a teacher used writing to document the learning taking place in social studies and asked the young children to give her more details about "what you want, but don't need to survive." In an elementary classroom during math time, the teacher asked the children to restate what they meant so that they could clarify what they were trying to say.

Many classrooms supported the learning of specialized vocabulary. One junior school non-ELA teacher stated, "It [subject area] does involve vocabulary, anchor charts, architecture, engineering," and the subject was "vocabulary heavy." Another ELA teacher at that school said that students need to learn the vocabulary of writing and reading, including "metaphor, alliteration, foreshadowing, flashback." Specialized vocabulary teaching was taking place in an early childhood social studies lesson where the teacher taught vocabulary associated with text features: "These symbols mean days of sunshine."

Classroom instruction and materials support this notion of writing with clarity by texts in the classroom, including graphic organizers (plot map) and mentor texts. Mentor texts allowed the students to reread for many different purposes and become different writers from one day to the next. Similarly, many of the classrooms were print-rich; the anchor charts located within supported clarity in writing. In one junior school ELA classroom, there were an abundance of anchor charts on the walls referring to the writer's craft.

Goal 3: Writing for a Purpose. I want my students to write for various purposes in and out of school (e.g., communicate their ideas, their beliefs, and their learning).

This goal and the fourth goal (see below) received 97% "yeses" by teachers. This goal appeared in the top five rank-ordered goals of 120 teachers and was the top choice of 30 teachers. In some cases, teachers engaged students in writing for a purpose as it related to genre ("make believe" in a primary grade), while in other cases to show what you know (e.g., expert writing in primary grade). Teachers used mentor texts to support learning related to this goal (e.g., use of children's author Donald Crews's work to teach "expert writing"). In interviews students stated that they engaged in and valued opportunities to write for personal reasons (e.g., "I have time to read and time to freely write <about whatever I want> every other day for about 10 minutes or so" in a junior school ELA classroom).

Teachers used writing purposefully in content areas (e.g., "Bring your journals for notes" in a junior school non-ELA classroom), indicating that they engaged students in writing for a purpose (e.g., writing like a historian or a scientist). In the elementary grades, teachers used writing as a strategy to compare/contrast concepts in the content areas and to "explain the math they are working on not just answer the questions or master a skill." Note-taking appeared to be the primary purpose for writing in the content-area classrooms that were observed, although there was one junior school non-ELA classroom where a teacher said that "[Writing serves to] communicate in the world. Talk to other people. Write to other people."

Some primary grade students said that the purpose of phonics instruction was "so you become a better writer," indicating that they may believe writing is about spelling words correctly. Several teachers stated that writing served the purpose of growing as people. A junior school ELA teacher said that writing served to "help them become good human beings," and a primary school ELA teacher said that "writing can be a great strategy for expressing emotion." For some students, writing served to tell others what they were thinking: "No one knew what I was saying. Now they do. If you get better, then others can read my writing and I know what I am saying." Another said that writing is "a way to express yourself without giving away too much about yourself personally."

Goal 4: Writing Skills and Strategies: I want my students to use the necessary skills, conventions, and strategies to be successful writers and readers.

This goal appeared in the top five rank-ordered goals of 111 teachers and was the top choice of 18 teachers. In many cases, the skills and strategies related directly to the state standards. One young child said, "My teacher wants us to learn about capitals and the beginning of a sentence, and question marks and sometimes commas." Another young child said the lesson was important because "Sometimes we see a sneaky E." A junior school ELA teacher made connections to reading strategies: "This is where the author wants us to make an inference. She wants us to

infer Saul's feelings. Have you noticed she does this a lot?"

Goal 5: Value for Literacy Processes: I want my students to value the connections between writing, reading, listening, speaking, and thinking.

While this goal came in as the fifth most important, there was a high level of consensus around this goal (96%). This goal appeared in the top five rank-ordered goals of 111 teachers and was the top choice of 19 teachers. Teachers valued the connection between the components of the language system because it allowed the teachers to "cover more ground at school together as a community" (junior school ELA teacher). Some teachers used the connections so as not to miss opportunities to value children's thinking: "I have a lot of other people to talk to, can you work on putting your ideas on paper?" (early elementary teacher).

In all, there was much observational evidence that reading and writing were a communal event in many classrooms where students were reading and talking to one another about what they were reading, *and* writing and talking to one another about their writing. Students were very aware of the connections between reading and writing. As one junior school student said, "So that it can help us with our writing skills. So that when we read, we can learn a little bit more and learn how to write. When you read, there's dialogue and great word choice. It tells us good ways to write."

Actions and Students

All the classroom observations and the interviews (of teachers and students) were coded. Collectively, the data confirmed that the five goals identified from the Delphi survey were important to teachers across grades, subject areas, and campuses. The goals teachers had explicated in the Purposes component of the self-evaluation were clearly demonstrated in their teaching and in the ways in which they and their students talked about their writing routines and practices.

Two additional goals emerged from the analysis. Although these two could have been subsumed into one of the five previously identified goals, the teachers were very clear about the importance of these as separate goals as a way of maintaining the integrity of observations, materials analysis, and interviews.

***Goal 6: Community. I want my students to partici-
pate in a community of writers who take risks together.***
Analysis of observations and interviews indicated
that teachers engaged students in participating in a
community of writers. In fact, it was surprising that
that goal did not appear on the list of top 5 goals
between the initial survey and the Delphi survey because there were so many instances of community in
the observational data.

Teachers across grades, campuses, and disciplines
worked to build a community of learners in their
classrooms. They encouraged students to engage
with others in their classrooms by using practices
such as turn-and-talk (e.g., "Talk with your group
about what they could have 'tasted' on Halloween
night"). They drew on the strengths of students in
the classroom to support one another. In the junior
school, one ELA teacher stated, "My goal was for
the kids to demonstrate higher-order thinking in a
structured conversation where they built on each
other's contributions, using text evidence."

***Goal 7: Writing process: I want my students to value
writing as a process (e.g., selecting a topic, drafting, revising, editing, publishing/sharing work).*** Although there
were very few instances of this goal being enacted
compared to the other goals, teachers in a handful of
classrooms across campuses did engage students in
the writing process. There was clear attention to children's portfolios (in early elementary grades) and the
planning that goes on around those portfolios (e.g.,
"Tell me your plan for today"). In upper elementary
classrooms, students turned easily to one another to
brainstorm the topic for their writing. In the junior
school ELA classrooms, there was evidence of peer
review and other components of a workshop model.

Standards

Attention was then turned to how well the previously described and analyzed data mapped onto
the priorities of the district and the International
Literacy Association's (2018) standards for literacy
professionals.

ILA's Standard 1: Foundational Knowledge. The data
from the surveys, interviews, and observations indicated that the district was meeting this standard except for "disciplinary-specific literacy processes that
serve as a foundation for all learning."

ILA's Standard 2: Curriculum and Instruction. There
were observations of the curriculum enacted by
teachers in the classroom visits/observations. The
findings aligned nicely with this standard except for
"provide a coherent and motivating academic program that integrates disciplinary literacy."

ILA's Standard 3: Assessment and Evaluation. While
AHISD is not a "test-driven" district, it was felt that
there should be cognitive attention to assessment
and evaluation. The data indicated that the district
did not inform families and colleagues about the
function/purpose of assessments.

ILA's Standard 4: Diversity and Equity. There was
very little attention to diversity and equity across
data sources. This was identified as another need for
attention in the district, especially given the opportunity gaps between achievement of students who
are White and those who are Latinx and Black.

***ILA's Standard 5: Learners and the Literacy
Environment.*** The findings aligned with this standard,
except for two: "incorporate . . . disciplinary literacy
and the learning environment" and "incorporate the
safe and appropriate ways to use digital technologies in literacy and language learning experiences"
(e.g., digital citizenship).

***ILA's Standard 6: Professional Learning and
Leadership.*** The findings aligned with this standard
except for creating classrooms where everyone (including and especially the teacher) carries the identity of writer and engages in the rituals of the practice
of writing.

In summary, the standards analysis indicated several areas in which the district needed to place its
attention: disciplinary literacies, digital literacies,
involvement of families and the community in assessments and in bridging home/school connections,
attention to diversity and equity, and ensuring that
educators consider themselves part of a writing
community.

SUPPORT THE CHANGE PROCESS

***Principle: Plan for ways to systematically support the
change process and use assessments to personalize the
support offered for change.*** Innovations, as described

in this chapter, are changes made to improve the quality of teaching and learning. Innovations can be simple and text-driven (e.g., a new handwriting book for 2nd grade) or complex, layered, and conceptual (e.g., team teaching). An innovation that enters a school as the result of a careful evaluation process has a greater likelihood of impact than one that has been brought in simply by external fiat or mandate.

At AHISD, the Literacy Leadership Team took the data gathered and analyzed and created a plan for focusing on writing and writing instruction in the district, across campuses, grade levels, and disciplinary areas. As with the evaluation using the PASS model, the team drew heavily on the expertise of the teachers and campus leaders in the district not only to create the model that would be used as the focus plan, but also to instantiate the plan.

To that end, recommendations for a 3-day Open Institute focused on writing were aligned with the plan. The Open Institute was held that following summer and secured the services of an exemplary writing teacher to facilitate the workshop. The overarching goals of the workshop included the following:

1. Create spaces and support where teachers of all disciplines engage as writers themselves, publishing at least one product;
2. Engage teachers in theory and research about the teaching of writing within the discipline;
3. Engage teachers in dialogue about instructional practices that support students in growing as writers, including practices that support digital citizenship, disciplinary writing, and building lifelong writers in a writing community.

The institute began with a conversation about communities of practice, how disciplines share some literacy practices, and how students can be brought into these practices. The 3-day workshop provided lots of time for writing, reflecting on writing, and sharing the writing of the participants. All the workshop participants were invited to work on a piece of their choosing; the genre or product was not stipulated. Rather, the presenters modeled what they should do in their classrooms—provide lots of opportunities for young writers to explore their

discipline through the act of writing. The teachers were engaged in mini-lessons throughout the institute, which gave them time to work with partners and in their writing groups. Discussions centered on metacognition and reflections of being a writer and a teacher of writing inside their own disciplines.

The Open Institute followed the plan of a mini-conference, with each day beginning with a whole-group activity/speaker (e.g., keynote on a topic that transcends all participants). The remainder of each day contained breakout sessions that addressed various topics teachers might find interesting. Lunch revolved around writing groups so that teachers could work on a piece of writing with their writing partners. The day ended with teachers sharing their work and thoughts for the day.

SUSTAIN CHANGE

Principle: No changes are important if they cannot be sustained. Good evaluation supports a cycle of growth. In a cycle of growth, teachers are empowered to shape their school and are encouraged to connect to one another, and not isolate themselves from one another. The Literacy Leadership Team played a crucial role in the process of supporting change. Far too many schools suffer today from mandated changes that come from the latest fad or most popular guru. High-stakes testing has resulted in enormous pressure for change that focuses only on certain outcomes. Yet there are many examples of literacy specialists who have found ways to encourage local autonomy and consensus building within their schools (see Au, 2001, 2005).

Sustainable change is not about supporting change to a final point, but to always "stay changing" in ways that reflect growth. This is not change for change's sake. A staff that has embraced change as the path for growth is taking control of the future. The power that comes with this control makes anything possible. Michael Fullan (2007) argued that the problem in schools today is not the absence of change (in fact, there are too many changes underway); rather, it is the lack of coherency among changes that is the problem.

Effective change requires leadership. Literacy leaders such as those at AHISD found themselves in the role of change agents. They were the ones encouraging change and keeping everyone on track.

The effective change agent finds the right balance between pressuring for change and supporting change (Fullan, 2007; Huberman & Miles, 1984; McLaughlin, 1987). Although it could be helpful to involve someone from the outside to support the change process, the insiders were the driving force behind the changes seen in teachers' attitudes toward writing and writing instruction and the shifts in students' writing achievement. Outside experts do play a role in supporting change. They offer perspectives that can be lost as change agents are immersed in change. It is important that outside experts not confuse the role of leadership with that of ownership. The ownership of the program has to rest with those making the changes.

ACCEPT THE MANDATE FOR CONTINUOUS IMPROVEMENT

Principle: The literacy leader's work is never done because it is focused on the cultural change imperative to foster coherence through a systematic process. The "evaluator's life" represents a way of thinking about professional work in relation to improvement. This involves learning to puzzle through challenges and possibilities in a systematic way. Literacy leaders must see their role as one of constantly linking to others inside and outside the immediate setting (Hood, 1982) with the mindset, "We can do better." The next set of innovations is already taking shape while the current ones are just settling into place. As with the Literacy Leadership Team at AHISD, local experts learn to enjoy the uncertainty of change, but also to enjoy the systematic, data-driven aspects of evaluation. Literacy leaders question themselves constantly about their role in the processes of evaluation and change and become "meta" in their reflections. These practices can assist them in becoming mindful of the importance of the moral imperative to meet the needs of learners as a way of accepting and promoting issues of social responsibility. This determination can enable them in making changes that fit into a coherent whole and will go a long way toward creating a vision of what can and should be, which is at the forefront of thinking about change.

CONCLUSION

Effective evaluation for improvement is not something that outside "experts" come in and do, but rather is a process that educators do as a learning community that serves learners. Change is grounded in reflective practices by teachers and the systems that support them. The work at AHISD is just one example of the change that can take place when local schools and school districts take ownership for the kind of change they want to make and when they involve all stakeholders. In order to do so, it is important to create and nurture a process of community building that empowers a professional stance toward education. It is important to create and nurture a system based on the notion of learning as a lifelong process. It is important to create a culture that can turn state and federal standards into an asset and not a diversion. The case that we presented in this chapter is one such way these beliefs instantiate themselves.

REFLECTION QUESTIONS

1. What is your motivation for change within your districtwide literacy program? What informs this motivation? Who else is committed to making the changes needed so that the schoolwide literacy program has positive effects on teaching and learning? What other stakeholders should be committed to make these changes with you? How can you get them on board?

2. What outside mandates does your district face? From within? How do those mandates inform the literacy instruction in your school?

3. What is the culture that you are trying to establish in your district? What is your vision for what the schoolwide literacy culture will be? How will you identify the right balance between pressuring for change and supporting change? Who can you bring in (an outsider) to assist you in supporting the change process? What would that person's role be?

PROJECT ASSIGNMENT

Develop a plan to evaluate your schoolwide literacy program that uses the principles provided in this chapter as a framework. Implement your plan and see how well the goals you develop instantiate themselves in the implementation.

REFERENCES

Au, K. H. (2001). Elementary programs in the context of the standards movement. In S. B. Wepner, D. S. Strickland, & J. T. Feeley (Eds.), *The administration and supervision of reading programs* (2nd ed., pp. 42–58). Teachers College Press.

Au, K. H. (2005). Negotiating the slippery slope: School change and literacy achievement. *Journal of Literacy Research, 37,* 267–288.

Fullan, M. (2007). *The new meaning of educational change* (4th ed.). Teachers College Press.

Green, R. A. (2014). The Delphi Technique in educational research. *SAGE Open, 4*(2), 1–8. https://journals.sagepub.com/doi/pdf/10.1177/2158244014529773

Hoffman, J. V. & Sailors, M. (2014). Evaluation, change and program improvement: The role of the literacy specialist. In S. B. Wepner, D. S. Strickland, & D. J. Quatroche (Eds.), *The administration and supervision of reading programs* (5th ed., pp. 145–166). Teachers College Press.

Hood, P. D. (1982). *The role of linking agents in school improvement: A review, analysis, and synthesis of recent major students.* Far West Laboratory for Educational Research and Development.

Huberman, A. M., & Miles, M. B. (1984). *Innovation up close: How school improvement works.* Plenum.

International Literacy Association. (2018). *Standards for the preparation of literacy professionals 2017.*

McLaughlin, M. W. (1987). Learning for experience: Lessons from policy implementation. *Educational Evaluation and Policy Analysis, 9*(2), 171–178.

Stake, R. (2000). Program evaluation, particularly responsive evaluation. In D. Stufflebeam, G. Madaus, & T. Kellaghan (Eds.), *Evaluation models: Viewpoints on educational and human services evaluation* (2nd ed., pp. 344–362). Kluwer-Nijhoff.

Steinmetz, A. (2000). The discrepancy evaluation model. In D. Stufflebeam, G. Madaus, & T. Kellaghan (Eds.), *Evaluation models: Viewpoints on educational and human services evaluation* (2nd ed., pp. 121–143). Kluwer-Nijhoff.

Part IV

INTERCONNECTIONS

A literacy program's richness comes from its diversity of components and students. For a literacy program to work effectively, all members of the school and community must work together to create and improve literacy. This part of the book includes five chapters that provide specialized literacy professionals with the necessary tools to create a fully effective program that attends to the diversity of students and the communities in which they live.

Chapter 12, written by Julie K. Kidd and M. Susan Burns, explains literacy leaders' role in developing teachers' knowledge of teaching writing and ways to integrate writing with reading and learning. Included in this chapter are an in-depth look at writing and the reading-writing-learning connection, and specific guidelines for developing goals, curriculum, and instruction that are based on standards. A specific professional development framework that focuses on teachers' needs is described so that they can develop, refine, and use culturally relevant instructional practices that promote students' writing competencies.

In Chapter 13, MaryEllen Vogt discusses the important role of literacy leaders in supporting teachers of English learners, and in monitoring and evaluating instructional approaches and programs for teaching language, literacy, and academic content to English learners. She provides an overview of the diverse characteristics of English learners in schools as a backdrop to a discussion of six principles for culturally responsive, exemplary teaching of these learners. These principles focus on knowledge of the learners, conditions for language learning, lesson quality, lesson delivery, monitoring and assessment of language development, and the importance of teachers' professional development. The SIOP (Sheltered Instruction Observation Protocol) Model is described as an instructional framework within which these six principles can be realized.

In Chapter 14, Jennifer L. Goeke and Kristen D. Ritchey discuss the role of literacy leaders and other administrative personnel in meeting the needs of students with reading disabilities and other learning challenges through Multi-Tiered Systems of Support (MTSS). They explain that MTSS is a multi-tiered system of services and supports for academics, behavior, and social–emotional learning that focuses on the whole child through communication and collaboration among both general and special educators. They demonstrate how RTI (Response to Intervention), which provides academic support, and PBIS (Positive Behavioral Interventions and Supports), which provides behavioral and social emotional support, can work together under the umbrella of MTSS to provide effective interventions.

Given the rapidly changing influence of new online technologies, Elena Forzani, Clint Kennedy, and Donald J. Leu in Chapter 15 discuss what leaders of literacy need to think about when it comes to redefining reading, writing, communication, and learning. As the authors share, with new online tools emerging daily, classroom instruction must keep up with technological changes to prepare students for this continuously shifting landscape. Ten principles, along with specific instructional ideas, are presented for specialized literacy professionals to use to support teachers' instruction with technology.

The final chapter of this book, Chapter 16, written by Patricia A. Edwards, Lisa M. Domke, and Marliese R. Peltier, discusses what leaders of literacy can and should do to promote parent involvement in children's learning. The authors focus on the importance of understanding school demographics and adopting asset-based mindsets as a starting point for developing parent engagement strategies and programs that are accessible to families from diverse cultural, linguistic, and economic backgrounds. Specific ideas are provided that communicate an awareness of and sensitivity to parental needs for helping their children succeed in school.

This last part of the book suggests that important links or interconnections to different programs, initiatives, and populations are essential for a literacy program's success in today's richly diverse and technologically savvy society.

CHAPTER 12

Promoting Writing With Reading and Learning

Julie K. Kidd and M. Susan Burns

- Developing teachers' knowledge of teaching writing and of ways to integrate writing with reading and learning is an important aspect of the work literacy specialists and supervisors do with teachers.
- Effective professional development is essential for educators to remain current on trends, issues, research, and policies in writing.
- For teachers to effectively integrate writing into the curriculum in ways that enhance writing development and promote learning across the content areas, professional development needs to focus on key knowledge and skills in teaching writing to students who bring a variety of assets to the classroom.

As this chapter begins, we want to introduce four administrators and supervisors who have responsibilities for offering effective professional learning opportunities for teachers who provide writing instruction for students in diverse community settings. First, let's meet Vita and Anna. Vita is a school administrator in a large suburban school district, and Anna is a literacy curriculum specialist in a small city school district. Vita and Anna work in neighboring school districts that represent many of the school settings across the country, diverse in racial, ethnic, cultural, and linguistic background and family-income levels. They are keenly aware of the intersectionality of these factors. Vita knows that writing has been identified as an area for growth in her district. She wants to provide professional development that focuses on writing assessment and instruction that emphasizes both the basics needed for students' success and the creative aspects of writing. Professional development also needs to address authentic measures of students' writing ability, given the diversity of the learners in her school. Vita, like many school administrators, is concerned to provide professional development that meets the needs of the teachers in her charge; assessment of district professional development indicates dissatisfaction on the part of teachers, including a sense that it lacks relevance for working with students in the district who are racially, culturally, linguistically, and socioeconomically diverse. She is pursuing effective professional development that meets the needs of teachers and other specialists in her district.

Anna shares many of the same issues as Vita. Working in a school district with students with a variety of linguistic and cultural backgrounds as well as diverse abilities, she realizes the need to approach the diversity of the students and their families as a strength as she addresses external issues that influence writing instruction. She is aware that teachers need support as they develop knowledge and competencies that will help them implement evidence-based practices in ways that facilitate writing development for each student.

Next we introduce Kerry, who is a Team Leader for Instructional Specialists with a focus on early childhood education for an inner-city school district. Like many other mentors, she is accountable for ensuring that students in her district meet state writing standards at the prekindergarten and primary grade levels. As an early childhood educator, Kerry wonders what she needs to consider in her work with pre-K teachers. She is pleased with the emphasis on writing but recognizes that professional development is needed to enable teachers to align their instructional practices with state writing standards.

Finally there is Fred, an administrator at a middle and high school for students with disabilities. (This middle and high school for students with disabilities serves students from multiple local school systems, including those of Kerry, Anna, and Vita. The students are sent from their home school system when their needs are too complex for their own system to address.) Fred, like many school administrators, is concerned about writing in the school's literacy program, and is determined to offer effective professional development that is worth faculty and literacy specialists' time. Faculty and literacy specialists in the school are keenly aware that they have in-depth knowledge of the extremely diverse skills in writing of students in their charge. Fred needs to harness that knowledge while also addressing evidence-based practices and standards, integrating these knowledge bases to meet the students' needs and writing development.

All these educators strive to keep up with research on effective professional development for teachers and on the most important areas to emphasize in effective writing methods. They know that the trend is to avoid one-time workshops focused on isolated content in 1- to 3-hour blocks of time (Desimone & Garet, 2015). Vita, Anna, Kerry, and Fred have seen educators mark time sitting in mandated workshops and have witnessed educators throw handouts in the trash as they exit such workshops. They recognize that these one-time workshops are ineffective and "understand the importance of sustained, content-focused PD [professional development] and are directing resources to ensuring teachers have access to such activities" (Desimone & Garet, 2015, p. 257). They want to provide meaningful, effective professional development focused on evidence-based instructional practices that promote positive learning outcomes for students who bring diverse assets to the classroom.

PROFESSIONAL DEVELOPMENT

As administrators and supervisors of literacy programs, Vita, Anna, Kerry, and Fred recognize the importance of keeping on top of current trends, issues, and policies in writing and professional development that support effective writing instruction. They believe that being aware of the research in these areas helps administrators and supervisors support their teachers and make informed and deliberate decisions. They recognize that in their roles as instructional leaders, it is important that they seek out professional learning opportunities to ensure that they continue to stay abreast of new developments. For this reason, they are members of professional organizations, such as the Association for Supervision and Curriculum Development (ASCD), the International Literacy Association (ILA), and the National Council of Teachers of English (NCTE), that provide journals, books, conferences, webinars, networking, and other services. They also involve themselves in research organizations, such as the Association of Literacy Educators and Researchers (ALER) and the Literacy Research Association (LRA), that offer research journals, conferences, and other resources that can inform evidence-based practices in their districts.

Vita, Anna, Kerry, and Fred also recognize the importance of cultivating relationships with experts on writing instruction within their schools and school districts as well as regionally. They find that these networks help them stay abreast of current trends and help them make informed decisions about writing instruction and appropriate professional development for teachers. By engaging in their own professional learning, Vita, Anna, Kerry, and Fred stay up to date in at least two relevant areas of research to practice focused on effective professional development and evidence-based writing instruction. Being knowledgeable about professional development designed to promote effective writing instruction is essential for administrators and supervisors committed to ensuring that students who bring racial, cultural, linguistic, ability (disability), and socioeconomic diversity to the classroom are provided with high-quality writing instruction that leads to student success.

Understanding Key Aspects of Professional Development for Teachers

Administrators and supervisors must understand key aspects of teacher professional development if they are to support and provide contextually relevant and culturally responsive learning opportunities that are informed by adult learning theories. These learning experiences build upon teachers' existing knowledge and prior experiences and acknowledge the varying interests, strengths, and needs teachers bring to their learning. This is important because research suggests that teacher learning is influenced by teachers' beliefs, content and pedagogical knowledge, and prior experiences (Covay Minor et al., 2016). Contextually relevant experiences situate learning locally within teachers' classrooms and school communities. Contextualized learning builds upon teachers' existing practices; focuses on the students they teach; and links new knowledge about teaching writing directly to their school and classroom goals, curriculum, and instructional practices.

In a study focused on listening to the voices of 2nd- and 3rd-grade teachers of writing, McKeown et al. (2019) found that these teachers value professional development with the characteristics of culturally responsive and contextually relevant professional development noted above. Additional components of effective professional development include

- Experiences that engage teachers in interactive learning and provide ample opportunities for practice
- Group sizes that are small enough for teachers to build relationships and trust but large enough to form an interactive learning community
- Room to differentiate and adapt instructional lessons, practices, and strategies

The teachers also indicated the importance of the modeling, support, and feedback provided by experienced writing teachers. They appreciated curricular materials that provided detailed writing content, materials, and lesson plans to support their implementation of effective writing strategies in their classrooms. Overall, the teachers found that professional development "based on these characteristics and components was a powerful mechanism for learning to implement a complex evidence-based practice" (McKeown et al., 2019, p. 785).

Utilizing the LEARN Framework

In our own work with professional development, we found the LEARN framework to be helpful in conceptualizing a multifaceted approach to professional development. LEARN provides opportunities for teachers to (L) learn new knowledge, (E) enact this knowledge in their classrooms, (A) assess the effectiveness of their instructional practices, and (R) reflect on experiences to make informed instructional decisions with the support of a (N) network of colleagues and mentors (Kidd et al., 2019; Snow et al., 2005). By using LEARN to frame their approach to planning and implementing professional development opportunities for teachers, administrators and supervisors ensure that there is a focus on engaging teachers in developing and refining their knowledge of effective instructional practices that promote students' writing competencies.

We return to Anna, who is a literacy curriculum specialist, to illustrate how the LEARN framework supports a contextualized and culturally responsive approach to providing professional learning opportunities. Anna recognizes that, like the 2nd- and 3rd-grade teachers in the McKeown et al. (2019) study described above, the teachers in her school district would benefit from professional development focused on writing instruction, including an emphasis on self-regulated strategy development (SRSD) in writing. SRSD is an evidence-based strategy for developing writing strategies that are specific to different genres of writing and for enhancing writing strategies across the writing process (Graham et al., 2013; McKeown et al., 2019). Anna began by working with the building-based literacy specialists in her school district to engage teachers in a self-assessment of their knowledge of SRSD and their perceptions about their effectiveness at implementing various components of the strategy. Using this information, Anna and the literacy specialists developed a year-long professional development plan focused on enhancing writing instruction with a focus on SRSD that was designed to be responsive to the evolving interests and needs of the teachers.

Anna and the literacy specialists decided that these learning opportunities would take place at institutes for learning with teachers in schools across the school district, within teachers' classrooms, and in small-group, supportive learning communities within their own schools (Kidd et al., 2019). They began by bringing teachers together for an institute at the beginning of the school year for 3 full days of professional development focused on evidence-based writing instruction. They brought the teachers back together for institute days on their

scheduled professional days throughout the year. These institutes focused on developing teachers' content and pedagogical knowledge. Anna and the literacy specialists engaged teachers in readings, videos, large-group discussions, and small-group activities designed to build teachers' knowledge of evidence-based writing instruction and specifically SRSD. They built opportunities for teachers to enact their learning by including activities that enabled them to practice with their peers. They also engaged teachers in experiences that prompted them to assess and reflect on the effectiveness of their enactment and next steps. By working with a network of teachers across the school district, the participants learned new knowledge and made plans for implementing what they learned in their own classroom context.

Between institutes, Anna worked with literacy specialists to ensure that all participating teachers had opportunities for in-classroom mentoring and coaching. The literacy specialists scheduled time in each teacher's classroom. Prior to the in-classroom experience, the teacher and literacy specialist identified a specific strategy for the focus of the visit. Teachers also indicated whether they wanted the literacy specialist to model the strategy, co-teach while implementing the strategy, or observe while the teacher implemented the strategy. After the session, the literacy specialist and teacher debriefed by assessing the impact of the enacted strategy on student learning and reflecting on how to modify or follow up to enhance learning.

Recognizing the importance of having a supportive network for learning, the literacy specialists also brought teachers together at least monthly as supportive, small-group learning communities. These learning communities included five to six teachers who had common interests (e.g., taught the same grade level) and often were located geographically close together (e.g., in the same hall or in the same pod). These community meetings were used to introduce and develop new content specific to the teachers' interests, needs, and contexts and to provide opportunities for teachers to share their experiences, problem-solve, and generate new ideas.

Across professional development opportunities, knowledgeable administrators and supervisors used what they knew about the teachers' interests, strengths, and needs to engage them in experiences designed to develop and refine their knowledge of writing development and instructional practices that promote positive outcomes for their students. They also provided teachers with opportunities to enact what they learned by practicing with peers and implementing instructional writing strategies in their own classrooms with the support of an expert mentor. By linking professional learning to classroom teaching, the program made sure that professional development opportunities were contextually relevant. Coming together in small, supportive learning communities enabled teachers to support and learn from one another as they talked about instructional writing practices pertinent to their classroom and school context. Fostering supportive networks within schools ensures that professional learning is ongoing and focused on developing content and pedagogical knowledge relevant to enhancing the writing development of students who bring diversity to the classroom. By utilizing an evidence-based approach, like the LEARN framework, that has been shown to be effective, administrators and supervisors can increase the likelihood that professional learning opportunities that are sustained over time will positively impact teachers' enactment of the targeted instructional practices (Kidd et al., 2019).

KNOWLEDGE ABOUT WRITING AND THE READING-WRITING-LEARNING CONNECTION

Thinking through the provision of professional development, Vita, Anna, Kerry, and Fred understand that there are aspects of professional development that they, as administrators and supervisors, may not have considered. They are concerned about the multifaceted curriculum content that they and their professional staff need to know about writing. Anna recognizes that helping teachers integrate writing with reading and learning is an important aspect of her work with teachers. She believes that in order to help teachers and improve programs, administrators and supervisors need knowledge of the writing process and the reading-writing-learning connection. She needs to review the current evidence base for her understanding. Fred (special education school director) knows that his extremely diverse students need explicit writing instruction for the basics, but he also wants his teachers to understand the evidence base for digital and multiple-modal literacies so that the teachers can help their students present their knowledge across content

areas. Anna and Fred as well as Vita and Kerry need to make writing happen for the students in their charge. They need help identifying the writing knowledge and skills that are evidence-based so that they can be prioritized in professional development. In this section, we present an overview of key considerations for writing instruction.

What Is the Writing Process?

Writing is a complex process that involves planning, drafting, revising, editing, and publishing text. Because this process involves the writer, possible collaborators, and an audience, it is influenced by social conventions and cultural practices (Bazerman, 2016). This means that as part of the planning or reflective process, writers consider the audience and purpose for writing, decide on a form or genre of writing, and generate and organize ideas for writing. As writers draft, they produce text, read the text produced, reflect, and produce additional text (Hayes, 2006). In doing so, they may revise by adding, deleting, changing, or rearranging the written text. In addition, they may edit or make changes to the text to ensure correct capitalization, punctuation, grammar, and spelling. The published version is considered the final product and is shared with the intended audience.

How Are Reading and Writing Related?

Reading and writing are interactive and complementary processes. Both readers and writers must know word meanings and spelling. For a reader, the reading-writing interaction involves comprehending a writer's message (Kintsch, 2004; Shanahan, 2016). For a writer, it involves alternating roles as reader and writer. A writer is usually a reader—often reading others' work before writing. That can give the writer a deep appreciation both of what was read and how it was written. Writers read their own work throughout the writing process (Hayes, 2006). Students continually alternate roles as readers and writers as they move back and forth between the two processes (Collins et al., 2017)

How Does Writing Promote Learning?

Writing is a tool for thinking that promotes and extends student learning across the content areas

(Graham & Perin, 2007; Kostos & Shin, 2010). Writing gives students concrete evidence of their feelings, observations, and actions, and it lets them revisit and review these ideas. It enables them to "make inferences, draw upon prior knowledge, and synthesize material" (Gammill, 2006, p. 760). By writing, students can explore the known and the new, and they can manipulate language to communicate with themselves and others. When students read and write about concepts in the content areas of English, mathematics, science, and social studies, they process ideas and information more deeply and have a better chance of remembering that material than by just listening or reading (Kostos & Shin, 2010). In this way, students write to learn (Fidalgo, Harris, & Braaksma, 2018).

What Needs to Be Considered When Planning Instruction?

While reading and writing overlap, they are not mirror images of each other, and their integration does not automatically lead to learning. This means that although it makes sense to integrate reading and writing in meaningful ways, it is also essential to provide direct instruction in the skills and strategies of each process for students at all levels. For example, 3rd-graders may need explicit instruction in creating good leads and conclusions in their writing, and 10th-graders may need instruction in the use of their senses and precise vocabulary to create imagery in their writing. Third-grade teachers and their students can read and compare the work of authors like Pam Conrad, Seymour Simon, and Arnold Lobel, and teachers can model lessons using this literature to show students how these authors write leads and conclusions. Tenth-grade teachers and students can read the poetry of Edgar Allan Poe or Emily Dickinson, and teachers can model lessons with this literature to show students how these writers evoke images. This intentional integration of reading and writing includes direct explanation, instruction, and practice to enhance learning of the targeted writing skills and strategies.

DEVELOPING WRITING GOALS, CURRICULUM, AND INSTRUCTION

For teachers to effectively integrate writing into the curriculum in ways that enhance writing development and promote learning across the content areas, teachers, administrators, families, and students need to know what is to be accomplished. These goals should reflect thoughtful consideration of writing development research, state standards and local assessments, and what is valued by members of the school community. They should account for the cultural and linguistic diversity of students and their socioeconomic differences, as well as their diverse abilities (disabilities). These goals guide instructional decisions and are the basis for establishing criteria used for assessing and evaluating student progress.

Likewise, teachers and administrators must be knowledgeable about effective ways to reach the goals. One way is to develop curriculum and plan instruction that builds across students' academic careers. To achieve this, some districts assemble districtwide or school-based efforts involving principals, literacy specialists, literacy coaches, teachers, students, and families. Even when schools and districts include teachers in such decision-making, often not every teacher's voice is heard (Engel & Streich, 2006). As teachers participate in professional development, time must be taken to listen to all teachers' ideas and concerns (Kidd et al., 2019; McKeown et al., 2019).

In districtwide or schoolwide efforts, and in professional development, educators (at a minimum including reading/writing specialists, grade-level teams of teachers, special education teachers, and teachers of English for speakers of other languages) refine the writing curriculum that builds upon the writing skills and strategies introduced to and practiced by students in previous grades. These educators rely on (1) research on writing development; (2) local, district, and state standards; (3) their own knowledge of what students can and should do; and (4) what the members of the school community value. The outcome of this work might be the development of goals similar to the ones listed below:

- Fluency—to write and type easily, legibly, and quickly enough to communicate with an audience, whether it be oneself or others.
- Competence—to write accurately and proficiently in a variety of forms or genres for different purposes and audiences.
- Independence—to choose and enjoy writing and possess the necessary skills and strategies to be able to write on one's own with a minimum of help and support.

With these goals established, instructional guidelines for curriculum and instruction in writing can be specified. Examples of these guidelines are listed below:

- Recognize students' diverse languages, cultures, and abilities (disabilities);
- Integrate technology and teach the new literacies;
- Use writing to construct meaning across curriculum in a variety of genres;
- Provide direct instruction in composing and writing conventions (including spelling);
- Promote choice and authenticity in writing for a variety of purposes and audiences;
- Create an environment that provides writing time, tools, and models.

Recognize Students' Diverse Cultures, Languages, and Abilities (Disabilities)

Students bring to their writing the richness of their cultural knowledge, linguistic backgrounds, and diverse abilities. Teachers can better teach their students by building upon students' knowledge and ways of knowing and becoming acquainted with students and their families within the context of their home and community (Banks, 2020; Kiyama, 2011; Moll et al., 2006; Moll & Gonzalez, 2004; Rodriguez, 2013). One way to do this is to promote two-way communications between the school and the home and community that "help families understand school programs" and "help schools understand families' cultures, strengths, and goals" (Hidalgo et al., 2004, p. 645). By understanding the richness of families' experiences and literacy practices, teachers provide opportunities for students to build upon their home literacy practices as they write about what is known and link new information to the knowledge they possess. Teachers enhance learning by recognizing and building upon students' diverse cognitive strengths, including those not traditionally recognized in schools (Sternberg, 2006). Sternberg explains, "When we teach students in a way that fits how they think, they do better in school" (p. 33).

Students need to write on a daily basis for a variety of purposes and share their writing with others. We also know that most students with disabilities need explicit instruction and practice with all aspects of writing, that is, planning, drafting, and revising as well as using the mechanics of writing such as grammar, punctuation, and spelling (Burns et al., 2010; Graham et al., 2014). This is the case for many students with learning disabilities, those with specific language impairments, or those with high-functioning autism (Accardo et al., 2020). Students with severe disabilities can learn to write, although traditional definitions of conventional writing need to be expanded to include multiple literacies (Keefe & Copeland, 2011; Ruppar, 2017).

Create an Environment that Provides Writing Tools, Time, and Models

Creating an environment that fosters writing entails setting aside time that is devoted to writing. Isolated skill instruction can be accomplished in short segments of time, but integrated instruction focused on meaningful learning with application in authentic contexts requires larger blocks of time (Graham et al., 2012). This kind of instruction also requires appropriate tools and models provided in an environment that promotes writing as a stimulating and engaging activity. Today Information and Communications Technology (ICT) needs to be considered carefully in providing comprehensive tools for writing (De Smedt & Van Keer, 2014). Tools are especially important for students with disabilities. Assistive technology is available at all levels of the writing process; for example, graphic organizers—both in paper form and through sophisticated computer software programs—are available for planning what one wants to write, speech-to-text systems are available for encoding, and text-to-speech systems are available for reviewing and revising (Dell et al., 2011; Evmenova et al., 2020). Tools such as Braille writers and computer keyboards provide a substitute or complement to pen and paper (Luckner et al., 2015).

One way to create this type of atmosphere is to schedule a consistent time for writing workshop (Calkins, 1994; Graham et al., 2012). Using a workshop approach to teaching writing and reading includes such activities as mini-lessons; work time for planning, writing, and revising; conferring with peers, response groups, and the teacher; and share sessions and publication celebrations (Calkins, 1994).

Promote Choice and Authenticity in Writing for a Variety of Purposes and Audiences

Writing for lots of different reasons and audiences builds fluency, competence, and independence

(Myhill et al., 2012). Students need to write for various purposes: to entertain, inform, persuade, and narrate. They also should have opportunities to write for a variety of audiences, including, for example, their peers, family members, teachers, businesses, and people across the country and around the world, as well as themselves.

Finding a balance between the writing process that incorporates choice and authenticity and the writing required in assessments of one's learning is also important. Some student writing as a means of assessment has a time limit; often, it includes a prompt that must be addressed, for example a summary or log of a science activity or a response to literature. Process writing focuses on teaching children to plan, draft, revise, edit, and publish for an audience and often spans the course of several days or weeks. Although writing for assessment with a short time limit may ask students to plan, draft, edit, and publish, there is often little time for students actually to revise their written work.

Provide Direct Instruction in Composing and the Conventions

Another aspect of sound writing instruction is direct and systematic instruction accompanied by time to write (Graham et al., 2012; Harris et al., 2006). Embedded in integrated instruction should be opportunities for lessons, guidance, and practice that allow students to become accomplished writers. For example, 3rd-grade students may need specific instruction on organizing their writing into paragraphs, and 8th-grade students might benefit from lessons on transitioning among paragraphs. Instruction that includes explanations, modeling, guided practice, and independent practice helps students identify strengths and needs in their own writing and put new or refined skills into practice as they write. De Smedt, Graham, and Van Keer (2020) support the impact of these strategies compared to "instruction as usual" and provide evidence of the benefits of peer-assisted explicit writing instruction, as well.

Earlier in this chapter we mentioned the Self-Regulated Strategy Development (SRSD) approach (Fidalgo et al., 2018; Graham et al., 2014; Harris et al., 2006; Saddler & Asaro, 2007), which promotes self-regulation in writing. Students learn the strategies that in turn make writing a task that requires less cognitive processing. As a result, students can focus on the content they want to communicate in their writing (Fidalgo et al., 2018; Graham et al., 2014). For example, students are taught to use a mnemonic, such as TREE, when writing an opinion essay (McKeown et al., 2019). They learn that when writing an opinion essay, they must state a topic (T) that tells what they believe, include at least three reasons (R) that support the belief, write an ending (E) that brings the essay to a conclusion, and examine (E) the essay to make sure they have included all of the parts. Strategies are taught in an explicit and systematic manner so that students learn the skills and understandings needed for writing while also learning to use the strategies themselves and to monitor their progress while writing. The SRSD approach utilizes a six-stage approach to instruction: (1) Develop and activate background knowledge, (2) discuss the strategy, (3) model the strategy, (4) memorize the strategy, (5) support the strategy, and (6) promote independent performance (Harris et al., 2002, pp. 112–113). SRSD uses four components of self-regulation combined or in isolation to promote the acquisition and use of strategies: "self-instruction, goal setting, self-monitoring, [and] self-reinforcement" (Harris et al., 2002, p. 112). It also "allows teachers to use the level of support (e.g., explicit instruction, guided discovery, and/or individualized assistance) needed for student success" (Harris et al., 2002, p. 112).

Use Writing to Construct Meaning Across the Curriculum in a Variety of Genres

Four types of writing in a typical pre-K–12 writing curriculum include expository, persuasive, descriptive, and narrative. Most good writing in everyday life contains elements of each of the four types. For example, a well-written newspaper article about a national park may be expository in style overall but include descriptive imagery, a narration of the park's history, and a persuasive style to influence readers to visit the park. Teaching each of the four types of writing separately makes sense, but the ultimate goal is for students to use elements of the four types together to produce well-crafted writing. Pre-K–12 students should write in every genre for authentic purposes (Duke et al., 2011) to show what they have learned and to build new knowledge in science, social studies, math, and other content areas. This includes, for example, journal writing, expository writing, or creative writing. Tenth-grade students can use poetry in social studies to relate the agony of war as they study world conflicts, or 2nd-graders can write persuasive letters to a community leader about the need for a hiking and biking trail along a local river.

Integrate Technology and Teach the New Literacies

As supervisors and administrators work with teachers to implement sound writing instruction, use of technology and technology integration is an important part of the conversation. Educators recognize the support technology provides for writing, and many are knowledgeable about the advancements of the available technology equipment and the increased use of technology tools to support writing and learning.

In addition to thinking about technology as a useful tool, supervisors and administrators also should focus on the integration of technology with writing. They should identify the skills and strategies students need to communicate proficiently using technology, through (for example) email, the Internet, and multimedia. Educators need to respond by providing instruction in the new literacies, the literacy skills and strategies required to communicate via ever-changing technologies (Hicks, 2018). Therefore, it is not sufficient for supervisors and administrators to focus only on the tools to support writing. They must also stay informed about the changing technologies and the new literacies needed for students to communicate successfully. (For more information, see Chapter 15 in this book.)

CONCLUSION

Vita, Anna, Kerry, and Fred are committed to promoting student writing along with reading and learning. They are fully aware of the challenges of supervising and administering schoolwide and districtwide English Language Arts programs, especially at a time when schools are held accountable for the achievement of their students. They understand the importance of being knowledgeable about writing and the connections among writing, reading, and learning. They also recognize the importance of engaging families in the instructional process and drawing upon the richness of students' cultural

knowledge, linguistic backgrounds, and diverse abilities. Developing writing programs based on long-range goals and sound writing instruction is a focus of the work they do. To that end, they stay up to date with the literacy field and advances in technology. They also provide opportunities for teachers to engage in professional development that keeps them informed of literacy research and practices and encourages them to be involved in communities of learners.

REFLECTION QUESTIONS

1. What professional development opportunities do teachers in your school need and/or want in order to stay current on trends, issues, research, and policy that affect classroom writing instruction?
2. What are current school or district practices that promote writing to read and learn? What role can you play in supporting teachers as they identify clear goals, develop a sound writing curriculum, and plan and implement effective writing instruction?
3. How can you promote access to quality professional development for teachers in your school or district?

PROJECT ASSIGNMENT

Invite a group of three or four teachers who are willing to be audio-recorded when they meet with you to discuss their students' writing. Ask them to bring two examples of their students' writing from different writing contexts or activities. When you convene the discussion group, give individual teachers an opportunity to share and discuss the writing they selected by asking them to explain the context from which the writing came, the reason the students produced the writing, and what they noticed about the writing. Encourage others to share their thoughts about the writing sample being discussed. After the teachers have had an opportunity to share and discuss the students' writing samples, ask them to talk about what they noticed across the writing samples and what patterns, if any, they noticed with students' strengths and areas of potential improvement. Engage them in a conversation about what goals, curriculum, instructional practices, and resources are in place within the classroom and across the school that promote students' writing. Also, encourage them to talk about what they see as the next steps for fostering students' writing development in their classrooms and across the school or school district, e.g., Is there a genre of writing that needs more attention? Are there specific skills and/or strategies that need development? Do we need to explore more effective ways to integrate technology to support writing?

After the discussion, transcribe the audio recording or listen to the discussion several times and take notes. Identify the themes that emerge from their discussion and consider ways that you can use what you learned from their discussion to support and enhance writing across your school or district.

Write a paper or participate in a discussion with others who held discussion groups that includes the following:

a. a description of the participants and context of the discussion,
b. discussion of the themes that emerged from the discussion,
c. a discussion on what you learned about the teachers' perceptions of writing curriculum and instruction, and
d. a reflection on how you can use the information you gained from the teachers' discussions to support teachers' professional development.

REFERENCES

Accardo, A. L., Finnegan, E. G., Kuder, S. J., & Bomgardner, E. M. (2020). Writing interventions for individuals with autism spectrum disorder: A research synthesis. *Journal of Autism and Developmental Disorders, 50*(6), 1988–2006.

Banks, J. A. (2020). *Cultural diversity and education: Foundations, curriculum, and teaching* (6th ed.). Pearson.

Bazerman, C. (2016). What do sociocultural studies of writing tell us about learning to write? In C. A. MacArthur, S. Graham, & J. Fitzgerald (Eds.), *Handbook of writing research* (pp. 11–23). Guilford Press.

Burns, M. S., Kidd, J. K., & Genarro, T. (2010). Writing: Underutilized for young children with disabilities? In T. Scruggs & M. Mastropieri (Eds.), *Advances in learning and behavioral disabilities* (Vol. 23, pp. 175–204). Emerald Group Publishing.

Calkins, L. (1994). *The art of teaching writing*. Heinemann.

Collins, J. L., Lee, J., Fox, J. D., & Madigan, T. P. (2017). Bringing together reading and writing: An experimental study of writing intensive reading comprehension in low-performing urban elementary schools. *Reading Research Quarterly, 52*(3), 311–332.

Covay Minor, E., Desimone, L., Caines Lee, J., & Hochberg, E. D. (2016). Insights on how to shape teacher learning policy: The role of teacher content knowledge in explaining differential effects of professional development. *Education Policy Analysis Archives, 24*(61). https://doi.org/10.14507/epaa.24.2365

De Smedt, F., Graham, S., & Van Keer, H. (2020). 'It takes two': The added value of structured peer-assisted writing in explicit writing instruction. *Contemporary Educational Psychology, 60*, 101835. https://www.sciencedirect.com/science/article/pii/S0361476X19304400?via%3Dihub

De Smedt, F., & Van Keer, H. (2014). A research synthesis on effective writing instruction in primary education. *Procedia - Social and Behavioral Sciences, 112*, 693–701.

Dell, A. G., Newton, D. A., & Petroff, J. G. (2011). *Assistive technology in the classroom: Enhancing the school experiences of students with disabilities* (2nd ed.). Pearson.

Desimone, L. M., & Garet, M. S. (2015). Best practices in teachers' professional development in the United States. *Psychology, Society and Education, 7*(3), 252–263.

Duke, N., Caughlan, S., Juzwik, M., & Martin, N. (2011). *Reading and writing genre with purpose in K–8 classrooms*. Heinemann.

Engel, T., & Streich, R. (2006). Yes, there is room for soup in the curriculum: Achieving accountability in a collaboratively planned writing program. *The Reading Teacher, 59*(7), 660–679.

Evmenova, A. S., Regan, K., & Hutchison, A. (2020). AT for writing: Technology-based graphic organizers with embedded supports. *TEACHING Exceptional Children, 52*(4), 266–269.

Fidalgo, R., Harris, K. R., & Braaksma, M. (2018). *Design principles for teaching effective writing*. Brill.

Gammill, D. M. (2006). Learning the write way. *The Reading Teacher, 59*(8), 754–762.

Graham, S., Gillespie, A., & McKeown, D. (2013). Writing: Importance, development, and instruction. *Reading and Writing, 26*(1), 1–15.

Graham, S., Harris, K. R., & McKeown, D. (2014). The writing of students with learning disabilities, meta-analysis of self-regulated strategy development writing intervention studies, and future directions: Redux. In H. L. Swanson, K. R. Harris, & S. Graham (Eds.), *Handbook of learning disabilities* (pp. 405–438). Guilford Press.

Graham, S., McKeown, D., Kiuhara, S., & Harris, K. R. (2012). A meta-analysis of writing instruction for students in the elementary grades. *Journal of Educational Psychology, 104*(4), 879–896.

Graham, S., & Perin, D. (2007). A meta-analysis of writing instruction for adolescent students. *Journal of Educational Psychology, 99*(3), 445–476.

Harris, K. R., Graham, S., & Mason, L. H. (2006). Improving the writing, knowledge, and motivation of struggling young writers: Effects of self-regulated strategy development with and without peer support. *American Educational Research Journal, 43*(2), 295–340.

Harris, K. R., Graham, S., Mason, L. H., & Saddler, B. (2002). Developing self-regulated writers. *Theory Into Practice, 41*(2), 110–115.

Hayes, J. R. (2006). New directions in writing theory. In C. MacArthur, S. Graham, & J. Fitzgerald (Eds.), *Handbook of writing research* (pp. 28–40). Guilford Press.

Hicks, T. (2018). The next decade of digital writing. *Voices from the Middle, 25*(4), 9–14.

Hidalgo, N. M., Siu, S., & Epstein, J. L. (2004). Research on families, schools, and communities: A multicultural perspective. In J. A. Banks & C. A. McGee Banks (Eds.), *Handbook of research on multicultural education* (pp. 631–655). Jossey-Bass.

Keefe, E. B., & Copeland, S. R. (2011). What is literacy? The power of a definition. *Research & Practice for Persons with Severe Disabilities, 36*(3–4), 92–99.

Kidd, J. K., Burns, M. S., & Nasser, I. (2019). *Promoting intentional teaching: The LEARN professional development model for early childhood educators.* Paul Brookes Publishing.

Kintsch, W. (2004). The construction-integration model of text comprehension and its implications for instruction. In R. B. Ruddell & N. J. Unrau (Eds.), *Theoretical models and processes of reading* (5th ed., pp. 1270–1328). International Reading Association.

Kiyama, J. M. (2011). Family lessons and funds of knowledge: College-going paths in Mexican American families. *Journal of Latinos and Education, 10*(1), 23–42.

Kostos, K., & Shin, E. (2010). Using math journals to enhance second graders' communication of mathematical thinking. *Early Childhood Education Journal, 38*(3), 223–231.

Luckner, J. L., Bruce, S. M., & Ferrell, K. S. (2015). A summary of the communication and literacy evidence-based practices for students who are deaf or hard of hearing, visually impaired, and deafblind. *Communication Disorders Quarterly, 37*(4), 225–241.

McKeown, D., Brindle, M., Harris, K. R., Sandmel, K., Steinbrecher, T. D., Graham, S., Lane, K. L., & Oakes, P. (2019). Teachers' voices: Perceptions of effective professional development and classwide implementation of self-regulated strategy development in writing. *American Educational Research Journal, 56*(3), 753–791.

Moll, L. C., Amanti, C., Neff, D., & González, N. (2006). Funds of knowledge for teaching: Using a qualitative approach to connect homes and classrooms. In N. Gonzalez, L. C. Moll, & C. Amanti (Eds.), *Funds of knowledge: Theorizing practices in households, communities, and classrooms* (pp. 83–100). Routledge.

Moll, L. C., & Gonzalez, N. (2004). Engaging life: A funds-of-knowledge approach to multicultural education. In J. A. Banks & C. A. McGee Banks (Eds.), *Handbook of research on multicultural education* (pp. 699–715). Jossey-Bass.

Myhill, D., Jones, S., Lines, H. & Watson, A. (2012). *The SAGE handbook of writing development.* SAGE Publications.

Rodriguez, G. M. (2013). Power and agency in education: Exploring the pedagogical dimensions of funds of knowledge. *Review of Research in Education, 37*(1), 87–120.

Ruppar, A. L. (2017). "Without being able to read, what's literacy mean to them?": Situated beliefs about literacy for students with significant disabilities. *Teaching and Teacher Education, 67*, 114–124.

Saddler, B., & Asaro, K. (2007). Increasing story quality through planning and revising: Effects on young writers with learning disabilities. *Learning Disability Quarterly, 30*(4), 223–234.

Shanahan, T. (2016). Relationships between reading and writing development. In C. A. MacArthur, S. Graham, & J. Fitzgerald (Eds.), *Handbook of writing research* (pp. 194–207). Guilford Press.

Snow, C. E., Griffin, P., & Burns, M. S. (Eds.). (2005). *Knowledge to support the teaching of reading: Preparing teachers for a changing world.* Jossey-Bass.

Sternberg, R. J. (2006). Recognizing neglected strengths. *Educational Leadership, 64*(1), 30–35.

CHAPTER 13

Reaching Linguistically Diverse Students Through Exemplary Language, Literacy, and Content Teaching

MaryEllen Vogt

- English learners are a diverse group of students with a variety of assets that teachers can build upon while teaching English literacy skills and strategies.
- Emerging bilinguals/multilinguals need highly effective and appropriate instruction in and practice with core reading skills, academic language, vocabulary, oral language proficiency, and grade-level content concepts.
- Literacy leaders and other administrators have an important role in supporting teachers of English learners, and in monitoring and evaluating instructional approaches and programs for teaching language, literacy, and academic content to English learners.

Picture a classroom in which you teach and think about the beginning of the school year when you review your class list for the first time. You see the names of five students who are designated as English learners.[1] Upon talking with your school's ESL (English as a second language)/ ESOL (English to speakers of other languages) teacher and/or contacting the district ESL/ESOL coordinator, you learn the following about these students:

---

1. At the time of this writing, there are a variety of terms used for identifying students who are acquiring English as a second or multiple language, such as English language learners, language learners, multilingual learners, and emerging bilinguals/multilinguals. The official governmental designation is "English learners," so this term will be used throughout this chapter.

- Isabella has been attending a local school in your district since kindergarten. Her home language is Spanish, and she lives in a multigenerational home with her mother, two brothers, and her grandparents, who emigrated from Mexico before Isabella's birth. She "dislikes school, has trouble reading, and feels defeated when it comes to academic work."
- Estuardo, from Guatemala, was held in detention with his father, mother, and two younger sisters for 5 months before recently arriving in your community, where he and his family now live with Estuardo's grandmother, a U.S. citizen. When it was safe, he went sporadically to school in Guatemala; he speaks a little bit of conversational English.
- Laurence has attended school in the United States for the past 2 years. She was born in Belgium; her mother is an attorney and her father is a professor. A nanny cares for Laurence, an older brother, and twin toddlers. Her first language is French and she studied English in a private school in Brussels. She and her family have recently relocated to your community.
- Tan immigrated to your town from Vietnam 4 years ago and he has attended ESL classes in your school since his arrival. Several other Vietnamese classmates have helped Tan become proficient with conversational English. His knowledge of grade-level academic language, however, remains limited, and he struggles with school.
- Kungawo is new to your school and community. A recent arrival from South Africa, his registration form indicates that he speaks Zulu, some Ndbele, and South African Sign Language, the latter so he can communicate with his father. He appears confident and eager, although he knows no English except for "Hi! My name is Kungawo."

From these brief scenarios, what do you know about each of these students that might impact their language and literacy development, one way or another? What else do you need to know about them to meet their language, literacy, and academic needs?

This chapter has a dual focus that addresses the following issues:

- English learners such as Isabella, Estuardo, Laurence, Tan, and Kungawo, must do double the work at school because while they are learning English, they are also expected to learn and master challenging grade-level content concepts and vocabulary (Short & Fitzsimmons, 2007).
- Teachers need support and assistance from literacy leaders, supervisors, and administrators in providing access to quality professional learning opportunities, language assessments and results, and proven, highly effective, and appropriate methods for teaching academic language, literacy, and content concepts to English learners.

OVERVIEW OF ENGLISH LEARNER DEMOGRAPHICS

As English learners, Isabella, Estuardo, Laurence, Tan, and Kungawo represent a group of students whose numbers continue to increase in schools in the United States. At the beginning of the school year in 2017, according to the most recent data available, there were 5 million English learners, representing 10.1% of the students enrolled in K–12 classrooms. The five states that had the highest percentage of English learners were California (19.2%), Texas (19.2%), Nevada (17.1%), New Mexico (16.3%), and Colorado (11.9%) (National Center for Education Statistics, 2020). At present, English learners are found in schools at all grade levels throughout the country, with the largest numbers in urban areas. Between the school years of 2000–2001 and 2015–2016, 43 states saw increases in the population of English learners as a percentage of total student enrollment (National Clearinghouse of English Language Acquisition, 2020).

The English Learners in Our Schools

Many educators and others view and refer to English learners as a homogeneous group simply because these students share one important characteristic: they are learning English as a new language. Some school districts use designations for English learners for program planning and placement, with current labels including SLIFE (Students with limited or interrupted formal education); SIFE (Students with interrupted formal education); LTEL (Long-term English learners); and newcomers. Other districts are abandoning such labels for English learners and instead are referring to students who are acquiring English as a second or multiple language as *emerging bilinguals* or *emerging multilinguals*.

During 2016–2017, Spanish was the most common language spoken by English learners in 46 of 50 states and the District of Columbia. For the remaining four states, the most common language was: Alaska—Yupik (38.81%); Hawaii—Iloko (18.22%); Maine—Somali (31.28%); and Vermont—Nepali (23.86%) (National Center for Education Statistics, 2020).

There are many programs in U. S. schools that focus on developing students' English and academic proficiency. The Department of Education's Office of English Language Acquisition (OELA, 2020) provides information about each of them, including Sheltered English Instruction, Content-Based ESL, Dual Language, Two-Way Dual Language, Transitional Bilingual, and so forth. See OELA for more information on each of these and more at https://www2.ed.gov/about/offices/list/oela/index.html. In addition, see the International Literacy Association's (ILA) Leadership Brief, *The Role of Bilingualism in Improving Literacy Achievement* (2019).

At this point, take a minute to reread the descriptions of the students in the chapter opening. Note that each student carries the designation of English learner and perhaps could fall under another label or two, such as:

- Estuardo is a newcomer, with limited, interrupted formal schooling.
- Isabella is a long-term English learner.
- Laurence is bilingual.
- Kungawo is a multilingual newcomer.
- Tan appears to have learning problems.

It is important to recognize the possible impact of using designations and labels for English learners (and perhaps any student, for that matter):

- Many labels focus on deficits, such as LTEL, SLIFE, newcomer, and/or learning problems.

These labels identify what is *missing* or *wrong* with a student. Even the designation *English learner* has been shown to have a negative connotation in terms of teacher expectations.
- Two of the labels ascribed to Laurence and Kungawo, however, are considered by most to be assets: bilingualism and multilingualism.

So, designations and labels matter. Why, then, do we continue to use designations and labels? The answer may be twofold:

- Designations are used by the U. S. Department of Education for data collection and analysis. School districts have co-opted the designations for program planning and development. Not surprisingly, for ease of use, the designations and labels have reached the classroom.
- Some educators use labels because, unfortunately, they view English learners as "belonging" to someone other than themselves, such as the ESL teacher or bilingual coordinator. With the number of English learners increasing in most states, it is incumbent on all teachers to take ownership of these students to close the achievement gap between them and their native-English speaking peers.

English Learners' Academic Achievement

Think for a moment about the English learners in your school and/or district. Are many of them lagging academically? The answer is most likely yes. On the National Assessment for Educational Progress (NAEP) exams for reading and math, there continues to be a significant gap between English learners and their English-proficient peers. For example, the 2019 NAEP results for reading showed that for all three grades (4, 8, 11) the average scaled scores for English learners were considerably lower than those of native English speakers, even though, in grade 4, English learners' scores showed improvement in reading as compared to the 2017 report (National Center for Education Statistics, 2019). The ongoing difference between English learners' and non-English learners' performance on the NAEP in reading is disturbing, even accounting for the fact that English learners are taking the test in a language other than their primary language. In addition, without appropriate instruction, English learners face a 13% chance of not graduating from high school, and Hispanic English learners are almost twice as likely to drop out of school as non-Hispanic, native-English speaking, White peers (Office of English Language Acquisition, 2020).

That said, there are reasons to be optimistic about the impact of some educational reforms that benefit English learners' language, literacy, and academic development (Short et al., 2017; Vogt, 2020b). Among recent reforms are:

- School improvement plans that include upgraded educational services for English learners, such as district-wide implementation of the SIOP Model (Sheltered Instruction Observation Protocol) (Echevarría et al., 2017).
- Teachers and administrators who regularly monitor English learners' language proficiency data, adjusting instruction and programs as needed.
- Professional learning opportunities for improving instruction for English learners that are available to districts through federal and state funding sources.
- The Every Student Succeeds Act of 2015, which has technically expired but is still in place, requiring more accountability from states for ensuring equitable instruction for all students. In an *Education Week* article, Jillian Balow, Wyoming Superintendent of Instruction, stated, "Instead of trying to skim over inequities, or put the good data out front to hide the bad data, one thing that ESSA has done is allowed us all an opportunity to reveal inequities. The equity indicator has allowed us to really rethink everything we do at the state education agency" (Ujifusa et al., 2019, p. 2).

EXEMPLARY LANGUAGE, LITERACY, AND CONTENT TEACHING FOR ENGLISH LEARNERS

TESOL International Association has published a document titled *The 6 Principles for Exemplary Teaching of English Learners* (TESOL International, 2018). The six principles are intended for all

educators who work with English learners, and they are applicable across varied educational and program contexts. Developed by a team of language experts, the principles are grounded in research, with contributions from educators around the world. According to TESOL, the six principles will help educators:

- Respect, affirm, and promote students' home languages, cultural knowledge, and experiences as resources
- Celebrate multilingualism and diversity
- Support policies that promote individual language rights and multicultural education
- Guide students to be global citizens

The remainder of this chapter will be organized around the six principles. As you read the next sections, reflect on what else you—as a literacy teacher, specialist, supervisor, and/or administrator—need to know about the language and literacy needs and strengths of Isabella, Estuardo, Laurence, Tan, and Kungawo, in order to make informed and appropriate instructional decisions for each of them.

Principle 1. Know Your Learners

For many of our students, especially those who don't believe their lives sufficiently matter, it's up to us to validate them—to honor their cultures, respect their families, encourage them to speak the truths, and to seek out and value their stories. We need to know and really "see" the students we interact with every day. (Routman, 2018, p. 289)

As literacy educator Regie Routman so eloquently states, knowing our students is the most important prerequisite for teaching them. Principle 1 encourages us to gather information about our students who are English learners, including their educational backgrounds, heritage or home languages (L1), talents, interests, cultures, and families. So, who are these students in our classrooms?

- Some immigrant students enter school in the United States with strong academic backgrounds, years of schooling, and proficient language and literacy skills in their L1. Think about Laurence and Kungawo. These students are among those who can transfer their knowledge, academic language, and language learning experiences from their L1 to learning in English. This asset, transferring knowledge and skills from one language to another, can be used by the teacher when planning instruction, whether for academic content or language.

- Other students arrive at school with little or no previous education, interrupted schooling, and little or no academic language in their L1. Think of Estuardo, who left a war-torn country with limited, interrupted schooling experiences. He is likely undocumented (note: another label). But this student, who has been through so much, undoubtedly has life experiences from which to draw connections to his new learning, if his teachers will recognize the assets he brings and then facilitate those connections.
- Still other English learners, a majority of those in U.S. schools, are native-born students who speak a language other than English at home and have not developed sufficient academic language proficiency in either their L1 or English. Reflect on Isabella, a child of first-generation immigrants, who has been in a classroom in the United States since she was five years old. Why do you think that she hasn't been able to exit from the ESL program? Is it due to test scores? Her reading ability?
- And then, of course, there are many other English learners all along the continuum with unique academic and language needs and strengths. Think of Tan, who is proficient in conversational English but is struggling with academic language in his content classes.

It is only by fully knowing Tan and the other students depicted in the scenarios that you will be able to provide them with appropriate language, literacy, and content instruction. Knowing students well means that teachers can leverage their assets and enrich lessons with the personal resources that these students bring to the classroom This begins by acknowledging that English learners are *not a group*. They are individuals who are as diverse as any other students in the school, and even though their names may look and sound different, their names matter. These students matter.

Figure 13.1 provides a list of some factors that contribute to English learner diversity. Each of these should be considered when creating instructional programs and lessons for English learners.

In addition, it is important to know the personal characteristics of your students, but especially those who are English learners (Short, 2020). Use a simple interest inventory, either electronic, in print, or via an interview, to gather important information, such as the following:

- Age
- Levels of language and literacy proficiency in the home language (L1)
- Levels of language and literacy proficiency in English (L2)
- Life experiences
- Special needs
- Students' access to supportive resources, such as people who speak English proficiently, materials written in English, access to a television or radio, and so forth
- Educational background (years and nature of schooling)
- Learning preferences
- Interests
- Gifts and talents
- Life goals

With this information, you can capitalize on a student's home language, knowledge, and cultural assets.

Principle 2. Create Conditions for Language Learning

In our work with teachers, we have found that many do not recognize the teachable moments in their lessons . . . they recognize moments when students have an "aha" reaction to key content concepts, but they are less cognizant of the "aha" language moments and less prepared to elicit or take advantage of them. (Short & Echevarría, 2016, p. 18)

Principle 2 suggests that it is educators' responsibility to provide all students with a safe place where they can take risks. This requires that *essential conditions* be in place to facilitate language learning (TESOL International, 2018; Short, 2020). These include student motivation, emotional well-being (such as lack of stress), appropriate academic input

Figure 13.1. Examples of Diverse Characteristics of English Learners

Educational History

- History of no formal schooling in L1 (home language)
- Formal schooling history in L1
- History of interrupted schooling in L1
- Home schooling in L1
- History of schooling in English
- History of interrupted schooling in English
- Schooling history as a long-term English learner

Home Language (L1) Proficiency

- Oral language proficiency in L1
- Written language proficiency in L1
- Reading proficiency in L1

Knowledge of English

- Experience with an alphabetic language system
- Proficiency in speaking and writing in English
- Multilingual proficiency (knowledge of multiple languages)

Sociocultural Factors

- Poverty
- Transience
- Refugee or asylum status
- Experience with stressors, such as violence and/or abuse

Educational Services:

- Special Education
- Gifted and Talented
- Migrant Services
- Title I

and feedback, and practice opportunities that are linked to language learning targets. Which of these *essential conditions* do you think are under the influence of the teacher?

In addition, there are *beneficial conditions* that have been found to promote language development, including the relationship between a student's L1 (first language) and L2 (English), such as both languages' being alphabetic; L1 language skills that transfer to L2; high-quality language, literacy, and content instruction; avid reading by the student; knowledge of the new culture; prior foreign language learning; opportunities to use the L2; and access to competent speakers of the L2. Consider how beneficial both Laurence's and Kungawo's bilingual/multilingual experiences are to their acquisition of English. Of the *beneficial conditions*, which could be provided by the teacher?

There are also *challenging conditions* that can be a hindrance to language learning. These include socioemotional factors, such as lack of encouragement or acceptance; limited formal schooling; special needs; being an older learner or long-term English learner; the confusing spelling rules of English; and so forth. Of the *challenging conditions*, which, if any, could the teacher lessen or ameliorate?

When creating a classroom environment for English learners, teachers need to attend not only to these conditions, but also to the physical setup (such as placement of desks, tables, chairs), purposeful use of supplementary materials, language supports, and creation of a risk-free culture that promotes interaction and collaboration.

Principle 3. Design High-Quality Lessons for Language Development

Principle 3 represents the core of instruction. The lessons, whether delivered in an English language class or general education class, must have clear outcomes and use varied inputs to present information to students. High-quality language lessons encourage the practice of authentic language coupled with relevant and meaningful content. (TESOL President Deborah Short, 2018, p. 3)

High-Quality Literacy Lessons for English Learners. During the past two decades, researchers have advanced our understandings of what English learners need to become proficient readers and writers in English:

- English learners who have learned to read and write in their first language can transfer that knowledge and experience to reading and writing in English (Goldenberg, 2008).
- The same five core reading elements (phonological awareness, phonics, fluency, vocabulary, comprehension), as identified by the National Reading Panel (2000), are equally important for native English speakers and English learners (August & Shanahan, 2008).

However, English learners must also receive instruction in and practice with oral language (International Literacy Association, 2017).

- High-quality vocabulary instruction for English learners must be provided throughout the day with a focus on essential content words, language processes such as summarizing, and language functions such as asking questions (Echevarría et al., 2017; Shearer et al., 2019; Short & Echevarría, 2016; Vogt, 2020a).
- Most of the instructional techniques, methods, and activities that teachers use when teaching reading to native English speakers are also appropriate for English learners. However, there a few that are especially beneficial for English learners' reading instruction, including:

  » *Language Experience Approach* (LEA). This tried-and-true reading approach, which has been researched and discussed in publications for over 80 years, has been rediscovered by educators who are working with English learners, struggling readers, and beginning readers (Dorr, 2006; Lee, 2020). Older English learners who are learning to read in English (with little to no reading in their L1) and those who are experiencing reading problems in English benefit from the relatively simple LEA steps (Nessel & Dixon, 2006; Vogt, 2020b). (To view the steps of LEA with young children who are English learners, please see https://www.youtube.com/watch?v=28JVhicjz34. To see LEA in action with high school students who are English learners, see https://www.youtube.com/watch?v=taH4pzbNt6k.)

  » *Academic Language Frames and Sentence Starters.* These scaffolds can be helpful to English learners when they are used judiciously and purposefully—and when the sentence frames are removed when they are no longer necessary. See Short and Echevarría (2016, pp. 80, 82) for sample frames that are grouped by language function. For example, for define/describe:

    ✓ ____ means ____
    ✓ ____ is an example of ____
    ✓ ____ looks like ____ because (or so) ____
    ✓ It has ____, but it doesn't have ____.

  » *Predictable Routines*. Students of all ages who are acquiring English benefit from predictable routines, such as attendance procedures, reviewing learning goals, and picking up and returning materials. The routines are introduced, modeled, and rehearsed before students are expected to do them on their own.

  » *Written and Posted Instructions*. Another important routine for English learners is for teachers to consistently write step-by-step instructions for tasks, experiments, assignments and so forth on chart paper or the whiteboard. Use picture support as necessary.

  » *Accessible Academic Language*. Learning to read and write academic language is a challenge for many English learners and for native-English speakers as well (Short & Echevarría, 2016).

High-Quality Content and Academic Language Instruction: The SIOP Model. As of this writing, there is but one instructional model that, when implemented to a high degree, has been proven effective for English learners (Echevarría et al., 2006; Short et al., 2012). For more than 20 years, the empirically validated Sheltered Instruction Observation Protocol model (SIOP) has been used successfully in classrooms in every state in the United States and in numerous countries throughout the world (Echevarría et al., 2017).

Extensive research on the SIOP model has found that when teachers implement in their lessons SIOP's 30 instructional features, grouped within eight components, consistently and systematically, English learners and other students, including native English speakers and other subgroups, outperform similar students in non-SIOP classrooms. The SIOP students demonstrate gains in academic English and content knowledge as measured by standardized tests (Echevarría, Richards-Tutor, Canges, & Francis, 2011; Echevarría, Richards-Tutor, Chinn, & Ratleff, 2011).

As you read about the eight SIOP components, think about how each supports the principles that you have read about to this point: Principle 1: Know your learners; Principle 2: Create conditions for language learning; and Principle 3: Design high-quality language lessons. Components of the SIOP model include (Echevarría et al., 2017):

- **Lesson Preparation.** Teachers plan lessons carefully, paying particular attention to content and language objectives, appropriate content concepts, the use of supplemental materials, adaptation of content, and meaningful activities.
- **Building Background.** Teachers make explicit links to their students' background experiences, knowledge, and past learning, and teach and emphasize key vocabulary.
- **Comprehensible Input.** Teachers use a variety of techniques to make instruction understandable, including speech appropriate to students' English proficiency, clear academic tasks, and modeling.
- **Strategies.** Teachers provide students with instruction in and practice with a variety of learning strategies, scaffolding their teaching with techniques such as think-alouds, and they promote higher-order thinking through questions and tasks at a variety of cognitive levels.
- **Interaction.** Teachers provide students with frequent opportunities for interaction and discussion, group students to support content and language objectives, provide sufficient wait time for student responses, and appropriately clarify concepts in the students' first language, if possible and as necessary.
- **Practice & Application.** Teachers include in lessons opportunities for students to practice and apply new learning through hands-on activities that involve reading, writing, listening, and speaking in English.
- **Lesson Delivery.** Teachers implement lessons that clearly support content and language objectives, use appropriate pacing, and have high levels of student engagement.
- **Review & Assessment.** Teachers provide a comprehensive review of key vocabulary and content concepts, regularly give specific, academic feedback to students, and conduct assessment of student comprehension and learning throughout the lesson.

High-implementing SIOP teachers—those who consistently teach content, language, and literacy lessons that include the 30 SIOP features—engage in culturally responsive teaching and differentiated instruction, because they

- Connect to a student's prior knowledge, interests, and cultural/familiar traditions and experiences
- Plan for culturally appropriate activities and materials
- Accept cultural communication norms that may be different from their own
- Develop a classroom culture around communication and participation
- Encourage the sharing of cultural ways of knowing
- Tap into problem-solving and other critical thinking skills
- Reduce cultural bias in assignments (Echevarría, 2020)

SIOP teachers become more aware of what it means to be culturally responsive when they consistently implement the SIOP features in their lessons. The SIOP framework operationalizes culturally responsive teaching.

Principle 4. Adapt Lesson Delivery as Needed

Teachers can modulate the questions they ask students according to their levels of language proficiency. If they plan them in advance, they can still ask questions that generate higher-order thinking, but the language of the questions can be simplified. (Echevarría et al., 2017, pp. 213–214)

As we all know, the best-laid lesson plans do not always end up as intended. A detailed, fantastic lesson plan can be derailed by any number of things. Of more consequence, however, is when a lesson fails because students do not understand what is being taught and, as a result, they are unable to participate fully with the class.

With SIOP, on-the-spot adjustments are minimized by anticipating what will need to be adapted in a lesson so all students, including English learners, can meet the content and language goals. SIOP teachers think through lesson elements in advance, adapting instruction and materials in a variety of ways, such as presenting information in a different manner, adjusting speech, having available adapted texts and/or activities, carefully planning explanations and questions in advance, and supporting student understandings with supplemental materials. During lesson delivery, additional modifications may need to be considered, but they are not done on the fly. Rather, adaptations for individual students' needs are included in every SIOP lesson plan.

Principle 5. Monitor and Assess Student Language Development

> The best lesson is worthless if students haven't learned anything at the end of it. (TESOL President Deborah Short, 2018, p. 5)

Monitoring and assessing English learners' language development and academic performance is fundamental for effective instruction. In addition to more formal means of assessment, the Review & Assessment component (Features 27–30) in SIOP emphasizes the importance of ongoing, informal assessment of students' knowledge of academic content and language before, during, and after a lesson is taught (Echevarría et al., 2017). SIOP teachers provide feedback to English learners throughout a lesson, replacing the ubiquitous "Nice job!" with a specific reference to a student's academic and/or language performance on a task.

While ESL/ESOL teachers are the educators who usually assess English development on more formal assessments, literacy educators are also responsible for obtaining that information to tailor reading and writing lessons, inform content teachers' lesson planning and delivery, and measure language growth over time. In some districts, ESL/ESOL teachers are responsible for several schools, so assessment of English learners may fall under the purview of the school's literacy teachers and/or specialist. In addition, it is important to review achievement data on English learners who have exited ELD (English Language Development)/ESL programs but have yet to be redesignated as English proficient because of not meeting reading and/or math standards. All these data should help guide programmatic decision making by literacy leaders for English learners.

Principle 6. Engage and Collaborate Within a Community of Practice

> Professional learning occurs in the midst of engagement with authentic problems, in examining possibilities and different perspectives, and in implementing practices that will resolve these problems. (Risko & Vogt, 2016, p. 2).

At present, many states in the United States still do not require that preservice teachers take coursework in second language acquisition and methodology for teaching English learners. As a result, many teachers report that they feel underprepared to meet the language, literacy, and content needs of English learners. It is incumbent on schools and school districts to provide all educators who work with English learners professional learning opportunities and ongoing support that focuses on theories of second language acquisition, and academic language, literacy, and content teaching techniques, within a proven instructional model for teaching English learners.

High-quality content and academic language instruction for English learners requires a combination of coaching; substantive, ongoing and dynamic professional learning activities; collaboration; time for co-planning; and a shared belief that all students, including English learners, can become capable readers, writers, and thinkers. When professional learning is highly personal and is situated in teachers' own classrooms with their own students, they are more likely to find relevance and ownership in their learning (Risko & Vogt, 2016). Whether the solution is to have teachers engage in a Professional Learning Community or another format, we, as language and literacy leaders and administrators, can no longer allow substandard teaching for over 10% of our student population in this country. Therefore, it is up to us, collaborating with our ESL/ESOL and bilingual colleagues, to demand the highest quality of instruction for all students, not just those for whom English is a first language. (For more information about the principles, see TESOL International, 2018.)

CONCLUSION

With increasing numbers of English learners in schools throughout the United States, it is incumbent on all educators to understand and respond to the language and literacy needs of these students. English learners are not a group—rather, they are as diverse as any other students. As literacy leaders, we need to assist teachers in creating culturally responsive classrooms in which students of different linguistic and cultural backgrounds are taught equitably and effectively. *The 6 Principles for Exemplary Teaching of English Learners* (TESOL, 2018) provide pedagogical foundations that every teacher, literacy leader, and administrator should know. The SIOP Model provides the instructional framework within which the six principles can be realized.

REFLECTION QUESTIONS

1. In this chapter, you were briefly introduced to five students who are English learners. Did you notice their ages and grade levels were not mentioned? That was intentional, because the hope is that for each of these students, you can see one of your own students, who may or may not be similar, but who is an individual who needs high-quality instruction in literacy, academic language, and academic content. What can you do, in your present role, to make this happen for the English learners in your school and/or district? Who will you tap to work with you? What goals do you hope to achieve?

2. The role of culture and language is powerful as children and adolescents develop their sense of who they are. How would you define your culture? Is it defined by your race, gender, language spoken? By your family, or community, job, or church? What else? By defining and describing our own cultures (we may have several), we can better recognize, honor, and validate the cultures of others, while creating a culturally responsive school, classroom, and district.

3. Reflect on when and how you learned a new language, whether as a traveler or as a student. As a traveler, how did you feel when you were immersed in a community where you did not understand the language? What did you do to accommodate? If you learned a language in school, what did the teacher do to make the learning comprehensible for you? Or what do you wish the teacher had done to make the learning more comprehensible? What are the implications of these questions for your own classroom, school, or district?

PROJECT ASSIGNMENT

1. *For teachers:* Using the SIOP overview, create a lesson plan about a topic you teach, and focus the instruction on the academic language related to your specific topic. Try to include some of the SIOP components. If possible, record yourself teaching the lesson and then see how many of the SIOP components were observable during your lesson. What, if any, differences did you see in how your students responded to your lesson? If you were to teach the lesson again, what would you do to make it more comprehensible for English learners?

2. *For administrators:* If you are new to SIOP, refer to the description of the SIOP components while you observe an effective teacher's lesson and determine which SIOP components were evident and which were not. If you were to conference with the teacher, especially if there were English learners in the class, what would you suggest for improving the lesson for another time? (Remember that SIOP is not about teacher evaluation; it's about lesson planning, discussing, and delivering more effective lessons. Also, remember that SIOP research studies have definitively shown that when teachers implement the 30 SIOP features within the eight components to a high degree, all students have been shown to make academic gains on standardized tests).

REFERENCES

August, D., & Shanahan, T. (Eds.). (2008). *Developing reading and writing in second-language learners: Lessons from the Report of the National Literacy Panel on Language-Minority Children and Youth.* Routledge.

Dorr, R. E. (2006). Something old is new again: Revisiting language experience. *The Reading Teacher* (138–146). https://ila.onlinelibrary.wiley.com/doi/epdf/10.1598/RT.60.2.4

Echevarría, J. (2020, July). *What research says about teaching English learners* [Keynote]. National SIOP Conference (Virtual).

Echevarría, J., Richards-Tutor, C., Canges, R., & Francis, D. (2011). Using the SIOP model to promote the acquisition of language and science concepts with English learners. *Bilingual Research Journal, 34*(3), 334–351.

Echevarría, J., Richards-Tutor, C., Chinn, V., & Ratleff, P. (2011). Did they get it? The role of fidelity in teaching English learners. *Journal of Adolescent and Adult Literacy, 54*(6), 425–434.

Echevarría, J., Short, D. J., & Powers, K. (2006). School reform and standards-based education: An instructional model for English language learners. *Journal of Educational Research, 99*(4), 195–211.

Echevarría, J., Vogt, M. E., & Short, D. (2017). *Making content comprehensible for English learners: The SIOP model* (5th ed.). Pearson.

Goldenberg, C. (2008). Teaching English language learners: What the research does and does not say. *American Educator, 32*(2), 8–23, 42–44. https://www.aft.org/sites/default/files/periodicals/goldenberg.pdf

International Literacy Association. (2017). *Second-language learners' vocabulary and oral language development* [Literacy Leadership Brief].

International Literacy Association. (2019). *The role of bilingualism in improving literacy achievement.* [Literacy Leadership Brief].

Lee, L. (February 20, 2020). *A fun, experiential approach to strengthen reading and writing skills: Language Experience Approach.* Edutopia. https://www.edutopia.org/article/fun-experiential-approach-strengthen-reading-and-writing-skills

National Center for Education Statistics. (2019). *National student group scores and score gaps.* The Nation's Report Card, U.S. Department of Education. https://www.nationsreportcard.gov/reading/nation/groups/?grade=4

National Center for Education Statistics. (2020). *Percentage of English learners by state: Fall, 2017.* https://nces.ed.gov/programs/coe/indicator_cgf.asp

National Clearinghouse for English Language Acquisition. (2020). *English learners: Demographic trends.* https://www.ncela.ed.gov/files/fast_facts/19-0193_Del4.4_ELDemographicTrends_021220_508.pdf

National Reading Panel. (2000). *Teaching children to read: An evidence-based assessment of the scientific research literature on reading and its implication for reading instruction.* National Institute of Child Health and Human Development.

Nessel, D. D., & Dixon, C. (2008). *Using the Language Experience Approach with English language learners: Strategies for engaging students and developing literacy.* Corwin.

Office of English Language Acquisition. (2020). *National and state-level high school graduation rates for English learners: 2015–2016.* https://ncela.ed.gov/files/fast_facts/GraduationRatesFactSheet.pdf

Risko, V. J., & Vogt, M.E. (2016). *Professional learning in action: An inquiry approach for teachers of literacy.* Teachers College Press.

Routman, R. (2018). *Literacy essentials: Engagement, excellence, and equity for all learners.* Stenhouse Publishers.

Shearer, B. A., Carr, D. A., & Vogt, M. E. (2019). *Reading specialists and literacy coaches in the real world* (4th ed.). Waveland Press.

Short, D. J. (2018, October). How does SIOP align with TESOL's 6 Principles? *Reflections on teaching English learners.* www.janaechevarria.com/?p=1138

Short, D. J. (2020, July). *Beyond SIOP.* [Keynote]. National SIOP Conference (Virtual).

Short, D. J., & Echevarría, J. (2016). *Developing academic language with the SIOP model.* Pearson.

Short, D., Fidelman, C., & Louguit, M. (2012). Developing academic language in English language learners through sheltered instruction. *TESOL Quarterly, 46*(2), 333–360.

Short, D. J., & Fitzsimmons, S. (2007). *Double the work: Challenges and solutions to acquiring language and academic literacy for adolescent English language learners.* Report to the Carnegie Corporation of New York. Alliance for Excellent Education.

Short, D., Vogt, M. E., & Echevarría, J. (2017). *The SIOP model for administrators* (2nd ed.). Allyn & Bacon.

TESOL International. (2018). *The 6 principles for the exemplary teaching of English learners.* https://www.tesol.org/the-6-principles/

Ujifusa, A., Blad, E., & Burnette, D. (2019, December 9). ESSA voices: The Every Student Succeeds Act, four years later. *Education Week.* https://www.edweek.org/ew/articles/2019/12/10/essa-voices-the-every-student-succeeds-act.html

Vogt, M. E. (2020a). Academic language and literacy development for English learners. In A. S. Dagen & R. M. Bean (Eds.), *Best practices of literacy leaders: Keys to school improvement* (2nd ed., pp. 325–343). Guilford Press.

Vogt, M. E. (2020b, July). *Developing literacy and oral language proficiency with the Language Experience Approach (LEA)* [Keynote]. National SIOP Conference (Virtual).

CHAPTER 14

Meeting the Needs of Students With Reading Disabilities Through Multi-Tiered Systems of Support (MTSS)

Jennifer L. Goeke and Kristen D. Ritchey

- Meeting the needs of students with reading disabilities through Multi-Tiered Systems of Support (MTSS) requires detailed understanding of the literacy learning problems of students with disabilities and other at-risk populations.
- MTSS emphasizes supporting the whole child through communication and collaboration among all educators—both general and special—across a multitiered system of services and supports focused on academics, behavior, and social emotional learning.
- Administration and supervision professionals play a key role in MTSS for students who have diverse reading and writing needs.

In recent decades, the education landscape has shifted dramatically with respect to students with disabilities. Nearly 96% of students with disabilities are now educated in local or neighborhood public school buildings, and approximately 76% of students with disabilities are educated in general education classrooms for at least 40% of the school day. Of that 76%, approximately 28% of students with disabilities are educated in general education classes full time (U.S. Department of Education, 2020). At the same time, general education teachers have increased responsibility for teaching students with disabilities, often in collaboration with special educators, reading specialists and coaches, and other school personnel. Recent policy mandates along with the adoption of the Common Core or other reform-based standards have only heightened this responsibility.

SERVICE-DELIVERY MODELS FOR STRUGGLING LEARNERS

To address the needs of struggling learners with and without disabilities, states and local school districts have increasingly moved toward systems-level, service-delivery models such as Response to Intervention (RTI) or Multi-Tiered Systems of Support (MTSS). In addition to being a service delivery model, RTI is included in the Individuals with Disabilities Education Improvement Act (IDEIA, 2004) as a method for determining special education eligibility under the category of learning disabilities (LD). Tiered approaches to services have been adopted and promoted nationally (Berkeley et al., 2009; Zirkel & Davis, 2010), and such approaches continue to advance the conversation regarding the improvement of evidence-based teaching in both general education and special education.

Although educators often use the terms RTI and MTSS interchangeably, they bear some important distinctions. RTI is a multitiered intervention approach focused on providing direct academic services and supports to at-risk students as a way of reducing the number of students referred for special education. RTI models are often conceptualized as a pyramid, with the bottom section of the pyramid representing Tier 1 (core instruction delivered to all learners) and the two upper sections representing Tiers 2 and 3 (progressively intensive interventions delivered to at-risk learners). RTI tiers are flexible; students are able to move into and out of intervention as their needs for support are met.

A weakness of RTI models is that the focus on the academic needs of individual students may prevent educators from addressing the needs of the whole child and from identifying systemic barriers that prevent RTI models from being successful. At times, RTI models fail to produce measurable results because systemic factors such as weak leadership, lack of teacher expertise, or poor implementation are left unaddressed. For example, a system that ignores weak core instruction at Tier 1 while funneling struggling learners into Tiers 2 and 3 will ultimately fail. MTSS extends the original concept of RTI, but incorporates a focus on systemic barriers, as well as the needs of both teachers and students. Table 14.1 presents the differences between the elements of RTI and MTSS.

WHAT IS MTSS?

Multi-tiered systems of support is defined by the American Institutes for Research's Center on Multi-Tiered System of Supports (n.d.) as a prevention framework that organizes building-level resources to address each individual student's academic and/or behavioral needs within intervention tiers that vary in intensity. MTSS allows for the early identification of learning and behavioral challenges and timely intervention for students who are at risk for poor learning outcomes. It also may be called a *multilevel prevention system*. The increasingly intense tiers (e.g., *Tier 1, Tier 2, Tier 3*), sometimes referred to as *levels of prevention* (i.e., *primary, secondary, tertiary* prevention levels), represent a continuum of supports.

Why are the differences between RTI and MTSS (shown in Table 14.1) important to literacy administrators and supervisors? First, as more schools and districts adopt MTSS, a key responsibility of administrators and supervisors is to ensure that practices, policies, and programs are aligned across classroom, school, and district levels. This means that in addition to focusing on student support, literacy leaders must provide coherent, systemwide professional development and instructional support for teachers and support staff who deliver literacy instruction, and must promote increased collaboration between general and special educators. As a result, literacy administrators and supervisors must be able to identify where a system is vulnerable and work to ensure consistency, accountability, and quality across the tiers of MTSS.

Second, one of the most important aspects of MTSS is that it provides a mechanism for the creation of teams—problem-solving teams, grade-level teams, student support teams, or building leadership teams—who assume collective responsibility for

Table 14.1. Comparison of Key Elements of RTI and MTSS

RTI	MTSS
Identifies and supports struggling students	Integrates academic and behavioral supports with the understanding that both are essential to student success
Focuses on academic supports	Focuses on curriculum design
All students receive screening and high-quality core instruction in Tier 1	Families are involved in collaborative problem-solving
Struggling students receive targeted small-group intervention in Tier 2 and/or intensive, individualized intervention in Tier 3	Promotes teacher learning and collaboration
Involves frequent progress monitoring and data-based decision-making	May include the 3 tiers of RTI as well as Positive Behavioral Interventions and Supports (PBIS)

both system-level and student-level problem solving and decision-making. As members or leaders of a problem-solving team, literacy administrators and supervisors play a critical role in determining whether core instruction is effective, why student problems are occurring, and what solutions are likely to make a difference.

Finally, a benefit of MTSS is an emphasis on the collective responsibility of all teachers to prevent academic failure and support the whole child. Because MTSS is a general education model, it helpfully dispels the illusion of two distinct groups of students: "typically achieving" and "special education." Students who have difficulty with reading and writing exist in nearly every general education classroom, and many of these students are not identified with a disability. Difficulties with reading and language skills are the most common of all learning problems (U.S. Department of Education, 2020). Students without disabilities who are at risk for reading failure, students who are culturally diverse and/or English learners, and low-achieving students all can benefit from effective instructional programs in literacy. Administrators and supervisors of reading programs play a key role in determining how students with literacy learning problems can best be

served through multitiered systems of support. This chapter addresses these issues.

MTSS might be conceptualized as the umbrella under which both RTI (academic supports) and PBIS (Positive Behavioral Interventions and Supports) are arranged. Within MTSS, RTI can be a model for schoolwide academic interventions for all students and/or as part of the special education identification process for students with LD. RTI provides instructional interventions to students who are not responding to effective general education instruction, providing a significant improvement in the efficiency with which student learning problems can be addressed. For example, English learners who need academic interventions but do not have a disability can receive supports within RTI. For students with disabilities, the special education eligibility evaluation process can take 6–12 months from referral to initial implementation of an Individual Education Program (IEP), but RTI interventions can begin almost immediately. In this chapter, RTI refers to the academic interventions component within MTSS. Below is a brief description of the characteristics of learners who would benefit from MTSS in reading.

STUDENTS WHO WOULD BENEFIT FROM MTSS IN READING

For far too many years, students with reading disabilities were considered the responsibility of special education teachers and served in separate special education settings. MTSS systems offer an approach to meeting the needs of students with a variety of learning needs beyond reading-based specific learning disabilities. There is a range of students with reading needs, both with and without identified special education classifications. A variety of factors may contribute to students reading below grade-level expectations. Skilled reading requires the development and coordination of foundational knowledge and processes. The Simple View of Reading (Hoover & Gough, 1990) posits that reading is the product of decoding and linguistic comprehension. Scarborough (2001) elaborated this model and identified key aspects of decoding and language comprehension (see Table 14.2). These provide a way of considering students with word-level or decoding difficulties, students with comprehension-specific reading difficulties, and students with combined reading difficulties.

Table 14.2. Components of Word Recognition and Language Comprehension

Word Recognition	Language Comprehension
• phonemic awareness • phonological awareness • awareness of the alphabetic principle • decoding • sight word recognition	• background knowledge • vocabulary • language structures • verbal reasoning • literacy knowledge

Students With Word-Level Reading Needs

For younger students, difficulties at the word level are often most pronounced. Most evidence suggests that the majority of students who have difficulty with early literacy have difficulties with phonological awareness, awareness of the alphabetic principle, beginning decoding, and early sight word recognition (Connor et al., 2014; Vellutino et al., 2004). For some students, their early reading needs are the result of lack of early literacy experiences. For students with reading disabilities, dyslexia is the most common form of this difficulty.

Dyslexia is defined by the International Dyslexia Association, the National Center for Learning Disabilities, and the National Institute of Child Health and Human Development (International Dyslexia Association, 2020, About Dyslexia, para. 1) as

> a specific learning disability that is neurobiological in origin. It is characterized by difficulties with accurate and/or fluent word recognition and by poor spelling and decoding abilities. These difficulties typically result from a deficit in the phonological component of language that is often unexpected in relation to other cognitive abilities and the provision of effective classroom instruction. Secondary consequences may include problems in reading comprehension and reduced reading experience that can impede growth of vocabulary and background knowledge.

Dyslexia falls under the specific learning disability educational classification under the Individuals with Disabilities Education Act. As noted in the definition above, a deficit in understanding the phonological components of language causes difficulties in word-level reading. These word-level reading difficulties, then, in turn, are related to poor fluency and comprehension.

Students With Language-Comprehension Reading Needs

Not all reading disabilities are related to dyslexia. There is increasing evidence of a group of students with adequate or perhaps mild word reading abilities, but primary deficits may manifest in the area of comprehension. These students may also be missed by universal screening in earlier grades (Catts et al., 2012; Silverman et al., 2019), as screening efforts generally focus on word reading risks.

Children may have inadequate language proficiency especially in areas of semantic processing (i.e., vocabulary and understanding word/phrase meaning) and advanced syntactic processing (i.e., how words are ordered for meaning). This could include English learners who are learning to read in a second (or perhaps third) language. For students with disabilities, this could be related to language impairments, which are communication disorders that affect students' ability to use oral and written language (receptive, expressive, or combined). The difficulty of these students with receptive *oral* language comprehension could affect their abilities with receptive *written* language comprehension. There is also emerging evidence that students with autism may have specific difficulties with reading comprehension related to vocabulary, language processing, and inferential comprehension (Davidson et al., 2018; McIntyre et al., 2017).

While the focus on reading disabilities should be on the components of reading that are areas of concern, it is important not to ignore the social and emotional consequences of reading problems. Motivation has been studied widely as related to reading achievement (see Van Ryzin, 2010, for a review), and many teachers report that students with reading problems are less likely to be highly motivated to engage in challenging reading activities. These students are also at risk for potentially more serious social and emotional outcomes, in many cases stemming from frustration. MTSS provides the comprehensive support system necessary to address both the reading and the social and emotional needs of students with reading disabilities.

THE THREE MTSS TIERS

For each of the three tiers of MTSS, this section shows how RTI literacy intervention might be implemented, focusing on instruction, assessment, and collaboration. Also provided is a brief description of how PBIS might work in parallel fashion with RTI at each tier to form a full multitiered system of support.

Decision-Making at Tier 1

A critical consideration at Tier 1 is examining the effectiveness of core instruction. Recognizing that what is often accepted as "typical" literacy instruction may be ineffective for many students, Tier 1 intervention works first to provide highly effective teaching for all students, including those with special needs, within the general education classroom. All students (not just those who might be at risk) are screened, and those who are identified as needing help receive additional and progressively more intensive intervention.

Instruction in Tier 1. The defining characteristic of Tier 1 instruction is that there is an adopted core general education curriculum that meets standards for evidence-based practices (e.g., reading/language arts instruction), and that instruction is differentiated for student needs. The first step to implementing RTI is to focus on Tier 1 instruction and to carefully evaluate the existing curriculum and materials to ensure that curriculum focuses on the major components of reading and includes evidence-based practices. Within RTI, a goal should be moving 80% of students toward mastery of the benchmark criteria established by the screening process. If this percentage falls below 80%, there is a danger that districts will not have sufficient resources to intervene. Even if districts had unlimited resources for intervention, it is impossible to adequately compensate for weak core instruction through expanded intervention. Strengthening core instruction must be a critical task for literacy administrators and supervisors within MTSS.

Other considerations in Tier 1 beyond the adopted curriculum are also important to ensure high-quality core instruction for all learners. Sufficient uninterrupted instruction time (e.g., 90–120 minutes per day) must be provided, as insufficient time, frequent disruptions, or schedule changes (assemblies, announcements, etc.) can interfere with implementation of high-quality instruction. In Tier 1, a variety of instructional grouping options (e.g., whole-group instruction, small-group instruction, and independent centers) are included to provide differentiated opportunities to learn. These components help to establish that students receive appropriate instruction, acknowledging that learning problems are not common to all students in the class. In situations where many students in a class are considered at risk, changes to core reading instruction may be the most effective first step to ensure a productive instructional environment.

Ms. Baker is a 1st-grade teacher in a diverse suburban school. She begins the day with her students seated on a carpet for whole-class instruction. First, she leads an explicit instruction lesson on phonemic segmentation and decoding. Students use cheerleader pom-poms to "cheer out" each sound in a list of words. Next, she reviews previously learned letters, letter sounds, and key words for each letter (s, /s/, snake). As she reveals each colorful card, the students respond chorally as they trace the letter in the air. Students are instructed on the new sound/spelling for the day using a key word. They decode words with that pattern, and read sentences containing those words.

Later in the day, students are once again seated on the carpet as Ms. Baker leads them through several rounds of phoneme segmentation and blending exercises using the Elkonin boxes procedure ("say it and move it"). All students have a few plastic disks laid out in front of them. Ms. Baker provides a word and students chorally segment it into sounds, moving a block toward themselves for each sound or segment of the word that they hear. The students then work together to spell the word as Ms. Baker models the spelling on a small whiteboard. Work on segmentation and blending continues later as Ms. Baker pulls small reading groups to the round table to provide differentiated small-group instruction using the same technique. Four to five students read a short, leveled text and then work to segment and blend new words they identify from the story.

Three times per year, Ms. Baker and her colleagues screen all of the students in 1st grade for academics, behavior, and social-emotional learning. If a student is identified as potentially at risk (e.g., for reading comprehension, math calculation, or self-regulation), the screening helps to target specific areas for intervention. To facilitate screening, the teachers share assessment roles, as some teachers, the reading specialist, and the school psychologist conduct the screening while other teachers provide instruction to groups of students from across the 1st-grade classrooms. In this way, screening efforts do not interfere with instruction. Once screening data are combined, the teachers and other members of the Problem Solving Team meet to discuss the results.

At regular intervals (e.g., weekly, biweekly), the teachers and staff also reflect on and evaluate their own actions and decisions within MTSS. While the overarching goal is to improve outcomes for students, MTSS interventions are planned and delivered by adults who must continuously adjust the ways they work, improve collaboration and communication, and balance the needs of the school population with the resources available.

Assessment in Tier 1. Assessment in Tier 1 of RTI includes universal screening, or brief assessments of all learners to determine which students may be at risk for reading problems (as well as math and behavior/SEL problems). Figure 14.1 presents screening data for the 1st-grade students in the case study above, and the students at risk are identified with stars. Screening tools are designed to be efficient to administer and score (<10 minutes per student) and are administered at least three times per year, although some schools screen four times a year. Fall, winter, and spring schedules are most common. Universal screening tools are widely available at most grades (with fewer tools for secondary students) and often apply principles of curriculum-based measurement (CBM) (Deno, 1985). CBM originated as a special education tool, but has been applied within general education contexts and includes commercial products such as Dynamic Indicators of Basic Early Literacy Skills (DIBELS) (Good & Kaminski, 2003), AIMSWeb (Edformation, 2006), and easyCBM (www.easy-cbm.com) systems. Other screening tools exist, including several that are computer-based, which may serve to facilitate screening efficiency. The National Center on Intensive Intervention (https://intensiveintervention.org) provides a list of screening tools that can be used across grade levels.

Figure 14.1. Universal Screening Data: Winter

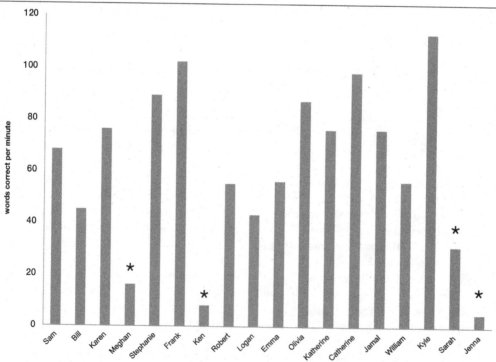

Collaboration in Tier 1. In Tier 1, grade-level or cross-grade-level teams may schedule weekly or bi-weekly planning data meetings, or problem-solving teams. These teams work together to set goals, plan instruction, and review assessment data including classwork, screening data, and progress-monitoring data. Teams may work to identify ways to address student needs in all tiers, as what works in Tier 1 can affect what happens in Tiers 2 and 3. Membership could include reading specialists, special education teachers, counselors, psychologists, administrators, and literacy coaches. Professional Learning Communities (PLCs) may also work in this manner.

Professional development and coaching may also be needed to help support implementation of high-quality instruction. In many schools, principals, assistant principals, and literacy coaches may regularly visit classrooms using "walk-through" protocols to help identify instructional activities that are supporting high-quality instruction and to identify areas that may need improvement. Coaching is often targeted for novice teachers, but even experienced teachers can benefit from professional development and additional support, especially when implementing new practices or working with challenging students.

PBIS as part of MTSS in Tier 1. The holistic structure of MTSS allows educators to address students' academic and behavioral needs simultaneously. When academic interventions are combined with positive behavioral supports, students can improve in all areas. Thus, PBIS implementation allows schools to foster a more positive culture while addressing the behavioral needs of individual students. As with RTI, key elements of PBIS are teams, consistent schoolwide expectations, tiered systems of support, professional development, and ongoing data analysis. As part of MTSS, PBIS helps focus both teachers and students on positive interactions rather than punishment, creating a school climate that supports student success in all areas, including literacy development.

At Tier 1, a universal screening tool such as the Social, Academic, Emotional, and Behavior Risk Screener (SAEBRS; Kilgus & von der Embse, 2014) may be used to screen all students for social–emotional and behavioral problems. Schools may also use additional strategies such as office discipline referrals, teacher nominations, or parent recommendations to identify students who need additional behavioral

support. Tier 1 intervention focuses on the prevention of unwanted behaviors; therefore, positive behavioral interventions and supports consist of establishing clear rules and routines, acknowledging and reinforcing appropriate behavior, and arranging the physical environment to prevent instances of behavior that are targeted for change.

Decision-Making at Tier 2

For students who are identified as at risk through universal screening and/or after being provided with high-quality Tier 1 instruction, Tier 2 instruction is provided. Students continue to participate in Tier 1 instruction, with other activities including collaboration continued in Tier 2.

Instruction in Tier 2. This tier of instruction is characterized as supplemental instruction or tutoring that is provided in addition to regular instruction (the National Center on Intensive Intervention has reviews of potential interventions: https://charts.intensiveintervention.org/aintervention). In most models, Tier 2 instruction is delivered three to five times per week for 20 to 30 minutes, and intervention lasts 8 to 12 weeks. Gersten et al. (2008) recommend that the focus of Tier 2 intervention be no more than three of the five foundation skills in reading (i.e., phonemic awareness, phonics, fluency, vocabulary, comprehension). Most models require that Tier 2 interventions be provided by professionals with expertise in interventions (e.g., reading specialists and special education teachers), but some models have classroom teachers or highly trained paraprofessionals implement Tier 2 instruction (Causton-Theoharis et al., 2007; Nelson et al., 2011). School resources and the amount of professional support may determine who the Tier 2 implementer is, but the individual must be trained and qualified to provide intervention (i.e., not a volunteer).

Within Tier 2 instruction, students with similar learning problems (e.g., decoding) are given a standard research-based intervention that has documented effectiveness for students with similar difficulties. A standard protocol is then applied while fidelity of implementation is assessed. This approach provides an appropriate emphasis on evidence-based practices for students with learning problems and results in more students likely to receive the same intervention, as well as greater treatment fidelity.

Based on the screening data, four children in Ms. Baker's class were identified as at risk. On the screening measures, these students have not met the January benchmark established for passage reading (refer to Figure 14.1). These students are discussed by the school-based Problem Solving Team, made up of 1st-grade teachers, the literacy coach, and an administrator. They discuss the students and make plans for how to address their needs.

Because the four students have similar difficulties reading words with short and long vowel patterns, the literacy specialist, Ms. Kurtis, tailors a small-group intervention specifically to their needs. Specifically, she begins small-group instruction within the general education classroom as a supplement to their existing guided reading groups and adds several activities to target these skills during center time. She works with these students 4 days a week for 15 minutes each day. The Elkonin box procedure ("say it and move it") is implemented in combination with other activities to strengthen students' skills in the identified area of weakness. She continues to collect assessment data on the students' progress and monitors the fidelity of the interventions for 8 weeks.

Progress-monitoring assessments (also assessing passage-reading fluency) are administered weekly to determine if the interventions are effective and the students are making progress that suggests they will no longer be at risk. The data are graphed, and the slope of these lines is estimated to determine rate of growth (using a formula in database software) to show the improvement during Tier 2 intervention. The slope is an estimate of the mean increase in the number of words per minute each week. Meghan and Sarah have made good growth (i.e., have responded to Tier 2 intervention), while Jenna and Ken have made little or no growth (i.e., have not responded to Tier 2 intervention).

The Problem Solving Team meets a second time to discuss the progress of Jenna and Ken. Tier 2 instruction is modified to include 5 extra minutes of sight word practice each day and continues for another 4 weeks for these students.

The team also determines that in addition to a lack of progress in literacy, Ken's behavior screening and office discipline referrals indicate that there has been an escalation in acting-out behaviors during class (e.g., talking out of turn and getting out of his seat to roam the classroom without permission). The team identifies the function of Ken's behavior as seeking attention. As a result, they decide to implement a Check-in/Check-out procedure in which Ken must receive feedback about his behavior from the classroom teacher 5–7 times per day. Ken may experience this increased adult attention as reinforcing, while more frequent opportunities for positive interaction and reinforcement from the teacher may help to promote and sustain positive behavior.

Assessment in Tier 2. Progress is monitored during Tier 2 to determine if students are responding (or responsive) to intervention and if reading performance is improving. The measures that are used for screening in most cases can also be used for monitoring progress. Unlike screening, in which all students are assessed three times per year, students who receive Tier 2 intervention are assessed weekly or biweekly. Data can be displayed on a graph (with the rate of growth, or slope, estimated) to determine if progress is sufficient. Figure 14.2 displays progress-monitoring data (with a slope estimate) for four students receiving Tier 2 intervention. A visual-inspection process can be used to determine the extent of students' response (for more information, see Hosp et al., 2007; Riley-Tillman & Burns, 2009).

Collaboration in Tier 2. As in Tier 1, teachers continue to collaborate. This collaboration can include ongoing data teams or problem-solving teams, and information about students who are receiving this type of intervention is also discussed. A challenging aspect of collaboration at Tier 2 (and also at Tier 3) is scheduling and management of resources (materials, people, and time). Some schools have adopted schoolwide intervention times during each day (staggered by grade) so that all students are available for intervention and there are sufficient staff to provide instruction to a variety of students. For example, from 10:00 to 10:30 all 1st-grade students work in an intervention group—for some students, it is their special education services; for some students, it is Tier 2 reading intervention or Tier 3 reading intervention; and for others, it may be reading enrichment or acceleration.

PBIS in Tier 2. Students who are not successful with Tier 1 prevention alone may be recommended for Tier 2 intervention. Team members with behavior expertise (e.g., behaviorist) help determine the

Figure 14.2. Progress-Monitoring Data During Tier 2 Instruction

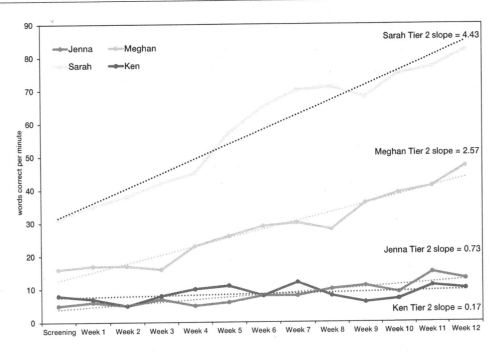

function (underlying reason) for a students' problem behavior so that the chosen intervention can be appropriately aligned with the student's needs. Tier 2 intervention often consists of small groups focused on areas such as social skills or self-management; the groups work on increased instruction and practice with targeted skills. During Tier 2, the team continues to collect and monitor data regarding student performance in both PBIS and literacy intervention to gain the fullest possible picture of a student's progress within the MTSS. They also ensure that interventions are scheduled to preserve participation in core instruction.

Decision-Making at Tier 3

Tier 3 intervention is provided for students who are identified as at risk through universal screening and who do not respond to high-quality Tier 1 and Tier 2 instruction.

Instruction in Tier 3. Tier 3 involves increased intensity of intervention. This can be provided by using smaller groups of students (e.g., three students), which allow more student–teacher interaction, and by increasing the frequency and amount of time for

each intervention session (e.g., 60 minutes per day in Tier 3 versus 20 minutes several times per week in Tier 2). In Tier 3, instruction is also individualized as it addresses areas of need (note, this is *not* individually delivered instruction or one-on-one teaching, but instruction that is tailored to each student in the group). Intervention also could include social or emotional aspects of learning, such as motivation, or behavioral components to improve areas, such as attention or on-task behavior. Tier 3 intervention is delivered by specialists and provides research-based intervention that is monitored for fidelity.

Assessment in Tier 3. As in Tier 2, progress-monitoring assessment continues to be administered, and data are collected. In some cases, progress might be monitored using grade-level materials (4th-grade students are administered 4th-grade progress-monitoring materials) or instruction-level materials (4th-grade students working on the 2nd-grade reading level are administered 2nd-grade progress-monitoring materials). Likewise, diagnostic assessment tools could be administered to help identify student needs and match intervention at Tier 3 to instructional needs.

Ms. Kurtis has implemented the Tier 2 instructional program with fidelity for 12 weeks, and Jenna and Ken have made some slow and inconsistent progress. They both continue to have difficulty with all aspects of phonological awareness (i.e., cannot blend three or four isolated sounds to produce a word, difficulty isolating initial phonemes in words). An additional meeting is scheduled to discuss their progress with the Problem Solving Team. At this point, a more specialized instructional approach is discussed. The team also decides that an educational evaluation may be needed to determine if either student has a disability.

In the meantime, the students begin working with Mr. Pickwick, one of the reading specialists, who is trained in the Lindamood Phonological Sequencing Program (LIPS) program (Lindamood & Lindamood, 1998). LIPS is an intensive instructional program designed to explicitly teach phonological awareness, and the program is implemented for 30 minutes per day, 5 days per week. Two other students from another classroom who are experiencing the same types of difficulty join this group. Mr. Pickwick carefully coordinates the schedule and content with Ms. Baker. After 4 weeks in the program, one of the students from Ms. Baker's class is making more consistent growth, but one student is not showing the same progress. The intervention is continued for another four weeks.

After 8 weeks, the Problem-Solving Team is reconvened to discuss the data for these students and potential evaluation for special education services. Jenna is considered to no longer be at risk, but the team will continue to monitor her progress, as she may need additional, intermittent intervention. Ken has not responded to Tier 3 instruction and is likely to need continued intensive instruction to improve his academic outcomes.

The team also reviews Ken's Tier 2 PBIS data, which reveals a slight decrease in disruptive classroom behaviors since the implementation of the Check-in/Check-out procedure. The team decides to continue with the Check-in/Check-out intervention and reanalyze the data in another 8 weeks. In addition, Ken is referred to participate in a small group led by the behavior specialist that meets once a week for 30 minutes to teach and practice self-management skills.

Data collected during Tier 2 and Tier 3 interventions can be used as a test for the evaluation process for special education as a student with LD. The progress-monitoring data highlight considerable deficits in Ken's literacy development. Rather than identifying him for special education, however, the team decides to continue monitoring Ken until the end of the marking period in light of his progress with the LIPS intervention. The team posits that if Ken continues to make moderate progress in literacy, his classroom behavior and motivation may also improve. At that point, Ken's entire instructional and behavioral program will be reviewed and special education identification reconsidered.

Collaboration in Tier 3. Many of the collaboration efforts that occur during Tier 1 and Tier 2 continue for students who are receiving Tier 3 services. Data analysis meetings and intervention planning may continue to occur, with special attention to students who are not making progress. Figure 14.3 presents the type of progress-monitoring data that are used across Tier 2 and Tier 3 to determine intervention planning. In Tier 3, additional personnel may be directly involved in working with students, such as special education teachers or other instructional or behavioral experts. Lastly, many schools may be working together with members of the IEP team, and parents or other community members may be invited to become involved in more meaningful ways for students receiving Tier 3 instruction.

PBIS in Tier 3. As with academic interventions, Tier 3 behavior supports are increasingly intensive and individualized, and may involve parents or other members of the student's local community. At Tier 3, interventions typically include a formal Functional Behavior Assessment to ensure that any intervention addresses the reasons for the student's problem behavior, along with a Behavior Intervention Plan. Interventions may also include wraparound supports, which involve both formal, evidence-based interventions and the student's natural support systems, and analysis of strengths and needs, as well as consideration of alternatives to suspension or expulsion. Tier 3 supports are also considered in light of a student's cultural and contextual influences, such as race, ethnicity, language, and neighborhood environment. It is critical that Tier 3 interventions be administered by a professional who has expertise in applied behavior as

Figure 14.3. Progress-Monitoring Data during Tier 3 Instruction

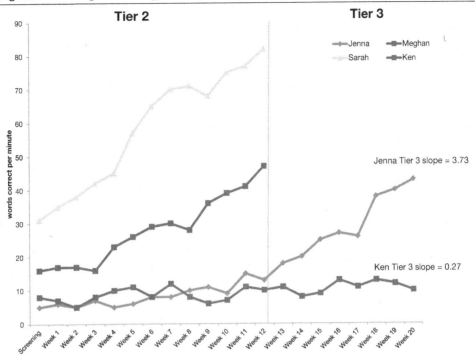

THE ROLE OF LITERACY LEADERS WITHIN MTSS

Within an MTSS framework, reading professionals play a key role in academic interventions for students who have reading and writing needs. It is important to note that intervention can also occur for mathematics (although fewer school districts implement RTI in math at this time). Tier 1, Tier 2, and Tier 3 activities may be occurring simultaneously at any point during a school year, as students move across tiers based on progress and as necessary to meet their needs.

There are many roles and responsibilities for reading professionals as a school or district begins to adopt MTSS. The first role could be as the expert in instruction and curriculum, which requires assessing the available resources and identifying what additional resources are needed. The core curriculum in reading/language may need to be reviewed and evaluated for content coverage and any need for additional resources. Likewise, the professional resources in a school building may need to be evaluated to determine which individuals in a building have the experience and/or expertise to implement Tier 2 and Tier 3 interventions and decide on the type of any additional professional development found to be necessary.

A second role of reading professionals could be as the individuals who provide professional development for new practices and as coaches to support implementation efforts. MTSS requires continuing development and expansion of teachers' skills, with coordinated professional development across a school or district to enhance system quality and coherence. These efforts are essential to ensure that teachers develop the skills to meet the needs of students with the most significant learning disabilities. For example, many teachers would benefit from additional professional development to meet the literacy needs of students who are English learners and have limited English proficiency. Coaching can provide support and feedback to teachers and other professionals as they implement instruction at all tiers. (For more information on coaching, see Chapter 3.)

A final role of reading professionals is as manager and facilitator of RTI efforts within a building (although this role could be the shared responsibility of many professionals). This role requires cultivating an atmosphere of collaboration and teamwork that can replace the "my students" and "your students" mindset that is common among educators. MTSS emphasizes the provision of effective supports and services by all educators—both general and special—and a mindset of "our students." The primary responsibility of some reading professionals may also include the many practical aspects of RTI implementation such as scheduling meetings and instruction, preparing and managing materials, supervising paraprofessionals, organizing data, and leading team meetings.

CONCLUSION

MTSS models represent a significant advance in our efforts to prevent students from developing serious learning and behavior problems, and to address systemic factors that make interventions unsuccessful. When literacy intervention occurs within a holistic structure that addresses a student's behavioral and social–emotional needs and includes collaboration and communication among educators, there is an increased likelihood of success. Nonetheless, widespread adoption of MTSS is still emerging, as these models are complex to create, implement, and sustain. As a result, questions continue to arise. For example, scholars and professionals continue to question and identify how RTI procedures will merge with existing special education policies and procedures. Also, the body of existing research on RTI models focuses primarily on reading instruction and intervention for elementary students; less is known about how RTI models might be implemented with older students (Denton et al., 2007; Pyle & Vaughn, 2012,). A broad set of evidence-based interventions is also missing, especially for older students and in areas such as reading comprehension and writing. However, the implementation of MTSS holds promise for improving the behavioral and academic outcomes for students, including those in reading.

REFLECTION QUESTIONS

1. What are some of the advantages and disadvantages of MTSS, and how could it address local issues faced by your school or district?
2. What are the implications for professional development (both at the school level and through graduate or continuing education)?
3. How are Tier 2 and Tier 3 similar to or different from special education services? In what ways might the two types of existing services need to remain separate, and in what ways might the two types of services be combined and streamlined?

PROJECT ASSIGNMENT

If your school or district is implementing MTSS, interview a school staff member to determine what is in place, how well it is working, and what improvements could be made. If your school or district is not implementing MTSS, ask school staff to brainstorm which aspects of MTSS could be a good first step to implementing MTSS in your building.

REFERENCES

Berkeley, S., Bender, W. N., Peaster, L. G., & Saunders, L. (2009). Implementation of response to intervention: A snapshot of progress. *Journal of Learning Disabilities, 42*(1), 85–95.

Catts, H. W., Compton, D., Tomblin, J. B., & Bridges, M. S. (2012). Prevalence and nature of late-emerging poor readers. *Journal of Educational Psychology, 104*(1), 166–181.

Causton-Theoharis, J. N., Giangreco, M. F., Doyle, M., & Vadasy, P. F. (2007). Paraprofessionals: The "sous-chefs" of literacy instruction. *Teaching Exceptional Children, 40*(1), 56–62.

Center on Multi-Tiered System of Supports (MTSS Center). (n.d.). https://www.air.org/centers/center-multi-tiered -system-supports-mtss-center

Connor, C. M., Alberto, P. A., Compton, D. L., & O'Connor, R. E. (2014). *Improving reading outcomes for students with or at risk for reading disabilities: A* synthesis of the contributions from the Institute of Education Sciences Research Centers (NCSER 2014-3000). National Center for Special Education Research, Institute of Education Sciences, U.S. Department of Education. https://ies.ed.gov/ncser/pubs/20143000/

Davidson, M. M., Kaushanskaya, M., & Ellis Weismer, S. (2018). Reading comprehension in children with and without ASD: The role of word reading, oral language, and working memory. *Journal of Autism and Developmental Disorders, 48*(10), 3524–3541.

Deno, S. L. (1985). Curriculum based measurement: The emerging alternative. *Exceptional Children, 52*(3), 219–232.

Denton, C., Bryan, D., Wexler, J., Reed, D., & Vaughn, S. (2007). *Effective instruction for middle school students with reading difficulties: The reading teacher's sourcebook.* Vaughn Gross Center for Reading and Language Arts at The University of Texas at Austin.

Edformation, Inc. (2006). *Assessment and improvement monitoring systems* (AIMSweb).

Gersten, R., Compton, D., Connor, C. M., Dimino, J., Santoro, L., Linan-Thompson, S., & Tilly, W. D. (2008). *Assisting students struggling with reading: Response to Intervention and multi-tier intervention in the primary grades. A practice guide* (NCEE 2009-4045). National Center for Education Evaluation and Regional Assistance, Institute of Education Sciences, U.S. Department of Education. https://ies.ed.gov/ncee/wwc/Docs/PracticeGuide/rti_reading_pg_021809.pdf

Good, R. H., & Kaminski, R. A. (2003). *Dynamic indicators of basic early literacy skills* (DIBELS). University of Oregon Center on Teaching and Learning.

Hoover, W. A., & Gough, P. B. (1990). The simple view of reading. *Reading and Writing: An Interdisciplinary Journal, 2*, 127–160.

Hosp, M. K., Hosp, J. L., & Howell, K. W. (2007). *The ABCs of CBM: A practical guide to curriculum-based measurement.* Guilford Press.

Individuals with Disabilities Education Improvement Act. (2004). NYSED. http://www.p12.nysed.gov/specialed/idea/

International Dyslexia Association (2020). *Definition consensus project.* https://dyslexiaida.org/definition-consensus-project/

Kilgus, S. P., & von der Embse, N. P. (2014). *Social, academic, and emotional behavior risk screener.* https://www.fastbridge.org/saebrs/

Lindamood, P., & Lindamood, P. (1998). *The Lindamood Phoneme Sequencing Program for reading, spelling, & speech: The LIPS program* (3rd ed.). ProEd.

McIntyre, N. S., Solari, E. J., Gonzalez, J. E., Solomon, M., Lerro, L. E., Novotny, S., Oswald, T. M., & Mundy, P. C. (2017). The scope and nature of reading comprehension impairments in school-aged children with higher functioning Autism Spectrum Disorder. *Journal of Autism and Developmental Disorders, 47*(9), 2838–2860.

Nelson, J., Vadasy, P. F., & Sanders, E. A. (2011). Efficacy of a Tier 2 supplemental root word vocabulary and decoding intervention with kindergarten Spanish-speaking English learners. *Journal of Literacy Research, 43*(2), 184–211.

Pyle, N., & Vaughn, S. (2012). Remediating reading difficulties in a response to intervention model with secondary students. *Psychology in the Schools, 49*(3), 273–284. doi:10.1002/pits.21593

Riley-Tillman, T. C., & Burns, M. K. (2009). *Evaluating education interventions: Single-case design for measuring response to intervention.* Guilford Press.

Scarborough, H. S. (2001). Connecting early language and literacy to later reading (dis)abilities: Evidence, theory, and practice. In S. Neuman & D. Dickinson (Eds.), *Handbook for research in early literacy* (pp. 97–110). Guilford Press.

Silverman, R. D., McNeish, D., Speece, D. L., & Ritchey, K. D. (2019). Early screening for decoding- and language-related reading difficulties in first and third grade. *Assessment for Effective Intervention, 46*(2), 99–109. https://eric.ed.gov/?id=EJ1286397

U.S. Department of Education. (2020). *Forty-second annual report to Congress on the implementation of the Individuals with Disabilities Education Act.* https://www2.ed.gov/about/reports/annual/osep/2020/parts-b-c/42nd-arc-for-idea.pdf

Van Ryzin, M. J. (2010). Motivation and reading disabilities. In A. McGill-Franzen & R. L. Allington (Eds.), *Handbook of reading disability research* (pp. 242–252). Routledge.

Vellutino, F. R., Fletcher, J. M., Snowling, M. J., & Scanlon, D. M. (2004). Specific reading disability (dyslexia): What have we learned in the past four decades? *Journal of Child Psychology and Psychiatry, 45*(1), 2–40.

Zirkel, P., & Davis, L. B. (2010). State laws for RTI: An updated snapshot. *Teaching Exceptional Children, 42*(3), 56–63.

CHAPTER 15

Providing Classroom Leadership in New Literacies

Preparing Students for Their Future

Elena Forzani, Clint Kennedy, and Donald J. Leu

- New literacies pose a continuing and fundamental challenge—but also an opportunity—for literacy educators: The reading and writing skills students will require tomorrow include ones that are not known today.
- The nature of new literacies can best be understood on two different levels: a variety of lowercase new literacies and a common uppercase New Literacies.
- Ten principles can be applied in school and in online classrooms to direct New Literacies instruction. These are especially important as teachers and students see the need and opportunity for more virtual learning experiences.

We have entered a markedly new era for literacy education using the Internet, particularly as the COVID-19 pandemic has significantly expanded remote instruction across the globe. The continuously changing nature of online technologies means that online reading and writing skills will also keep changing. This creates a fundamental challenge—but also an opportunity—for literacy educators: The reading and writing skills students will require tomorrow will include ones that are unknown today. This simple fact requires educators to think in new ways about how to teach, administer, and supervise classroom programs in the English language arts.

The COVID-19 pandemic impelled educators to think in new ways about how to teach with new technologies and within new literacy learning contexts. As schools closed their physical buildings and teaching and learning moved to remote spaces, teachers had to rapidly adapt by learning new techniques for teaching over Zoom or other virtual platforms. Teachers employed apps and other digital tools, such as Google Classroom and Jamboard, to make the most of these spaces, each with new literacies required for their effective use. Such spaces and tools will likely continue to provide both challenges and opportunities for teachers and learners.

THE CONTINUOUSLY CHANGING NATURE OF LITERACY

Today, new online technologies continuously appear for literacy that redefine reading, writing, communication, and learning. Consider just a few of the more recent arrivals in addition to the older incumbents: Zoom, Twitter, Facebook, Instagram, Dropbox, Skype, Chrome, iMovie, and any of thousands of mobile apps. Each requires additional reading and/or writing skills to take full advantage of their affordances. Moreover, additional literacy tools will appear with additional new literacies required to use them effectively.

Thus, when we speak of new literacies in an online age, we mean that literacy is not just new today; it becomes new every day of our lives. Proficiency in these online new literacies will define students' success in both school and life. How teachers adapt to a new and dynamic definition of literacy in the classroom will define their students' future.

Some believe that there is little to teach, that today's students are already "digital natives" (Prensky, 2001), skilled in online literacies. It is true that these students have grown up in a digital world and are developing proficiency, from out-of-school experiences, with gaming, social networking, video, and texting (Alvermann et al., 2012; Zickuhr, 2010). However, this does not necessarily mean that they are skilled in online information use (Bennett et al., 2008). Indeed, recent research shows that students are relatively unskilled at locating, critically evaluating, and comprehending online information (Forzani, 2018; Kiili et al., 2018).

THE NEW LITERACIES OF ONLINE RESEARCH AND COMPREHENSION

The fact that literacies change poses a fundamental problem for thinking about theory. How can we develop adequate theory when the object that we seek to understand continuously changes, being redefined by new technologies, new contexts, and new conceptions of literacy? New Literacies theory (Leu et al., 2019) proposes that we solve this conundrum by thinking about theory on two levels: lowercase (new literacies) and uppercase (New Literacies). Lowercase new literacies refers to a set of new literacies required by a specific technology and its social practices; for example, text messaging (Lewis & Fabos, 2005); a disciplinary base, such as the semiotics of multimodality in online media (e.g., Kress, 2003); or a distinctive, conceptual approach, such as new literacy studies (Street, 1995, 2003). These literacies rapidly change as new technologies change and new contexts for reading and writing emerge.

New Literacies, as the broader concept, benefits from work taking place in the multiple lowercase dimensions. Common findings from research in lowercase new literacies, across multiple perspectives, define a broader, more stable, uppercase New Literacies theory. Leu et al. (2019) suggest that New Literacies theory currently includes these common findings:

1. The Internet is this generation's defining technology for literacy and learning within the global community.
2. The Internet and related technologies require new literacies to fully access their potential.
3. New literacies are deictic, meaning that their significance depends on the contexts in which they are used, and such contexts rapidly change, carrying new meanings with them.
4. New literacies are multiple, multimodal, and multifaceted; as a result, our understanding of them benefits from multiple points of view.
5. Critical literacies are central to new literacies.
6. New forms of strategic knowledge are required with new literacies.
7. New social practices are a central element of new literacies.
8. Teachers become more important, though their role changes, within new literacy classrooms. (p. 1158)

The new literacies of online research and comprehension (Leu et al., 2019) are an example of a lowercase theory and may be especially important to classroom reading programs. This perspective frames online reading comprehension as a process of problem-based inquiry involving the new skills, strategies, dispositions, and social practices that take place as the Internet is used to conduct research, solve problems, and answer questions. At least five processing practices occur during online research and comprehension; they include: (1) reading to identify important questions, (2) reading to locate information, (3) reading to evaluate information critically, (4) reading to synthesize information, and (5) writing to communicate information. These processing practices require specific skills and strategies that are distinctive to online research and comprehension.

How does the nature of reading and writing change on the Internet? What, if any, new literacies are required? Researchers are just discovering the answers to these questions (Afflerbach & Cho, 2008). First, it appears that online reading comprehension often takes place within a research and problem-solving task (Coiro & Castek, 2010). Second, online reading becomes tightly integrated with writing, as users communicate with others to learn about the questions they explore and then communicate their own interpretations. A third difference that exists is that new technologies such as browsers, search engines, learning management systems, blogs, email, and many others are used online. Additional skills are required to use each of these technologies effectively.

Finally, and perhaps most important, online reading may require increased emphasis on higher-level thinking compared to offline reading. In a context in which anyone may publish anything, higher-level thinking skills such as the critical evaluation of information and understanding an author's point of view become especially important. Emerging research has provided the following additional insights:

- Some readers who are challenged in offline contexts may read better in online contexts, even compared to those students who read well offline but who lack online reading skills (Castek et al., 2011).

- Prior topic knowledge may contribute less to online research and reading comprehension than offline reading comprehension, since readers may gather required prior topic knowledge online as a part of the reading paths they follow (Coiro, 2011).
- Students often learn many online research and comprehension skills from other students as a result of challenging activities designed by the teacher (Kiili et al., 2012).
- Students may be motivated in somewhat different ways in online, compared to offline, contexts (Forzani et al., 2020).

These insights will be important to our work in the administration and supervision of literacy programs. They will also become important to the new contexts for learning that are emerging online, such as the original MOOCs (Massive Open Online Courses) and other virtual learning contexts, as well as the changing nature of online communities led by newer platforms such as Discord. Discord is a free, invite-only community. Users can create channels for different purposes where they can chat, collaborate, and share with one another. Students will require these new reading skills to successfully participate in new online contexts for learning that will define their future.

NEW LITERACIES STANDARDS

A growing number of communities are beginning to recognize the changes to literacy that are taking place in an online age. They are changing educational standards so their students are better prepared for work and life in an online information age.

Canada: Manitoba

The province of Manitoba, Canada, for example, developed an educational framework called Literacy with ICT Across the Curriculum (Minister of Manitoba Education, Citizenship, and Youth, 2006). This initiative outlines skills and includes standards required in the 21st century in all aspects of their curriculum, such as:

identifying appropriate inquiry questions; navigating multiple information networks to locate relevant information; applying critical thinking skills to evaluate information sources and content; synthesizing information and ideas from multiple sources and networks; representing information and ideas creatively in visual, aural, and textual formats; crediting and referencing sources of information and intellectual property; and communicating new understandings to others, both face to face and over distance. (Minister of Manitoba Education, Citizenship, and Youth, 2006, p. 18)

International Society for Technology in Education

The International Society for Technology in Education (ISTE) is a global community of educators interested in using technology to transform education. ISTE has several sets of standards around the integration of technology in education, including standards for students, educators, education leaders, and coaches. The standards for educators focus on developing educators who are collaborative learners, designers, facilitators, and analysts, and who inspire students to contribute responsibly within digital contexts. The standards for education leaders include strands such as advocating for equity, visioning and strategic planning, empowering educators, designing systems and teams, and staying connected to emerging technologies. You can download the standards and free resources at https://www.iste.org (International Society for Technology in Education, 2018).

The United States

In the United States, the Common Core State Standards (CCSS) Initiative (2010) sought to establish more uniform standards across states that better prepare students for college and careers in the 21st century. One of the key design principles in the CCSS, research and media skills, indicates that it is essential to integrate new literacies into the classroom. It states:

To be ready for college, workforce training, and life in a technological society, students need the ability to gather, comprehend, evaluate, synthesize, and report on information and ideas, to conduct original research in order to answer questions or solve problems, and to analyze and create a high volume and extensive range of print and nonprint texts in media forms old and new. The need to conduct research and to produce and consume media is embedded into every aspect of today's curriculum. (Common Core State Standards, 2010, p. 4)

Three changes are especially noticeable in the English/Language Arts Standards of CCSS:

1. There is a greater focus on reading informational texts.
2. Higher-level thinking is emphasized.
3. Digital literacies are integrated throughout the English/language arts standards.

Each of these reflects the shift in reading from page to screen. While there is more that can be done (Drew, 2012), a number of anchor standards now include new literacies required by digital technologies (Leu et al., 2019). Despite differences in how they integrate new literacies into national, state, provincial, and organizational standards, all represent the changes taking place in literacy education as reading shifts from page to screen. Global economic competition and workforce preparation are causing governments to rethink the literacy preparation of their youth.

TEN PRINCIPLES TO INFORM CLASSROOM LEADERSHIP AND INSTRUCTION IN NEW LITERACIES

As you think about integrating these new literacies into your classrooms, it may be useful to consider ten research-based principles that can inform the administration and supervision of classroom literacy programs in this area:

1. Recognize that a new literacies journey is one of continuous learning.
2. Begin teaching and learning new literacies as early as possible.
3. Use new literacies to help the last student become the first.
4. Recognize that online search skills are important to success in new literacies.
5. Use online reading experiences to develop critical thinking skills with students who are flexible skeptics.

6. Integrate the Internet into classrooms through online communication.

7. Open doors for teachers by starting with a pilot program, especially in resistant schools and districts.

8. Use performance-based assessments for evaluating new literacies.

9. Use Internet Reciprocal Teaching (McVerry et al., 2009) as an effective strategy to teach the new literacies of online research and comprehension in one-to-one computing classrooms.

10. Engage students in collaborative online learning experiences with classroom partners in other parts of the world.

Below, we define these principles and include specific instructional practices that can be used to implement them.

1. Recognize That a New Literacies Journey Is One of Continuous Learning

As new technologies appear on the Internet, new literacy requirements and opportunities appear (Leu, 2000). Consider, for example, one student who was reading online about how rainbows are formed. She encountered an unfamiliar word, "refraction." A second student noticed the problem and showed her a strategy that had become possible with an update to the Google search engine. This second student went to the Google search box in the browser and typed in "define: refraction." She knew that using the keyword "define:" plus an unfamiliar word generates results limited to online dictionary entries for the target word. Reading several entries in the search results made the meaning of this unfamiliar word clear to the first student, who had acquired a new online reading skill.

Examples like this take place regularly as users encounter new affordances within older technologies or as new technologies appear. These developments are reminders that engagements with the new literacies are really a journey, not a destination. This regular appearance of new literacies requires additional roles for school leaders, teachers, and students.

If you are a school leader, your role includes developing a vision for working within this continuously changing landscape. This means living an active,

online professional life so that you might become more familiar with the new literacies that new technologies require. Your role may also be enhanced by working to build supportive online communities among teachers so they can share and exchange new skills and new technologies that they discover.

As a school leader, keep a running list of the best new online tools and resources that you encounter. Regularly distribute these through your school's social network, wiki, or blog. Alternatively, send a weekly email message to the teachers with whom you work, pointing them to new online tools and resources that may be useful in their classrooms. Encourage teachers to share the best online resources that work effectively in classrooms to support learning, or develop a collaborative list using a Google doc. This will quickly build a community around the effective integration of online new literacies into classrooms.

If you are a teacher, your role includes integrating online literacy experiences into the classroom in a regular and thoughtful fashion. This will require knowing which online reading and writing skills are the most important to support. It will also mean developing learning experiences to help students take up these practices. In addition, it means learning about new online skills and resources from other colleagues, an important source of information in a world where it is hard for any one person to keep up with all the changes. It also means being on the lookout for new skills and strategies that students in your class manifest so you can then distribute these skills to your other students and to fellow teachers.

For students, developing new literacies requires regular, consistent, and safe access to online technologies in the classroom and at home. When this is not possible at home, it becomes even more important for access to be available at school. It also means expanding an interest in learning new literacy skills and developing the ability to share these effectively with others.

2. Begin Teaching and Learning New Literacies as Early as Possible

Schools should begin to integrate the Internet and new literacies into the classroom as soon as children begin their literacy education program, and should not wait until they have learned to read offline. A useful first step is to begin Internet integration within the earliest grades, using online resources that serve to teach initial offline reading skills. These programs teach early offline reading skills at the same time they provide experiences with navigating an online interface. *Starfall* is an exceptional resource for children that supports the development of early offline reading skills; it is located at http://www.starfall.com/. *ReadWriteThink* is another valuable resource for teachers that provides an extensive set of K–12 lessons that teach offline reading and writing skills to young children, and is located at http://www.readwritethink.org/.

3. Use New Literacies to Help the Last Student Become the First

As a teacher, instruct students who struggle with offline literacies in a simple set of new literacies associated with a new technology tool before you teach these tools to anyone else. This enables readers and writers who struggle to become literate in this new technology before other, higher-performing students do. For example, when you begin to use email, learning management systems, and blogs in your classroom, use these opportunities to help the last become the first. Teach readers who struggle how to make wiki and blog entries first. Then have them show others how to use these new tools. Also, have them be available to support those who require assistance. Unfortunately, the opposite often happens: Readers who struggle are frequently denied access to online experiences because their offline literacy skills are thought to be insufficient (Castek et al., 2011).

4. Recognize That Online Search Skills Are Important to Success in New Literacies

The reading ability required to locate online information (Guinee et al., 2003) is a gatekeeping skill. A user who cannot locate information will be unable to solve a given problem. New online reading skills and strategies are required to generate effective keyword search strategies (Bilal, 2000; Guinee et al., 2003), to read and infer which link might be most useful within a set of search engine results (Henry, 2006), and to efficiently scan for relevant information within websites (Rouet et al., 2011). Each is important to integrate into classroom literacy programs.

Create new search engine skills. Search engines regularly add new search capabilities that are not always known to users. To keep up to date with those that are added to Google, visit Google's "Search Education" resources at http://www.google.com/insidesearch/searcheducation/index.html/. Here you will find lesson plans, activities to improve your own search skills, daily search challenges for your students, and training webinars for both you and your students. Less skilled online readers often "click and look" their way down a list of search results, skimming each site without making inferences from information in the results. This is very inefficient and often leads students to miss the best site when it does not appear as they expect.

Play "One Click." To develop better inferential comprehension skills during the reading of search results, play "One Click." Conduct a search for any topic you are teaching in class. See if students can locate the best link on the search results page for each question that you ask, such as, "Which link will take you to a site developed by an Egyptologist?" or "Which site on this page is a commercial site that might be trying to sell you something?" Each question should require students to make an inference from the limited information appearing in the search results. If you have an interactive whiteboard and projector, you can ask students to come to the board, show the answer they think is correct, and explain their reasoning.

5. Use Online Reading Experiences to Develop Critical Thinking Skills With Students Who Are Flexible Skeptics

A central objective of any instructional program in new literacies is to develop students who read as flexible skeptics. Students should be open to considering multiple perspectives but also critical of those perspectives. In online contexts, students need to learn how to question the information they read for relevancy and accuracy, infer the bias or point of view of the author, and question the credibility of the sources they encounter.

Critically evaluating online information includes the ability to read and judge the level of accuracy, credibility, and bias of information (Center for Media Literacy, 2005). Although these skills have always been necessary to comprehend and use offline texts (Bråten et al., 2009; Bråten et al., 2011), the online proliferation of unedited information and merging of commercial marketing with educational content (Fabos, 2008) presents additional challenges that are quite different from those of traditional print and media sources, requiring new strategies.

Without explicit training in these new literacy skills, many students become confused and overwhelmed when asked to judge the quality of information they encounter online (Sanchez et al., 2006; Sundar, 2008). Teachers' leadership in this area will ensure that their students gain the critical evaluation skills required for an online age.

Frontline Judge. Ask students to take on the role of a judge during an online research project. This will help students take a critical but flexible stance toward the information they encounter. As the frontline judge, they must consider multiple perspectives on an issue by reading different texts and learning about the purposes and biases of different sources. They must also weigh different evidence across these texts. This process will encourage students to

- Consider conflicting perspectives
- Examine and integrate evidence across the three tiers of *content* (i.e., knowledge claims and evidence), *source* (i.e., author or publisher), and *context* (i.e., document characteristics such as text type; currency, or date of publication or presentation)
- Deliberate before forming a "verdict," or coming to a reasoned conclusion about the issue they are investigating (Forzani, 2020)

Source Plus. Schools increasingly require students to list the sources for any online information that is used in a report. Take this one step further and require students also to indicate how they determined that each source was credible.

6. Integrate the Internet Into Classrooms Through Online Communication

It may be easiest to integrate the Internet into classrooms through the use of online communication tools such as email, wikis, and blogs, as well as child-safe social networks for schools. Each creates

a wonderfully natural way in which to develop a culture of effective online information use in classrooms (Zawilinski, 2011). Importantly, they may be used to keep parents informed about what is taking place in classrooms.

As educators begin to integrate these online communication tools into classrooms, they should not ignore concerns about child safety. Communication should be restricted to students and a community of trusted people, such as parents and other teachers and classes. Many tools provide these protections in one of two ways. First, most permit you to restrict access. Typically, you can list the addresses of people you wish to be able to view, add, or edit information. Second, many tools permit you to review messages before they are sent. Child-safe email systems are also available, such as those offered by ePals and Gaggle.

Many new apps now exist for connecting teachers, students, and families virtually, such as *Seesaw* (https://web.seesaw.me) and *Bloomz* (https://www.bloomz.net). These tools allow teachers to send messages and post pictures and videos to individual families, certain groups of students, or a whole class. They also enable students to develop digital portfolios that can be shared with their teacher, classmates, families, and others who are given access. Tools such as these allow for multiple points of connection among students, teachers, and families beyond the classroom walls. Social networking tools have been an especially important method of developing and maintaining classroom and school community during COVID-19 school shutdowns, when many students were learning remotely.

7. Open Doors for Teachers by Starting With a Pilot Program, Especially in Resistant Schools and Districts

Technology coordinators often place restrictions on classroom access to Internet tools. As a literacy leader, you should determinedly work to make child-safe access to online tools and resources easier for teachers. A useful strategy is to simply suggest that a pilot program be implemented in a single classroom for each new online technology. Present the case, describing what the technology does, how it will increase opportunities for students, and how the teacher can ensure child safety. Also suggest that a note be sent to parents to inform them about what will be taking place and why it is important, and to request their permission. Anxieties will be reduced in the school or district, and after a successful pilot, there may be more willingness to try additional innovations.

Use Voicethread (http://voicethread.com/) **or FlipGrid** (http://flipgrid.com) as a supportive tool for classroom learning and communication, especially for readers who struggle and for younger readers. Teachers can post an image, a video, or a text and invite others to respond by voice, video, or text. That students can respond in these ways makes full participation possible for younger children or readers and writers who struggle. It is also a child-safe tool where access can be limited only to students in a single classroom. As a literacy leader, you could propose and conduct a pilot of this tool in one classroom to evaluate its potential for other classrooms in relation to the costs for the district.

Use Google Workspace for Education. Google offers a free suite of collaborative online tools, including Google Docs for word processing, spreadsheets, forms, presentations, and drawing pages. Word processing and other files may be used by anyone with permission from the creator. Thus, multiple students and teachers can collaboratively work on a single document at once. Additionally, Google offers video and chat features that allow teachers and students to connect virtually. Teachers can also use Google Classroom to post announcements and assignments, organize classwork into modules or units, and keep track of student grades. Using these tools as part of a pilot is a low-risk way to begin implementing technology in the classroom.

8. Use Performance-Based Assessments and Informal Observations for Evaluating New Literacies

Good instruction is informed by good assessment. Thus, it is important to have assessments capable of measuring new literacies in ways that inform instruction (Forzani et al., 2020). Performance-based assessments provide diagnostic information gathered as students perform an authentic task that is required in life and in the classroom.

While no assessment is a perfect solution (Darling-Hammond, 2010), performance-based assessments can work better than many other forms of assessment (Wiggins, 1998).

Models for assessing the new literacies of online research and comprehension have appeared. For example, the PISA Reading Assessment (Organisation for Economic Co-operation and Development, 2018) evaluated 15-year-olds in a number of different countries on their reading skills and incorporated digital reading in the assessment. PISA has also developed a framework to assess Information and Communication Technologies (ICTs) across multiple disciplines (Organisation for Economic Co-operation and Development, 2019).

The ePIRLS version of PIRLS, or Progress in International Reading Literacy Study, is another new assessment of online reading (Mullis et al., 2017). The ePIRLS (https://timssandpirls.bc.edu) is an innovative, performance-based assessment of students' ability to read and learn online in science and social studies. Students have to navigate and learn from multiple webpages, information graphics, animations, and pop-up windows; an avatar guides students through the online reading, research, and learning tasks.

Yet a third approach is the Online Research and Comprehension Assessment, or ORCA (Leu et al., 2009). Each online research task in science is directed through chat messages from an avatar student within a social network. Along the way, students are asked to locate four different websites and summarize the central information from each in their notepad. They also evaluate the credibility of a website and write a short report of their research in either a wiki or an email message. The assessments have demonstrated good levels of both reliability and validity (Leu et al., 2012). This format and the performance-based nature of the assessment may provide a model for others. To gain greater understanding of what these types of assessments look like, you may view a video overview of the assessments posted by ORCA at https://www.youtube.com/watch?v=aXxrR2wBR5Y. (For more information on assessment, see Chapter 10 in this book.)

In addition to performance-based assessments, you can use informal observations of students conducting online research to gain important diagnostic information about their ability. Look carefully at how they locate, evaluate, synthesize, and communicate information online during their research. You can also ask students to think aloud as they conduct this research, or ask students to come to an interactive whiteboard and think aloud so that the entire class can see their strategies.

9. Use Internet Reciprocal Teaching as an Effective Strategy to Teach the New Literacies of Online Research and Comprehension in One-to-One Computing Classrooms

As schools move toward one-to-one computing classrooms, where students have their own laptops (cf. Argueta et al., 2011), educators will be challenged to teach new literacies. Teachers may have only a few seconds of their students' attention to teach a new online skill if their laptops are open. If students' laptops are closed, attention may not be substantially greater. Consider this central issue: How do you teach a new online research and comprehension skill in the 15 seconds or so that you have students' attention? One way is to embed the skill that you seek to teach in a research problem for groups of students to solve. When you see a student figure out the target skill that you have embedded into the research problem, have that student share and explain what he or she did so that others can also solve the problem. This approach, a part of Internet Reciprocal Teaching (Leu et. al, 2008), has demonstrated efficacy in the classroom for developing online research and comprehension skills (Leu & Reinking, 2010).

In one-to-one classrooms, you might consider the use of monitoring software on your screen. Monitoring software places a thumbnail image of each student's screen on the teacher's screen. Thus, for example, if several students are visiting a popular singer's site inappropriately, you can simply pause students' screens, alerting them that they are off task. Students will close the site quickly, and they will be more likely to stay on task in the future. More important, though, this tool may be used to display a student's screen when the student is teaching a new skill to the class. There are many different monitoring software programs, including Apple Remote Desktop, LanSchool, Netop Vision, and others.

10. Engage Students in Collaborative Online Learning Experiences with Classroom Partners in Other Parts of the World

Some teachers are beginning to explore the future of instruction. They connect with other classrooms around the world to engage in collaborative projects. These classrooms use Google, student blogging tools, email, wikis, learning management systems, and web development tools to conduct research, exchange information, and learn. With these projects, students increase their new literacies skills, develop a richer understanding of content, and gain a greater understanding of the differences that define our world. Most important, participating in such projects provides students with preparation for the world they will soon enter, especially in the workplace.

You can use ePals tools like "Find Connections" (https://www.epals.com/#/connections) to identify classrooms around the world for a pen pal exchange. You can also visit "Explore Collaborations" (https://www.epals.com/#/ExploreExperience) to create or participate in a classroom learning project. Some teachers are also leveraging students' familiarity with broadly used tools such as FlipGrid and Twitter by using popular social media hashtags (e.g., #langchat or #flteach) in instruction. Students can post videos of themselves and partner with students at a school abroad for an authentic digital pen pal experience.

CONCLUSION

The nature of reading is changing in an online world of information and communication. Teachers encounter new literacy tools, requiring new literacy skills nearly every day. It is essential that teachers include instruction in these new literacies within their classrooms, since today's students are not fully prepared for them (Forzani, 2018; Kennedy, Leu, & Rhoads, 2016).

It is equally important to begin thinking about reading and literacy in a new way. It may be that a continuously shifting landscape of new literacies means that learning how to learn becomes more important than mastering a fixed and static set of literacy skills that will need to be continuously updated as new technologies appear. What may become fundamental to create are classrooms in which learning is organized around the social practices of continuously new online literacies, not a set of specific skills that may alter over time.

The world of new literacies requires school leaders and teachers with the understanding of what is taking place and a vision of what is now possible for our students. It is an exciting world for leaders who are interested in supporting change and development. One thing is very clear—the leadership that they provide will determine what the present students will achieve in the future.

NOTE

Portions of this material are based on work supported by the U.S. Department of Education under Award No. R305G050154 and R305A090608. Opinions expressed herein are solely those of the authors and do not necessarily represent the position of the U.S. Department of Education, Institute of Educational Sciences.

REFLECTION QUESTIONS

1. Which of the ideas in this chapter best suit the instructional opportunities of your teachers and classrooms? Why? How could they be adapted to support student learning in new literacies?
2. Is one or several of the instructional principles described in this chapter most important to K-12 education? Which one(s)? Why?
3. How could you use this chapter to organize and conduct a 2-hour workshop for the teachers at your school? Plan this workshop and the set of experiences that you would provide.

PROJECT ASSIGNMENT

Explore ePals, FlipGrid, Google Workspace for Education, and other tools discussed in this chapter. Identify one or more tools that could be used in a classroom, and send an email to colleagues describing the tool(s) and how they might be used. If your district blocks these tools, have a meeting with the appropriate person to request that the tools be unblocked for one classroom so that this teacher might conduct a "pilot." Prepare a presentation for this meeting that explains the function and importance of each tool and how each can be used in a child-safe fashion.

REFERENCES

Afflerbach, P. A., & Cho, B. Y. (2008). Determining and describing reading strategies: Internet and traditional forms of reading. In H. S. Waters & W. Schneider (Eds.), *Metacognition, strategy use, and instruction* (pp. 201–255). Guilford Press.

Alvermann, D., Hutchins, R. J., & DeBlasio, R. (2012). Adolescents' engagement with Web 2.0 and social media: Research, theory, and practice. *Research in the Schools, 19*(1), 33–44.

Argueta, R., Huff, J., Tingen, J., & Corn, J. (2011). *Laptop initiatives: Summary of research across seven states.* North Carolina State University, College of Education. https://www.fi.ncsu.edu/wp-content/uploads/2013/05/laptop-initiatives-summary-of-research-across-seven-states.pdf

Bennett, S., Maton, K., & Kervin, L. (2008). The "digital natives" debate: A critical review of the evidence. *British Journal of Educational Technology, 39*(5), 775–786.

Bilal, D. (2000). Children's use of the Yahooligans! Web search engine: Cognitive, physical, and affective behaviors on fact-based search tasks. *Journal of the American Society for Information Science, 51*(7), 646–665.

Bråten, I., Strømsø, H. I., & Britt, M. A. (2009). Trust matters: Examining the role of source evaluation in students' construction of meaning within and across multiple texts. *Reading Research Quarterly, 44*(1), 6–28.

Bråten, I., Strømsø, H. I., & Salmerón, L. (2011). Trust and mistrust when students read multiple information sources about climate change. *Learning and Instruction, 21*(2), 180–192.

Castek, J., Zawilinski, L., McVerry, G., O'Byrne, I., & Leu, D. J. (2011). The new literacies of online reading comprehension: New opportunities and challenges for students with learning difficulties. In C. Wyatt-Smith, J. Elkins, & S. Gunn (Eds.), *Multiple perspectives on difficulties in learning literacy and numeracy* (pp. 91–110). Springer.

Center for Media Literacy. (2005). *Literacy for the 21st century: An overview and orientation guide to media literacy education. Part 1 of the CML MediaLit kit: Framework for learning and teaching in a media age.* www.medialit.org/cml-medialit-kit

Coiro, J. (2011). Predicting reading comprehension on the Internet: Contributions of offline reading skills, online reading skills, and prior knowledge. *Journal of Literacy Research, 43*(4), 352–392.

Coiro, J., & Castek, J. (2010). Assessment frameworks for teaching and learning English language arts in a digital age. In D. Lapp & D. Fisher (Eds.), *Handbook of research on teaching the English language arts* (3rd ed., pp. 314–321). Routledge.

Common Core State Standards Initiative. (2010). *Common Core State Standards for English language arts and literacy in history, social studies, science and technical subjects.* http://www.corestandards.org/ELA-Literacy

Darling-Hammond, L. (2010). Performance-based assessment and educational equity. *Harvard Educational Review, 64*(1), 5–31.

Drew, S. (2012). Open up the ceiling on the Common Core State Standards. *Journal of Adolescent & Adult Literacy, 56*(4), 321–330.

Fabos, B. (2008). The price of information: Critical literacy, education, and today's Internet. In J. Coiro, M. Knobel, C. Lankshear, & D. Leu (Eds.), *Handbook of research on new literacies* (pp. 839–870). Erlbaum.

Forzani, E. (2018). How well can students evaluate online science information? Contributions of prior knowledge, gender, socioeconomic status, and offline reading ability. *Reading Research Quarterly, 53*(4), 385–390. doi: 10.1002/rrq.218

Forzani, E. (2020). A three-tiered framework for proactive critical evaluation during online inquiry. *Journal of Adolescent and Adult Literacy, 63*(4), 401–414. doi: 10.1002/jaal.1004

Forzani, E., Corrigan, J., & Slomp, D. (2020). Reimagining literacy assessment through a New Literacies lens. *Journal of Adolescent and Adult Literacy, 64*(3), 351–355. https://doi.org/10.1002/jaal.1098

Forzani, E., Leu, D., Li, E., Rhoads, C., Guthrie, J., & McCoach, B. (2020). Characteristics and validity of an instrument for assessing motivations for online reading to learn. *Reading Research Quarterly.* Advance online publication. https://doi.org/10.1002/rrq.337

Guinee, K., Eagleton, M. B., & Hall, T. E. (2003). Adolescents' Internet search strategies: Drawing upon familiar cognitive paradigms when accessing electronic information sources. *Journal of Educational Computing Research, 29*(3), 363–374.

Henry, L. (2006). SEARCHing for an answer: The critical role of new literacies while reading on the Internet. *The Reading Teacher, 59*(7), 614–627.

International Society for Technology in Education (ISTE). (2018). *ISTE Standards for Education Leaders.* https://www.iste.org/standards

Kennedy, C., Rhoads, C., & Leu, D. J. (2016). Online research and learning in science: A one-to-one laptop comparison in two states using performance based assessments. *Computers & Education, 100,* 141–161.

Kiili, C., Laurinen, L., Marttunen, M., & Leu, D. J. (2012). Working on understanding during collaborative online reading. *Journal of Literacy Research, 20*(10), 1–36.

Kiili, C., Leu, D. J., Marttunen, M., Hautala, J., & Leppänen, P. H. T. (2018). Exploring early adolescents' evaluation of academic and commercial online resources related to health. *Reading and Writing, 31,* 533–557. doi: 10.1007/s11145-017-9797-2

Kress, G. (2003). *Literacy in the new media age.* Routledge.

Leu, D. J. (2000). Literacy and technology: Deictic consequences for literacy education in an information age. In M. L. Kamil, P. Mosenthal, P. D. Pearson, & R. Barr (Eds.), *Handbook of reading research* (Vol. 3, pp. 743–770). Erlbaum.

Leu, D. J., Coiro, J., Castek, J., Hartman, D., Henry, L. A., & Reinking, D. (2008). Research on instruction and assessment in the new literacies of online reading comprehension. In C. C. Block & S. Parris (Eds.), *Comprehension instruction: Research-based best practices* (pp. 111–153). Guilford Press.

Leu, D. J., Coiro, J., Kulikowich, J., & Cui, W. (2012, November). *Using the psychometric characteristics of multiple-choice, open Internet, and closed (simulated) Internet formats to refine the development of online research and comprehension assessments in science: Year three of the ORCA project.* Paper presented at the annual meeting of the Literacy Research Association, San Diego, CA.

Leu, D. J., Kinzer, C. K., Coiro, J., Castek, J., & Henry, L. A. (2019). New Literacies: A dual level theory of the changing nature of literacy, instruction, and assessment. In D. E. Alvermann, N. J. Unrau, M. Sailors, & R. B. Ruddell (Eds.), *Theoretical models and processes of literacy* (7th ed., pp. 1150–1181). Taylor & Francis.

Leu, D. J., Kulikowich, J., Sedransk, N., & Coiro, J. (2009). *Assessing online reading comprehension: The ORCA project.* Research grant funded by the U.S. Department of Education, Institute of Education Sciences.

Leu, D. J., & Reinking, D. (2010). *Final report: Developing Internet comprehension strategies among adolescent students at risk to become dropouts.* U.S. Department of Education, Institute of Education Sciences Research Grant.

Lewis, C., & Fabos, B. (2005). Instant messaging, literacies, and social identities. *Reading Research Quarterly, 40*(4), 470–501.

McVerry, J. G., Zawilinski, L., & O'Byrne, W. I. (2009, September). Navigating the Cs of change. *Educational Leadership, 67*(1). http://www.ascd.org/publications/educational-leadership/sept09/vol67/num01/Navigating-the-Cs-of-Change.aspx

Minister of Manitoba Education, Citizenship, and Youth. (2006). *Literacy with ICT across the curriculum: A resource for developing computer literacy.* https://en.unesco.org/icted/sites/default/files/2019-04/75_manitoba_literacy_with_ict.pdf

Mullis, I. V. S., Martin, M. O., Foy, P., & Hooper, M. (2017). *ePIRLS 2016 international results in online informational reading.* International Association for the Evaluation of Educational Achievement.

Organisation for Economic Co-operation and Development. (2018). *PISA 2018 results (Volume I: What students know and can do.* https://www.oecd.org/pisa/publications/pisa-2018-results-volume-i-5f07c754-en.htm

Organisation for Economic Co-operation and Development. (2019). *PISA 2021 ICT framework.* https://www.oecd.org/pisa/sitedocument/PISA-2021-ICT-Framework.pdf

Prensky, M. (2001) Digital natives, digital immigrants. *On the Horizon, 9*(5), 1–6. http://dx.doi.org/10.1108/10748120110424816

Rouet, J.-F., Ros, C., Goumi, A., Macedo-Rouet, M., & Dinet, J. (2011). The influence of surface and deep cues on primary and secondary school students' assessment of relevance in web menus. *Learning and Instruction, 21*(2), 205–219.

Sanchez, C. A., Wiley, J., & Goldman, S. R. (2006). Teaching students to evaluate source reliability during Internet research tasks. In S. A. Barab, K. E. Hay, & D. T. Hickey (Eds.), *Proceedings of the seventh international conference on the learning sciences* (pp. 662–666). International Society of the Learning Sciences.

Street, B. (1995). *Social literacies.* Longman.

Street, B. (2003). What's new in new literacy studies? *Current Issues in Comparative Education, 5*(2), 1–14.

Sundar, S. S. (2008). The MAIN model: A heuristic approach to understanding technology effects on credibility. In M. J. Metzger & A. J. Flanagin (Eds.), *Digital media, youth, and credibility* (pp. 73–100). MIT Press.

Wiggins, G. (1998). *Educative assessment: Designing assessments to inform and improve student performance.* Jossey-Bass.

Zawilinski, L. (2011). *An exploration of a collaborative blogging approach to literacy and learning: A mixed method study* [Unpublished doctoral dissertation]. University of Connecticut.

Zickuhr, K. (2010). *Generations 2010.* Pew Research Center. https://www.pewresearch.org/internet/2010/12/16/generations-2010/

CHAPTER 16

Working With Parents and the Community

Patricia A. Edwards, Lisa M. Domke, and Marliese R. Peltier

- Educators' expectations for parent engagement influence how parents are positioned and the types of access and power they have—all of which impact the success of parent-engagement initiatives.
- As teachers and administrators, we need to develop a fuller and deeper understanding of the ways cultural, linguistic, and economic differences impact parents' participation in traditional forms of engagement in their children's schooling.
- Adopting asset-based mindsets, developing cognitive flexibility, learning about school demographics, and considering factors impacting parent engagement can provide a starting point for developing engagement strategies and programs that are accessible to families of diverse cultural, linguistic, and economic backgrounds and productive in supporting their children's school success.

When children enter school, both the students themselves and their parents are impacted by the new school environment (Edwards, 1993, 2016). Delpit (1995) noted that "Teachers cannot hope to begin to understand who sits before them unless they can connect with the families and communities from which their children come" (p. 209). Classroom teachers must face the reality that they will most likely teach students who come from different cultural, ethnic, linguistic, racial, and social class backgrounds than their own. Understanding a school's demographics can inform how teachers work through issues related to school segregation, redistricting, funding, equity, instruction, and assessment.

LEARNING ABOUT STUDENTS' FAMILIES AND COMMUNITIES

Although U.S. schools have become increasingly racially and ethnically diverse, these changes have played out differently across the country. Each year, teachers interact with a group of students who are unique and different from all previous classes. In order to recognize each group's diverse backgrounds and needs, it is helpful to create a demographic profile (see Edwards, 2004, 2009). A demographic profile describes the parent community within individual classrooms and the school building as a whole. Edwards (2016) lists the benefits of making a demo profile:

- Allows teachers to develop tailor-made, parentally appropriate activities
- Helps teachers to take a look at the history of parent involvement at the school level
- Allows teachers to determine whether parental involvement has been effective or not
- Gives teachers a way to pinpoint where problems may be occurring
- Allows teachers to interact with families in ways that are specific to their needs
- Provides teachers with an in-depth look at the strengths of a family/community
- Gives teachers real data and removes the guesswork/judgments/assumptions about families (p. 7)

Especially for the many teachers living outside the boundaries of the district where they teach, it is helpful to seek information about the communities in which they work—specifically, the school's individual identity and the characteristics of the area around the school. Sweeney (2012) stated that "in order to know students, families and their communities, teachers need to hone their abilities to deeply notice in ways that assist them in recognizing opportunities that allow them to teach in the most fair and equitable ways" (p. 3). This might refer to noticing what is happening not only inside schools, but also within the surrounding community. To assist with a deeper level of noticing and the construction of a demographic profile, teachers and administrators might first consider the school's characteristics, such as its type, setting, and special programs. Then principals and teachers might walk around the community, visiting neighborhoods, stopping in local stores, and observing residents' activities and the ways in which they interact. It is especially important to look for activities and funds of knowledge (Moll et al., 1992) that might be incorporated into classroom practices. This information begins to construct a picture of the families who live in the neighborhood and their lifestyles.

Knowing the community is important to have successful parent involvement. In a broad sense, parent involvement, now framed as parent or family engagement, includes home-based activities that relate to children's education in school. It might also include school-based activities where parents actively participate in events that take place during the school day. Parent engagement is the participation of parents in every facet of children's education and development from birth through adulthood, accompanied by the recognition that parents are the primary influence in children's lives (Edwards, 2009). However, unless teachers understand the cultural, linguistic, and socioeconomic diversity that exists within their school communities, they may have difficulty reaching out to a wide range of parents and others involved in their students' education. It is important that teachers acknowledge all those who are involved in a child's education because not just parents, but other adults such as grandparents, aunts, uncles, stepparents, and guardians may carry the primary responsibility for a child's education and development.

Demographic profiles support teachers to know their classrooms, families, and communities in deep ways. However, we need to be cognizant that developing this deep knowledge is not a one-time task, but an ongoing process. Every year classes change, and students have different situations and needs. H. Richard Milner recommends to educators, "Start where you are, but don't stay there" (as cited in Pace, 2014, para. 1). Educators need to push beyond the familiar parent involvement activities to engage in activities that meet families' needs instead. Because families' needs differ each year, teachers must embrace *cognitive flexibility*, which supports the kinds of learning needed to apply knowledge in evolving real-world contexts (Spiro, 2015). Cognitive flexibility is the ability to adapt to a constantly changing environment. Edwards and her colleagues (2019) employed Cognitive Flexibility Theory in a series of parent-involvement modules to provide teachers with strategies to use when confronting challenging situations and, more important, to broaden teachers' perspectives on parents. Then teachers can identify and attempt to address the underlying needs and situational factors affecting parents' actions instead of finding deficits in the parents (and students) themselves. Cognitive flexibility is important because each situation and case differs from every other; therefore, it is not possible to rely on a checklist of prescribed behaviors that will work in every situation. Instead, teachers employ cognitive flexibility by integrating their prior knowledge and experiences with information from the specific case to address that particular situation (Spiro, 2015). In the following sections, we list contextual factors that may influence the ways in which parents engage with schools. Educators can take note of these factors so that they can prepare to adapt their approaches to their students.

FACTORS INFLUENCING PARENT ENGAGEMENT

Too often, parent engagement is viewed in terms of White middle-/upper-middle-class expectations such as helping with homework, volunteering for class parties/events/field trips, and reading books aloud to children (e.g., Auerbach, 2007). However, differences between home and school languages, or literacy issues that place a barrier between parents and school communications, may complicate parents' ability to engage in school-specified activities. Parents may have work schedules that conflict with the school day; they may lack access to transportation. Their own experiences with schooling such as different grading systems in other countries,

learning different concepts or ways of completing school tasks, or lack of school support/success may make them less comfortable engaging in school activities (e.g., Auerbach, 2007; Ji & Koblinsky, 2009; Rah et al., 2009). Parents may also have different cultural views of teachers and schooling, such as viewing teachers as experts who should not be questioned, which can make parents reluctant to help with homework or approach teachers with concerns (Colombo, 2006).

However, it is important to recognize that parents may be contributing to their children's education in other ways. For example, families may emphasize having a strong work ethic, the importance of education, or other important life and character advice (Alfaro et al., 2014; Auerbach, 2007; López, 2001). Therefore, before lamenting that parents do not care, educators need to get to know families— their strengths, challenges they face, and viewpoints. Creating a demographic profile (Edwards, 2009), as described at the beginning of this chapter, is a helpful first step. Teachers can also ask parents via a questionnaire, phone call, or in-person conversation about their child's likes, dislikes, and learning style, as well as whether parents' needs are being met by the classroom and school and what else can be done to better meet their needs (Edwards et al., 2017).

All of this information can help educators consider underlying factors that could affect the ways in which families engage with schools. This has been conceptualized in terms of power, prestige, positioning, and access (Edwards et al., 2019). Parents are their children's teachers throughout life. Thus, they should have a degree of *power* or control over what happens to their children. When parents experience a loss of power, they may feel fear and anxiety (Foy et al., 2014). *Prestige* relates to the degree of power that an individual experiences and the status that the individual is granted because of that power. If a parent experiences a loss of prestige, they may blame themselves for the loss or attribute the cause to another individual. When parents blame themselves, they may experience shame, embarrassment, or depression. In contrast, the parents may feel anger if they blame another individual as the cause for their decreased prestige (Foy et al., 2014). An individual's *positioning* is another factor that influences how a parent or student will react in a situation. When teachers and schools position parents as being knowledgeable, they are sharing power and validating the parent's role as a contributor to their children's education. Last, an individual's *access*, or the ability to obtain and use the necessary resources for daily living and learning, reflects one's power, prestige, and positioning.

The four concepts of power, prestige, positioning, and access relate to Maslow's (1943) Hierarchy of Needs. Briefly, Maslow suggested that there are five hierarchical levels of need. The foundational levels of the hierarchy relate to an individual's physiological needs (e.g., food, water, shelter) and safety needs (e.g., security, health). The middle level identifies an individual's need for a sense of belonging or love. The top two levels address an individual's needs for esteem (e.g., recognition, independence, and recognition) and self-actualization (e.g., self-fulfillment).

We suggest that when administrators, teachers, and other educational stakeholders identify a family's underlying needs, then they can identify meaningful solutions that benefit all parties. Educational stakeholders can focus on how the family's underlying needs intersect with how the parents might perceive the actions of the school and educational stakeholders as a threat to their power, prestige, positioning, or access. Educational stakeholders need to take an asset-based perspective when considering these intersections. Working from an asset-based perspective, administrators and teachers can determine ways that families contribute to the children's learning as well as identify the needs or potential threats that might limit the families' contributions. Working as a collaborative team with parents has the potential to positively impact children's educational success and contribute to lifelong benefits (Centers for Disease Control and Prevention, 2012).

MEDIATING CHALLENGES TO PRODUCTIVE PARENT ENGAGEMENT

Because families face unique situations, administrators and teachers must acknowledge that parent engagement is not a "one-size-fits-all" endeavor. Rather, the ways in which parents are able to engage in their children's schooling depends on the particular type of challenge that each family must manage or overcome. Effective parent engagement initiatives should involve *differentiated parenting* and *parentally appropriate* activities (Edwards, 2004; 2009).

Differentiated parenting thinking tells schools not to expect the same types of engagement from every family. Rather, teachers must get to know parents and work with them to discover their individual and family needs, such as their access to information and school opportunities, and consider how they are positioned to preserve their power. Then they develop a plan for parent engagement that can realistically be attended to, given the family's daily routines and background. Attention to *parental appropriateness* acknowledges that "because parents are different, tasks and activities must be compatible with their capabilities" (Edwards, 2009, p. 83). This is not to say that parents' goals for their children vary greatly—they all want their children to succeed in school. Rather, their situations, perspectives, and abilities may affect their capacity to support their children in particular ways.

For example, many literacy teachers, reading specialists/literacy coaches, and administrators lament children not reading at home or submitting completed, signed reading logs as records of their reading. In the following sections, we will look at this situation through potential contextual factors to help you consider issues of parental appropriateness and the ways in which issues of power, prestige, positioning, and access may impact how parents engage with schools.

Multilingual Learners

One possible explanation for students not seeming to read at home or return signed reading logs is that their parents speak languages other than English. Therefore, when information about reading logs and the importance of reading at home is sent home in English, they do not have access to the information. Furthermore, parents' languages and knowledge lose power and prestige when their home languages are positioned as unimportant when compared to English knowledge, or worse, if they are positioned as detrimental to learning English. (Such an assumption is unfounded; studies have shown that knowledge of one language helps students learn additional languages, and that they can apply literacy skills across language, e.g., Bialystok, 2006; Goldenberg, 2011). Educators can improve parents' access to information by translating information sent home through help from multilingual school staff, community organizations, other caregivers, or, if necessary, Google Translate.

Colorín Colorado (https://www.colorincolorado.org/) also provides multilingual tips about reading for families.

In addition, it is important to value families' home languages and make sure parents know how reading to their children in their home languages and/or providing opportunities for children to read in their home languages helps them develop biliteracy, or literacy skills in multiple languages. Not only does this need to be communicated explicitly, but educators can also help families access multilingual texts from, for example, the International Children's Digital Library (http://childrenslibrary.org) and publishers such as Lee & Low and Mantra Lingua. In addition, educators can acknowledge the value of families' reading of diverse texts such as local newspapers or religious texts written in home languages.

Work Schedules

Another potential challenge to completing reading logs may be families' work schedules. Within the past 15 years, patterns of work in the United States have shifted dramatically. For example, parents may work longer hours, atypical hours (e.g., nights or weekends), multiple jobs, or even return to higher education (Tankersley, 2014). These changes intersect with the roles that parents can play in their children's formal schooling. For example, parents may work during the evening hours, meaning that formal child care centers, relatives, or friends may assume the role of supporting children with the completion of nightly reading logs. In these circumstances, teachers and administrators might position parents as undervaluing their children's education or not wanting to be engaged with the school. It is important to acknowledge that parents' devotion to their children has not changed, but the nature of caregiving has changed. With this change in caregiving, most parents would agree that developing collaborative partnerships between families and schools becomes even more essential to supporting children's educational success (Applebaum, 2009).

One way to develop a collaborative partnership with families is to develop an understanding of the family at the beginning of the year (Edwards et al., 2019). Often, teachers will send home forms in the students' home languages that ask parents to share information about the student. These forms can be expanded to include information about the family's

caregiving structure. Parents retain their power and prestige, since the school values their knowledge about their children and uses it to inform educational decisions. By developing an understanding of the family, teachers and literacy specialists can identify ways to support the completion of at-home reading logs and determine if alternative accountability documentation would be appropriate if parents are not available to sign the nightly logs.

In addition, the school can identify if the family has access to literacy materials for the nightly reading assignments (Edwards et al., 2019). Families' complex work schedules may prevent them from being available to visit their public libraries when they are open. They may have limited financial resources to purchase books, since the national average median household income continues to decline (Pew Research Center, 2016). To mitigate the lack of access to books, schools might increase the number of library books the children can check out from the school, provide books from donated materials, or look to nonprofit book programs (e.g., Imagination Library, Reach Out and Read).

Trauma

Challenges related to trauma could also impact at-home literacy practices. Prior to 2020, research indicated that almost one in every four children had experienced a traumatic event before the age of three (Briggs-Gowan et al., 2010; Mongillo et al., 2009). The global events of 2020 surely heighten the need for trauma-informed teaching and teachers who understand and appreciate the impact that traumatic events have on children. The National Child Traumatic Stress Network (2003) defined trauma as an experience that negatively affects an individual's physical, physiological, or emotional well-being. The death of family members due to COVID-19, sustained and repeated experiences associated with systemic racial discrimination, or the adverse experience of reduced social contact with same-age peers are all potential sources for trauma for our children.

Since so many children are affected by trauma, teachers and literacy specialists can prepare for when they may need to support a student who experiences trauma. Educational stakeholders can establish collaborative and trusting relationships with the family (The National Child Traumatic Stress Network, n.d.). Teachers can create safe, stable, and caring classrooms where children are positioned as valuable participants and have access to the tools needed to address their trauma (Perry, 2009).

Teachers and literacy specialists should be aware that children are affected by trauma differently. For example, sudden changes in completion of nightly reading logs may be an indicator that the teacher should check in with the family. Through collaborative conversations with the parents, teachers can determine if and how to alter the nightly reading assignment. Some children may need time and space to recover from traumatic events, necessitating a temporary reduction or alternation of educational expectations.

While trained professionals (i.e., school counselors, mental health professionals, and social workers) will determine and facilitate appropriate intervention efforts, teachers and administrators can learn to recognize triggers and maintain collaborative communication with the family. For instance, a teacher might recognize that particular books may trigger traumatic responses in a student. The teacher can then assign an alternative text for nightly reading so as not to trigger such responses in the student.

For additional contextual factors such as parents facing low literacy levels, caregivers challenging teachers or administrators, and families preferring limited school engagement, as well as tips for working with families, see *Partnering with Families for Student Success: 24 Scenarios for Problem Solving with Parents* (Edwards et al., 2019).

CONCLUSION

Substantial evidence supports the importance of home–school partnerships (e.g., Henderson & Mapp, 2002; Jeynes, 2003; Sheldon, 2007), but there is also wide agreement that educators and policymakers often recommend and/or expect parent engagement strategies that are a poor match for many of the families who populate the schools (e.g., Auerbach, 2007; Edwards, 2009). As teachers, reading specialists/literacy coaches, and administrators, we are responsible for becoming deeply knowledgeable about our children's families—to get to know how they perceive their roles in their children's education; to become fully aware of the intellectual, emotional, cultural, and social resources at their disposal; and to understand the obstacles that might

prevent them from being engaged in their children's schooling in sustained and productive ways. As we develop a clear profile of the families, their resources, and their challenges, we must then develop a responsive plan of action—one that *can and will* be put into practice. This plan should meet families' needs and address any threats to the family's power, prestige, positioning, or access (Edwards et al., 2019). Doing so may require that we leave behind the practices with which we are most familiar, for example, back-to-school nights, parents as field trip chaperones, and parents as classroom helpers. We need to conceptualize practices that effectively fit the full range of abilities, demands, and challenges that confront families.

REFLECTION QUESTIONS

1. Consider the parents in the school setting in which you teach. What challenges might they face related to engaging in school, and what engagement strategies could be effective for developing a sustained home–school partnership?
2. If you were to design and implement a before- or after-school program for the students in your school or community, what information would you need to gather to plan a program that would accommodate the needs of children and their families?
3. What can you and your colleagues do to learn as much as possible about parents' availability, as well as the assets they bring, for working with their children to ensure their school success (e.g., parents' before- and after-school schedules, child care arrangements, homework help, areas of expertise, and supportive encouragement they provide)?

PROJECT ASSIGNMENT

Identify and implement a parent engagement activity that you consider fundamentally important to the success of the children in your school. Next, consider how power, prestige, positioning, and access might limit full engagement among the caregivers of your students. Using some of the ideas and suggestions described in this chapter, as well as others, develop a plan to mediate the obstacle(s) or challenge(s). For example, should you provide parent training on the activity to increase parent efficacy? Should you offer the event at a different time (or multiple times) of day? In what languages should you communicate the information? At the completion of the parent engagement activity, evaluate your efforts. Did it result in more widespread participation? Did parents and children report engagement and enjoyment? Did children demonstrate greater knowledge of the target strategy? If you were to implement this activity again, describe ways that you would modify your plan as a result of this analysis.

REFERENCES

Alfaro, D. D., O'Reilly-Diaz, K., & López, G. R. (2014). Operationalizing consejos in the P–20 educational pipeline: Interrogating the nuances of Latino parent involvement. *Multicultural Education, 21*(3/4), 11–16.

Applebaum, M. (2009). *How to handle hard-to-handle parents*. Corwin.

Auerbach, S. (2007). From moral supporters to struggling advocates: Reconceptualizing parent roles in education through the experience of working-class families of color. *Urban Education, 42*(3), 250–283.

Bialystok, E. (2006). The impact of bilingualism on language and literacy development. In T. K. Bhatia & W. C. Ritchie (Eds.), *The handbook of bilingualism* (pp. 577–601). Blackwell Publishing.

Briggs-Gowan, M. J., Ford, J. D., Fraleigh, L., McCarthy, K., & Carter, A. S. (2010). Prevalence of exposure to potentially traumatic events in a healthy birth cohort of very young children in the northeastern United States. *Journal of Traumatic Stress, 23*(6), 725–733.

Centers for Disease Control and Prevention. (2012). *Parent engagement: Strategies for involving parents in school health*. U.S. Department of Health and Human Services. https://www.cdc.gov/healthyyouth/protective/pdf/parent_engagement_strategies.pdf

Colombo, M. W. (2006). Building school partnerships with culturally and linguistically diverse families. *Phi Delta Kappan, 88*(4), 314–318.

Delpit, L. (1995). *Other people's children: Cultural conflict in the classroom*. The New Press.

Edwards, P. A. (1993). Before and after school desegregation: African-American parent involvement in schools. *Educational Policy, 7*(3), 340–369.

Edwards, P. A. (2004). *Children's literacy development: Making it happen through school, family, and community involvement*. Allyn and Bacon.

Edwards, P. A. (2009). *Tapping the potential of parents: A strategic guide to boosting student achievement through family engagement*. Scholastic.

Edwards, P. A. (2016). *New ways to engage parents: Strategies and tools for teachers and leaders, K–12*. Teachers College Press.

Edwards, P. A., Domke, L. M., & White, K. L. (2017). Closing the parent gap in changing school districts. In S. B. Wepner & D. W. Gomez (Eds.), *Challenges facing suburban schools: Promising responses to changing student populations* (pp. 109–121). Rowman & Littlefield.

Edwards, P. A., Spiro, R. J., Domke, L. M., Castle, A. M., White, K. L., Peltier, M. R., & Donohue, T. H. (2019). *Partnering with families for student success: 24 scenarios for problem solving with parents*. Teachers College Press.

Foy, S., Freeland, R., Miles, A., Rogers, K. B., & Smith-Lovin, L. (2014). Emotions and affect as source, outcome and resistance to inequality. In J. D. McLeod, E. J. Lawler, & M. Schwalbe (Eds.), *Handbook of the social psychology of inequality* (pp. 295–324). Springer.

Goldenberg, C. (2011). Reading instruction for English language learners. In M. L. Kamil, P. D. Pearson, E. B. Moje, & P. Afflerbach (Eds.), *Handbook of reading research* (Vol. 4, pp. 684–710). Routledge.

Henderson, A., & Mapp, K. (2002). *A new wave of evidence: The impact of school, family, and community connections on student achievement. Annual synthesis, 2002*. National Center for Family and Community Connections with Schools, Southwest Educational Development Laboratory.

Jeynes, W. (2003). A meta-analysis: The effects of parental engagement on minority children's academic achievement. *Education & Urban Society, 35*(2), 202–218.

Ji, C. S., & Koblinsky, S. A. (2009). Parent involvement in children's education: An exploratory study of urban, Chinese immigrant families. *Urban Education, 44*(6), 687–709.

López, G. R. (2001). The value of hard work: Lessons on parent involvement from an (im)migrant household. *Harvard Educational Review, 71*(3), 416–438.

Maslow, A. H. (1943). A theory of human motivation. *Psychology Review, 50*(4), 370–396.

Moll, L. C., Amanti, C., Neff, D., & Gonzalez, N. (1992). Funds of knowledge for teaching: Using a qualitative approach to connect homes and classrooms. *Theory Into Practice, 31*(2), 132–141. https://doi.org/10.1080/00405849209543534

Mongillo, E. A., Briggs-Gowan, M. J., Ford, J. D., & Carter, A. S. (2009). Impact of traumatic life events in a community sample of toddlers. *Journal of Abnormal Child Psychology, 37*(4), 455–468.

National Child Traumatic Stress Network. (n.d.). *Families and trauma.* http://www.nctsn.org/resources/topics/families-and-trauma

National Child Traumatic Stress Network. (2003, Fall). What is child traumatic stress? *Claiming Children.* https://www.samhsa.gov/sites/default/files/programs_campaigns/childrens_mental_health/what-is-child-traumatic-stress.pdf

Pace, K. (2014, April 18). *"Start where you are, but don't stay there": Five strategies important to improving teaching and learning for diverse, young people.* Michigan State University Extension. https://www.canr.msu.edu/news/start_where_you_are_but_dont_stay_there

Perry, B. D. (2009). Examining child maltreatment through a neurodevelopmental lens: Clinical applications of the neurosequential model of therapeutics. *Journal of Loss and Trauma, 14*(4), 240–255.

Pew Research Center. (2016, May 11). *America's shrinking middle class: A close look at changes within metropolitan areas.* http://www.pewsocialtrends.org/2016/05/11/americas-shrinking-middle-class-a-close-look-at-changes-within-metropolitan-areas/

Rah, Y., Choi, S., & Nguyễn, T. S. T. (2009). Building bridges between refugee parents and schools. *International Journal of Leadership in Education, 12*(4), 347–365.

Sheldon, S. B. (2007). Improving student attendance with school, family, and community partnerships. *The Journal of Educational Research, 100*(5), 267–275.

Spiro, R. J. (2015). Cognitive flexibility theory. In J. M. Spector (Ed.), *Encyclopedia of educational technology* (pp. 111–116). Sage.

Sweeney, J. (2012). *Veteran teachers working in diverse communities: Noticing students, families and communities* (Publication No. 3508630). [Doctoral Dissertation, Michigan State University]. ProQuest Dissertations and Theses Global.

Tankersley, J. (2014, December 14). The devalued American worker. *The Washington Post.* http://www.washingtonpost.com/sf/business/2014/12/14/the-devalued-american-worker

About the Contributors

Peter Afflerbach is professor of education at the University of Maryland at College Park. His research interests include individual differences in reading, reading comprehension strategies for print and digital reading, reading assessment, and the verbal reporting methodology. Dr. Afflerbach has served on National Academy of Education and National Academy of Science committees related to literacy and literacy assessment. He is a member of the NAEP 2025 Reading Framework Development Committee and has served on the NAEP Standing Reading Committee and prior Reading Framework Committees. He was elected to the International Literacy Association's Reading Hall of Fame in 2009.

Hyoju Ahn is a PhD student in the literacy education program at the University of Maryland at College Park. Her research interests are online multimodal reading strategies and its instruction and assessment for K–12 students. Based on her teaching experience at South Korean public elementary schools, her research aims to examine how online reading strategies support different levels of students' reading comprehension and how students use and apply online information.

Rita M. Bean is professor emerita in the University of Pittsburgh School of Education. Her research focuses on professional learning of teachers, school change, literacy curriculum and instruction. She has studied extensively the role of the reading specialist/literacy coach, especially in supporting classroom literacy instruction. Her books include *The Literacy Specialist: Leadership and Coaching for the Classroom, School, and Community* (with V. Goatley), *Cultivating Coaching Mindsets* (with J. Ippolito), and *Best Practices of Literacy Leaders: Keys to School Improvement* (with A. S. Dagen). Dr. Bean served as a board member for the International Literacy Association and is a member of the Reading Hall of Fame.

William G. Brozo is emeritus professor of literacy at George Mason University. He is the author of numerous articles and books on literacy development for children and adolescents. His newest books are *Engaging Boys in Active Literacy: Evidence and Practice* and *Disciplinary and Content Literacy for Today's Adolescents*. As a national and international consultant, he has provided technical support to teachers, teacher leaders, and policy makers across the United States and around the world. Dr. Brozo's research focuses on international literacy assessments, content area/disciplinary literacy, and the literate lives of boys.

M. Susan Burns is professor emerita in the College of Education and Human Development at George Mason University. Prior to joining the faculty at Mason, Susan was study director at the National Research Council, producing the reports *Preventing Reading Difficulties in Young Children* (1998) and *Starting Out Right: A Guide to Promoting Children's Reading Success* (1999). Her research centers on the cognitive, language, and literacy development and learning of young children (birth through grade 3). Her work includes all children: those with diverse abilities (children with disabilities), those living in poverty, and those from multilingual and multicultural backgrounds.

Lisa M. Domke is an assistant professor of language and (bi)literacy education in the Department of Early Childhood and Elementary Education at Georgia State University. Her research focuses on elementary children's biliteracy development, as well as issues related to children's literature and disciplinary literacy. Lisa is a former elementary teacher who taught a range of grades and in a Spanish dual-language immersion program. In addition, she worked in a summer migrant education program and has taught various undergraduate and master's literacy and language courses.

Patricia A. Edwards is a member of the Reading Hall of Fame and a professor of language and literacy in the Department of Teacher Education at Michigan State University. She is the first African American president of the Literacy Research Association and the 2010–2011 president of the International Literacy Association. Her research focuses on issues related to families and children. She was named as the 2017–2018 Jeanne S. Chall Visiting Researcher at the Harvard Graduate School of Education. More recently, she received the 2019 AERA Scholars of Color Distinguished Career Contribution Award.

Toni Faddis has served as a public school educator for the past 27 years as a teacher, principal, and district leader. She currently coaches school principals and is passionate about addressing and eliminating opportunity gaps. Toni has authored a number of publications, including *The Ethical Line: 10 Leadership Strategies for Effective Decision Making* (Corwin Press, 2019).

Parker Fawson is the Emma Eccles Jones Endowed Chair of Early Education and professor as well as director of the Center for the School of the Future at Utah State University. He was previously the dean of the School of Education at Utah Valley University and president of the Association of Literacy Educators and Researchers. He served as a technical assistant for Utah's Reading First Grant (2003–2007) and has authored and coauthored refereed research reports on early literacy; he is coauthor of *Your Classroom Library: New Ways to Give It More Teaching Power*.

Douglas Fisher is chair of the Department of Educational Leadership at San Diego State University. He is a former president of the International Literacy Association and a teacher and administrator at Health Sciences High & Middle College. He has served as a teacher and a language and development specialist.

Miranda S. Fitzgerald is an assistant professor in the Department of Reading and Elementary Education at the University of North Carolina at Charlotte, where she teaches and studies elementary literacy instruction and assessment. Her research focuses on the integration of literacy and science instruction; supporting vocabulary and reading comprehension; and supporting teachers in applying research-based literacy practices. Fitzgerald completed her doctorate at the University of Michigan.

Elena Forzani is an assistant professor in literacy education at Boston University's Wheelock College of Education and Human Development, where she teaches courses in literacy instruction and assessment, with a focus on technology. Her research centers on using multiple methods to understand and support students' digital literacies practices. Following her doctoral work in educational psychology at the University of Connecticut, Elena worked at Boston College as the assistant research director for PIRLS and ePIRLS. She has published in journals such as *Reading Research Quarterly*, *Journal of Adolescent and Adult Literacy*, and *The Reading Teacher*. Elena taught 1st grade and high school English and reading.

Nancy Frey is a professor of educational leadership at San Diego State University. She has published articles in *The Reading Teacher, Journal of Adolescent and Adult Literacy,* and *English Journal* with coauthor Douglas Fisher. Nancy is a credentialed special educator, reading specialist, and administrator, and teaches at Health Sciences High & Middle College.

Jennifer L. Goeke is an associate professor of special education at Montclair State University. She holds a PhD from the University of Albany in educational psychology. Her research interests and publications are focused on the development of research-based teacher education pedagogy for inclusion and teacher preparation of middle and secondary special educators in the STEM areas.

James V. Hoffman is a professor of language and literacy at the University of North Texas and currently serves as the Meadows Chair for Excellence in Education. He was elected to the Reading Hall of Fame in 2002 and received the Oscar S. Causey Award for research in literacy from the Literacy Research Association in 2018. He has been active in international literacy projects in Central America, Africa, and Asia. The primary focus of his research has been on teaching and teacher preparation. He has published more than 150 articles, books, and chapters on literacy-related topics.

Jacy Ippolito is a professor and codirector of Educational Leadership Programs at Salem State University in Salem, MA, where he teaches courses in literacy and leadership. Jacy's research, teaching, and consulting focus on the intersection of adolescent literacy, literacy coaching, teacher leadership, and school reform. Jacy's recent books include *Disciplinary Literacy Inquiry and Instruction* (2019); *An UnCommon Theory of School Change* (2019); *Unpacking Coaching Mindsets* (2018); *Investigating Disciplinary Literacy* (2017); and *Cultivating Coaching Mindsets* (2016). Jacy completed his doctorate and master's in education at the Harvard Graduate School of Education. To connect with Jacy, visit him on Twitter (@ Jippolito).

Clint Kennedy is the director of education for PlayVS, an esports startup based in California. At PlayVS, Clint directs the relationship with the National Federation of High School State Associations and is the de facto commissioner for all state-based leagues. Following his doctoral work in educational psychology at UConn, Clint worked as the global director of IT for Whittle Schools and Studios. Clint has worked with K–12 schools, universities, and private companies for 20 years focused on integrating technology to improve learning and teaching. His research interests include educational technology, esports management, mastery-based learning, and the teaching of "soft skills."

Julie K. Kidd is a professor in the College of Education and Human Development at George Mason University and is director of the Division for Child, Family, and Community Engagement. Prior to joining the faculty at Mason, Julie was a reading specialist and classroom teacher. Julie's research focuses on teacher professional development as well as developing young children's cognitive, literacy, and numeracy abilities. She is coprincipal investigator on research grants funded by the Institute of Education Sciences and was principal investigator on a Head Start University Partnership Teacher Effectiveness research grant. Julie has published numerous research articles and book chapters.

Diane Lapp is a distinguished professor of education at San Diego State University. She has taught in elementary and middle school and is currently teaching English at an urban high school. Author of numerous articles, chapters, podcasts, webinars, and books, her major areas of research and instruction focus on issues related to struggling learners and their families from low-socioeconomic-status urban communities. Her many educational awards include Distinguished Research Lecturer from SDSU's Graduate Division of Research, IRA's 1996 Outstanding Teacher Educator of the Year, and IRA's 2011 John Manning Award for her work in public schools. She is a member of the California and the International Reading Halls of Fame.

Donald J. Leu started his teaching career in the Peace Corps and then taught in schools in California. He is now emeritus professor and Endowed Chair in Literacy and Technology at the University of Connecticut. He is also a member of the Reading Hall of Fame and past president of the Literacy Research Association. A graduate of Michigan State University, Harvard University, and the University of California, Berkeley, Don's work focuses on the new skills and strategies required to read, write, and learn with Internet technologies and instructional practices that prepare students for these new literacies.

Maryann Mraz is a professor in the Department of Reading and Elementary Education at the University of North Carolina at Charlotte, where she teaches graduate and undergraduate courses in literacy instruction. She is the author of over 80 books, articles, chapters, and instructional materials related to literacy education. Her professional interests include content-area reading, the role of the literacy coach, and the professional development of teachers. She is the coauthor of *Content Area Reading: Literacy and Learning Across the Curriculum* with Richard T. Vacca and Jo Anne L. Vacca.

Alejandro Gonzalez Ojeda is an assistant professor of educational leadership at San Diego State University, and a technology leader at Health Sciences High & Middle College. Alejandro has introduced innovative practices and led professional development around blended and distance learning through his work as a practitioner, researcher, and author.

Yadira Palacios is the academic dean at Alamo Heights Junior School in the Alamo Heights Independent School District. She earned her doctoral degree from Texas A&M University. She regularly presents at local and state conferences.

Moonyoung Park is an assistant professor in the Department of English Education in the College of Education at Jeju National University, Korea. His research has focused on language teacher education, assessment of aviation English, computer-assisted language learning, and language test development and validation. He is a member of the Literacy Assessment Task Force of the International Literacy Association and is the vice president of the Asia-Pacific Association for Computer-Assisted Language Learning (APACALL; www.apacall.org).

Marliese R. Peltier received her doctoral degree in curriculum, instruction, and teacher education with a specialization in language and literacy from Michigan State University. Her research examines how teachers understand and enact teaching practices that (dis)connect students' home and school literacy practices. Marliese has been published in *Reading and Writing Quarterly: Overcoming Learning Difficulties* and *Literacy Practice and Research*. She has coauthored a chapter in the *Handbook of Research on Reading Comprehension, 2nd Edition*. Marliese is a former special education teacher who provided both resource room and teacher consultant support.

Diana J. Quatroche, a professor in the Department of Teaching and Learning in the Bayh College of Education at Indiana State University, teaches undergraduate and graduate courses in reading and language arts. In addition to classroom teaching experience, she has supervised school reading programs and coordinated Title I reading programs. Her research interests include the role of graduate programs in preparing reading specialists as literacy leaders, and the effect of professional development on teacher practice and student learning. She served as executive director of her state reading association and has received numerous professional development grants.

Timothy Rasinski is a professor of literacy education at Kent State University, where he also holds the Rebecca Tolle and Burton Gorman Chair in Educational Leadership. He is a former classroom teacher and reading specialist. Tim has written over 200 articles and has authored or edited over 50 books or curriculum programs on reading education. Tim's scholarly interests include foundational reading and readers who struggle. His research on reading has been cited by the National Reading Panel and has been published in *Reading Research Quarterly* and *The Reading Teacher*. In 2010 Tim was elected to the International Reading Hall of Fame.

D. Ray Reutzel is a program specialist in the Center for the School of the Future at Utah State University. He is professor emeritus in the College of Education at the University of Wyoming. He is the author of more than 235 published works and has received more than $17 million in grants. He is the past editor of *Literacy Research and Instruction* and *The Reading Teacher* and current executive editor of the *Journal of Educational Research*. Dr. Reutzel is a member of the Reading Hall of Fame, of which he is a past president, and is the recipient of the 2019 William S. Gray Citation of Merit from the International Literacy Association.

Kristen D. Ritchey is a professor of special education at the University of Delaware. She holds a PhD from the University of Maryland, College Park. Her research interests and publications are focused on assessment and intervention for students with reading and writing disabilities in elementary school.

Misty Sailors is a professor of language and literacy studies and department chair of Teacher Education and Administration at the University of North Texas. She is a literacy researcher, reading specialist, and teacher educator. Sailors actively works with literacy teachers and literacy coaches in the United States and teachers, literacy coaches, and literacy specialists in Chile, Malawi, Mozambique, and South Africa. Her scholarly work focuses on professional development with reading teachers and literacy coaches, literacy program development, and literacy research methodologies. She has published over 75 research articles and book chapters and five books on literacy related topics.

Meghan Valerio is a doctoral student in curriculum and instruction (literacy emphasis) at Kent State University. Currently a literacy consultant, Meghan was an elementary public school classroom teacher for 5 years and reading specialist for 5 years, three of which were in a Title I school. She taught graduate and undergraduate literacy courses at two universities and continues to teach reading and writing development courses in her role as graduate assistant. Meghan's research interests include investigating literacy and cognitive development from a critical literacy perspective as well as exploring pre- and inservice teacher perspectives to enhance literacy instructional practices and experiences.

Jean Payne Vintinner is a clinical assistant professor in the Department of Reading and Elementary Education at the University of North Carolina at Charlotte. A former high school English and reading teacher, her academic interests include adolescent literacy, content-area reading, and motivating struggling readers.

MaryEllen Vogt, professor emerita, California State University, Long Beach, is an author of numerous literacy articles, chapters, and books, including the SIOP series. Dr. Vogt served as codirector of the CSU Center for the Advancement of Reading, has provided professional development throughout the United States, and served as a visiting scholar at the University of Cologne in Germany. She received CSULB's Distinguished Faculty Teaching Award, is a past president of the California Reading Association and the International Literacy Association, has been inducted into the California Reading Hall of Fame, and, in 2017, was inducted into the international Reading Hall of Fame.

Jimmie Walker is the executive director of curriculum and instruction at Alamo Heights Independent School District. Previously, she served as the academic dean for Elementary Instruction in the same district. She was a classroom teacher for 16 years and was the recipient of the HEB Excellence in Education Teacher of the Year award. She received her doctoral degree from Johns Hopkins University. She was awarded the National Dissertation of the Year award by the Carnegie Project.

Shelley B. Wepner is a dean and professor in the School of Education of Manhattanville College. She was a reading specialist, Title I teacher, and K–8 curriculum supervisor in three school districts before becoming a faculty member and administrator in higher education. She has published over 150 books, chapters, articles, and instructional materials. Her research focuses on partnerships between K–12 and higher education and leadership skills for effectively supporting teacher education and literacy development. Her most recent books are *Entrepreneurial Leadership: Strategies for Creating and Sustaining Partnerships for K–12 Schools* and *Challenges Facing Suburban Schools: Promising Responses to Changing Student Populations*.

Chase Young is an associate professor and director of the Literacy EdD program at Sam Houston State University. His research aims to develop reading fluency and support struggling readers in elementary school. His research has appeared in journals such as the *Journal of Educational Research, Journal of Research in Reading, Reading Psychology, The Reading Teacher*, and *Journal of Adolescent and Adult Literacy*. He is currently an editor of *Literacy Research and Instruction* and previously served as editor of the *Journal of Teacher Action Research* and the *Texas Journal of Literacy Education*. Previously, he taught elementary school and served as a reading specialist.

Index

AUTHORS

SUBJECTS